Riding CENTRAL OREGON *Horse Trails*

By Kim McCarrel

Happy Trails! Kim McCarrel

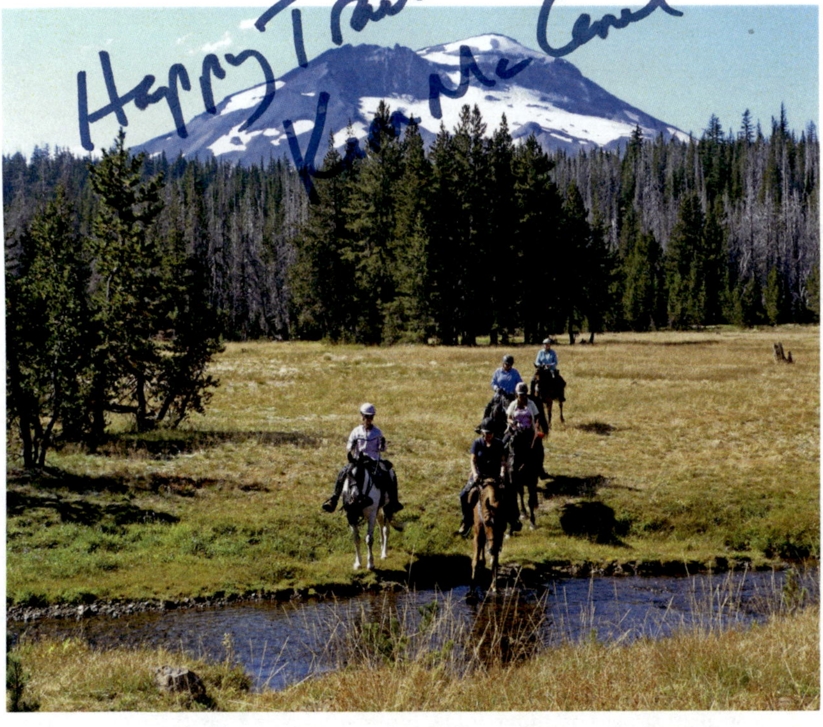

Over 150 Trails to Explore on Horseback

14 Horse Camps

Over 1,600 Miles of Trails

Ponderosa Press

Bend, Oregon

Riding Central Oregon Horse Trails

1st Edition 2005
2nd Edition 2012
3rd Edition 2018

ON THE COVER:
South Sister from Park Meadow

AT RIGHT:
Indian Prairie Trail, Ochoco Mountains

Published by

Ponderosa Press

64495 Old Bend Redmond Hwy., Bend, OR 97703
www.NWHorseTrails.com

ISBN 978-0-9826770-2-5

Safety Notice: Every effort has been made to ensure that the information in this guidebook is as accurate as possible at press time. However, horseback riding is an inherently dangerous activity, and you are responsible for your own safety on the trails. Ponderosa Press and the author are not responsible for any loss, damage, or injury that may occur to anyone using this book. The information contained in this guidebook cannot replace good judgment. The fact that a trail is described in this book does not mean it will be safe for you. Trail conditions can change from day to day, so always check local conditions and know your own limitations.

Do not go where the path may lead; go instead where there is no path, and leave a trail.

Ralph Waldo Emerson

Contents

Central Oregon Horse Trails Map

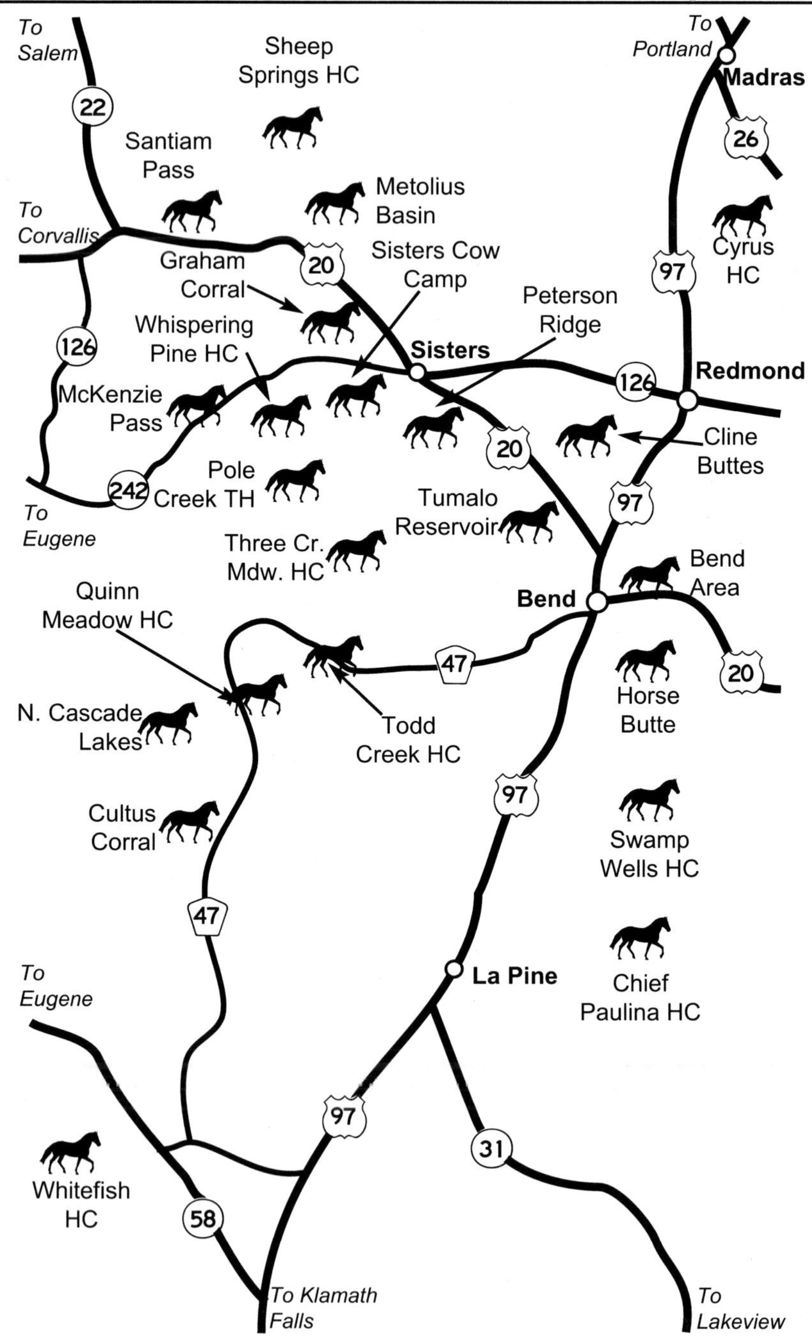

Central Oregon Horse Trails Map

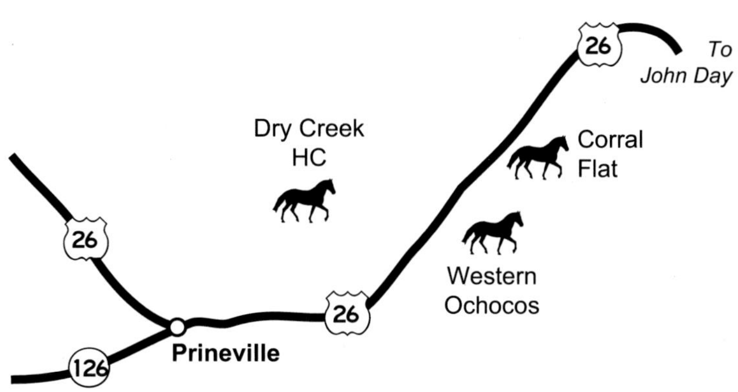

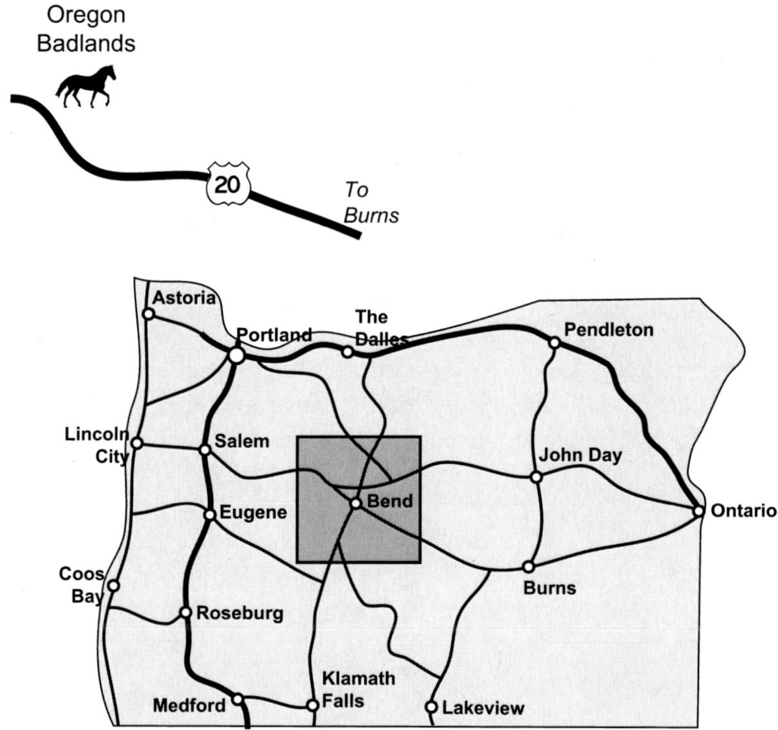

Foreword

Central Oregon is home to wonderful horse trails that are favorites of visitors and locals alike. The terrain is horse friendly, with excellent tread and few dropoffs. There are plenty of horse camps, most with excellent amenities. The scenery is spectacular, and the weather is dependably sunny.

In Central Oregon, you can ride through stands of shady hemlocks and firs, through park-like ponderosa pine forests, or across vast sagebrush deserts. You can visit pristine alpine lakes and ride beside bubbling streams lined with wildflowers. You can enjoy impressive views of jagged volcanic peaks. And, if you choose your trails appropriately, you can ride here year round.

The purpose of this guidebook is to provide the information you need to decide whether a particular trail is right for you: what the terrain is like, how difficult the ride is, how to find the trailhead, and what facilities you will find when you get there. We hope this book encourages you to try out some trails you haven't ridden yet.

Because of Central Oregon's popularity with visitors, some wilderness trails have become very, very crowded, especially on summer weekends. To address issues of overuse, the Forest Service is contemplating a permit system that would limit use to a certain number of visitors per day. As of our press date, the Forest Service hadn't yet announced what the permit system might look like or when it might be implemented, so please check the Deschutes National Forest website for updates on this proposal.

The information provided here is as accurate as possible as of its publication date. But of course, conditions change over time, so we've included information on how to contact local land managers for updated conditions.

See you on the trails!

Kim McCarrel

Saddlebag Savvy

The difference between a great ride and a lousy one, or between a mild misadventure and a disaster, may hinge upon whether you brought along the proper gear. Even on a short ride, it's a good idea to carry the "Ten Essentials" for survival, and know how to use them.

1. Navigation: Always carry a map of the area you'll be riding, even if you know the trail. Carry a compass and/or GPS and know how to use it. And of course, extra batteries for your GPS are a must.

2. Water: You can live for weeks without food, but only a few days without water. Carry extra water, along with water purification tablets or a water purifier just in case.

3. Extra Clothing: Always bring one more layer of clothing than you think you'll need. Rain gear, a hat, and gloves are the most important items, and an extra fleece jacket is a good idea. Extra packets of hand and toe warmers are easy to carry, and an emergency space blanket takes up little room but you'll be glad you have it if you have to spend a night on the trail.

4. Food: Bring along food for one more meal than you think you'll need. Trail mix, energy bars, dried fruit, and other snacks are good items to have on hand. A neat trick is to keep a can of tuna in your saddle bag. You won't be tempted to snack on it during a normal ride and it will keep forever, so if an emergency occurs and you need it, it will be there.

5. Light: If you have to spend the night on the trail, you'll be glad to have a flashlight and extra batteries on hand. A flashlight also comes in handy for signaling. Don't store the flashlight with the batteries inside, in case the flashlight gets accidentally switched on and drains the batteries. A headlamp is nice for keeping your hands free.

6. Fire: Waterproof matches and a fire starter like a candle stub can make a night stranded on the mountain a lot more comfortable.

7. Sun Protection: Sunglasses and extra sunscreen may not seem like survival essentials, but the lack of them can sure make your trip less enjoyable. Sunscreen needs to be reapplied occasionally for optimal effectiveness, so bring some extra along.

8. First Aid: Any Scout worth his or her salt knows you should carry a first aid kit. Equestrians should carry first aid items for people (bandaids, insect repellent, insect bite cream, antibiotic ointment, gauze pads, adhesive tape, a needle for removing splinters, ace bandage, small scissors, personal prescriptions, etc.) as well as first aid items for horses (vet wrap, equine thermometer, antiseptic scrub, Banamine, etc.) Be sure someone in your party has had training in first aid.

9. Knife: A good knife is essential, since it can help with fire building, first aid, and food preparation. A Leatherman-type tool will include other helpful gadgets in addition to a knife, like saws, tweezers, screwdrivers, scissors, can opener, etc.

10. Signal: With a cell phone and a fully-charged battery, you may be able to summon help in an emergency. However, cell coverage is not reliable, especially in the wilderness. A loud whistle and a metal signaling mirror can help rescuers find you faster. Three blasts or flashes mean "help needed." A Spot emergency locator beacon is a good idea, and walkie-talkies can help keep a group in contact if you get separated.

Bonus Ideas: It goes without saying that wearing a helmet may save your life. Other things that can come in very handy in a trail emergency include a large plastic garbage bag (can be used as a poncho, a tent, a ground cloth, or to carry water) and twine or a shoelace for tack repairs. Put your contact information in your saddle bag in case your horse gets loose and runs off. And be sure to carry your important medical information on your person (in your pocket, or tucked inside the inner rim of your helmet) in case you get hurt and are unconscious when paramedics arrive.

It's also important to consider which items should be on your person instead of in your saddlebag. Waterproof matches, your cell phone, and a knife are probably the bare minimum. If you and your horse get separated, all that great emergency equipment in your saddlebag won't do you any good. If your riding clothes are short on pockets, use a fanny pack or a Cashel Ankle Safe trail pouch to carry critical items.

Finally, always tell someone where you are going and when you'll be returning, then stick with your plan. That way if something goes wrong, they'll know where to start looking for you.

Ride safely, be prepared, and have fun!

Certified Feed Required

To help control the spread of invasive species in the Northwest, both the Forest Service and the Bureau of Land Management now require that any horse feed brought onto Federal land must be certified to be free of weed seeds.

The Forest Service's catchy name for this special horse feed is "Weed Seed-Free Feed." (Say that three times fast!) Most folks call it "certified feed" instead.

There are two types of certified feed: hay that a state agricultural inspector has deemed to be free of weed seeds, or heat-processed feed pellets. (The heat treatment kills the seeds and prevents them from germinating.)

The bottom line for horseback riders is that if you go on Federal land, you are allowed to have only certified feed in your trailer or at your campsite. If you violate this requirement, you can be ticketed and fined.

You can purchase certified hay or pellets from most feed stores, or go to http://www.oregon.gov/ODA/programs/MarketAccess/MACertification/Pages/WeedFreeForage.aspx for a list of certified hay producers.

The Three Sisters from the summit of Scott Mountain.

Leave No Trace Principles

Leave No Trace is a nationally-recognized outdoor skills and ethics education program. Its seven Leave No Trace Principles outline the ways that recreational users can minimize the impact we have on the land. The principles are listed below, followed by specific things we equestrians can do to ensure that the beautiful places we enjoy today will be preserved for generations to come.

Plan Ahead and Prepare

-- Educate yourself about the area you plan to visit. Talk with local land managers to find out about trail conditions. Know before you go.

-- Carry and use a map, and take responsibility for knowing your route and staying on it.

-- Tell someone where you are going, and stick with your itinerary.

Travel and Camp on Durable Surfaces

-- Water your horse directly from a stream or lake only at trail crossings or if there is a rocky or sandy bank. Otherwise, bring water to your horse using a collapsible bucket to protect fragile shoreline vegetation.

-- Above the tree line, please stay on the trails to avoid damaging fragile alpine environments.

-- Use trails designated for horse use.

-- When traveling cross-country, don't ride single file. Each rider should pick his own route to disperse hoofprints, staying on durable surfaces.

-- Avoid steep slopes and soft ground. Ride across slopes rather than straight up or down to reduce erosion.

-- To minimize damage, don't ride trails that are wet and muddy.

Dispose of Waste Properly

-- Pack out all garbage.

-- Disburse any manure piles after rest breaks on the trail.

-- When you stop for a bathroom break, make sure you're at least 200 feet (that's about 75 steps) away from any streams, lakes, or springs. Bury all waste, and carry out your used toilet paper.

Leave What You Find

-- Use certified feed to help prevent the spread of invasive species. Start feeding it to your animals three or more days before entering the forest so their digestive systems are clear of weed seeds.

-- Fill in pawed ground to help the vegetation regrow.

-- Do not allow horses to paw or chew vegetation.

Minimize Campfire Impacts

-- Build fires only if the weather is safe, and use only dead and downed wood that is smaller than your wrist. Make sure your campfire is dead out before leaving it.

Respect Wildlife

-- Control your dog. Electronic collars work well on the trail.

Be Considerate of Other Visitors

-- Please keep horses out of lakes in the wilderness, as these lakes are used for drinking water by backpackers.

-- Keep horses off designated bike trails. Horse hooves break up the firm trail tread that bicyclists enjoy.

-- If you encounter other trail users that are not familiar with horse traffic, greet them and ask them to move off to the downhill side of the trail, and coach them as needed.

-- A friendly equestrian makes a lasting impression on other trail users.

For more information about Leave No Trace principles, go to www.lnt.org/programs/ principles.php.

A late fall ride at Green Ridge.

Wilderness Riding

This book covers trails in six designated wilderness areas: Three Sisters, Mt. Jefferson, Mt. Washington, Diamond Peak, Mill Creek, and Oregon Badlands. These areas are permanently protected by Congresss in order to preserve their special characteristics, and to protect fish and wildlife habitat, water quality, and vegetation.

Wilderness areas are managed differently than other federal land, with emphasis on environmental protection, solitude and primitive recreation. As a result, wilderness riding is a different experience than front-country riding. The terrain is typically more rugged, the trails are more challenging, and you'll see fewer signs along the way.

In the Deschutes National Forest, wilderness trail junction signs have historically shown trail names and/or destinations. But as these signs reach the end of their useful lives, they are being replaced with signs that show only the trail numbers. This means you will need to carry a map and know how to use it. Wilderness maps are available from any forest service office.

Special regulations apply to designated wilderness areas, including:

-- Wilderness Permits are required. These free, self-issued permits (one per group) are available at all wilderness trailheads. They are important in locating injured visitors, and they provide the Forest Service with valuable information about trail usage patterns over time.

-- Groups should be no larger than 12 heartbeats (5 people, 5 stock animals, and 2 dogs, for example) in order to reduce impacts.

-- All wheeled devices (bicycles, carts, strollers) are prohibited to protect traditional wilderness values.

-- Horses must be secured more than 200 feet from water and main trails to protect fragile plants and keep water clean.

-- Bury human waste 6 inches deep and at least 200 feet (70 steps) from water and trails to prevent disease. Carry out toilet paper.

-- No entry is allowed in any site, area, or trail marked "Closed for Restoration."

-- Campfires, where allowed, must be at least 100 feet (35 steps) from all water and main trails. Fires must be out cold before you leave them.

Central Oregon Maps

One of the most important items in your saddlebag is your map. You should always carry a map of the area you're riding, even if you know the trail. Of the maps listed below, the National Geographic and Adventure Maps are updated regularly and are printed on durable waterproof paper. The remaining maps are not updated on a regular basis, but are more comprehensive than the National Geographic and Adventure Maps.

National Geographic Bend/Three Sisters Map
National Geographic Mt. Jefferson/Mt. Washington Map
Adventure Map's Central Oregon Hiking-Trail Map

Deschutes National Forest Map
Ochoco National Forest Map

Bend Ranger District Map
Sisters Ranger District Map
Fort Rock Ranger District Map
Crescent Ranger District Map
Prineville Ranger District Map
Big Summit Ranger District Map

Three Sisters Wilderness Map
Mt. Jefferson Wilderness Map
Mt. Washington Wilderness Map
Diamond Peak Wilderness Map

Printable maps for LaPine State Park, Oregon Badlands Wilderness, and many BLM riding areas are available online.

Kim and Tex on the trail near Cyrus Horse Camp.

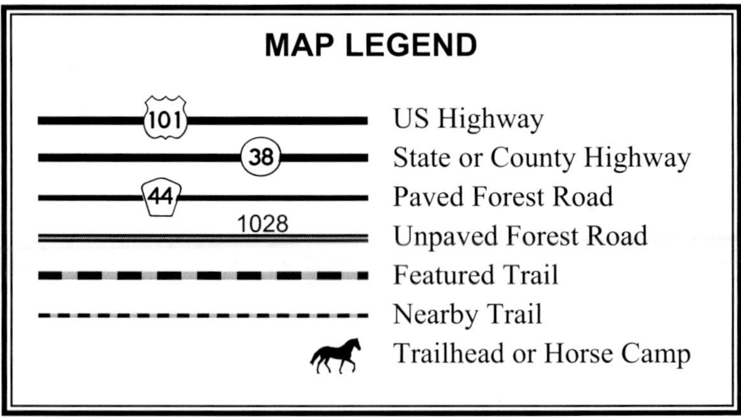

Bend Area Day Rides

Deschutes Natl. Forest & Bureau of Land Mgt.

Several trails and large tracts of public land near Bend offer very nice riding, and most are accessible year round.

On the west side of Bend, the Deschutes River Trail is a fabulous low-elevation trail along the Deschutes. It's a spectacular ride in the autumn when the brilliant fall foliage contrasts with the blue sky and water and the nearby black lava flows.

On the east side of Bend, you'll find many miles of riding at the Mayfield Pond and Juniper Woodlands Recreation Areas, at the Rickard Road area, and at Horse Ridge, all of which offer virtually year-round riding on dirt roads and trails. Juniper Woodlands and Horse Ridge have the added bonus of excellent mountain views.

Along the Deschutes River Trail, near the Slough Trailhead.

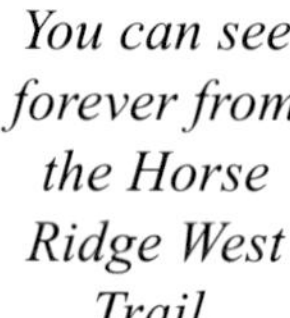

You can see forever from the Horse Ridge West Trail.

Debbie and Whitney ride Split and Dixie along the Deschutes River Trail.

Mayfield Pond reflects the snowcapped Three Sisters in early spring.

Bend Area Trailheads

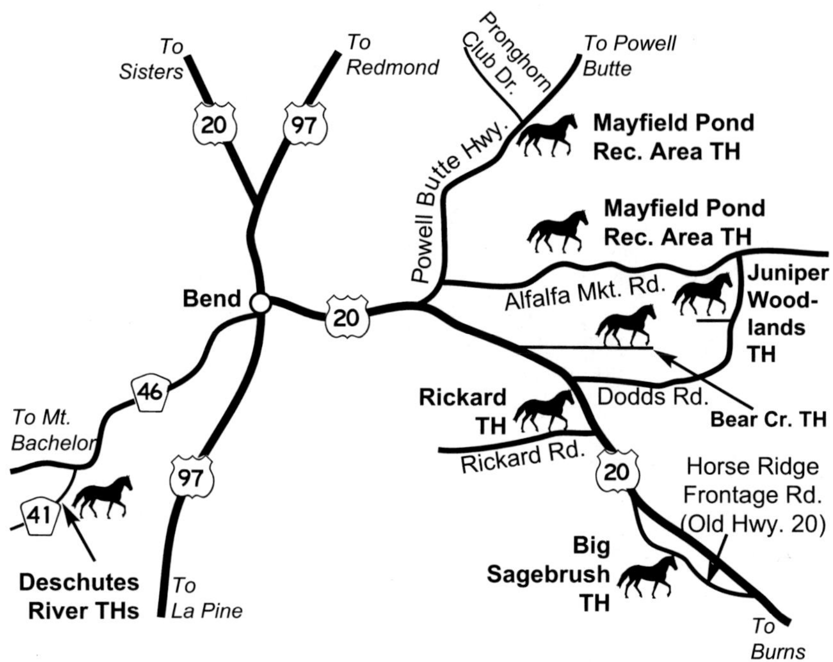

Bend Area Trails

Trail	Difficulty	Elevation	Round Trip
Deschutes River Trail	Easy	3,950-4,100	7.5-13.5 miles
Horse Ridge West	Moderate	3,750-4,650	6.5-10 miles
Juniper Woodlands	Easy	3,350-3,450	Varies
Mayfield Pond Rec. Area	Easy	3,200-3,500	Varies
Rickard Road Area	Moderate	3,600-3,900	Varies

Deschutes River Trail

Trailhead: The best trailer parking is at an unsigned dirt turnout just before the Lava Island Trailhead

Length: 7.5 miles round trip from Lava Island Trailhead to Dillon Falls, or 13.5 miles round trip to Benham Falls

Elevation: 3,950 to 4,100 feet

Difficulty: Easy

Footing: Suitable for barefoot horses

Season: Early spring through late fall

Permits: Northwest Forest Pass required.

Facilities: Toilets at each trailhead. Parking for 2-4 trailers just before Lava Island Trailhead. Additional parking possible at Big Eddy, Aspen, Dillon Falls, and Slough Trailheads, though heavy use by hikers and mountain bike riders may severely limit trailer parking. Stock water is available on the trail.

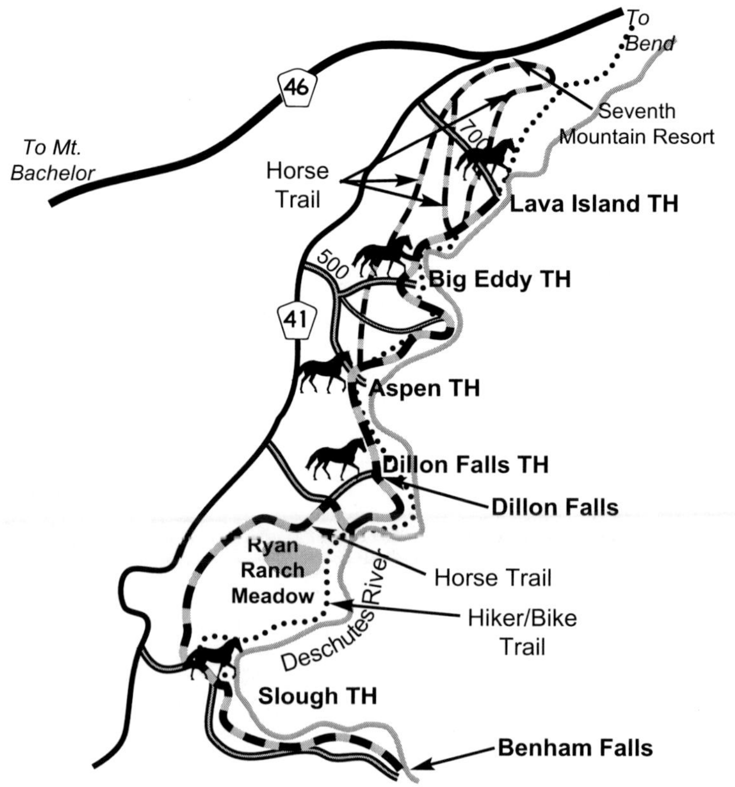

Highlights: The Deschutes River Trail offers excellent views of the river, the lush vegetation it supports, and the ancient lava flows on the east side of the river. In mid-October, the fall colors along this trail are spectacular. The horse trail is mostly separate from the hiking and mountain biking trail, and is signed with white diamond trailblazers on the trees. Dogs are required to be on leash on this trail from May 15th to September 15th.

Finding the Trailheads: From Hwy. 97 in Bend, take Exit 138 (Colorado Ave.) and head west on Hwy. 46 (the Cascade Lakes Hwy.) Follow the signs toward Mt. Bachelor for 7.5 miles and turn left on Road 41, the first road on the left after passing the Seventh Mountain Resort. In 0.5 mile, turn left to reach the Lava Island Trailhead, or continue along Road 41 and follow the signs to reach the other trailheads.

The Ride: The trail roughly parallels the river, with entry/exit opportunities at every trailhead but Benham Falls, where the parking area is too small for trailers. From Lava Island to Dillon Falls there are separate trails for horses, hikers, and bicyclists. From Dillon Falls to Slough the horse trail skirts around Ryan Ranch Meadow to the west on a closed forest road that has gates at both ends. From Slough to Benham Falls, all users share the same trail.

Riders enjoy the excellent views along the Deschutes River Trail.

Horse Ridge West

Trailhead: Start at Big Sagebrush Trailhead, an unimproved and unsigned parking area off the Horse Ridge Frontage Road (old Hwy. 20)

Length: 6.5 to 10 miles round trip

Elevation: 3,750 to 4,650 feet

Difficulty: Moderate -- steep hills to climb

Footing: Suitable for barefoot horses

Season: Nearly year-round -- trail is dusty in summer but offers good footing in spring, fall, and early winter

Permits: None

Facilities: Parking for 3 trailers. No stock water on the trail.

Highlights: Most of Horse Ridge is mountain bike territory. (Bikes are not allowed in the Oregon Badlands Wilderness just across Hwy. 20.) While horses are technically allowed on all the Horse Ridge trails, most are steep and narrow — not places you would want to suddenly

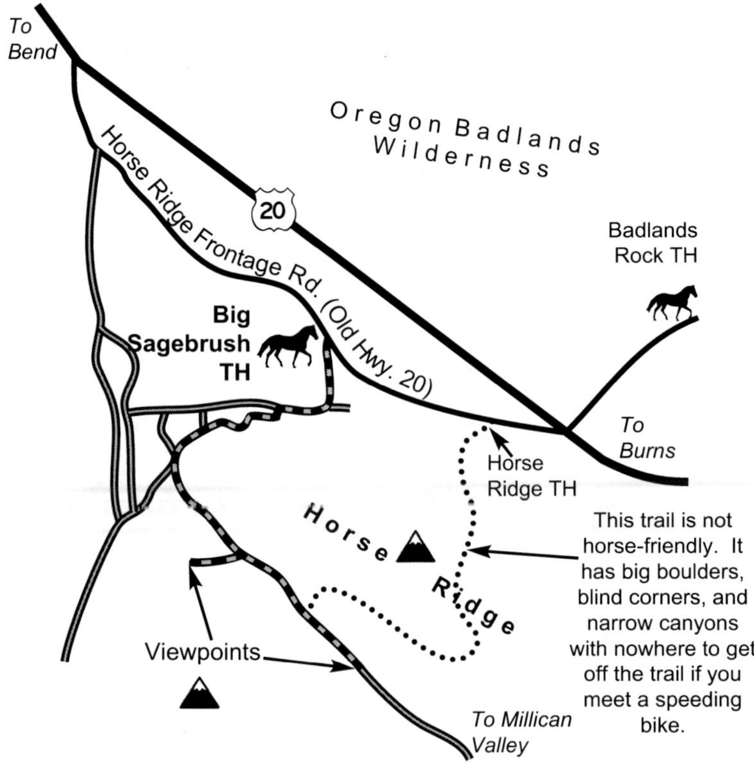

Whitney, Debbie, and Diana ride up Horse Ridge, with Mt. Washington, Black Butte, and Mt. Jefferson behind them.

encounter a speeding bike. The western-most Horse Ridge trail, however, gets much less bike traffic, and has long lines of sight so you can see cyclists coming. The views from this trail are fabulous. From several vantage points you can see Bend, Redmond, the Three Sisters, Mt. Jefferson, Mt. Hood, Pine Mountain, and Millican Valley. Some of the oldest junipers in the world can be found on this ridge.

Finding the Big Sagebrush Trailhead: From Bend, drive east on Hwy. 20 for 12.5 miles and turn right on the Horse Ridge Frontage Road, a paved but unsigned road that goes off to the right between mileposts 12 and 13. Drive 3.1 miles and turn right on an unsigned dirt road that runs between two rock cribs toward a gate on the far end of the trailhead parking area.

The Ride: Go through the gate and ride 0.5 mile, then when you come to a dirt road, turn right. Follow this road for several miles, keeping to the left at each junction. The road will take you up a steep hill, level out, and then climb again for a total elevation gain of 800 feet in 2 miles. When the road levels out for the second time, you'll be on the middle Horse Ridge. You are now about 3 miles from your trailer. Detour to the right on the next dirt road to reach an excellent viewpoint. Return to the road you rode up on, and continue for another 1.5 miles for a look down into the Millican Valley. After exploring the ridgetop and enjoying the views, retrace your steps to return to your trailer.

Juniper Woodlands

Trailhead: Start at the Juniper Woodlands Trailhead off Alfalfa Market Road, or at the Bear Creek Trailhead off Hwy. 20

Length: Varies -- multiple routes on about 12 miles of dirt roads

Elevation: 3,350 to 3,450 feet

Difficulty: Easy, but a GPS may come in handy

Footing: Some rocky spots, but overall fine for barefoot horses

Season: Year-round -- trails are dusty in summer but excellent in winter, spring, and fall

Permits: None

Facilities: Parking for 3-4 trailers at Juniper Woodlands Trailhead, or 1-2 trailers at Bear Creek Trailhead. Stock water is available on the trail during irrigation season.

Highlights: Trail 1, the Bobcat Trail, isn't the most interesting riding, since it's a long straight stretch that runs mostly along a power line. But it connects you to other trails and dirt roads to explore in the area. The terrain is fairly flat, punctuated by occasional rock outcroppings and covered with old-growth juniper. You'll even have some nice views of the Cascades.

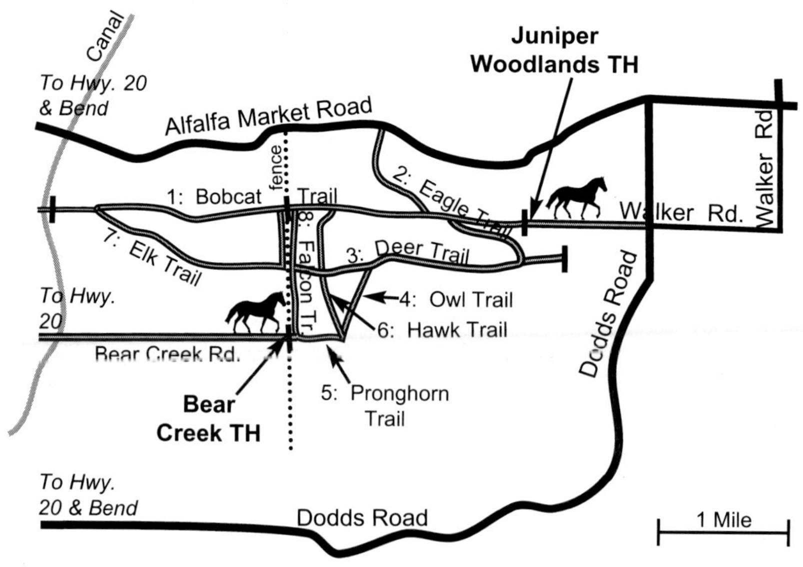

Teresa rides Kodie and Whitney rides Dixie along the Bobcat Trail at Juniper Woodlands.

Finding the Trailheads: Juniper Woodlands Trailhead: drive east from Bend on Hwy. 20 for 4.7 miles. Turn left on Powell Butte Highway, and in 0.9 mile take the first exit from the roundabout to turn onto Alfalfa Market Road. Follow it 8.5 miles and turn right on Dodds Road. In another mile, turn right on Walker Road. Continue 1 mile to the trailhead at the end of the road. Bear Creek Trailhead: take Hwy. 20 east from Bend for 6.9 miles and turn left on Bear Creek Road. In 2.2 miles the road turns to gravel, and the trailhead is 1.5 miles beyond that.

The Ride: Trail 1 starts at the Walker Road Trailhead and runs nearly straight for 2.5 miles. While the official trail ends where Trails 1 and 7 meet, you can continue straight ahead on a dirt road for another 0.4 mile to reach an irrigation ditch where you can water your horse (in summer). In addition to the official trails shown, several other dirt roads and game trails wind through the junipers, so you'll find plenty of ways to explore the area.

Mayfield Pond Recreation Area

Trailhead: Start at the Alfalfa Market Road Trailhead or the Powell Butte Highway Trailhead

Length: Varies -- multiple routes possible

Elevation: 3,200 to 3,500 feet

Difficulty: Easy, but a GPS may come in handy on these unsigned roads

Footing: Suitable for barefoot horses

Season: Year-round -- trails are dusty in summer but excellent in winter, spring, and fall

Permits: None

Facilities: Parking for 4-6 trailers at either trailhead. No stock water on the trail.

Highlights: Mayfield Pond Recreation Area is located a little north of the Oregon Badlands, in an area bounded by Alfalfa Market Road to

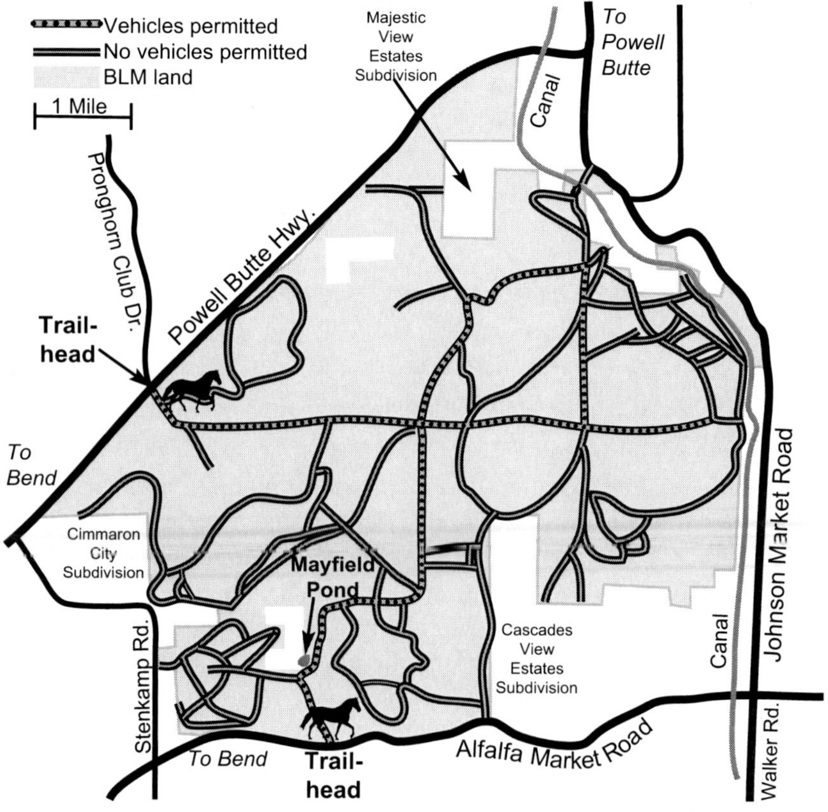

Debbie and Split explore the trails at Mayfield Pond Recreation Area on a sunny winter day.

the south, Powell Butte Highway to the west, and Johnson Market Road to the east. This 19,500-acre BLM area has a few roads where motor vehicle use is allowed, but most of the riding is on old dirt roads where motorized vehicles are not permitted. The terrain is fairly flat sagebrush and juniper country, with a few interesting rock outcroppings thrown in--good riding for green horses or inexperienced riders, and a nice place to ride to keep your horse conditioned in winter.

Finding the Trailheads: Alfalfa Market Road Trailhead: From Bend, drive east on Hwy. 20 for 4.7 miles. Turn left on Powell Butte Highway, and at the roundabout in 0.9 mile, take the first right onto Alfalfa Market Road. Follow it 4.5 miles to the trailhead on the left side of the road. Powell Butte Highway Trailhead: From Bend, drive east on Hwy. 20 for 4.7 miles. Turn left on Powell Butte Highway and continue 6.3 miles to the trailhead on the right side of the road, directly across from the entrance to the Pronghorn Resort. From Redmond, take Hwy. 26 east 6.5 miles to Powell Butte Hwy., turn right, and drive 12 miles to the trailhead on the left side of the road.

The Ride: The riding is easy and relaxed at the Mayfield Pond Recreation area. You can have fun exploring the old dirt roads in the area, or you can ride cross-country. It's a good idea to use a GPS here, because none of the dirt roads are signed and it's easy to get disoriented.

Rickard Road Area

Trailhead: Start at the Rickard Trailhead

Length: The closest southern loop is about 6.5 miles round trip, and several other loops of varying lengths are possible

Elevation: 3,600 to 3,900 feet

Difficulty: Moderate -- the riding is easy, but a GPS and BLM's on-line map of the Horse Butte area will come in handy on these unsigned roads

Footing: Suitable for barefoot horses

Season: Year-round -- trails are dusty in summer but have good footing in winter, spring, and fall

Permits: None

Facilities: Parking for 4 trailers. No stock water on the trail.

Highlights: This trailhead provides access to the northern part of the Horse Ridge area and offers several loop trails of varying lengths. Just north of the trailhead are trails with a combined length of about 2 miles

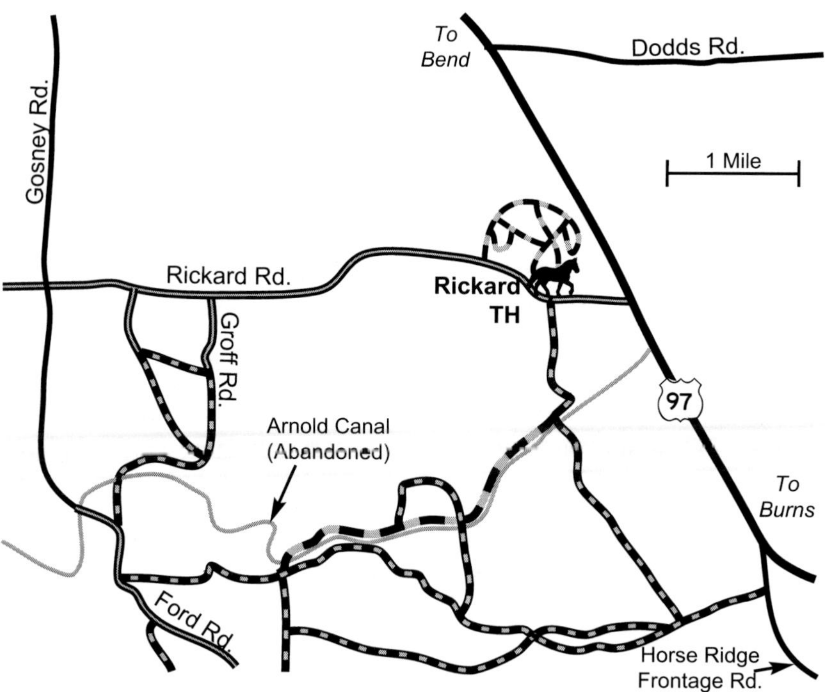

Connie, Lydia, Debbie, and Whitney take a winter ride from the Rickard Road Trailhead.

-- better suited to dog walking than horseback riding. Heading south from the trailhead, though, you can use the area's dirt roads and a few single-track trails to create some nice equestrian loops. The footing is great for barefoot horses, and the trails are easy. Much of the area is covered with juniper and sagebrush, but as you travel west you'll reach the area burned by the 1996 Skeleton Fire. This area has few trees so it offers good views of the Cascades. None of the roads are numbered and there isn't much variation in the terrain, so it can be easy to get lost. Be sure to carry a map and a GPS or compass.

Finding the Rickard Trailhead: From Bend, take Hwy. 20 eastbound and turn right on Rickard Road, next to the 11-mile marker. Drive 0.7 mile and turn right into the trailhead parking lot.

The Ride: You can ride several good loops from the parking area. To reach the trails south of the trailhead, ride east on Rickard Road for 200 feet and turn right to go through a gate that is partially blocked by large boulders (to exclude motor vehicles). Explore the area's roads and trails, but note that the trail beside the abandoned canal (really, a small ditch) is faint in places and can be easy to miss.

Debbie and Whitney on Mel and Dixie, on the Deschutes River Trail.

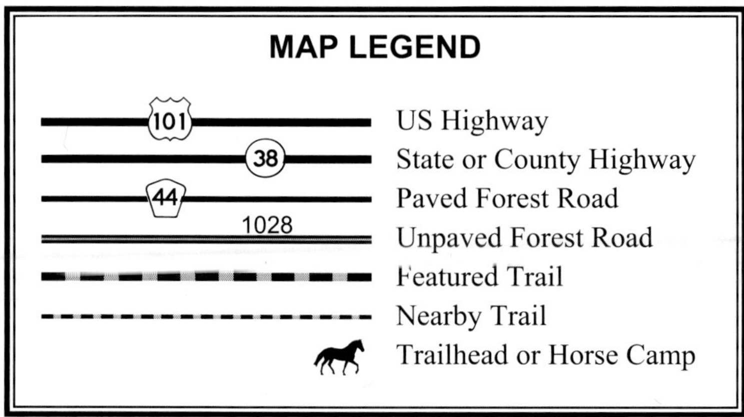

Chief Paulina Horse Camp

Newberry Natl. Volcanic Monument

Deschutes National Forest

Newberry National Volcanic Monument, located about 45 minutes south of Bend, was established in 1990 to preserve the unique geologic features of the Newberry Volcano. The volcano's caldera was formed when Newberry Volcano blew its top, and later volcanic eruptions occurred as recently as 1,300 years ago – little more than the blink of an eye in geologic terms. Paulina Lake and East Lake, in the bottom of the caldera, are popular for boating and fishing. From various points around the rim you are treated to panoramic views of the Three Sisters, Mt. Bachelor, Mt. Jefferson, and Fort Rock. At 7,985 feet, Paulina Peak is the tallest of the mountains that ring the crater, followed by North Paulina Peak at 7,467 feet. These peaks and the Monument's horse camp were named for Chief Paulina, a wily Snake Indian chief and skilled horseman who wreaked havoc on the settlers, miners, and trappers in the Oregon Territory. Chief Paulina Horse Camp provides both overnight camping and day-use facilities. La Pine State Park is located nearby, and can be accessed without entering the Monument.

From the Lost Lake Trail you can see Big Obsidian Flow, Paulina Lake, the Three Sisters, and Mt. Bachelor.

Getting to Chief Paulina

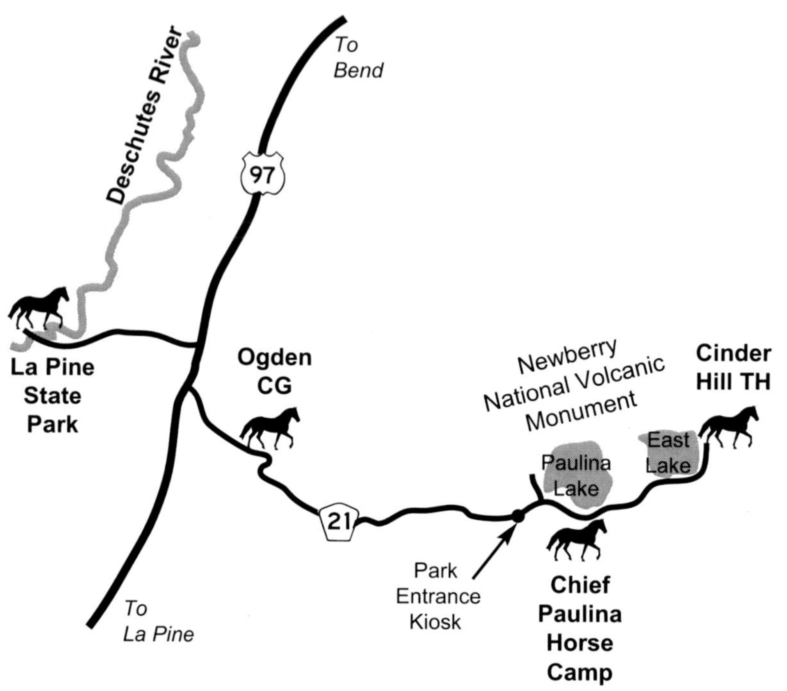

Newberry Crater Area Trails

Trail	Difficulty	Elevation	Round Trip
Crater Rim Loop	Difficult	6,400-7,700	25 miles
East Rim Loop	Moderate	6,400-7,400	11-23 miles
La Pine State Park	Easy	4,100-4,200	3-9 miles
Newberry Crater Trail	Moderate	6,300-7,300	3.5-17 miles
North Paulina Peak	Moderate	6,300-7,600	11.5 miles
North Rim Loop	Challenging	6,300-7,600	17 miles
Paulina Peak Loop	Difficult	6,300-7,700	13 miles
Peter Skene Ogden Trail	Moderate	4,300-6,400	16.5-20 miles
South Rim Loop	Moderate	6,400-7,300	13.5 miles

Chief Paulina Horse Camp

Directions: From Bend, take Hwy. 97 south for 23 miles and turn left on Paulina Lake Road (Road 21). Continue 11 miles to the park entrance kiosk, then drive 1 mile past it and turn right. The horse camp is ahead on the right in 1.2 miles.

Elevation: 6,400 feet

Campsites: 14 sites. Four sites have 4-horse corrals and the rest have 2-horse corrals. All are back-in, and 6 sites can accommodate 2 vehicles. The sites toward the back (south side) of the camp cannot accommodate larger trailers.

Facilities: Vault toilet, manure bin, stock water in a large trough. All sites have fire pits and picnic tables. No potable water. Day-use parking area holds 5-6 trailers.

Permits: Campsites may be reserved at www.recreation.gov. Call Hoodoo Recreation to be sure the stock water trough is filled. Fee for overnight camping; Northwest Forest Pass required for day use.

Season: May to October

Contact: Bend/Ft. Rock Ranger District: 541-383-4000
Concessionaire: 541-338-7869, www.hoodoo.com
Reservations: 877-444-6777, www.recreation.gov

Linda grooms Beamer in the corral at Chief Paulina Horse Camp.

Crater Rim Loop

Trailhead:	Start at Chief Paulina Horse Camp
Length:	25 miles round trip
Elevation:	6,400 to 7,700 feet
Difficulty:	Difficult -- long, with one very steep segment
Footing:	Hoof protection recommended
Season:	Late spring through fall
Permits:	Camping fee, or Northwest Forest Pass for day use
Facilities:	Toilet, stock water, and manure bin at the horse camp. Stock water is also available near Paulina Lake Lodge.

Highlights: This ride features expansive views and varied terrain. The trail up Paulina Peak is very steep and difficult and the loop is long, so this is a trail for well-conditioned horses and experienced riders only.

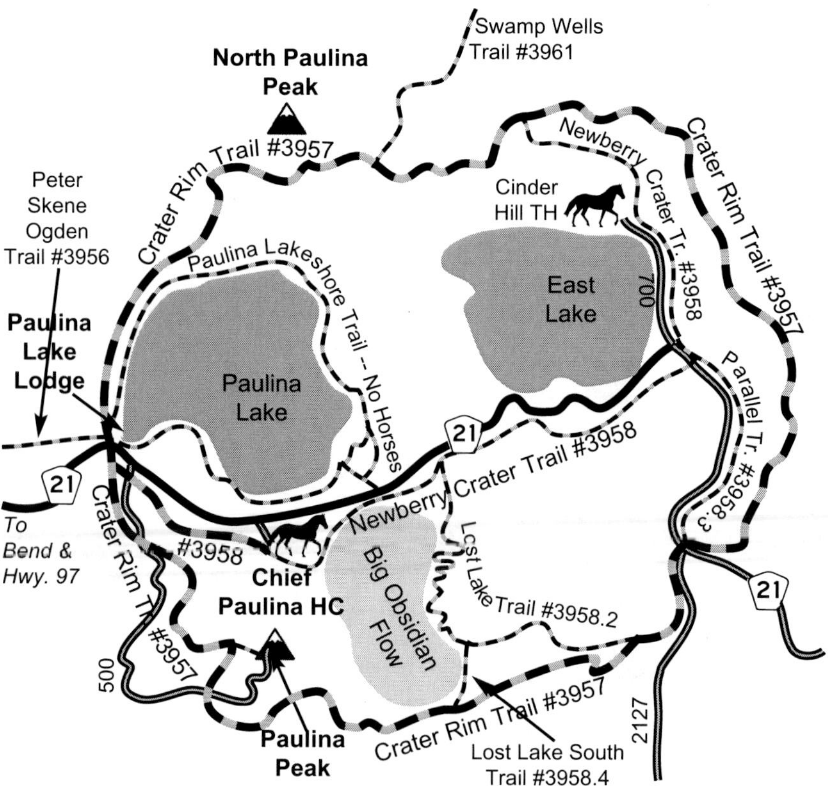

The Ride: From Chief Paulina Horse Camp, pick up the Newberry Crater Trail #3958 between campsites 9 and 10 and ride west for 1.5 miles. Turn left on Crater Rim Trail #3957 toward Paulina Peak. The trail climbs gradually for the next 1.1 mile, then it crosses Road 500 and starts climbing in earnest, gaining 1,300 feet of elevation in the next 1.5 miles. This section of the trail is difficult because in places it is extremely steep. The trail passes near the summit of Paulina Peak, offering breathtaking views. It then levels off for about 3 miles as it runs along the south side of Paulina Peak and past Big Obsidian Flow. After that, the trail heads gently downhill for about 6.5 miles, passing the junctions with the Lost Lake South #3958.4 and Lost Lake #3958.2 trails. Just after crossing Road 21, veer right to stay on the Crater Rim Trail and continue around the rim. You will reach the junction with the Newberry Crater Trail #3958 about 5.7 miles after crossing Road 21. About 1.6 miles after that, you'll pass the junction with the Swamp Wells Trail #3961. In 0.5 mile, you'll pass North Paulina Peak, then the trail will head steadily down for 6 miles to near the west shore of Paulina Lake. Return to the horse camp on the Newberry Crater Trail #3958.

The Crater Rim Trail circles the entire rim of Newberry Caldera.

East Rim Loop

Trailhead: Start at Chief Paulina Horse Camp or Cinder Hill Trailhead

Length: 11 miles round trip from Cinder Hill Trailhead, or 23 miles round trip from Chief Paulina Horse Camp

Elevation: 6,400 to 7,400 feet

Difficulty: Moderate

Footing: Suitable for barefoot horses

Season: Summer through fall

Permits: Camping fee, or Northwest Forest Pass for day use

Facilities: Toilet, stock water, and manure bins at the horse camp. Toilet at Cinder Hill Trailhead. Stock water is also available at East Lake.

Highlights: The views from Cinder Hill are a real treat -- you can see East Lake below you, plus Big Obsidian Flow, Paulina Peak, and

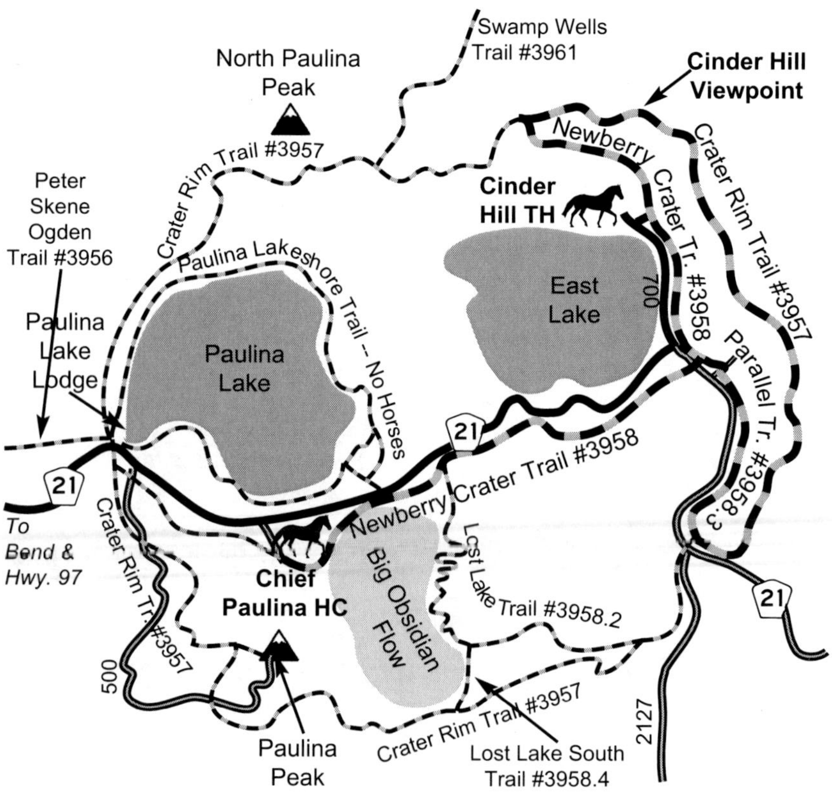

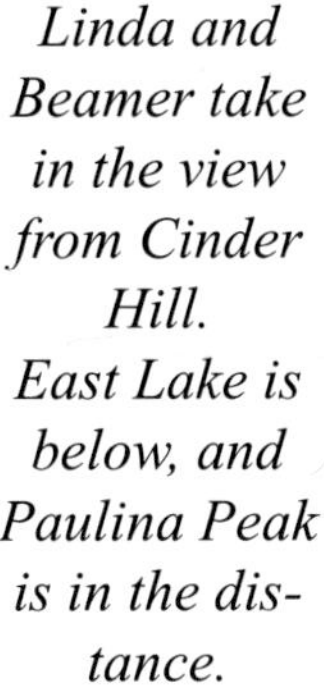

Linda and Beamer take in the view from Cinder Hill. East Lake is below, and Paulina Peak is in the distance.

Paulina Lake in the distance. Once you've made your way up to the crater rim, the trail is fairly level until it begins to descend gradually to the lake shore.

Finding the Cinder Hill Trailhead: From Chief Paulina Horse Camp, drive east on Road 21 for 4.5 miles. The road runs into the Cinder Hill campground, and about 0.5 mile after entering the campground you'll see the day-use parking area on the left.

The Ride: From the Cinder Hill Trailhead, a short spur trail takes you east to the Newberry Crater Trail #3958. Turn left on it, and in 2.2 miles you'll reach the crater rim, gaining 900 feet of elevation in the process. Turn right on the Crater Rim Trail #3957, and in 0.8 mile you'll arrive at the Cinder Hill viewpoint. After enjoying the views, continue along the rim for about 4.9 miles. When you reach the junction with the Parallel Trail #3958.3, turn right and ride down through the lodgepoles for 1.4 miles to a dirt road where the trail seems to disappear. Turn right on the dirt road, and in 200 feet veer left around a pile of tree stumps to find the trail again. In 0.6 mile you'll reach the Newberry Crater Trail. Turn right on it and in 1.3 miles veer left on the spur trail that will take you back to your trailer. From Chief Paulina Horse Camp, pick up the Newberry Crater Trail #3958 between campsites 2 and 3, and ride 5 miles to the junction with the Parallel Trail #3958.3 just across gravel Road 21. Veer left on the Newberry Crater Trail, and in 1.3 miles you'll reach the Cinder Hill Trailhead. Continue by following the directions above.

La Pine State Park

Trailhead: La Pine State Park has two equestrian trailheads, one on each side of the Deschutes River

Length: 3-9 miles, depending on route taken

Elevation: 4,100 to 4,200 feet

Difficulty: Easy

Footing: Suitable for barefoot horses

Season: Late spring through fall

Permits: No fee for day use

Facilities: Plenty of parking for horse trailers. Toilets at several locations around the park. Stock water is available on the trail.

Highlights: The La Pine State Park trails are accessible when the high country is still deep in snow, and they offer nice views of the Deschutes River and Fall River. La Pine State Park also boasts the largest

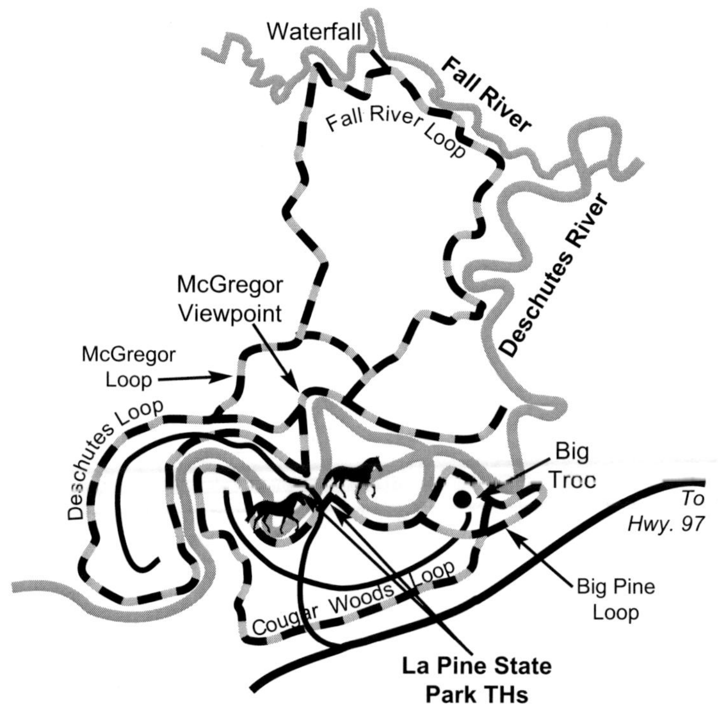

The Deschutes River from McGregor Viewpoint.

ponderosa pine in Oregon. At 191 feet high, 326 inches around, and 500 years old, it's an impressive sight. Several loop rides are possible within the park, so you can tailor your ride to fit your preferences.

Finding the La Pine State Park Trailheads: Take Highway 97 south from Bend for 22 miles (1 mile north of the turnoff to Newberry Crater). Turn right at the sign for La Pine State Park, drive 4 miles, then veer right into the park and continue straight ahead for 0.5 mile to reach the trailheads on either side of the Deschutes River.

The Ride: The park offers five trails that can be combined to make two loops, or you can link all of the loops to make one longer ride. The Big Pine and Cougar Woods Loops depart from the parking area on the east side of the river and can be combined to create a 3.8-mile loop. The Deschutes, McGregor, and Fall River Loops are accessible from the west side of the river and can be combined to create a 5-mile loop. Trail maps are posted at strategic locations throughout the park.

Newberry Crater Trail

Trailhead: Start at Chief Paulina Horse Camp

Length: 3.5 miles round trip from the horse camp to Paulina Lake Lodge, or 12.5 miles round trip to Cinder Hill Trailhead, or 17 miles round trip to the crater rim

Elevation: 6,300 to 6,500 feet for the lake shore portion of the trail, or 6,300 to 7,300 feet to the crater rim

Difficulty: Easy on the crater floor (along Road 21), moderate to the crater rim

Footing: Suitable for barefoot horses

Season: Summer through fall

Permits: Camping fee, or Northwest Forest Pass for day use

Facilities: Toilet, stock water, and manure bins at the horse camp. Stock water is also available near Paulina Lake Lodge and at East Lake.

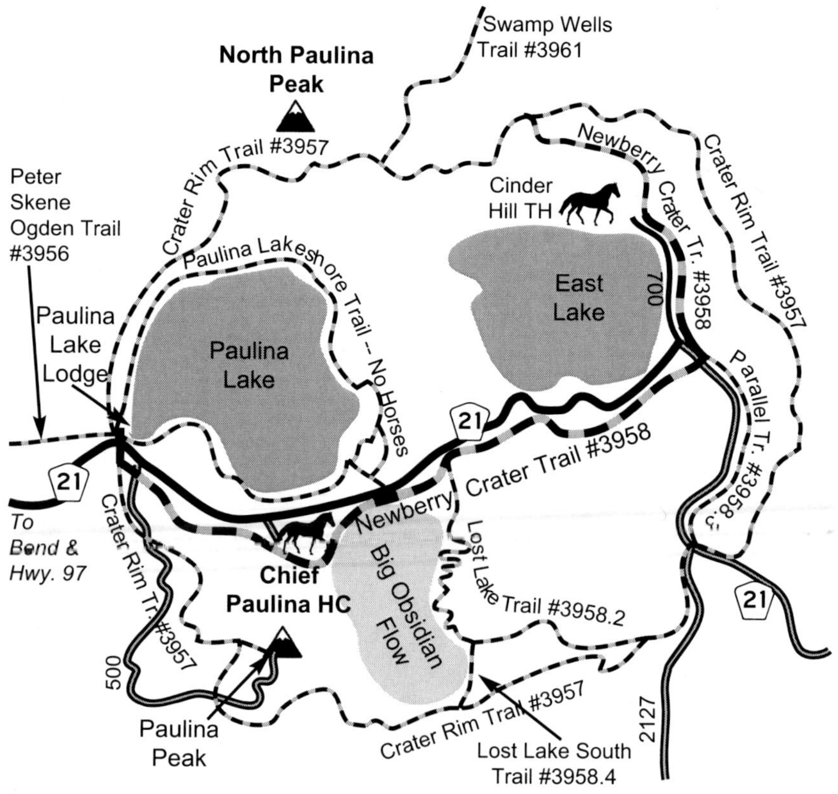

Highlights: The Newberry Crater Trail #3958 runs beside Road 21 at lake level all the way from Paulina Lake Lodge to the Cinder Hill Trailhead. From there it climbs to the Crater Rim Trail. This trail provides access to other trails that can take you to the crater rim, or you can ride it to Paulina Lake Lodge for lunch or dinner.

The Ride: From Chief Paulina Horse Camp, you can pick up the westbound Newberry Crater Trail #3958 between campsites 9 and 10 or the eastbound trail between campsites 2 and 3. Heading west, the trail runs mostly under the power lines for 1.5 miles. At the junction with the Crater Rim Trail #3957, you can veer right and cross Road 21 to reach Paulina Lake Lodge, the Peter Skene Ogden Trail #3956, and the Crater Rim Trail toward North Paulina Peak. Heading east, after 2.3 miles the Lost Lake trail #3958.2 goes off to the right. About 2.7 miles beyond that, the Newberry Crater Trail intersects with the Parallel Trail #3958.3. If you stay to the left you'll reach the Cinder Hill Trailhead, where you can detour to East Lake to give your horse a drink. If you continue on the Newberry Crater Trail, you'll climb to the Crater Rim Trail #3957 in another 2.2 miles.

Most of the Newberry Crater Trail has little elevation gain/loss. It has great footing for really moving out -- or for just moseying along.

North Paulina Peak

Trailhead: Start at Chief Paulina Horse Camp
Length: 11.5 miles round trip
Elevation: 6,300 to 7,600 feet
Difficulty: Moderate
Footing: Suitable for barefoot horses
Season: Summer through fall
Permits: Camping fee, or Northwest Forest Pass for day use
Facilities: Toilet, stock water, and manure bins at the horse camp. Stock water is also available near Paulina Lake Lodge.

Highlights: The ride is a steady but moderate climb to the crater rim. The views from the rim near North Paulina Peak are fabulous. As you gaze out at Paulina Lake and Paulina Peak, note that if the west side

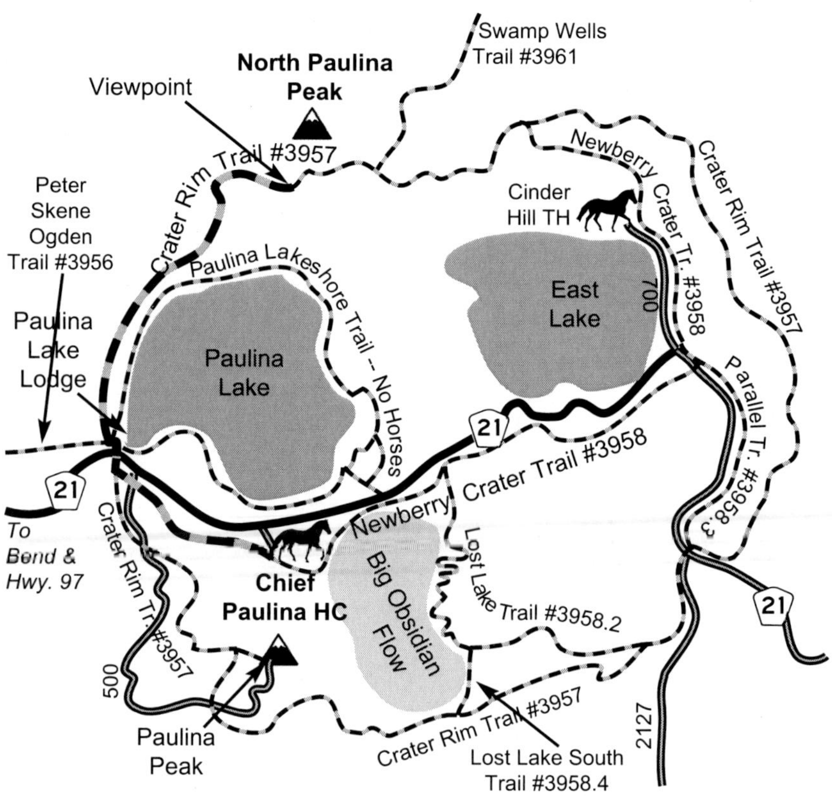

of the crater hadn't crumbled away and allowed Paulina Creek to flow out, Oregon would have had a second Crater Lake.

The Ride: From Chief Paulina Horse Camp, pick up the Newberry Crater Trail #3958 between campsites 9 and 10 and ride west for 1.5 miles. Turn right on the Crater Rim Trail #3957. Cross Road 21 and the bridge over Paulina Creek, then immediately turn left and go around the green metal gate to stay on the Crater Rim Trail #3957. (The Peter Skene Ogden Trail #3956 goes to the left, and the Paulina Lakeshore Trail (no horses allowed) goes to the right.) The trail climbs fairly steadily for 4 miles, following a forest road at first and then becoming a single-track trail. The trail then levels out and crosses a cinder-covered area that provides great views of the lake and the crater rim. If you continue 0.5 mile, you'll reach the junction with the Swamp Wells Trail #3961. About 1.6 mile later, you'll reach the junction with the Newberry Crater Trail #3958.

Whitney rides Dixie past a viewpoint near North Paulina Peak.

North Rim Loop

Trailhead: Start at Chief Paulina Horse Camp
Length: 17 miles round trip
Elevation: 6,300 to 7,600 feet
Difficulty: Challenging -- long
Footing: Hoof protection recommended
Season: Late spring through fall
Permits: Camping fee, or Northwest Forest Pass for day use
Facilities: Toilet, stock water, and manure bins at the horse camp. Toilet at Cinder Hill Trailhead. Stock water is also available near Paulina Lake Lodge and at East Lake.

Highlights: Though this ride is rather long, it's much easier than the Paulina Peak and Crater Rim loops. And it offers scenic views from the crater rim near North Paulina Peak.

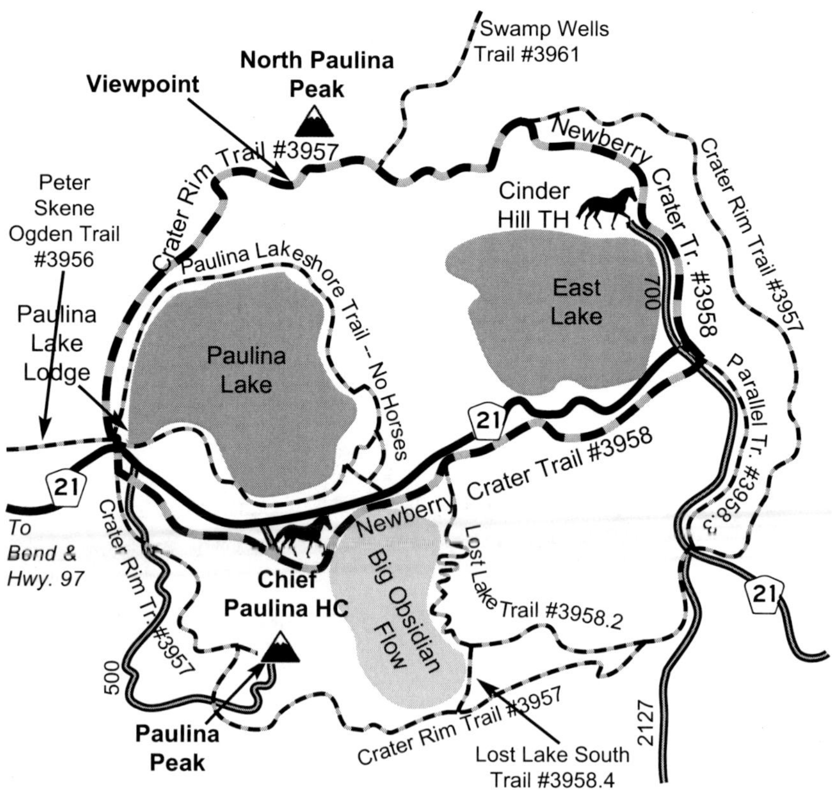

From the North Rim you have a splendid view of Paulina Lake and Paulina Peak.

The Ride: From Chief Paulina Horse Camp, pick up the Newberry Crater Trail #3958 between campsites 9 and 10. Ride west for 1.5 miles to the Crater Rim Trail #3957. Turn right on the Crater Rim Trail, then cross Road 21 and the bridge over Paulina Creek. Immediately turn left, go around the green metal gate, and pick up the Crater Rim Trail #3957 toward North Paulina Peak. The trail climbs fairly steadily for about 4 miles, following a forest road at first and then becoming a single-track trail. Then the trail levels out as it runs along the crater rim. About 2 miles after passing North Paulina Peak, turn right onto Newberry Crater Trail #3958 and follow it down to the shore of East Lake, about 2.2 miles. Continue another 1.3 miles to where the trail crosses Road 21, then veer right and follow the Newberry Crater Trail #3958 for about 5 miles, back to Chief Paulina Horse Camp. Along the way, you can water your horses at the boat ramp next to Paulina Lake Lodge and at East Lake near the Cinder Hill Trailhead.

Paulina Peak Loop

Trailhead: Start at Chief Paulina Horse Camp

Length: 13 miles round trip for the loop, or 13.6 miles round trip if you detour to the summit of Paulina Peak

Elevation: 6,300 to 7,700 feet for the loop, or 8,000 if you ride to the summit

Difficulty: Difficult -- very steep

Footing: Hoof protection recommended

Season: Late spring through fall

Permits: Camping fee, or Northwest Forest Pass for day use

Facilities: Toilet, stock water, and manure bins at the horse camp. Stock water is also available near Paulina Lake Lodge.

Highlights: If your horse is in good condition and you don't want to commit to the 25-mile ride around the entire rim of the crater, this trail is an alternative. You'll see the spectacular views from the top of

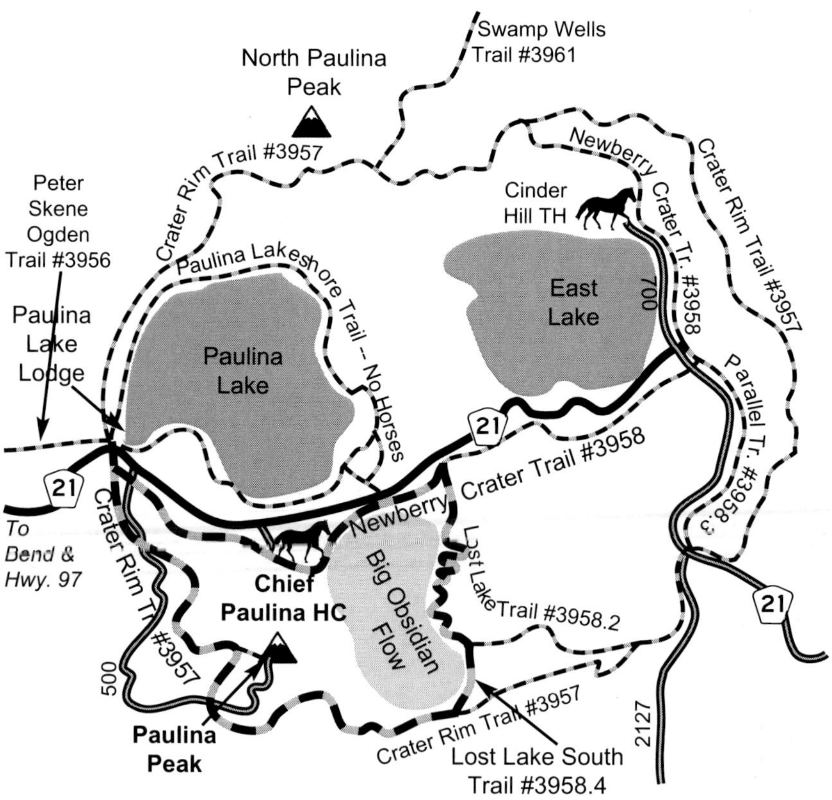

Paulina Peak and have an up-close look at Big Obsidian Flow. It's a challenging ride, though, because the first leg of the trail climbs very, very steeply.

The Ride: From Chief Paulina Horse Camp, pick up the westbound Newberry Crater Trail #3958 between campsites 9 and 10 and ride 1.5 miles. Turn left on the Crater Rim Trail #3957 toward Paulina Peak. The trail runs parallel to Road 500 for a mile or so, crosses it, and then climbs very steeply to near the summit of Paulina Peak, gaining 1,300 feet of elevation in 1.5 miles. The views from the top are amazing, but do not attempt this trail unless your horse is in very good condition. If you want to ride to the summit of Paulina Peak (which can also be accessed by car), veer left on the 0.3-mile spur trail. As you continue around the loop, the Crater Rim Trail levels out, and in 3.4 miles it reaches the junction with the Lost Lake South Trail #3958.4. Turn left on it, and in 0.7 mile turn left again on the Lost Lake Trail #3958.2. It will take you down a series of switchbacks along the eastern edge of the impressive Big Obsidian Flow. In 2.7 miles, turn left on the Newberry Crater Trail #3958 to return to the horse camp.

The summit of Paulina Peak offers a panoramic view.

Peter Skene Ogden Trail

Trailhead: Start at Chief Paulina Horse Camp or at Ogden Campground, 25 miles south of Bend on Hwy. 97

Length: 20 miles round trip from the horse camp to Ogden Campground, or 4 miles round trip to Paulina Falls. From Ogden Campground, it's 16.5 miles round trip to Paulina Falls or 17.5 miles round trip to Paulina Lake.

Elevation: 4,300 to 6,400 feet

Difficulty: Moderate

Footing: Suitable for barefoot horses

Season: Summer through fall

Permits: Camping fee, or Northwest Forest Pass for day parking at Chief Paulina Horse Camp. No fee at Ogden Campground.

Facilities: Toilets, stock water, plenty of parking at both Chief Paulina and Ogden Campground. Stock water is available on the trail.

Highlights: The trail winds along beside Paulina Creek, past lovely pools, waterfalls, and rapids. Wildflowers are abundant along the creek, which is often just a few feet from the trail. Paulina Falls, located about 0.5 mile from Paulina Lake, spills over a volcanic ledge into a canyon some 80 feet below. If you ride to the shore of Paulina Lake, you can get a delicious burger, ice cream, soda, or beer at Paulina Lake Lodge.

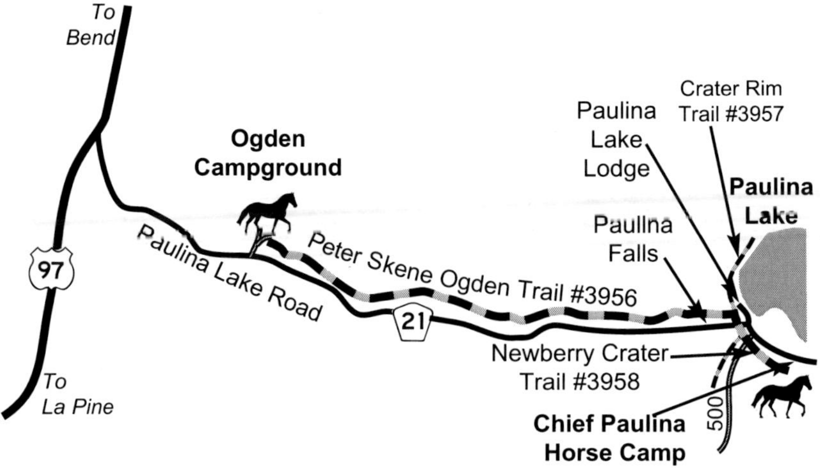

The double Paulina Falls drops an impressive 80 feet and is located right beside the trail.

Finding Ogden Campground: Take Hwy. 97 south of Bend for 23 miles and turn left on Paulina Lake Road toward Newberry National Volcanic Monument. Drive 2 miles and turn left into the campground. Park in the large gravel parking lot to the right of the campground entrance.

The Ride: <u>From Ogden Campground</u>, the trail leaves the gravel parking area, crosses Paulina Creek, and follows the creek steadily uphill to Paulina Lake. <u>From Chief Paulina Horse Camp</u>, pick up the westbound Newberry Crater Trail #3958 between campsites 9 and 10 and ride 1.5 miles. Turn right on the Crater Rim Trail #3957, then cross Road 21 and the bridge over Paulina Creek. Immediately turn left, go around the green metal gate, and pick up the Peter Skene Ogden Trail #3956 on the left. <u>All</u>, the scenery on this trail is quite varied, as the trail travels past riparian vegetation along the creek, across tree-covered hills, through dense stands of lodgepole pine, and across hillsides scarred by wildfire. You'll enjoy numerous waterfalls of varying sizes all along the creek. On the lakeshore, Paulina Lake Lodge offers toilets, a small general store, and a very good cafe. Note that bicyclists are permitted to ride uphill on the Peter Skene Ogden Trail but are required to ride downhill on a nearby forest road, appropriately known as the Paulina Plunge.

South Rim Loop

Trailhead: Start at Chief Paulina Horse Camp
Length: 13.5 miles round trip
Elevation: 6,400 to 7,300 feet
Difficulty: Moderate
Footing: Hoof protection recommended
Season: Summer through fall
Permits: Camping fee, or Northwest Forest Pass for day use
Facilities: Toilet, stock water, and manure bins at the horse camp. No stock water on the trail.

Highlights: This lollipop loop trail runs along the base of Big Obsidian Flow, which towers a hundred feet or more above the trail. It then climbs toward the crater rim on the Lost Lake Trail, offering amazing views of Big Obsidian Flow, Paulina Lake, Paulina Peak, and the Cascades before descending gently back to lake level.

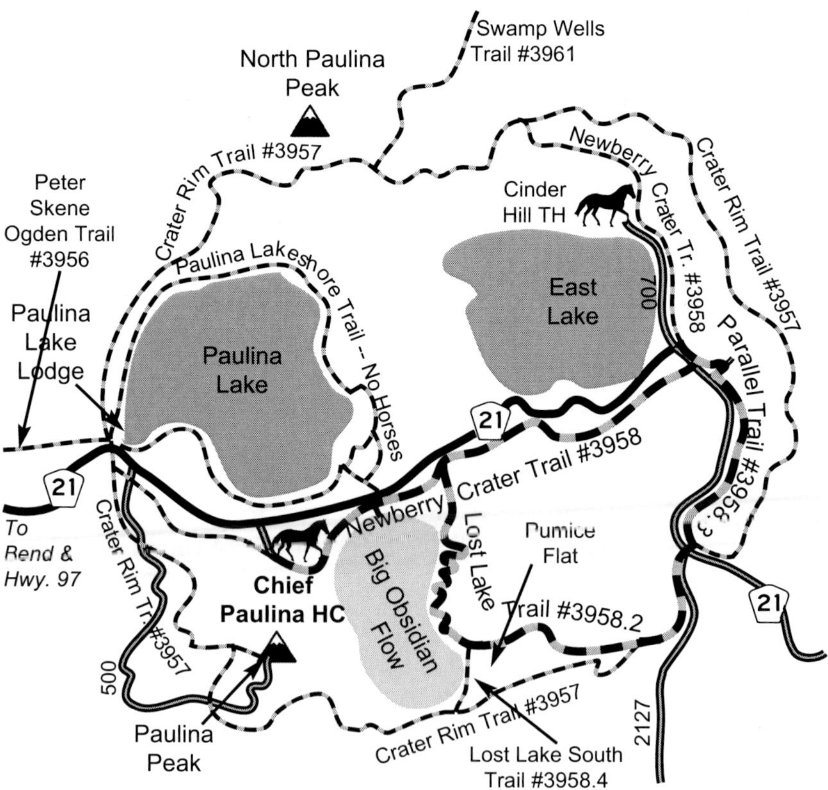

The Ride: Pick up the Newberry Crater Trail #3958 between campsites 2 and 3, and in 200 feet veer left at the junction. In 1.5 miles you'll cross the paved road that leads to the Big Obsidian Flow hiker trailhead. About 0.7 mile later, turn right at the junction with the Lost Lake Trail #3958.2. (Lost Lake is located at the base of Big Obsidian Flow, but you can't see it from the trail.) The trail climbs slowly for the next mile, then gains 700 feet of elevation on about 1.4 miles of switchbacks. The views in this section are panoramic. Then the trail descends for about 0.2 mile to a junction. Veer left on the Lost Lake Trail toward Pumice Flat, and in 1.5 miles the Lost Lake Trail meets the Crater Rim Trail #3957. Veer left on the Crater Rim Trail. In 1 mile, cross Road 21 and turn left on the Parallel Trail #3958.3. Follow it 1.4 miles to a dirt road where the trail seems to disappear. Turn right on the dirt road, and in 200 feet veer left around a pile of tree stumps to find the trail again. In another 0.6 mile, turn left on the Newberry Crater Trail #3958 and follow it 4.6 miles back to the horse camp. Where the trail runs through the decommissioned Hot Springs Campground the trail may at times be hard to follow. Just skirt around the base of the lava flow on your left and you'll soon pick up a clearer trail.

Diana rides Mo up the Lost Lake Trail beside the Big Obsidian Flow, part of the South Rim Loop.

Linda rides Beamer across Pumice Flat, on the Lost Lake Trail at Newberry Crater.

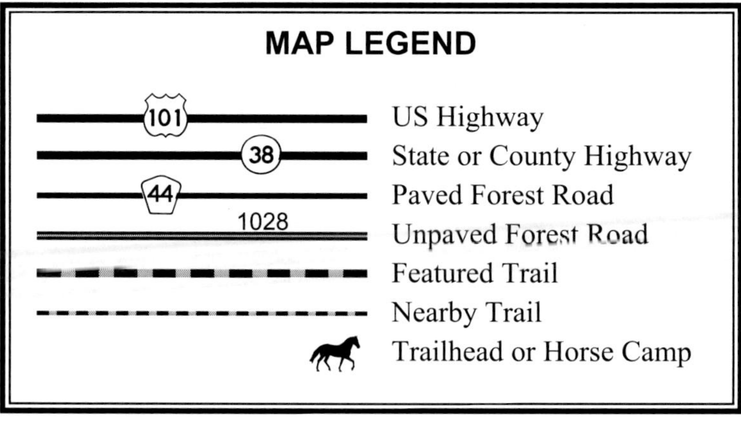

Cline Buttes Recreation Area

Bureau of Land Management

The Cline Buttes Recreation Area is a 50 square mile block of BLM land located between Bend, Redmond, and Sisters. Its dirt roads and sandy trails offer nearly-endless riding. While the trails can be dusty in summer, they offer excellent riding the rest of the year. And in most sections of Cline Buttes, horseback riders and mountain bike riders enjoy separate trails, as do motorized and non-motorized users.

Cline Buttes is a long-term project, as BLM is developing the recreation area's trail network in stages. Four trailheads currently offer horse trailer parking. As of this writing, BLM has completed the Maston, Tumalo Canals, and Cascade View Trailheads. The Fryrear Trailhead is scheduled to be moved to a new location and enlarged in 2018. Many of the equestrian trails are built, but other than at Maston they have not yet been signed. Until the signage is installed, keep a sense of adventure and have fun exploring the Cline Buttes trails.

Riders on Forgotten Fields Road, east of the Canals Trailhead.

Cline Buttes Recreation Area

The large trailheads at Cline Buttes offer easy parking for many trailers.

Teresa, Lydia, and Debbie ride Pops, Magic, and Split on a winter jaunt in the Maston area.

Getting to Cline Buttes Trailheads

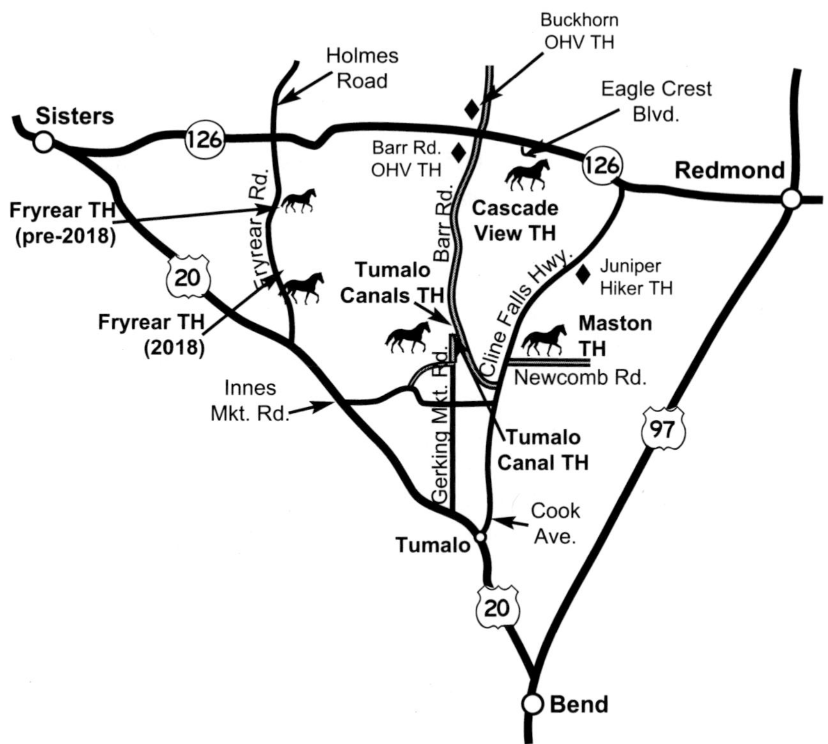

Cline Buttes Area Trails

Trail Area	Difficulty	Elevation	Round Trip
Cascade View Trails	Easy	3,050-3,300	4+ miles
Fryrear Trails	Easy	2,900-3,300	12+ miles
Maston Trails	Easy	3,050-3,300	15+ miles
Tumalo Canals East Trails	Easy	3,150-3,250	10+ miles
Tumalo Canals West Trails	Easy	3,150-3,450	15+ miles

Cascade View Trails

Trailhead: Start at Cascade View Trailhead

Length: About 4 miles of official trails for now, but more trails will be added in the future. You can also ride the trails used by Eagle Crest Stables.

Elevation: 3,050 to 3,300 feet

Difficulty: Easy, though as of our press date there are no trail signs

Footing: Suitable for barefoot horses

Season: Year-round

Permits: None

Facilities: Toilet, and parking for 8-10 trailers

Highlights: The Cascade View Trailhead is aptly named, with impressive mountain views from both the trailhead and the nearby trails. The heavy dashed line in the map below represents the only official horse trail out of the Cascade View Trailhead as of our publication

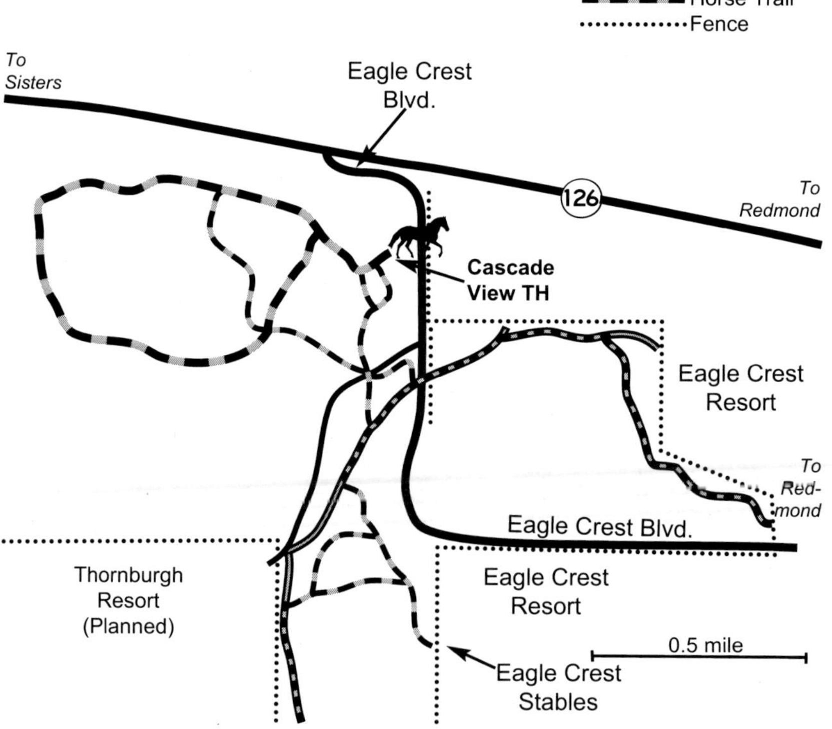

The Three Sisters and other Cascade mountains are visible from several vantage points along the Cascade View trails.

date. However, you can also ride the Eagle Crest Stables trails and the dirt roads, shown with narrower lines on the map. Plans call for additional trails to be built in the next couple of years, to connect the current trail with the trails in the Tumalo Canal, Maston, and Buttes areas. In the Cascade View area, horses and bikes are on separate trails.

Finding Cascade View Trailhead: From Bend, take Hwy. 20 to Tumalo and turn right on Cook Avenue, which soon becomes Cline Falls Hwy. After 10 miles, turn west on Hwy. 126 toward Sisters. In 2.9 miles, turn left on Eagle Crest Blvd. From Redmond, head west on Highland Avenue/Hwy. 126. Drive 7 miles and turn left on Eagle Crest Blvd. From Sisters, take Hwy. 126 east toward Redmond. In 12 miles, turn right on Eagle Crest Blvd. All, continue 0.3 mile on Eagle Crest Blvd. to the trailhead on the right.

The Ride: From the trailhead, go between the rock cribs in the fence and turn left on the trail. The trails here meander among the junipers, sagebrush, and bunch grass, and provide views of the Cascades from several vantage points. Trail junction signs are coming eventually, so please be patient.

Fryrear Trails

Trailhead: Start at the Fryrear Trailhead
Length: 12+ miles of trails
Elevation: 2,900 to 3,300 feet
Difficulty: Easy, though as of our press date there are no trail signs
Footing: Suitable for barefoot horses
Season: Year round
Permits: None
Facilities: The Fryrear Trailhead, to be built in 2018, will have a toilet, picnic tables, and parking for 12 trailers. No stock water on the trail.

Highlights: The canyons near Fryrear Trailhead are a delight. The basalt walls of Dry Canyon and Fryrear Canyon tower impressively

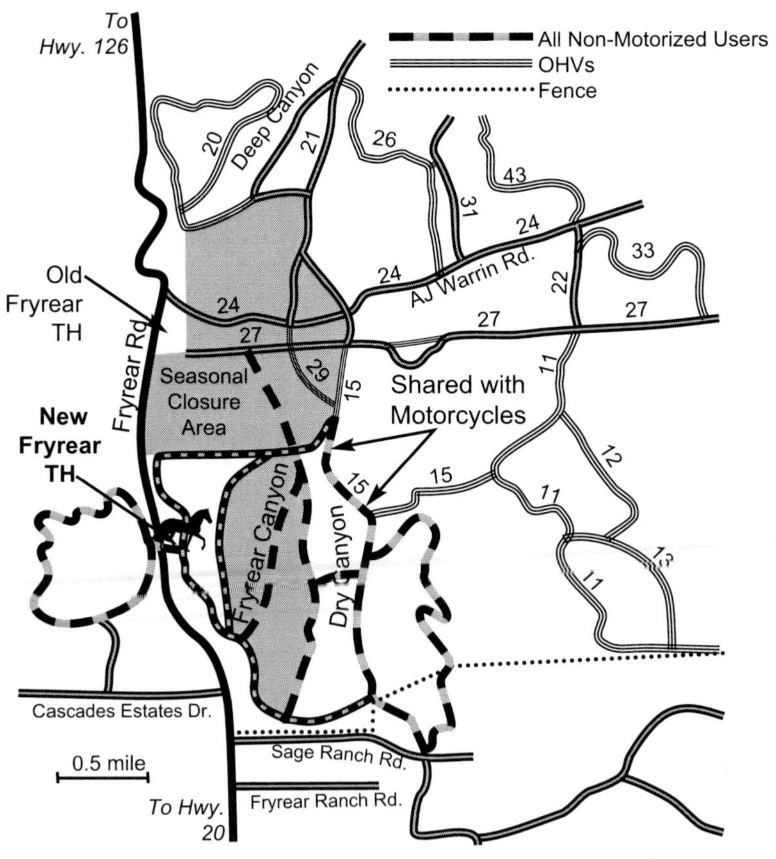

over the trail, and if you look carefully you can even find pictographs in Fryrear Canyon. Fryrear Canyon is closed from February 1 to August 1 to protect nesting raptors. You can ride around Fryrear Canyon during the closure period, but not through it. The area closure is serious, because the golden eagles nesting here will kill their young if you get too close to their nest. Dry Canyon is open year-round.

Finding Fryrear Trailhead: From Bend, drive northwest on Hwy. 20 for 13 miles, turn right on Fryrear Road, and continue 2.3 miles to the trailhead. From Redmond, drive west on Hwy. 126 for 13.5 miles, turn left on Fryrear Road, and continue 3.2 miles to the trailhead. From Sisters, drive east on Hwy. 126 for 5 miles, turn right on Fryrear Road, and continue 3.2 miles to the trailhead.

The Ride: To explore the canyons, head north or south from the new trailhead. The non-motorized trails near the Fryrear Trailhead are shared with mountain bikes, and part of the trail that runs through Dry Canyon is shared with motorcycles While the shared horse/motorcycle section is short, the canyon is very narrow there so it may be difficult to get off the trail if you need to. Use caution. Note that while OHVs are not permitted on the non-motorized trails, horses are allowed on the OHV trails. (Ride at your own risk.)

Lydia on Shadow and Diana on Tommy, traveling through Dry Canyon.

Maston Trails

Trailhead: Start at the Maston Trailhead
Length: 15+ miles of trails
Elevation: 3,050 to 3,300 feet
Difficulty: Easy
Footing: Suitable for barefoot horses
Season: Year-round
Permits: None
Facilities: Toilet, picnic tables, and parking for 18 trailers. No stock water on the trail.

Highlights: From the Maston Trailhead, you can access over 15 miles of easy equestrian trails. The terrain is fairly flat, and the footing is sandy. This is a popular mountain biking destination in the winter, but don't worry — the horse trails are completely separate from the

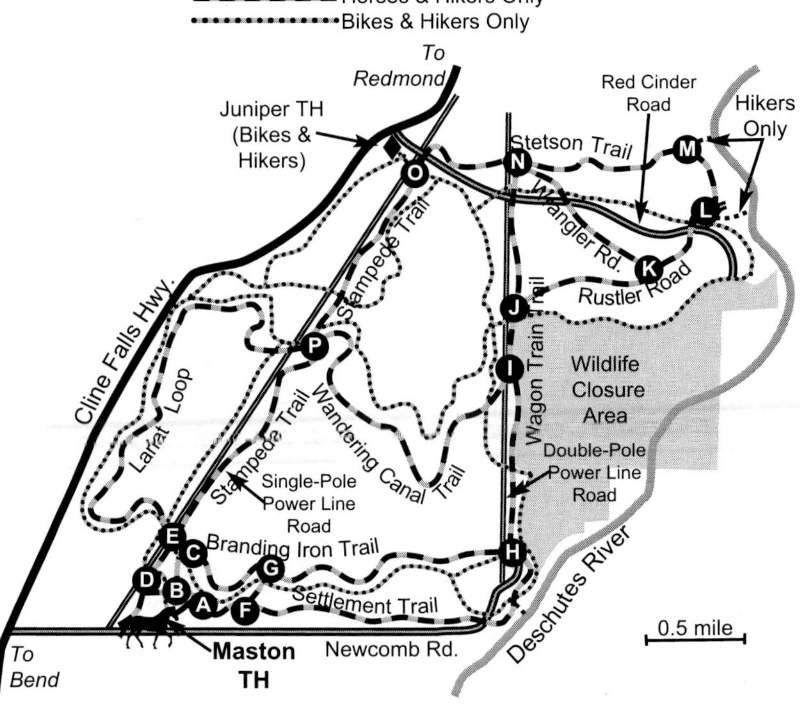

mountain bike trails. The two types of trails run roughly parallel to one another in order to leave large undisturbed tracts for wildlife habitat.

Finding Maston Trailhead: From Bend, take Hwy. 20 northwest for 6 miles. In Tumalo, turn right on Cook Ave., which soon becomes Cline Falls Hwy., and drive 4.5 miles. From Redmond, drive west on Hwy. 126 for 4.5 miles, turn south on Cline Falls Hwy. and continue 5.5 miles. From Sisters, drive east on Hwy. 126 for 15 miles, turn south on Cline Falls Hwy. and continue 5.5 miles. All, turn east on Newcomb Road and drive 0.9 mile to the trailhead.

The Ride: Interesting sights abound on the Maston trails. From the Stetson and Settlement Trails you'll have views of the Deschutes River and the canyon it flows through. The Wandering Canal Trail follows a canal that was dug to bring Tumalo Reservoir water to early-1900s homesteaders. This canal, and others in the area, never held water because the reservoir failed. When you ride the Settlement Trail, keep an eye out for the ruined foundations of an old homestead, likely abandoned because the promised irrigation water never came. Plus, you'll enjoy views of the Cascades from several vantage points.

Sue rides Bella along the Settlement Trail at Maston, with the Three Sisters on the horizon.

Tumalo Canals — East Trails

Trailhead: Start at the Tumalo Canal Trailhead
Length: 10+ miles of trails
Elevation: 3,150 to 3,250 feet
Difficulty: Easy, though as of our press date there are no trail signs
Footing: Suitable for barefoot horses
Season: Year round
Permits: None
Facilities: Toilet, picnic tables, and parking for 16 trailers. No stock water on the trail.

Highlights: From the Tumalo Canal Trailhead, you can cross Barr Road and access about 10 miles of easy trails and roads. One of the

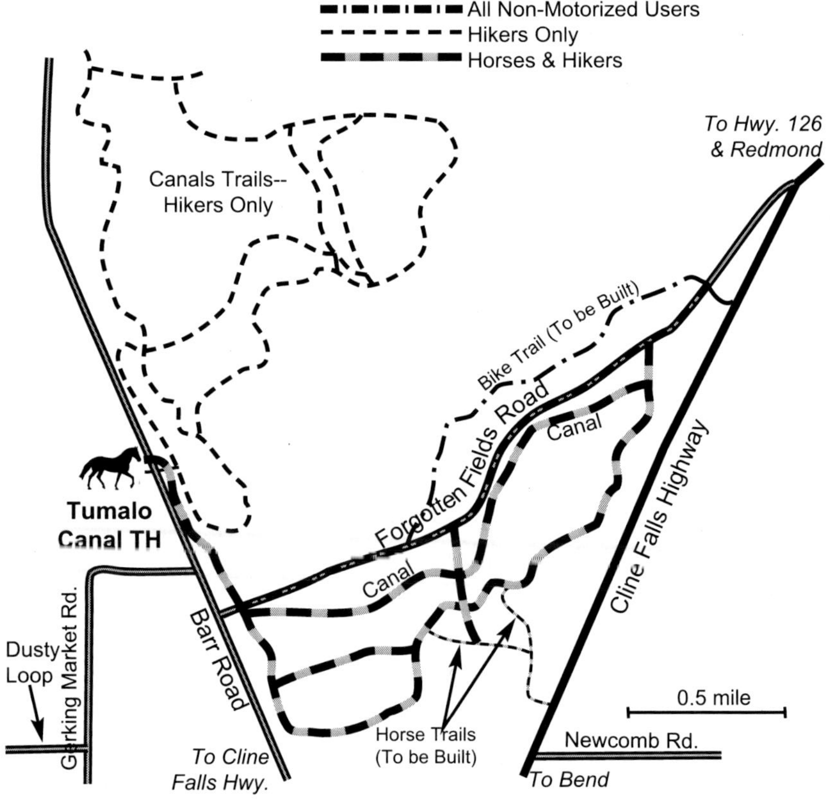

Whitney and Diana ride Misty and Tommy along the Forgotten Fields Road. What a view!

trails follows an abandoned canal, and Forgotten Fields Road provides a stunning view of the Cascades.

Finding Tumalo Canal Trailhead: From Redmond, take Hwy. 126 west for 4.5 miles, turn south on Cline Falls Hwy. and drive 6.5 miles, then turn right on Barr Road. Follow it for 1.5 miles to the trailhead. From Bend, take Hwy. 20 northwest for 5.5 miles to Tumalo and turn right on Cook Ave., which soon becomes Cline Falls Hwy. In 4 miles, turn left on Barr Road and follow it 1.5 miles to the trailhead. From Sisters, take Hwy. 20 toward Bend for 14 miles. Just before the highway heads downhill into Tumalo, turn left on Gerking Market Road. In 4.5 miles, turn left on Barr Road, then left again into the trailhead.

The Ride: From the trailhead parking area, cross Barr Road and pick up the horse trail that goes to the right, paralleling the road. After the trail crosses Forgotten Field Road, you can choose from several trails that wind among the area's juniper trees. Plans call for a trail to eventually cross Cline Falls Highway, connecting these trails with those in the Maston area.

Tumalo Canals – West Trails

Trailhead: Start at the Tumalo Canal Trailhead
Length: 15+ miles of trails
Elevation: 3,150 to 3,450 feet
Difficulty: Easy, though as of our press date there are no trail signs
Footing: Suitable for barefoot horses
Season: Year round
Permits: None
Facilities: Toilet, picnic tables, and parking for 16 trailers. No stock water on the trail.

Highlights: On the west side of Barr Road, the Tumalo Canal Trailhead provides access to many miles of easy riding on dirt roads, trails,

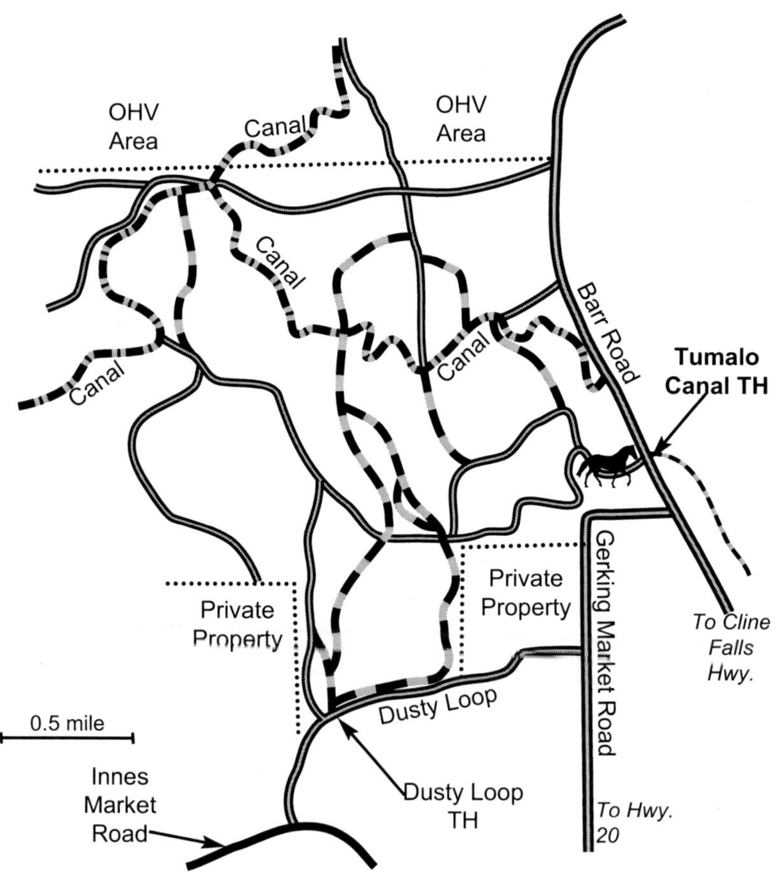

and along the banks of historic canals. The trails offer filtered views of the mountains from several vantage points.

Finding Tumalo Canal Trailhead: From Redmond, take Hwy. 126 west for 4.5 miles, turn south on Cline Falls Hwy. and drive 6.5 miles, then turn right on Barr Road. Follow it for 1.5 miles to the trailhead. From Bend, take Hwy. 20 northwest for 5.5 miles to Tumalo and turn right on Cook Ave., which soon becomes Cline Falls Hwy. In 4 miles, turn left on Barr Road and follow it 1.5 miles to the trailhead. From Sisters, take Hwy. 20 toward Bend for 14 miles. Just before the highway heads downhill into Tumalo, turn left on Gerking Market Road. In 4.5 miles, turn left on Barr Road, then left again into the trailhead.

The Ride: From the trailhead parking area, head west and go through the gate, then follow the dirt roads, single-track trails, and canals. The stretch of trail that parallels Dusty Loop features an interesting rock outcropping, and the canals are fun to follow. BLM plans to install signs at important junctions, but until that project is completed you may want to carry a compass or GPS so you can keep yourself oriented.

Debbie rides Split past a rock outcropping east of the Tumalo Canal Trailhead.

Dry Canyon, near the Fryrear Trailhead, is truly an impressive sight.

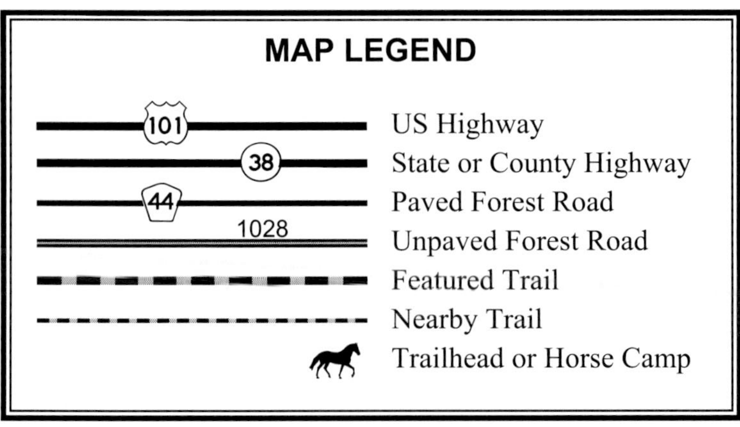

Corral Flat Dispersed Camp

Ochoco National Forest

Every year the Bandit Springs endurance race is staged at Corral Flat, a dispersed camping spot in one of the prettiest sections of the Ochoco Mountains. The area features tiny creeks, stately ponderosa pines and grand firs, and grassy meadows filled with seasonal wildflowers. The endurance trails run on a combination of single-track trails and forest roads, so it's important not to miss any junctions. However, the trails are not signed, and neither are many of the forest roads. You'll need a detailed map, a GPS or compass, and some wayfinding skills. Please keep a spirit of adventure and realize that you are doing a bit of exploring when you ride in this beautiful area.

Whitney rides Dixie through a flower-filled meadow along the Indian Prairie Trail.

Getting to Corral Flat

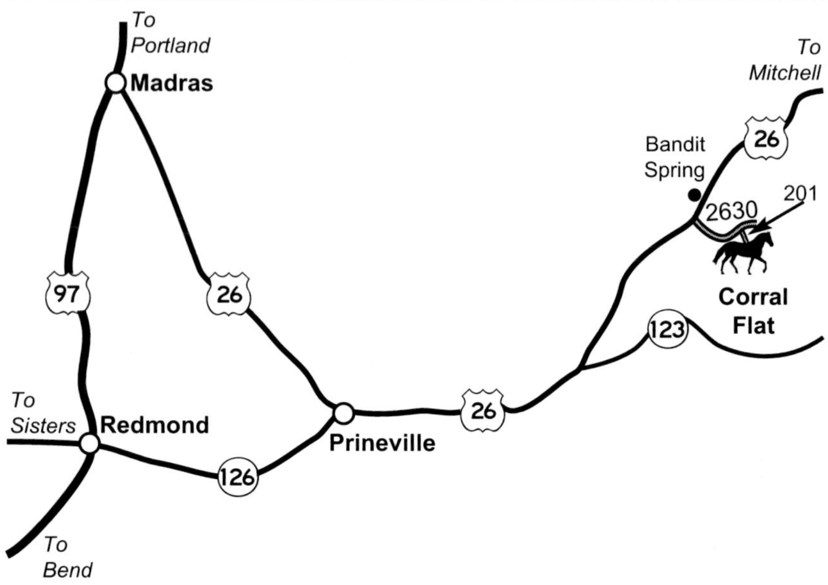

Corral Flat Trails

Trail	Difficulty	Elevation	Round Trip
Coyle Butte Loop	Moderate	4,600-5,500	10 miles
Indian Prairie	Moderate	4,800-6,000	18 miles
Old Stock Road Loop	Moderate	4,400-5,500	13 miles
Walton Lake	Moderate	4,800-5,500	12.5 miles

Corral Flat Dispersed Camping

Directions: To reach the Corral Flat dispersed camping area, take Hwy. 26 east from Prineville for 29 miles. Just after the 48-mile post, turn right on Road 2630 toward Marks Creek Sno-Park. Drive 1.9 miles and turn right on Road 201, a dirt road that runs beside a large meadow bordered by a rail fence. Continue 0.1 mile to the parking/ camping area.

Elevation: 4,750 feet

Campsites: Dispersed camping only — no defined campsites

Facilities: None -- no toilets, no water, no corrals

Permits: None

Season: Late spring through fall

Contact: Ochoco National Forest, 541-416-6500

Tommy and Tex hang out in their portable corrals at Corral Flat.

Coyle Butte Loop

Trailhead: Start at Corral Flat dispersed camping area

Length: 10 miles round trip

Elevation: 4,600 to 5,500 feet

Difficulty: Moderate -- the riding is easy and the trail is well-defined in most spots, but the route is unsigned, so a Prineville Ranger District map and a GPS will come in handy

Footing: Suitable for barefoot horses

Season: Late spring through fall

Permits: None

Facilities: Plenty of trailer parking at Corral Flat. Stock water is available on the trail.

Highlights: This trail is the route of the 10-mile fun ride held each year in conjunction with the Bandit Springs endurance race. The trail runs on a combination of single-track trails and open and closed forest roads that wind through beautiful forest and grassy meadows filled with wildflowers in season. An OHV trail network is planned for this area, which may affect this route in the future.

The Ride: Start on the south side of the Corral Flat camping area, next to the forest service kiosk. The trail goes over a low knoll and

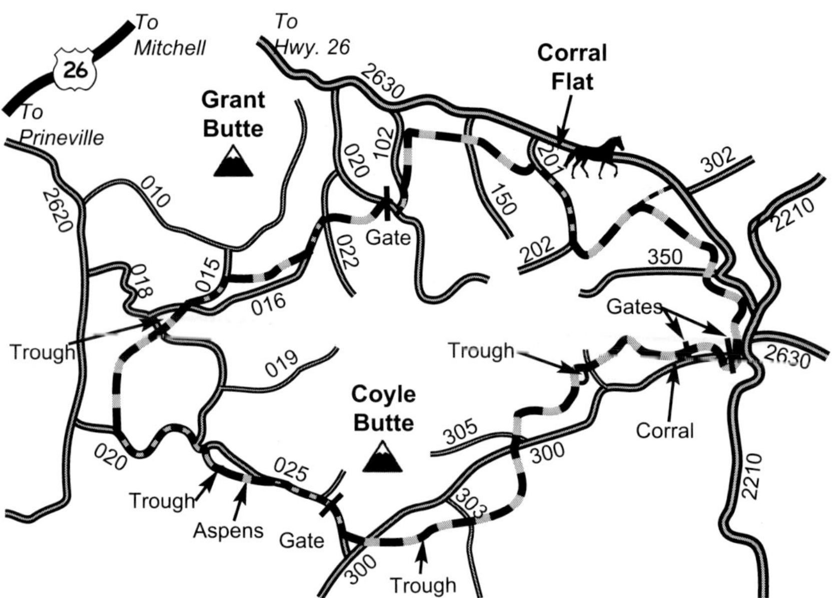

veers to the right. In 0.4 mile you'll cross closed Road 150, traverse a meadow, and travel beside closed Road 102. About 1 mile from the kiosk, you'll reach Road 020 and a cattle guard. Go through the gate. After another 1.0 mile you'll cross Road 016, and 0.1 mile later you'll arrive at a cattle trough. In another 0.5 mile, the trail turns left on another Road 020 and follows it 0.5 mile. When the road forks, go to the right on Road 025, then immediately veer right again on a less-distinct dirt road that runs uphill and becomes a single track. It parallels Road 025 for 0.7 mile, taking you to another water trough, along tiny Rush Creek, and past an exclosure fence around an aspen thicket. Then the trail rejoins Road 025, which begins running downhill and gets very eroded. In 0.2 mile Road 025 goes through a gate. In another 0.2 mile, veer left off the road on a single-track, which shortly crosses gravel Road 300. In 0.2 mile you'll reach another trough beside a boggy creek bed, and 0.4 mile later you'll cross Road 303. In 0.5 mile, you'll re-cross gravel Road 300. About 0.6 mile later, at a wire fence, a trail detours to the right to a dry water trough. Ignore it, and in 100 yards the detour trail rejoins the main trail. Continue for another 0.8 mile to a cattle-gathering corral. In 0.1 mile after that you'll go through another gate, and 0.2 mile later you'll cross Road 300, go through a gate next to a cattle guard, and re-cross Road 300. The trail then parallels Road 2630, crossing Road 350 after 0.5 mile. In another 0.5 mile the trail reaches a T-junction. Turn left, and in 0.4 mile you'll come to another T-junction with a wide ATV trail. Turn right here, and in 0.4 mile you'll arrive back at Corral Flat.

Lydia and Connie ride Shadow and Diamond through a sunlit meadow on the Coyle Butte Loop.

Indian Prairie

Trailhead: Start at Corral Flat dispersed camping area

Length: 18 miles round trip

Elevation: 4,800 to 6,000 feet

Difficulty: Moderate -- the riding is easy but the route is unsigned, so a Prineville Ranger District map and a GPS will come in handy

Footing: Hoof protection recommended

Season: Late spring through fall

Permits: None

Facilities: Plenty of trailer parking at Corral Flat. Stock water is available on the trail.

Highlights: This is a rather long ride, but it goes through easy terrain and the scenery is great -- lush meadows, beautiful forest, and nice views from several spots. Seeing the vast Indian Prairie nestled between Slide Mountain and Mt. Pisgah is worth riding the entire 18 miles.

The Ride: From Corral Flat, ride east on Road 201 (the road through the camping area), which soon becomes a trail. In 0.4 mile, turn left where Road 202 goes off to the right. At the junction in another 0.5

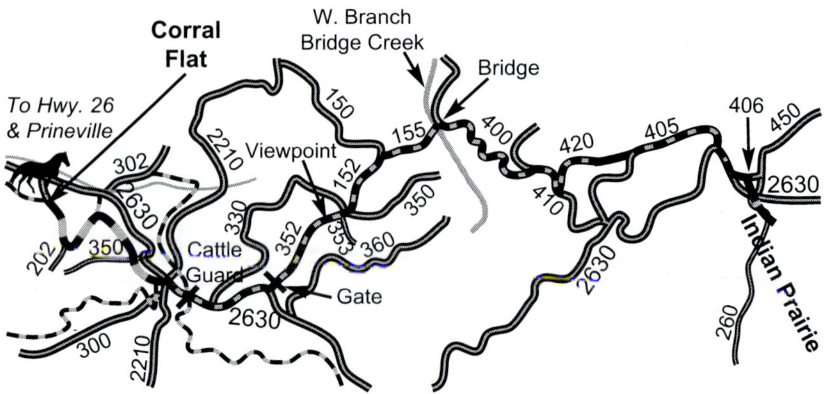

Lydia and Shadow stroll across Indian Prairie.

mile, turn right on a single-track trail. Continue 1 mile, and when you see the junction of gravel Roads 2630 and 2210, veer left and ride cross-country to the road junction. Go to the right on Road 2630, and in 0.2 mile go through the gate at the cattle guard, then continue along Road 2630 for another 0.7 mile. Turn left on Road 352, go through the wire gate, and ride about 0.9 mile. Look left for a nice view across a clearcut. In another 0.1 mile you'll reach a spot where a dirt road comes in on the left. About 100 feet later, Road 352 ends at gravel Road 350. Veer right on Road 350 and in 50 feet take a hard left down the embankment onto dirt Road 152. In 0.6 mile you'll reach another junction, with Road 150 going to the left and Road 155 going to the right. Turn right on Road 155, and in 0.6 mile you'll reach the bridge over the West Branch of Bridge Creek. Cross the bridge and turn right on Road 400. In 1.2 miles, a single-track trail goes off to the left. Follow it uphill, and it soon becomes Road 420. Stay on it for a total of 1.1 miles and you'll see another single-track trail depart on the left. Follow it for 1 mile, and when the trail forks go left again. In 0.7 mile you'll reach the beautiful Indian Prairie. The forest shelter and the aspen grove in the upper meadow are both worth exploring.

Old Stock Road Loop

Trailhead: Start at Corral Flat dispersed camping area

Length: 13 miles round trip

Elevation: 4,400 to 5,500 feet

Difficulty: Moderate -- the riding is easy but the route is unsigned, so a Prineville Ranger District map and a GPS will come in handy

Footing: Hoof protection recommended

Season: Late spring through fall

Permits: None

Facilities: Plenty of trailer parking at Corral Flat. Stock water is available on the trail.

Highlights: This loop mostly follows gravel and dirt forest roads up and down over low, forested ridges and through lush meadows. You'll have panoramic views to the north from several vantage points.

The Ride: From Corral Flat, ride Road 201 eastward. It soon becomes a single track, and in 0.4 mile Road 202 goes off to the right.

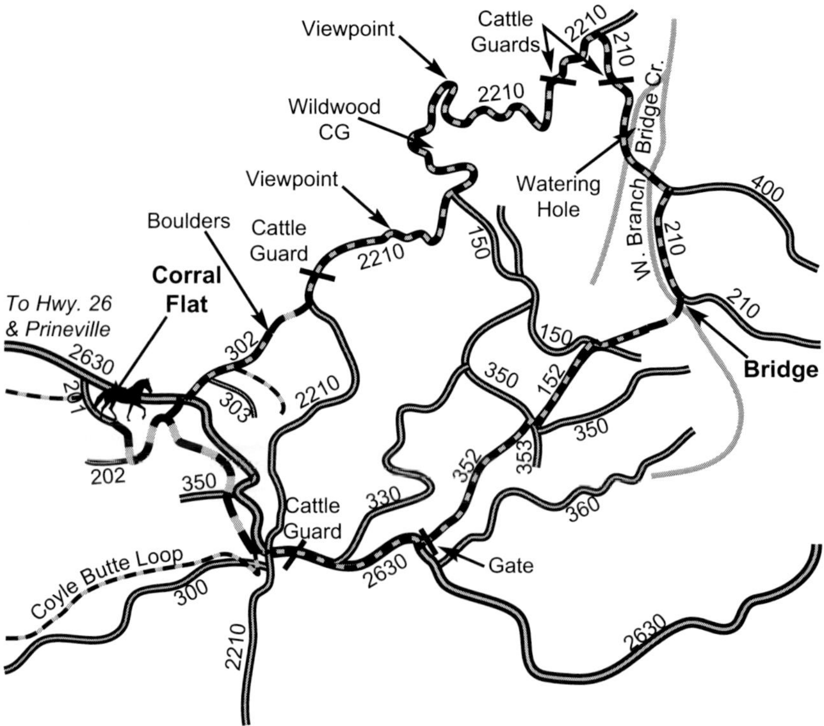

Whitney and Dixie enjoy the view from Road 2210.

Stay left, and in 0.5 mile go straight at a 3-way junction. In 0.2 mile you'll reach Road 2630. Jog slightly to the right and pick up Road 302. Follow it for 1 mile to where it ends at some boulders in the road. Go between the boulders and ride cross-country, straight up the hill, and in 0.2 mile you'll reach Road 2210. Turn left on the road and go through the gate next to the cattle guard. Follow Road 2210 for 0.5 mile to a viewpoint, then another 1.8 miles to an even better view-point, passing Wildwood Campground on the way. Road 2210 now begins to lose elevation, and in 1.2 miles you'll cross a cattle guard. About 0.3 mile after that, turn right on Road 210. You'll start gaining elevation now, and after 0.8 mile you'll find a short spur trail on the left that leads to a watering hole at the creek. About 0.8 mile beyond that, the road forks. Go the right and continue along the West Branch of Bridge Creek. Very Important: In 0.7 mile, turn right and cross the bridge over the creek. Follow the overgrown single-track that skirts the left side of the meadow, then follow the white diamonds on the trees. In 0.6 mile you'll reach Road 150. Turn right on it, and almost immediately veer left on Road 152. About 0.6 mile later you'll come to Road 350. Jog to the right and immediately turn left on Road 352. Follow it for 0.7 mile to a gate at gravel Road 2630. Go through the gate and turn right on Road 2630, following it for 1.0 mile, going through a gate at a cattle guard after 0.8 mile. When you reach gravel Road 2210, cross it and ride straight ahead cross-country for 50 feet, then turn right on the trail and follow it 1.9 miles back to Corral Flat.

Walton Lake

Trailhead: Start at Corral Flat dispersed camping area

Length: 12.5 miles round trip

Elevation: 4,800 to 5,500 feet

Difficulty: Moderate -- the riding is easy but the route is unsigned, so a Prineville Ranger District map and a GPS will come in handy

Footing: Hoof protection recommended

Season: Late spring through fall

Permits: None

Facilities: Plenty of trailer parking at Corral Flat. Stock water is available on the trail.

Highlights: This is a delightful ride that follows single-track trails and dirt roads to Walton Lake. It travels through ponderosa forest, fir groves, and lush flower-filled meadows. It's easy to make a wrong turn on these unsigned trails, so be sure to carry a map and a GPS or compass.

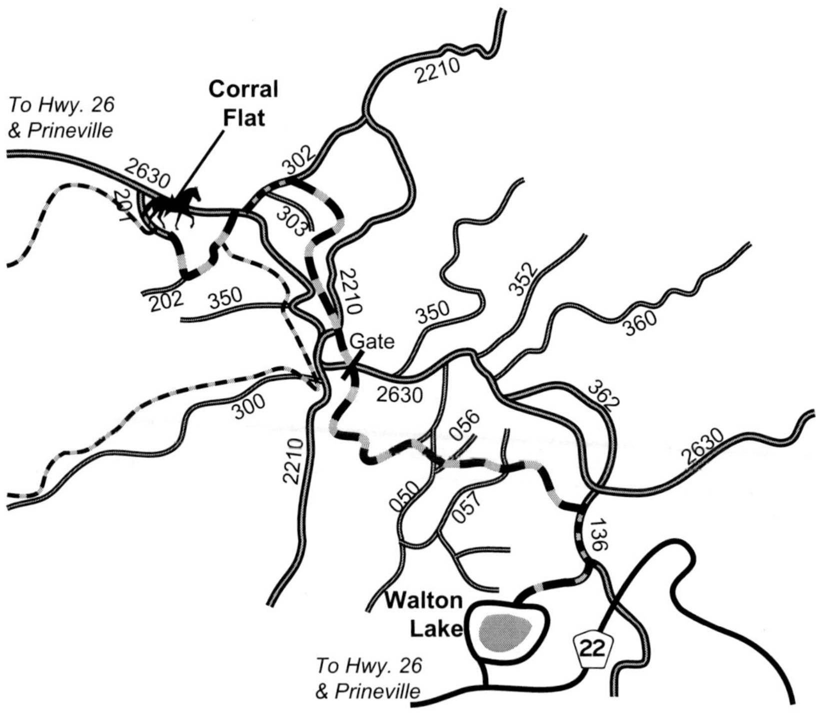

Diana rides Mo and Whitney rides Dixie through a meadow filled with wild asters.

The Ride: From Corral Flat, ride east on Road 201. It soon becomes a trail, and in 0.4 mile Road 202 goes off to the right. Stay left, and in 0.5 mile a single-track trail goes off to the right. Go straight, and in 0.2 mile you'll reach Road 2630. Jog slightly right and pick up Road 302. Follow it for 0.5 mile, passing Road 303 on the way. Turn right on a wide trail that is occasionally marked with white diamonds on the trees. Continue 1.3 miles and cross gravel Road 2210, then in 0.2 mile cross gravel Road 2630 next to the cattle guard. Go through the wire gate and ride 0.9 mile. At the junction with an unnumbered dirt road, stay to the right on the trail. In another 0.2 mile you'll cross dirt Road 050, then 200 feet later you'll cross dirt Road 056 and start seeing blue ski-trail diamonds on the trees. In 0.6 mile, continue straight ahead when the trail crosses a ski trail. In 0.2 mile after that, veer right on a wide trail marked by a white diamond. About 0.5 mile later, veer right onto dirt Road 136. In another 0.2 mile, turn right on an indistinct dirt road that leads downhill into a meadow filled with corn lilies. Follow it for 0.7 mile, then turn left on a wide trail and continue 0.2 mile to Walton Lake. Note that horses are not permitted in the campground that surrounds Walton Lake, so you'll need to tie your horse outside the campground and walk to the lake on foot.

Diana on Mo and Whitney on Dixie, on the trail to Walton Lake.

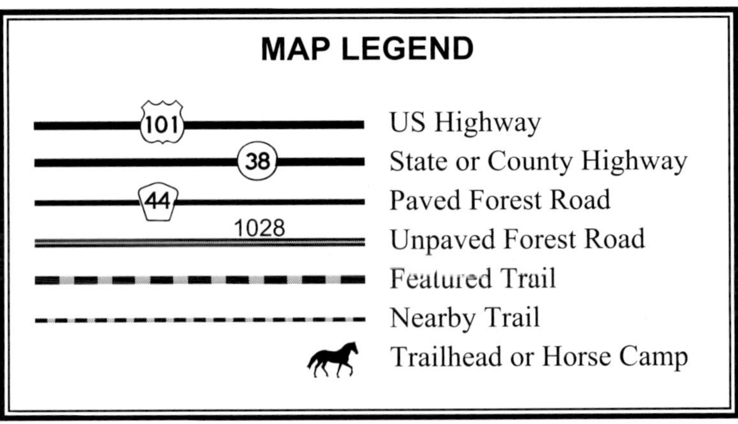

Cultus Corral

Cultus Lake Area

Deschutes National Forest

Cultus Corral Horse Camp is located a couple of miles from Cultus Lake, in the heart of the Cascade Lakes District about 50 miles southwest of Bend. The horse camp has corrals, large parking pads at each campsite, and plentiful shade provided by lodgepole pines. The trails will take you over Bench Mark Butte and to a variety of pretty lakes. The word "cultus" is Chinook jargon that means "worthless." It is believed that the term refers to the lack of adequate forage for horses in the area. It certainly doesn't refer to the nearby trails, which are a delight.

Connie, Diana, and Lydia on Mel, Diamond, and Shadow, ready to ride the Many Lakes Loop near Little Cultus Lake.

Getting to Cultus Lake

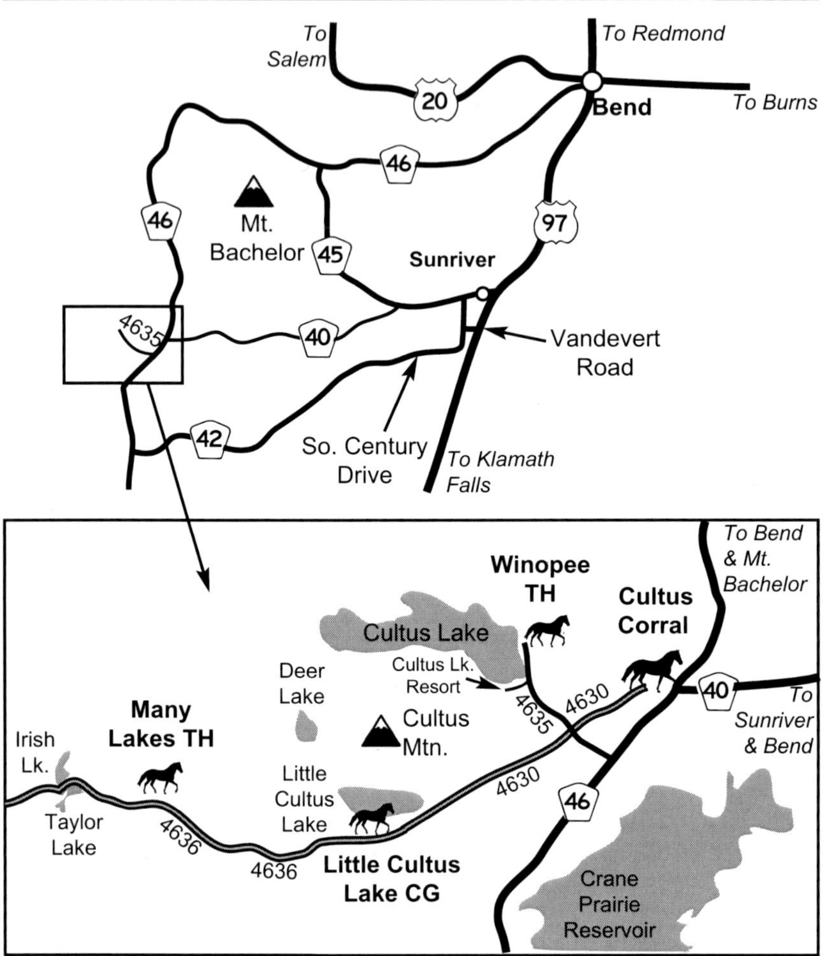

Cultus Lake Trails

Trail	Difficulty	Elevation	Round Trip
Bench Mark Butte	Moderate	4,450-4,800	9 miles
Bench Mark/Cultus Loop	Moderate	4,450-5,100	15.5 miles
Irish & Taylor Lakes	Easy	4,450-5,600	12-19.5 miles
Many Lakes Loop	Moderate	4,450-5,400	12-19.5 miles
Winopee Lake	Moderate	4,450-5,000	12.5-22.5 miles
Winopee Tie Trail	Easy	4,450-4,800	5-6 miles

Cultus Corral

Directions: From Bend, drive south on Hwy. 97 for 18 miles. Turn right on Vandevert Road and follow it for 1.0 mile. Turn left on South Century Drive, and in 1.1 mile veer right to stay on South Century Drive, which soon becomes Road 42. In 22.8 miles, turn right on Road 46. Drive 6.3 miles and turn left on Road 4635 toward Cultus Lake Resort. In 0.7 mile, turn right on Road 4630. The horse camp is on the right in 1.1 miles. The route is well signed. Alternatively, you can take Hwy. 46 (the Cascade Lakes Hwy.) past Mt. Bachelor to Road 4635.

Elevation: 4,450 feet

Campsites: 11 sites, 10 with 4-horse corrals and one with highline poles. All sites have fire pits and picnic tables, all are level and back-in, and most have room for 2 trailers.

Facilities: Vault toilet, manure bin, garbage cans. Stock water from a pump. Day-use parking for 8-10 trailers.

Permits: Camping fee, or Northwest Forest Pass for day use

Season: Summer through fall

Contact: Bend/Ft. Rock Ranger District: 541-383-4000
Hoodoo Recreation (concessionaire): 541-338-7869

Connie leads Moose out of his corral in preparation for a ride.

Bench Mark Butte

Trailhead: Start at Cultus Corral

Length: 9 miles round trip from the horse camp to the Corral Swamp Trailhead

Elevation: 4,450 to 4,800 feet

Difficulty: Moderate

Footing: Hoof protection recommended

Season: Summer through fall

Permits: Camping fee. No fee for day-use parking at Cultus Corral.

Facilities: Toilets, stock water, and day-use parking for 8-10 trailers at Cultus Corral. No stock water on the trail.

Highlights: This trail departs from Cultus Corral and runs over the flank of 5,028-foot Bench Mark Butte to the Corral Swamp Trailhead.

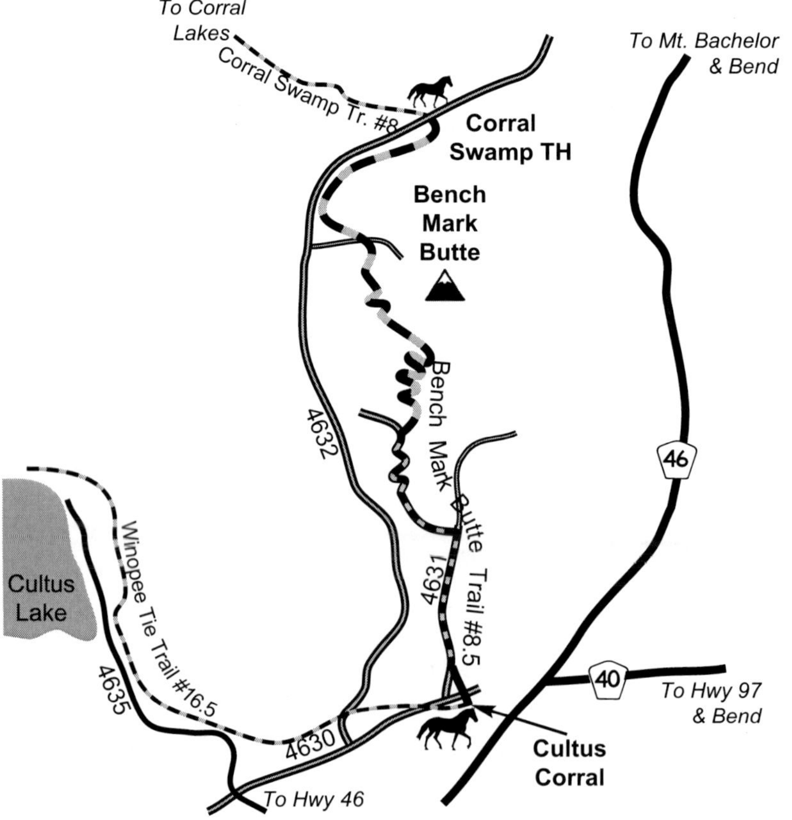

The trail runs on a combination of gravel roads and single-track trails and is signed with gray diamonds on the trees. It is fairly rocky in some sections, and has some switchbacks.

The Ride: Pick up the camp's perimeter trail between campsite 11 and the shelter, then in 150 feet make a hard right onto the Bench Mark Butte Trail #8.5. In 0.1 mile, the trail crosses Road 4630 and begins following gravel Road 4631. In 0.8 mile, veer left on a closed road that switchbacks up the butte for 1.2 miles. The route then veers onto a single-track on the right and continues 1.9 miles over Bench Mark Butte and down to the Corral Swamp Trailhead. On the north side of the butte, keep an eye out for some peek-a-boo views of Mt. Bachelor through the trees. Once you reach the Corral Swamp Trailhead, you can either continue on to the Corral Lakes on Trail #8 (about 3 miles farther) or retrace your steps to Cultus Corral. Before you ride, be sure to check with the Forest Service to make sure this trail has been cleared.

Whitney, Diana, Lydia and Connie make a switchback on the Bench Mark Butte Trail.

Bench Mark Butte/Cultus Lake Loop

Trailhead: Start at Cultus Corral
Length: 15.5 miles round trip
Elevation: 4,450 to 5,100 feet
Difficulty: Moderate
Footing: Hoof protection recommended
Season: Summer through fall
Permits: Camping fee. No fee for day-use parking at Cultus Corral.
Facilities: Toilets, stock water, and day-use parking for 8-10 trailers at Cultus Corral. Stock water is available on the trail.

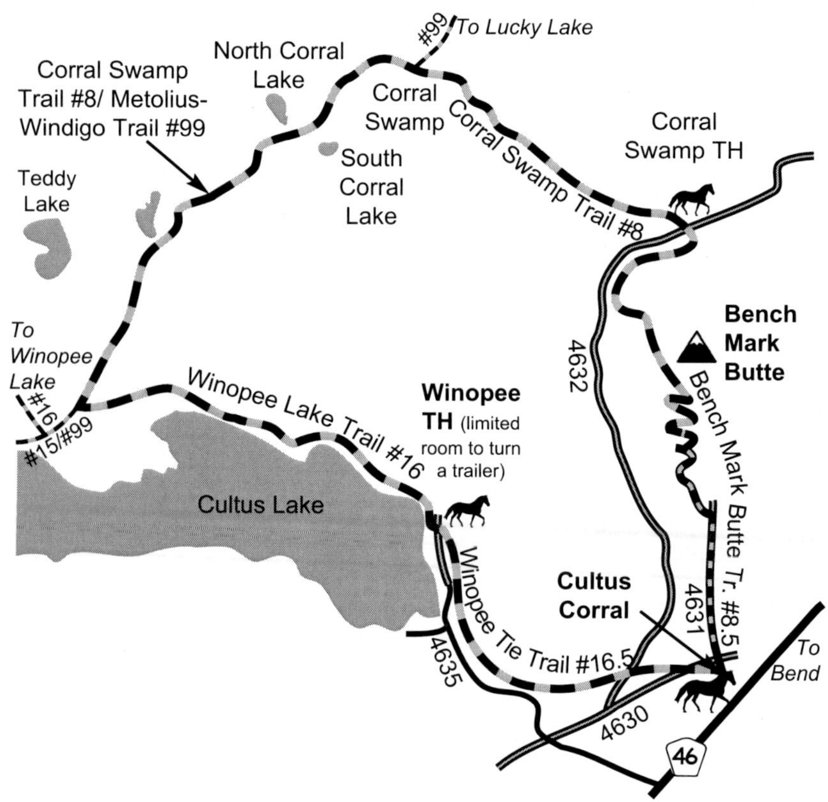

Connie on Diamond and Whitney on Dixie, on the Winopee Lake Trail along the shore of Cultus Lake.

Highlights: This scenic loop ride goes over the flank of Benchmark Butte; through forest of lodgepole pines, hemlocks and firs; past several pretty lakes; across meadows; and along the shore of Cultus Lake.

The Ride: Pick up the camp's perimeter trail between campsite 11 and the shelter, then in 150 feet make a hard right onto the Bench Mark Butte Trail #8.5. It will take you to the Corral Swamp Trailhead in 4.5 miles. Continue on the Corral Swamp Trail #8 for 2 miles. At the junction with the Metolius-Windigo Trail #99, turn left on the Corral Swamp/Met-Win Trail. After another mile you'll ride between North and South Corral Lakes. Continue 2.3 miles, turn left onto the Winopee Lake Trail #16, and continue 2.4 miles to the Winopee Trailhead. From there, take the Winopee Tie Trail #16.5 and follow it 3 miles back to Cultus Corral. For additional information, see the pages in this chapter for the Bench Mark Butte and Winopee Tie Trails.

Irish & Taylor Lakes

Trailhead: Start from Little Cultus Lake Campground or Cultus Corral

Length: 12 miles round trip from Little Cultus Lake, or 19.5 miles round trip from Cultus Corral

Elevation: 4,450 to 5,600 feet

Difficulty: Easy

Footing: Hoof protection recommended

Season: Summer through fall

Permits: Camping fee. No fee for day-use parking at Cultus Corral or on the road near Little Cultus Lake Campground.

Facilities: Toilet, stock water, and day-use parking for 8-10 trailers at Cultus Corral. Toilet, potable water, and parking for 2 trailers near Little Cultus Lake Campground. Stock water is available on the trail.

Highlights: This is a fun, easy road ride that goes past the trailheads for Lemish Lake and Many Lakes and ends at the beautiful Irish and Taylor Lake, at the junction of Road 4636 and the Pacific Crest Trail. You can start the ride at Cultus Corral, but we recommend trailering to Little Cultus Lake to start, because gravel Road 4630 is straight and boring.

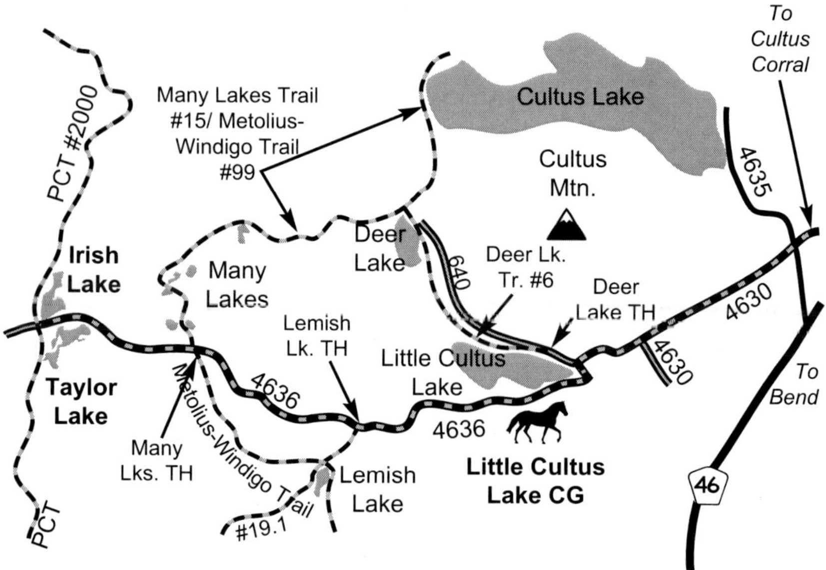

Whitney and Cody take in the view at Irish Lake.

Finding Little Cultus Lake Campground: Follow the directions to Cultus Corral at the beginning of this chapter, but instead of turning right on Road 4630, turn left. In 1.7 miles, the road number changes to 4636, and in another 1.2 miles you'll reach Little Cultus Lake Campground. You can either park in at the campground (and pay the camping fee) or drive through the campground to turn around and find a pull-off on the side of Road 4636 just east of the campground. Road 4636 is not suitable for trailers beyond Little Cultus Lake Campground.

The Ride: From Cultus Corral, ride Roads 4630 and 4636 west for 3.7 miles to Little Cultus Lake Campground. From Little Cultus Lake Campground, ride west on Road 4636. The road is too rough for horse trailers, but it makes a great ride on horseback. After 2.3 miles, you will pass Lemish Lake Trailhead, and in another 2 miles you'll pass the Many Lakes Trailhead. Continue on Road 4636 for 1.8 miles to Taylor Lake and Irish Lake. These two scenic lakes are directly across the road from one another, and the Pacific Crest Trail runs along their western edges.

Many Lakes Loop

Trailhead: Start from Little Cultus Lake Campground or Cultus Corral

Length: 12 miles round trip from Little Cultus Lake Campground, or 19.5 miles round trip from Cultus Corral

Elevation: 4,450 to 5,400 feet

Difficulty: Moderate

Footing: Hoof protection recommended

Season: Summer through fall

Permits: Camping fee. No fee for day-use parking at Cultus Corral or on the road near Little Cultus Lake Campground.

Facilities: Toilet, stock water, and day-use parking for 8-10 trailers at Cultus Corral. Toilet, potable water, and parking for 2 trailers near Little Cultus Lake Campground. Stock water is available on the trail.

Highlights: The Many Lakes Trail is aptly named, as it weaves among dozens of small lakes that lie scattered through the forest. There is little elevation gain or loss, so you could trot or canter if you wanted. But you won't want to go fast, because you'll be savoring the views of the lovely lakes and the beautiful hemlock and fir forest.

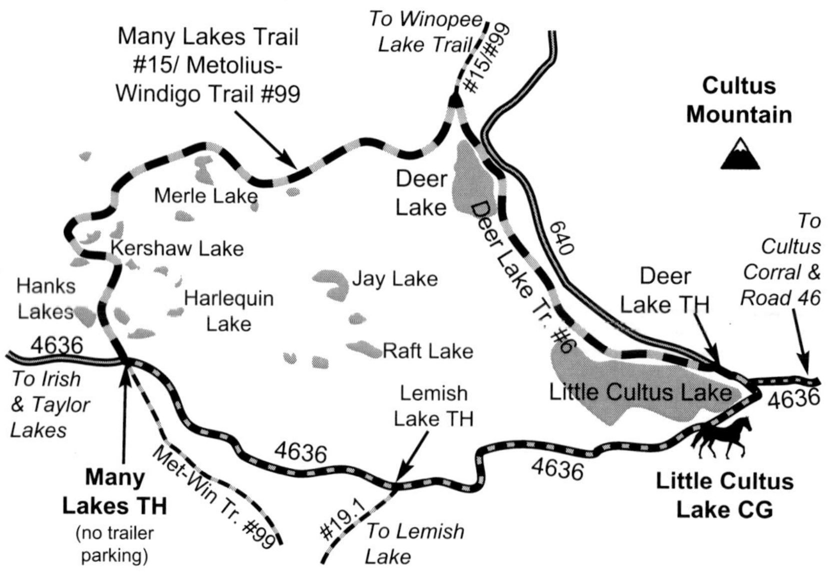

Lisa rides Mr. T past East Hanks Lake in the Many Lakes Basin.

Finding Little Cultus Lake Campground: Follow the directions to Cultus Corral at the beginning of this chapter, but instead of turning right on Road 4630, turn left. In 1.7 miles, the road number changes to 4636, and in another 1.2 miles you'll reach Little Cultus Lake Campground. You can either park in at the campground (and pay the camping fee) or drive through the campground to turn around and find a pull-off on the side of Road 4636 just east of the campground. Beyond Little Cultus Lake Campground, Road 4636 is too rough for trailers.

The Ride: <u>From Cultus Corral</u>, ride Roads 4630 and 4636 west for 3.7 miles to Little Cultus Lake Campground. <u>From Little Cultus Lake Campground</u>, ride west on Road 4636 about 4.3 miles to the Many Lakes Trailhead. Pick up the Many Lakes Trail #15/Metolius-Windigo Trail #99 heading north, and follow it as it winds among dozens of little lakes. After 4.7 miles it intersects with the Deer Lake Trail #6. Turn right at this junction and follow the Deer Lake Trail for 2.3 miles to the Deer Lake Trailhead. Follow Road 640 for 0.4 mile, then turn right on Road 4636 to return to your trailer at Little Cultus Lake Campground or turn left to ride back to Cultus Corral.

Winopee Lake Trail

Trailhead: Start at Cultus Corral or the Winopee Trailhead

Length: From Winopee Trailhead it's 6.5 miles to the Teddy Lakes, 12.5 miles to Muskrat Lake, or 16.5 miles to Winopee Lake round trip. From Cultus Corral it's 13.5 miles to the Teddy Lakes, 18.5 miles to Muskrat Lake, or 22.5 miles to Winopee Lake round trip.

Elevation: 4,450 to 5,000 feet

Difficulty: Moderate

Footing: Hoof protection recommended

Season: Summer through fall

Permits: Camping fee. No fee for day-use parking at Cultus Corral or Winopee Trailhead.

Facilities: Toilets, stock water, and day-use parking for 8-10 trailers at Cultus Corral. Possible parking for 1-2 trailers at the tiny Winopee Trailhead. Stock water is available on the trail.

Highlights: Depending on how far you want to ride, you can start at either Cultus Corral or at the Winopee Trailhead, and you can end up at the Teddy Lakes, Muskrat Lake, or Winopee Lake. Most of the

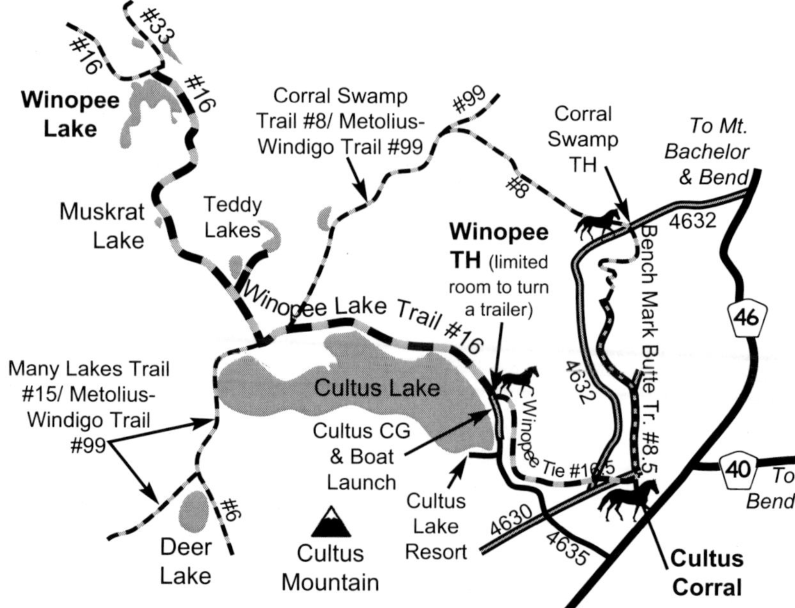

route is forested, and you'll ride along the shore of beautiful Cultus Lake and through several nice meadows along the way.

Finding Winopee Trailhead: Follow the directions to Cultus Corral at the beginning of this chapter, but instead of turning right on Road 4630, go straight on Road 4635 and follow the signs toward Cultus Lake Campground and Winopee Trailhead. The trailhead is very small, so on busy summer weekends you may not be able to turn your trailer around. Instead, turn around at Cultus Campground or the boat launch area and park beside Road 4635.

The Ride: From Cultus Corral, take the Winopee Tie Trail #16.5 to the Winopee Trailhead. (See the Winopee Tie Trail pages for more information.) From the Winopee Trailhead, follow the Winopee Lake Trail #16 along the northern shore of Cultus Lake for 2.5 miles, pass the junction with the Corral Swamp Trail #8, and in another 0.3 mile turn right on the Winopee Lake Trail where it intersects with the Many Lakes Trail #15. After 0.7 mile, the trail to Teddy Lakes goes to the right and takes you 0.5 mile to North Teddy Lake. Or, stay left and ride 1.2 miles more to reach Muskrat Lake and its derelict cabin. From Muskrat Lake, it's 1.4 miles to the south end of Winopee Lake or 2.0 miles to the north end.

In early summer, snow melt swells Muskrat Lake so it covers several acres.

By fall, Muskrat Lake shrinks to a tiny pond just 50 feet across.

Winopee Tie Trail

Trailhead: Start at Cultus Corral

Length: 6 miles round trip to Winopee Trailhead, or 5 miles round trip to Cultus Lake Resort

Elevation: 4,450 to 4,800 feet

Difficulty: Easy

Footing: Hoof protection recommended

Season: Summer through fall

Permits: Camping fee. No fee for day-use parking at Cultus Corral or Winopee Trailhead.

Facilities: Toilets, stock water, and day-use parking for 8-10 trailers at Cultus Corral. Toilets and potable water at Cultus Lake Campground. Stock water is available on the trail.

Highlights: This is an easy, fun ride through the forest from Cultus Horse Camp to the Winopee Trailhead on the shore of Cultus Lake. This trail connects with other trails in the area so you can create longer rides, or you can ride to Cultus Lake Resort for a good burger, shake,

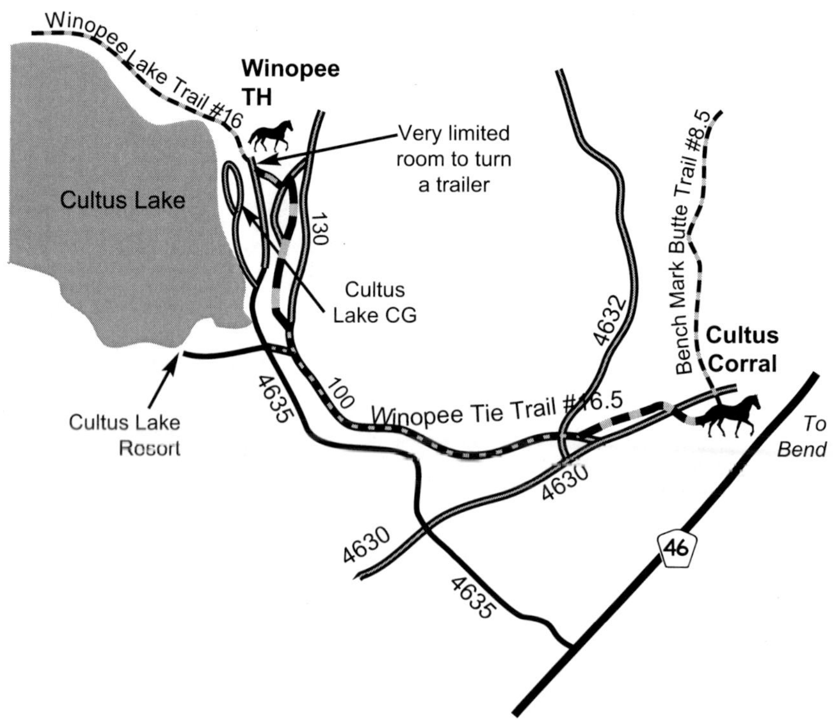

Whitney on Dixie and Diana on Mo, riding the Winopee Tie Trail from Cultus Corral to the Winopee Trailhead at Cultus Lake.

or beer. The Winopee Tie Trail is signed with gray diamonds, and includes both forest roads and single-track trails. The footing is excellent and the terrain slopes gently, creating good opportunities for trotting and cantering.

The Ride: The Winopee Tie Trail #16.5 departs from Cultus Corral between campsites 7 and 8 and takes you to the camp's perimeter trail. Turn right on it, and in 150 feet turn left on the Winopee Tie Trail. In the first 0.6 mile you'll cross gravel Roads 4630 and 4632 and begin traveling under the power lines and along gray-cinder Road 100. Follow it for 1.1 miles, then veer right on Road 130. In 0.2 mile, veer left on a closed dirt road indicated by the gray diamonds on the trees. It soon becomes a single-track trail, which you'll continue on for 0.7 mile. Turn left on another closed dirt road, again signed with gray diamonds. In 0.2 mile the route veers right on another closed road, and 0.1 mile later it comes out on gravel Road 4635. Turn right and continue 0.1 mile to reach Winopee Trailhead. Note: to reach Cultus Lake Resort, don't turn right on Road 130. Stay on Road 100 and it will take you to Road 4635 and the entrance to the resort in 0.3 mile. Ride 0.4 mile to the lodge, tie your horses in the trees, and go inside for a good meal or snack.

Lisa and Mr. T travel down the Winopee Lake Trail.

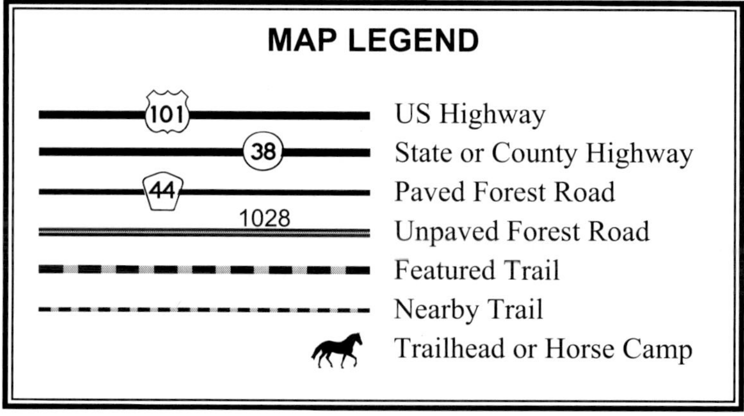

Cyrus Horse Camp

Gray Butte Area

Crooked River National Grasslands

If you're looking for a great place to ride nearly year round, with varied terrain, good footing, nice views, and wonderful spring wildflowers, then Cyrus Horse Camp is the destination for you. Located about 19 miles north of Redmond, Cyrus Horse Camp and the area around Gray Butte offer excellent riding during the shoulder seasons, when the higher-elevation trails are blanketed with snow. The Cole Loop and Warner Loop endurance trails run past the camp, or you can do shorter day rides by linking segments of the endurance trails with the dirt roads in the area. On some of these trails you are likely to encounter mountain bikes and grazing cattle, so be prepared. Additional trailheads are a short trailer ride from Cyrus Horse Camp.

The trails near Cyrus Horse Camp offer expansive views of the surrounding area.

Getting to the Gray Butte Area

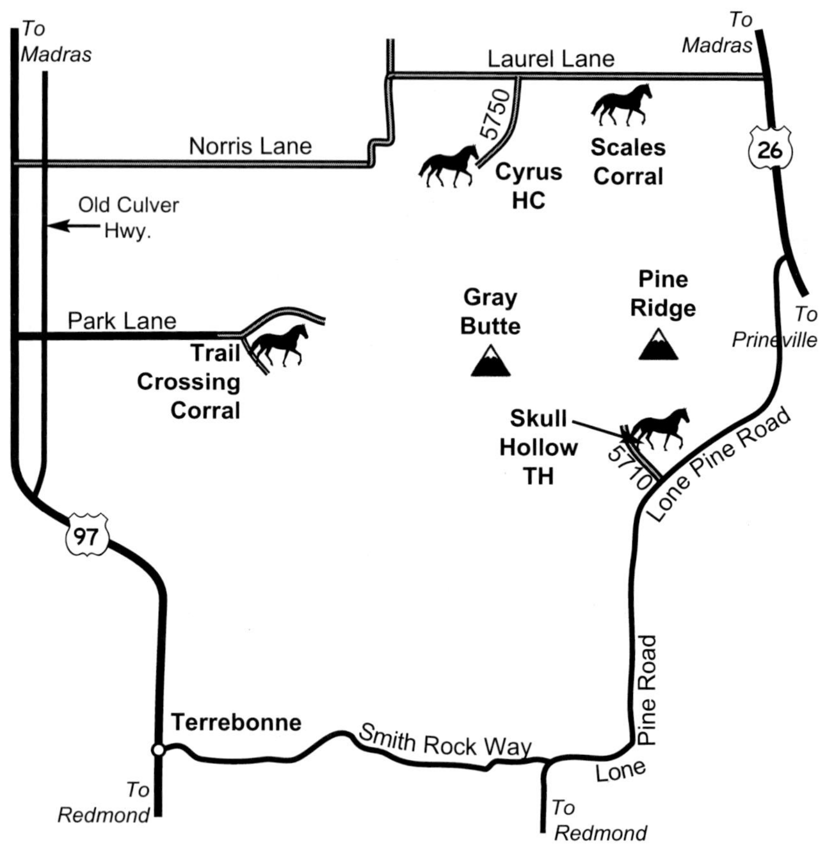

Gray Butte Area Trails

Trail	Difficulty	Elevation	Round Trip
Cole Loop	Challenging	3,000-4,000	25 miles
Gray Butte Trail	Challenging	2,700-4,250	13-23 miles
Henderson Flat OHV Trails	Moderate	2,900-3,400	Varies
Pine Ridge Loop	Moderate	3,000-3,900	8-15 miles
Scales Corral Loop	Moderate	3,200-3,800	11.5 miles
Skull Hollow Loop	Moderate	3,000-4,200	9-13 miles
Tam-a-lau Loop	Moderate	2,500-2,800	12.5 miles
Trail Crossing Corral Lp.	Challenging	2,900-4,250	9-15 miles
Warner Loop	Moderate	2,950-3,400	12.5 miles

Cyrus Horse Camp

Directions: From Redmond, take Hwy. 97 north for 5.5 miles. In Terrebonne, turn right on Smith Rock Way. Drive 4.9 miles, turn left on Lone Pine Road, and continue 7.4 miles. Turn left on Hwy. 26 and drive 2 miles. (Note: Norris Lane offers a more direct route, but the road is dusty, washboard gravel all the way.)
From Madras, drive south on Hwy. 26 for 13 miles.
From Prineville, drive northwest on Hwy. 26 for 15 miles.
All: Between mileposts 11 and 12, turn west on Laurel Lane. Continue 3 miles and turn left on Road 5750, then drive 1.2 miles to the horse camp.

Elevation: 3,350 feet

Campsites: 9 spacious campsites with 1-, 2-, or 4-horse corrals. All sites have room for 2 vehicles. Some sites are more level than others.

Facilities: Vault toilet, manure dump, fire pits, and picnic tables. No potable water, but stock water is seasonally available. Check with the Crooked River Grasslands office for stock water availability, 541-416-6640.

Permits: None

Season: Spring through early winter. In early spring the trails can be very muddy. To avoid damaging the trails, please wait until the terrain has dried.

Contact: Crooked River National Grasslands, 541-416-6640

Directions to Other Area Trailheads

Skull Hollow Trailhead: From Redmond, take Hwy. 97 north for 5.5 miles. In Terrebonne, turn right on Smith Rock Way. Drive 4.9 miles, turn left on Lone Pine Road, and continue 4.2 miles, then turn left on Road 5710 and park in the dirt parking area east of Skull Hollow Campground.

Scales Corral: Follow the directions toward Cyrus Horse Camp above, but 2 miles after turning onto Laurel Lane you'll come to Scales Corral on your left. Park next to the corrals.

Trail Crossing Corral: From Redmond, drive north on Hwy. 97 for 10 miles, turn right on Park Lane, and continue about 2 miles, past McPheeters Turf. When the road forks, turn left and drive 0.5 mile to the parking area. The Henderson Flat OHV staging area is a little farther up the road.

Cole Loop

Trailhead: Start at Cyrus Horse Camp, Scales Corral, Trail Crossing Corral, or Skull Hollow Trailhead

Length: 25 miles round trip

Elevation: 3,000 to 4,000 feet

Difficulty: Challenging — long distance

Footing: Hoof protection recommended

Season: Spring through early winter

Permits: None

Facilities: Toilet, corrals, and stock water in season at Cyrus Horse Camp. Parking but no other facilities at other trailheads. Stock water is available on the trail in season.

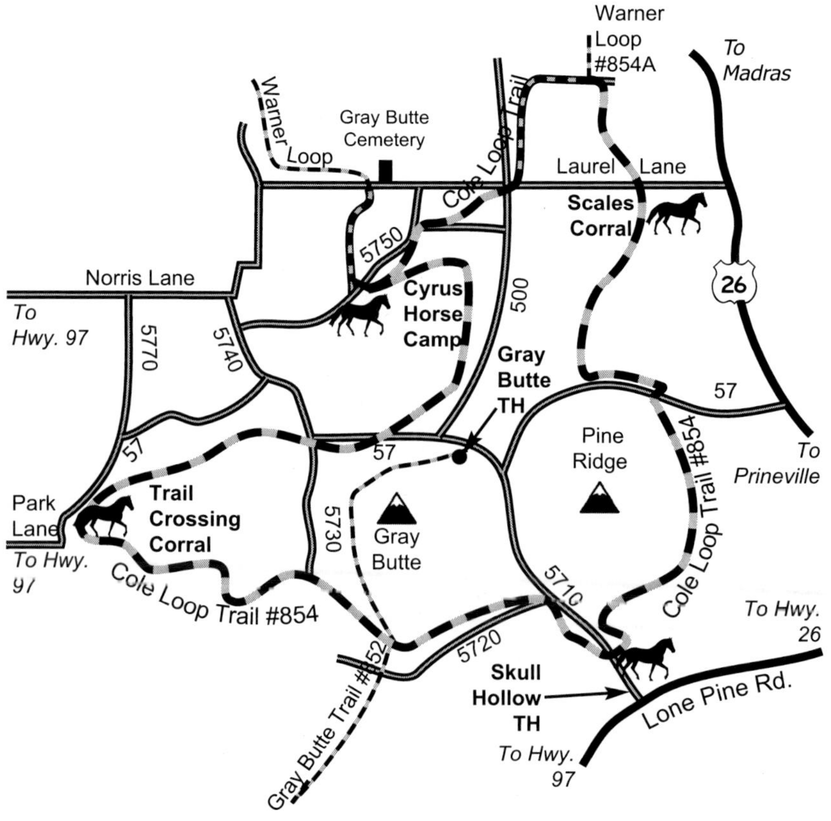

Highlights: Cole Loop is part of the Ridgeriders Endurance Trail system, the site of the annual Still Memorial Endurance Ride (named in honor of Cole and Charlotte Still, endurance riders who championed the development and maintenance of these trails). Cole Loop is rideable almost year round, although the segment of the trail on the north side of Gray Butte can be very muddy in winter and early spring.

The Ride: The Cole Loop trail travels through the sagebrush flats north of Cyrus Horse Camp, around the eastern flank of Pine Ridge, across the south side of Gray Butte, and through the canyons between Gray Butte and Trail Crossing Corral. The trail is only signed occasionally, but it is well maintained and easy to follow. By connecting segments of Cole Loop with other trails and forest roads, you can break this trail in to 4 shorter loop rides: Pine Ridge Loop, Scales Corral Loop, Skull Hollow Loop, and Trail Crossing Loop. See the descriptions of these trails in this chapter for more details.

Debbie and Mel stop at a scenic overlook on the Cole Loop Trail.

Gray Butte Trail

Trailhead: Start at Cyrus Horse Camp or Skull Hollow Trailhead

Length: Up to 23 miles round trip from Cyrus Horse Camp, or up to 13 miles round trip from Skull Hollow Trailhead

Elevation: 2,700 to 4,250 feet from Cyrus Horse Camp, or 2,700-3,700 from Skull Hollow Trailhead

Difficulty: Challenging--very steep side hills, plus mountain bike traffic

Footing: Hoof protection recommended

Season: Spring through early winter

Permits: None

Facilities: Toilet, corrals, and seasonal stock water at Cyrus. Huge trailer parking area at Skull Hollow, but no other facilities. Stock water is available on the trail in season.

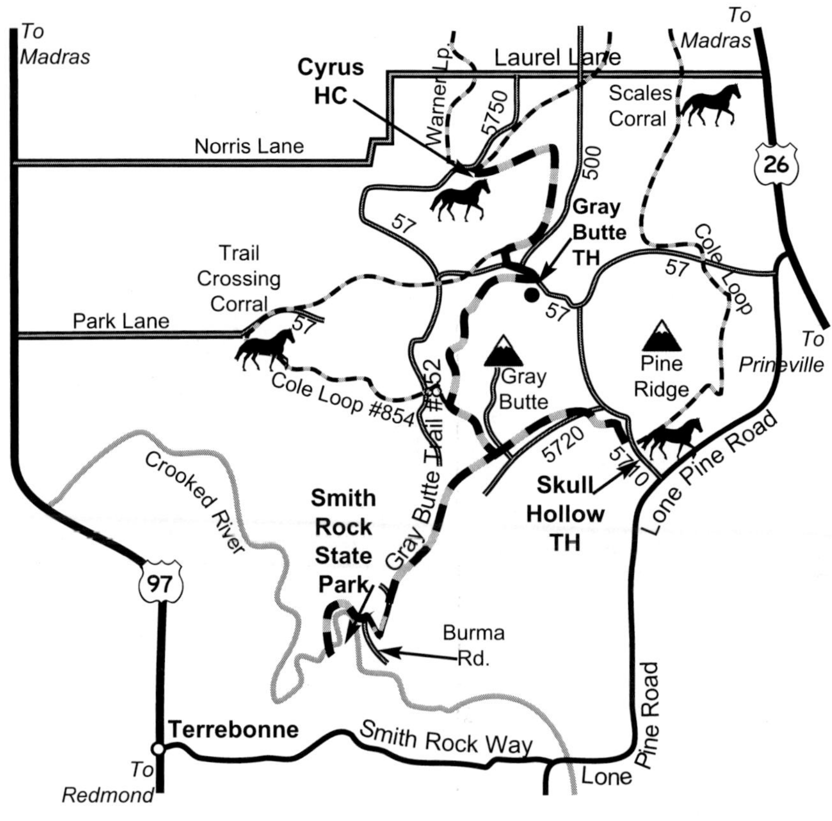

Lydia rides Shadow across a steep ridge toward Smith Rock on the Gray Butte Trail.

Highlights: The Gray Butte Trail is popular with mountain bikers, and the section that runs south toward Smith Rock State Park traverses a very steep ridge where it can be difficult to get off the trail if you meet a cyclist. However, equestrians with nerves of steel will be rewarded with great views of Smith Rock, the Cascades, and interesting rock outcroppings next to the trail.

The Ride: <u>From Cyrus Horse Camp</u>: Pick up the Cole Loop Trail on the east side of the campground, just to the right of the camp water supply. After 2 miles the trail drops into a small ravine, crosses a stream bed next to a wooden pole fence, then comes up out of the ravine into an area that has been cleared of juniper. Immediately turn left on an old dirt road and continue 0.1 mile to gravel Road 57. Turn left and ride Road 57 for 0.4 mile to the Gray Butte Trailhead at McCoin Orchard. Head west on the Gray Butte Trail. In 3.7 miles the trail forks, going left toward Skull Hollow or right toward Smith Rock. Go right. <u>From Skull Hollow Trailhead</u>: Pick up the trail next to the kiosk on the north end of the parking area. In 0.9 mile it crosses Road 5720 and veers left. Continue 1.6 miles. At the crest of the hill, the trail splits. Turn left toward Smith Rock. <u>All</u>: From the trail junction, the trail traverses a steep ridge for about 3 miles. Near the end of the ridge you'll encounter large geologic outcroppings similar to the ones that formed Smith Rock, plus panoramic views to the west. Continue another 2.5 miles and you'll reach Smith Rock State Park and the Crooked River, losing 800 feet of elevation in the process. Retrace your steps to return to your trailer.

Henderson Flat OHV Trails

Trailhead:	Start at Trail Crossing Corral Trailhead
Length:	18 miles of trails
Elevation:	2,900 to 3,400 feet
Difficulty:	Moderate
Footing:	Hoof protection recommended
Season:	December 1 - March 31
Permits:	None
Facilities:	Toilet, parking for several trailers. No stock water on the trail.

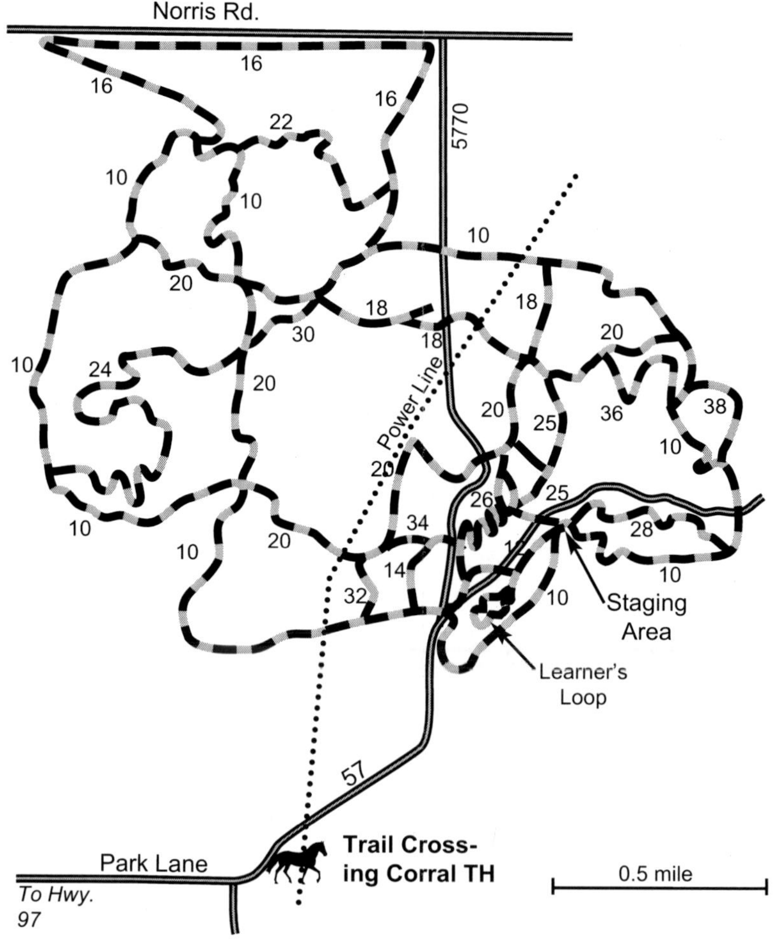

Highlights: While horses are allowed year-round on the Henderson Flat OHV Trail System, the best time of year to ride here is December 1 to March 31, when the area is closed to OHV use. The trails circle several buttes, run through the ravines that separate the buttes, and travel across the surrounding grassland. This is an excellent place for a winter ride.

The Ride: From the Trail Crossing Corral Trailhead, ride northeast on Road 57 to the Henderson Flat OHV Staging Area. From here you can pick up the trails. The Trail 10 loop is about 6.7 miles around, and Trail 20 is about 2.6 miles long. Have fun exploring!

Connie, Debbie, and Lydia ride the trails at Henderson Flat OHV Trail System, with Mt. Jefferson and Juniper Butte in the background.

Pine Ridge Loop

Trailhead: Start at Cyrus Horse Camp or Skull Hollow Trailhead

Length: 15 miles round trip from Cyrus Horse Camp, or 8 miles round trip from Skull Hollow

Elevation: 3,000 to 3,900 from Cyrus, or 3,000 to 3,700 feet from Skull Hollow

Difficulty: Moderate — easy trail, but some trail junctions are not signed

Footing: Hoof protection recommended

Season: Spring through early winter

Permits: None

Facilities: Toilet, corrals, and seasonal stock water at Cyrus. Huge trailer parking area at Skull Hollow, but no other facilities. Stock water is available in season along the trail from Cyrus, but not from Skull Hollow.

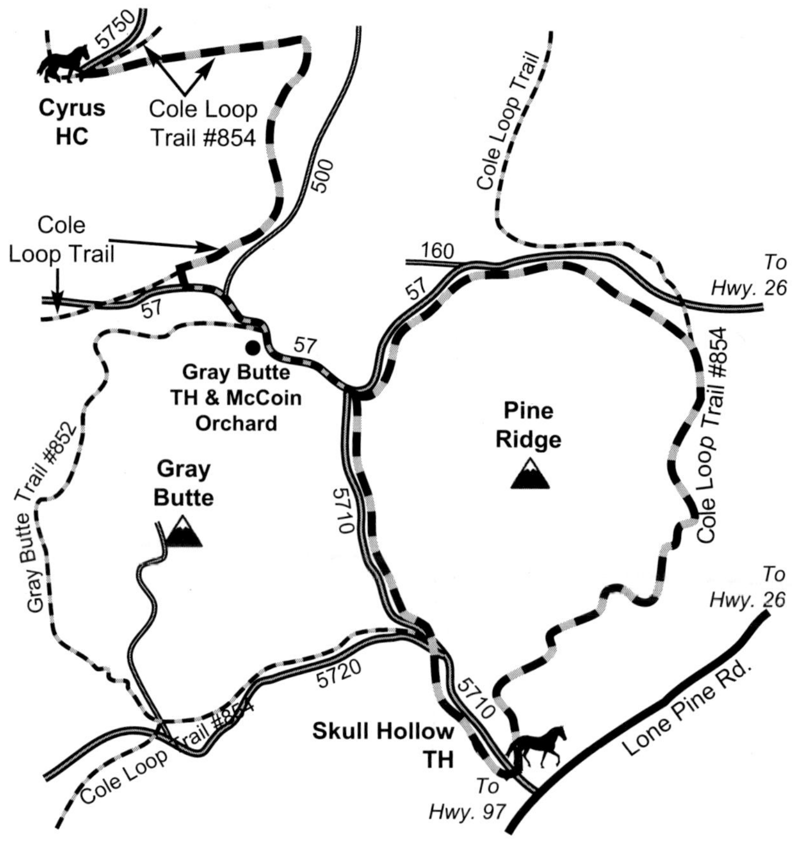

Highlights: This pleasant ride all the way around Pine Ridge links segments of the Cole Loop Trail with user-created trails that run beside the forest roads between Pine Ridge and Gray Butte.

The Ride: From Cyrus Horse Camp: Pick up the unmarked (no kiosk) Cole Loop Trail on the east side of the campground, just to the right of the camp water supply. After 2 miles, the trail drops into a small ravine, crosses a streambed next to a wooden pole fence, then comes up out of the ravine into an area that has been cleared of junipers. Immediately turn left on an old dirt road and continue 0.1 mile to gravel Road 57. Turn left and ride Road 57 for 0.4 mile to the Gray Butte Trailhead at McCoin Orchard. Continue along Road 57 for 0.6 mile and turn right on Road 5710. Ride the trail beside the road to the Skull Hollow parking area and follow the directions below.

From Skull Hollow Trailhead: Pick up the trail running eastward up onto the flank of Pine Ridge. Follow it counterclockwise around Pine Ridge. In 2.7 miles you'll reach 2 water tanks in a wire cattle enclosure. Ride through the enclosure and continue on the dirt road that runs along the side of the hill. In 0.3 mile, veer left off the dirt road onto the single track trail. After another 0.6 mile the trail splits and the Cole Loop Trail continues to the right. Veer left and continue around Pine Ridge. In 0.5 mile the trail reaches Road 57 and continues beside it. In 0.4 mile, Road 160 goes off to the right. Stay to the left beside Road 57 and in 0.9 mile, Road 5710 goes to the left. If you parked at Cyrus Horse Camp, turn right on Road 57 and retrace your steps back to the horse camp. If you parked at Skull Hollow, turn left and ride the trail beside Road 5710 back to the parking area.

Lydia on Shadow, and Connie on Diamond, on the north side of the Pine Ridge Loop.

Scales Corral Loop

Trailhead: Start at Cyrus Horse Camp or at Scales Corral
Length: 11.5 miles round trip
Elevation: 3,200 to 3,800 feet
Difficulty: Moderate — some sections of the trail are unsigned
Footing: Hoof protection recommended
Season: Spring through early winter
Permits: None
Facilities: Toilet, corrals, and seasonal stock water at Cyrus. Huge trailer parking area at Skull Hollow, but no other facilities. Stock water is available on the trail in season.

Highlights: This ride covers the north end of the Cole Loop Trail and completes a loop by following gravel roads and a user-created trail. It offers views of Gray Butte, Pine Ridge, and the open expanses to the north and east. The spring wildflowers are beautiful.

The Ride: From Cyrus Horse Camp, pick up the Cole Loop Trail on the east side of the campground, just to the right of the camp water

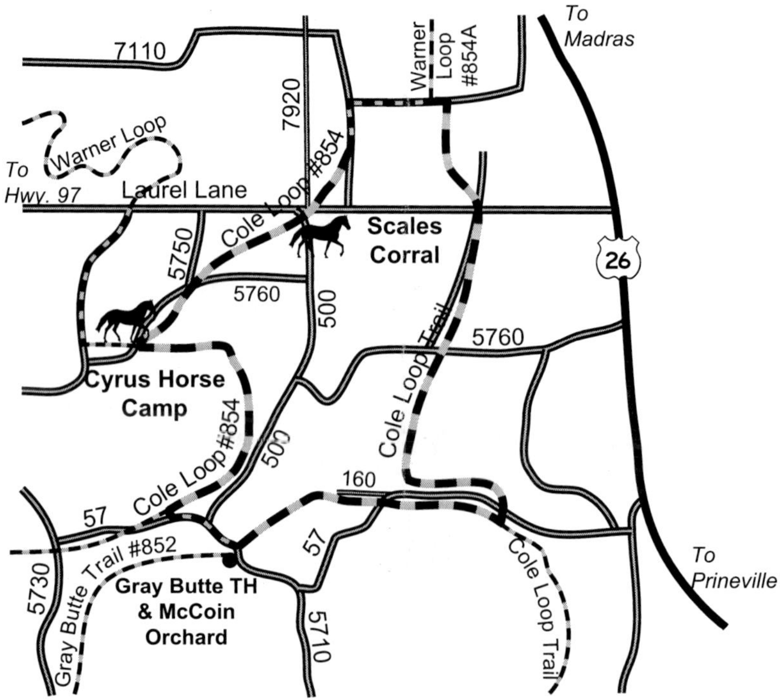

supply. After 2 miles the trail drops into a small ravine, crosses a streambed next to a wooden pole fence, then comes up out of the ravine into an area that has been cleared of junipers. Immediately turn left on an old dirt road and continue 0.1 mile to gravel Road 57. Turn left and ride Road 57 for 0.4 mile to the Gray Butte Trailhead at McCoin Orchard. Ride past the orchard and turn left along the orchard fence. Go through the gate and down the hill to the water trough. To the right of the trough, go through the gate (close it again if it is closed), and pick up the trail that continues downhill along the orchard fence. It runs for 0.9 mile and at times is indistinct, but you'll be able to see Road 57 ahead of you so aim toward it and the trail will reappear. The trail drops down to a seasonal creek, crosses it, and continues on the right side of Road 160, a well-travelled dirt road. In 0.3 mile, Road 160 intersects Road 57. Go left and pick up the trail that runs beside Road 57. In 0.7 mile, veer left on the Cole Loop Trail. The trail crosses Road 57, and 3.0 miles later it crosses Laurel Lane. In 0.8 mile the trail turns west and goes through a fence. In another 0.1 mile the Warner Loop trail goes off to the right. Continue straight ahead and in 0.6 mile the trail bends south. In 0.9 mile it reaches Laurel Lane and Scales Corral. From Scales Corral, the trail runs past the kiosk at Scales Corral, and in 1.6 miles it reaches Cyrus Horse Camp. From there, follow the directions above.

Linda and Beamer on the Scales Corral Loop trail, with Haystack Butte and Mt. Jefferson in the background.

Skull Hollow Loop

Trailhead: Start at Cyrus Horse Camp or at Skull Hollow Trailhead
Length: 13 miles round trip from Cyrus Horse Camp, or 9 miles round trip from Skull Hollow Trailhead
Elevation: 3,000 to 4, 200 feet
Difficulty: Moderate — some steep side hills
Footing: Hoof protection recommended
Season: Spring through early winter
Permits: None
Facilities: Toilets, corrals, and stock water in season at Cyrus. Huge trailer parking area at Skull Hollow, but no other facilities. Stock water is available on the trail in season.

Highlights: This well-maintained trail provides excellent views from the flanks of Gray Butte. It is popular with pleasure and endurance riders, as well as with mountain biker riders. The trail is accessible

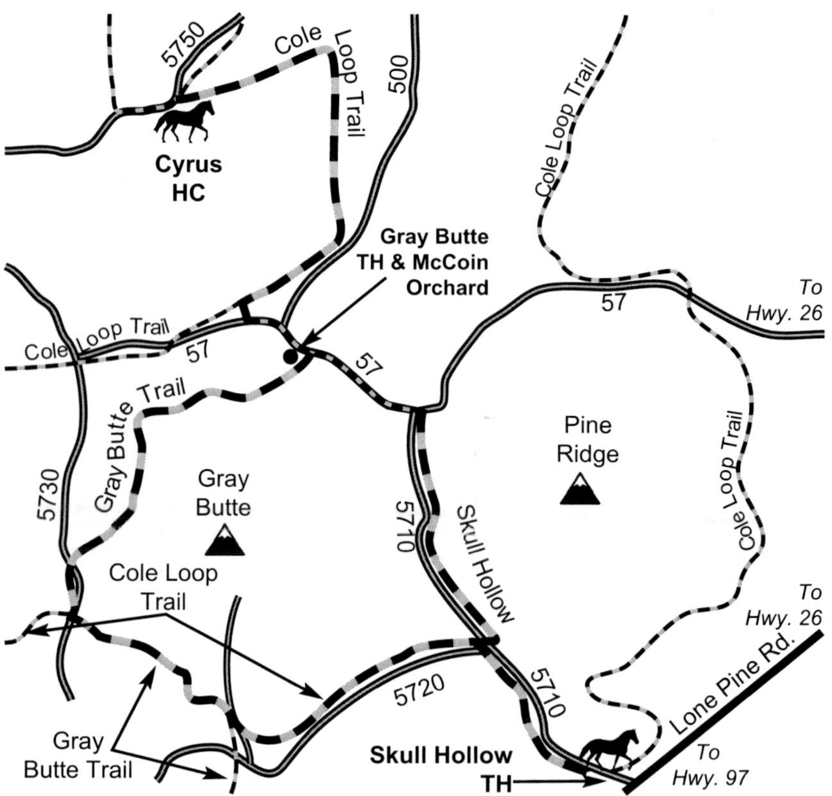

Debbie rides Split along the spectacular Tam-a-lau Loop on a clear winter day.

of the canyons, providing spectacular views of the canyon cliffs, and the rivers and Lake Billy Chinook 700 feet below.

Finding the Trailhead: The official Tam-a-lau Trailhead is off Highway 63 (which runs along the south shore of Lake Billy Chinook), but horses are not allowed on the trail that leads from the gorge to the top of the peninsula. Equestrians can access the trail from the north end of Crooked River Ranch. Take Highway 97 north from Redmond through Terrebonne, turn left on Lower Bridge Road, and follow the signs to Crooked River Ranch. Turn right on NE 43rd, then go left on Chinook and follow the signs to the fire hall. Turn right on SW Peninsula Road and follow it until it turns to gravel. Proceed another mile, cross the cattle guard, and park.

The Ride: From the parking area, Peninsula Road continues northward, but it is too rough for trailers. Ride along it for 3 miles, then turn left on Road 040. Follow it for 0.3 mile, then veer left again on the unsigned Road 041. Continue 0.7 mile, watching for a gate through the fence on the north side of the road. Turn right, go through the gate, and ride the dirt road for 0.4 mile to where the Tam-a-lau Trail crosses the road. The trail loops around the northern end of the peninsula and provides impressive views of Lake Billy Chinook and the Deschutes and Crooked Rivers, 700 feet below. After completing the loop, return to the parking area by retracing your steps.

Trail Crossing Corral Loop

Trailhead: Start at Cyrus Horse Camp or Trail Crossing Corral

Length: 15 miles round trip from Cyrus Horse Camp, or 9 miles round trip from Trail Crossing Corral

Elevation: 2,900-4,250 feet

Difficulty: Challenging (steep, rocky, some steep side slopes)

Footing: Hoof protection recommended

Season: Spring through early winter

Permits: None

Facilities: Toilet, corrals, and seasonal stock water at Cyrus Horse Camp. Parking for several trailers.but no facilities at Trail Crossing Corral. Stock water is available on the trail in season.

Highlights: This trail features panoramic views to the west, north, and east, and its significant elevation gains and losses provide good opportunities for conditioning your horse. The trailhead is next to the

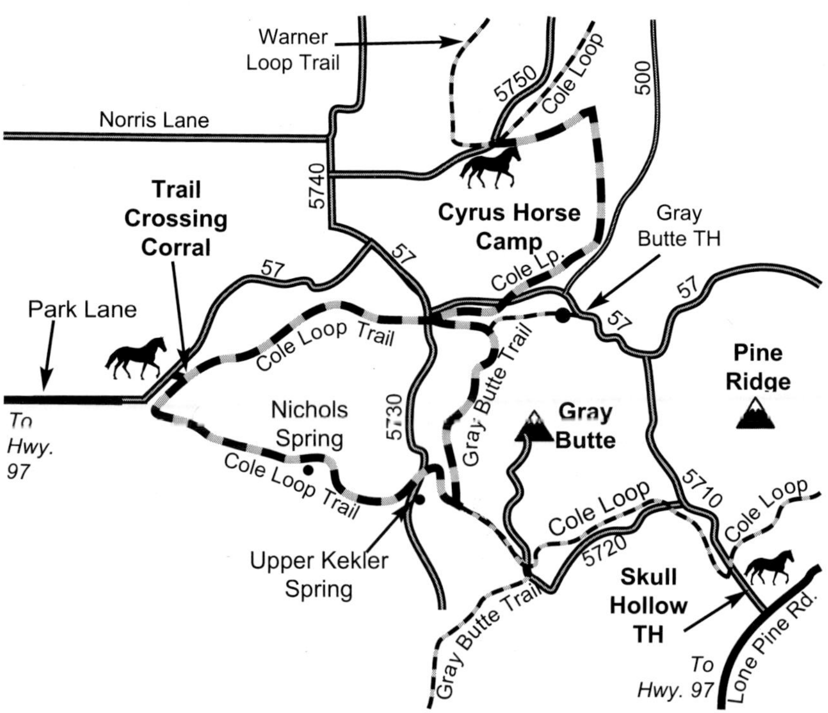

Lydia on Shadow and Connie on Diamond, on the Gray Butte Trail segment of the loop.

Henderson Flat OHV area, but while you may see and hear off-highway vehicles near the trailhead, OHVs are not allowed on this trail.

The Ride: From Trail Crossing Corral: Begin by going through the gate at the south end of the corral area and heading northeast. The trail gains elevation steadily for 3.5 miles. About 3 miles from the trailhead, it crosses the junction of Roads 57 and 5730. The Cole Loop Trail goes to the left and through a fence. Instead, continue straight ahead on a single-track trail that runs along the right side of the fence, and in 0.5 mile you'll reach a gate and the Gray Butte Trail. Turn right on the Gray Butte Trail (turning left will take you to the Gray Butte Trailhead) and follow it about 1.8 miles to a gate at a trail junction. Turn right on the Cole Loop Trail. The trail goes downhill for 0.8 mile to Upper Kekler Spring, then very steeply downhill for 1.6 miles to Nichols Spring. It then descends more gradually, and after 1.7 miles it reaches Road 57, which it follows back to the trailhead. From Cyrus Horse Camp: Pick up the unmarked Cole Loop Trail on the east side of camp and ride it 3.0 miles to the junction of Road 57 and Road 5730. Go through the fence and turn left on the single track trail that runs east along the fence, then follow the directions above.

Warner Loop

Trailhead: Start at Cyrus Horse Camp or at Scales Corral

Length: 12.5 miles round trip

Elevation: 2,950 to 3,400 feet round trip

Difficulty: Moderate. The trail is easy, but some trail junctions are unsigned.

Footing: Suitable for barefoot horses

Season: Early spring through early winter

Permits: None

Facilities: Toilet, corrals, and stock water in season at Cyrus Horse Camp. Parking for several trailers at Scales Corral, but no facilities. Stock water is available on the trail in season.

Highlights: Most of the trail runs across grassland and sagebrush flats, with nice views of Gray Butte, Pine Ridge, Haystack Butte, and Grizzly Mountain. The hilly segment on the west end provides views of Haystack Reservoir as well. It's an easy ride, and it's accessible most of the winter.

The Ride: From Cyrus Horse Camp, pick up the trail next to the kiosk on the north side of camp and follow it northeast for 1.6 miles to Scales

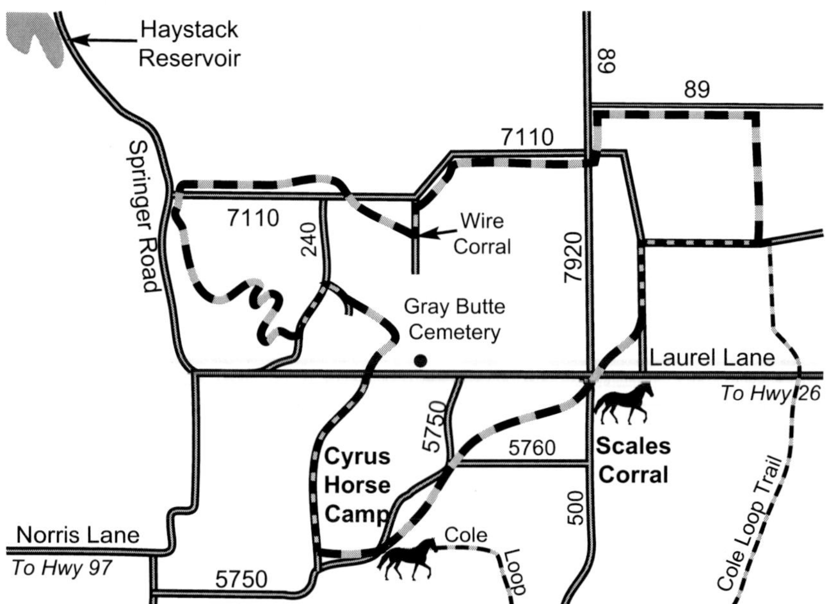

Corral. <u>From Scales Corral</u>, cross Laurel Lane and Road 7920 and pick up the single-track trail that runs northeast. After 0.5 mile it veers north on a dirt road. For the next 1.1 mile the road runs north, then east. At a fence line, the Cole Loop trail goes straight ahead and Warner Loop turns left. Go left, and for the next 2 miles the trail follows the perimeter of a fenced area. Then the trail crosses Road 7920 and continues east for another mile. When you reach a dirt road with a cattle guard, turn left and ride along the road for 0.2 mile to a barb-wire corral. Turn right and ride through the corral, picking up the trail just north of the corral. Continue westward beside Road 7110 for 1.6 miles to Springer Road. The trail veers left when it reaches Springer Road, then travels over a series of small hills that offer several good viewpoints. After 1.8 miles the trail comes out on a dirt road. Turn left and follow it 0.2 mile, then turn right on another dirt road. In 100 yards, veer left onto a single-track trail. Follow the trail 0.8 mile, cross Laurel Lane, go through the gate, and veer right on the dirt road just inside the gate. Follow it 1.1 miles, then turn left on a single-track trail and continue 0.4 mile to Cyrus Horse Camp. To return to Scales Corral, pick up the trail next to the kiosk on the north side of the horse camp.

Connie, Diamond, and Joylyn the dog move out on the Warner Loop Trail.

Teresa on Jane and Lydia on Shadow, on the trail near Cyrus Horse Camp.

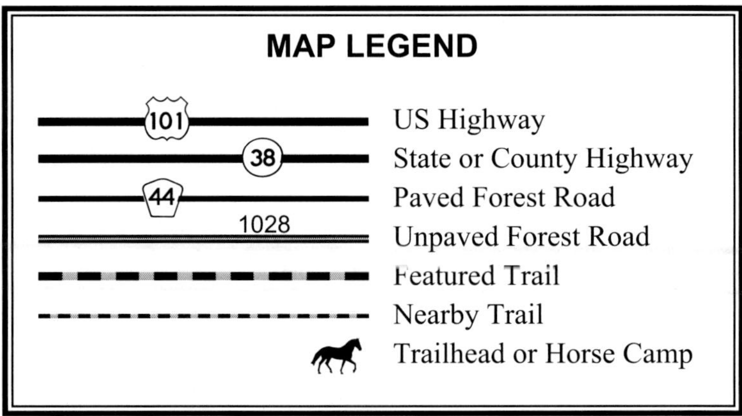

Dry Creek Horse Camp

Ochoco National Forest

Dry Creek Horse Camp is a nice, quiet spot in the hills about 30 miles east of Prineville. From the horse camp you can ride the Giddy Up Go Trail and the Brennan Palisades Trail. This may not sound like much, but both trails are a delight. Plus, the horse camp is only 2.5 miles from a paved road, so it's convenient to use Dry Creek as your base camp as you trailer out to explore additional day-riding trails not far way. These additional trails are covered in the Western Ochocos chapter. (Note that camping at trailheads is not permitted in the Ochoco National Forest.)

Diana and Tommy on the Giddy Up Go Trail.

Getting to Dry Creek Horse Camp

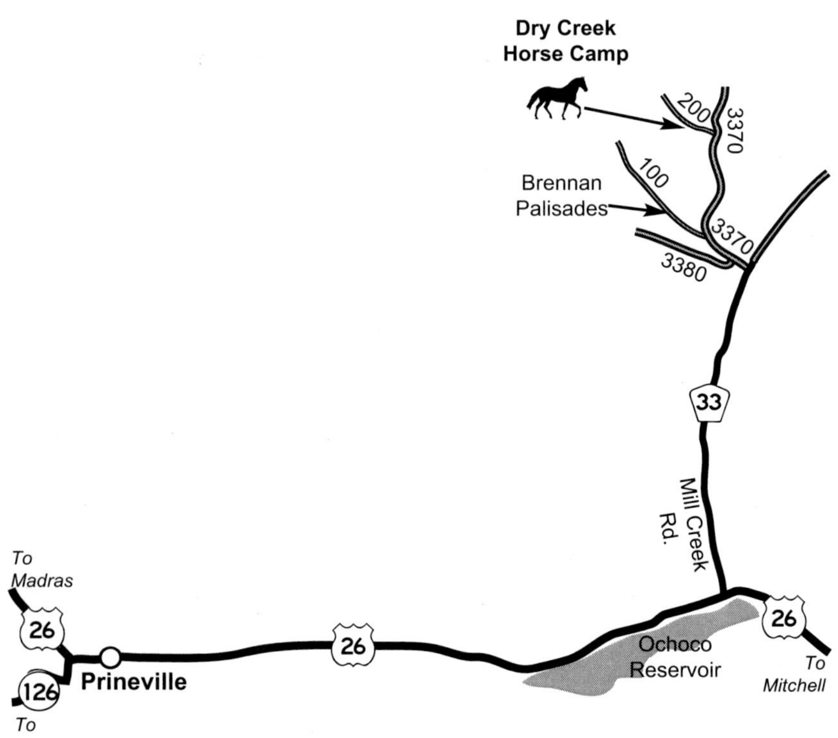

Dry Creek Trails

Trail	Difficulty	Elevation	Round Trip
Brennan Palisades	Moderate	3,350-3,900	5-7 miles
Giddy Up Go Loop	Challenging	3,900-5,100	11 miles

Dry Creek Horse Camp

Directions: From Prineville, head east on Hwy. 26. In 8 miles, just past the 28-mile marker, turn left on Mill Creek Road (Forest Road 33). Continue for 5 miles, then turn left on Road 3370, just before the pavement ends. Drive 2.5 miles, staying to the right when Road 3380 and Road 100 to Brennan Palisades each go to the left. Turn left on Road 200 to reach the horse camp.

Elevation: 3,900 feet

Campsites: Six sites. Two have 4-horse corrals and 4 have 2-horse corrals. All sites are back-in and several have room for 2 vehicles. Unfortunately, several of the parking pads are not very level.

Facilities: Vault toilet, manure pit. All sites have fire pits and picnic tables. Stock water is available in season from nearby Dry Creek, which lives up to its name by drying up by mid-summer. Bring your own stock water and drinking water.

Permits: None

Season: Summer through fall

Contact: Ochoco National Forest: 541-416-6500

Dry Creek Horse Camp

Brennan Palisades

Trailhead: Start at Dry Creek Horse Camp

Length: 5 miles round trip to Brennan Palisades, or 7 miles round trip to the old barn

Elevation: 3,350 to 3,900 feet

Difficulty: Moderate -- trail is easy except for small creek crossings and the downed logs you may encounter on this user-created trail

Footing: Hoof protection recommended

Season: Late spring through fall

Permits: None

Facilities: Parking for 2-3 rigs at the horse camp. Stock water is available on the trail.

Highlights: This trail runs through a beautiful riparian area beside Dry Creek, taking you to the impressive and quite unexpected Bren-

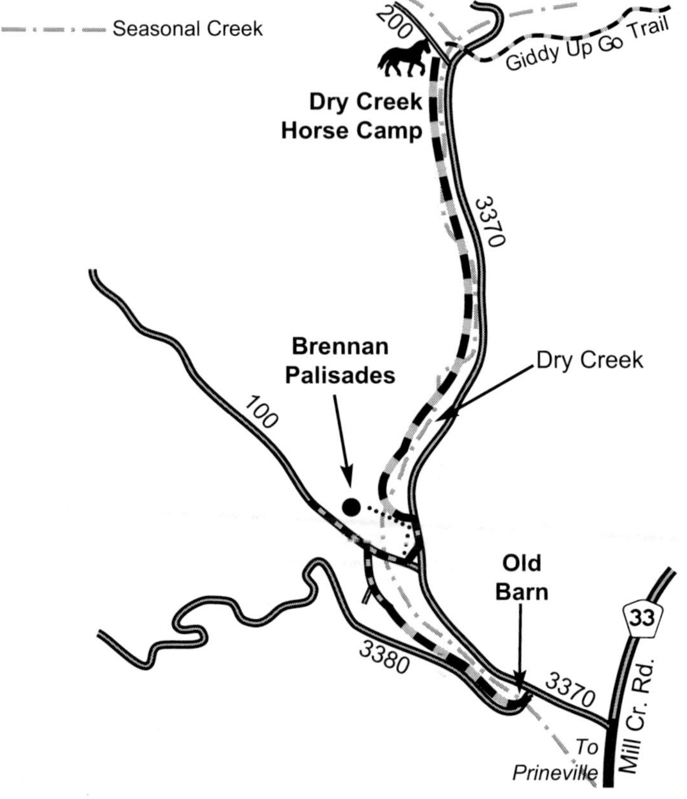

it climbs the ridges north of Dry Creek Horse Camp. Most of the trail is on single-track trail, though some sections follow old forest roads. The route is signed with yellow wood diamonds on the trees. On the trail, you'll travel through beautiful forest of ponderosa pines and grand firs, see the crumbling remains of some derelict cabins at Kidnap Spring, and enjoy an expansive view from the top of the ridge. Several stretches of the single-track are fairly steep, but there are no drop-offs.

The Ride: The Giddy Up Go Trail #830 departs across Road 200 from the horse camp. It crosses Dry Creek and heads to the left, climbing fairly consistently on a single-track trail for the first 3 miles as it gains about 1,200 feet. The best views are found near the high point of the trail. The Loop Trail then heads more gradually downward, at times following a single-track trail and at other times following forest roads. About 2.5 miles after the viewpoint, the Giddy Up Go Tie Trail goes off on the left. If you follow the Tie Trail you'll shorten your ride by about 2 miles and enjoy a very pretty stretch of trail. If you stay on the Loop Trail, you'll be on a combination of forest roads and single-track trail as you return to the horse camp.

Linda and Beamer enjoy the view along the Giddy Up Go Trail.

Diana and Tommy pause near Kidnap Spring on the Giddy Up Go Trail, next to the remains of a tumble-down cabin.

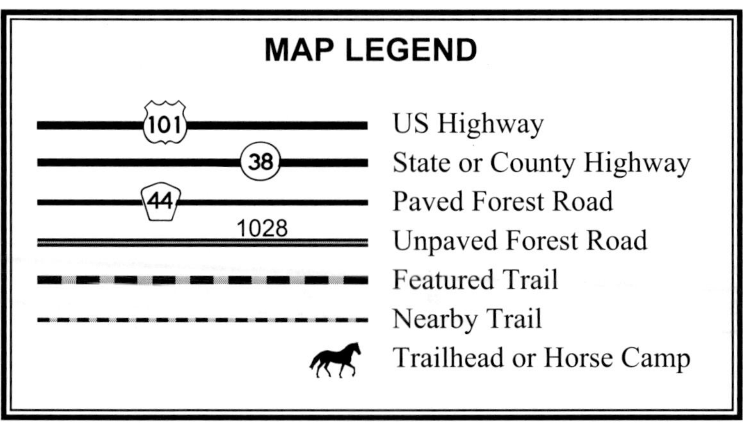

Graham Corral

Black Butte Area

Deschutes National Forest

Graham Corral is a horse camp located near Black Butte, a 6,000-foot cinder cone located about 7 miles northwest of Sisters. The riding in this area features open ponderosa pine forest and occasional impressive mountain views. Most of the trails have little elevation change. The snow is almost always gone from the area by April, so you can enjoy riding here for several months before the trails of the high Cascades are accessible. The Green Ridge Trail and the Sisters Tie Trail are two other fun trails that are a short trailer drive from Graham Corral. The trails near Graham Corral are easy and scenic, so they are popular with both local riders and out-of-towners who want to enjoy the Central Oregon sunshine.

Debbie and Split enjoy the view of the Sisters, Broken Top, and Glaze Meadow from the top of Gobblers Knob.

Getting to Graham Corral

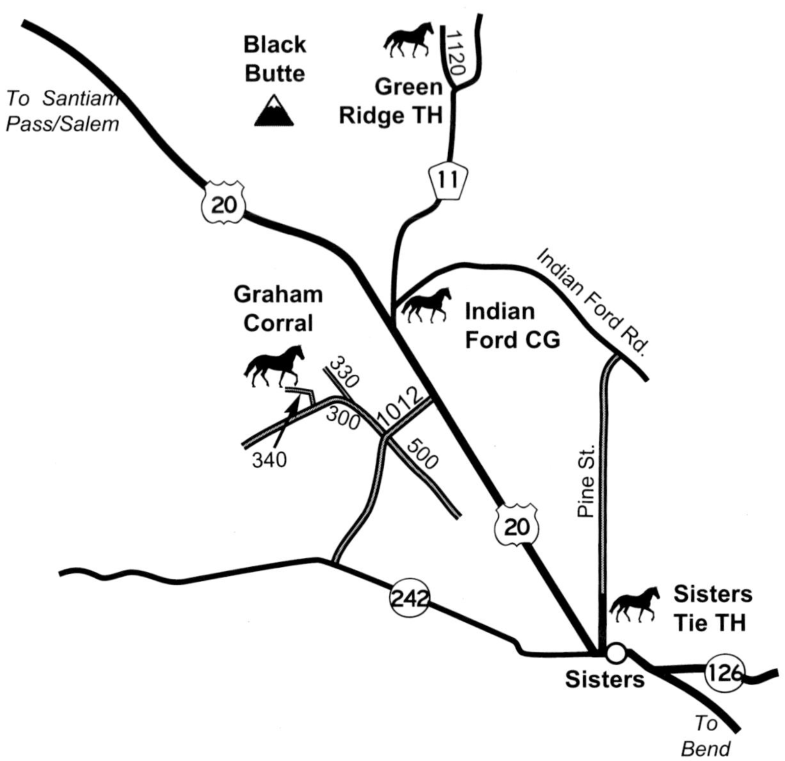

Graham Corral Area Trails

Trail	Difficulty	Elevation	Round Trip
Black Butte Stables Trails	Easy	3,300-3,450	5-12 miles
Fourmile Butte Loop	Easy	3,300-4,050	10 miles
Green Ridge Trail	Moderate	3,800-4,800	18 miles
Metolius River	Moderate	3,000-4,000	17 miles
Sisters Cow Camp	Easy	3,250-3,550	13.5 miles
Sisters Tie Trail	Easy	3,200-3,350	13-20 miles
Skylight Cave	Moderate	3,300-4,100	12.5 miles
Upper Butte Loop	Moderate	3,250-4,000	16-20 miles

Highlights: If you like to explore new trails, you'll enjoy riding in the Glaze Meadow area. You'll start on the Metolius-Windigo Trail, but when you reach Indian Ford Creek you'll veer off onto the trail network used by Black Butte Ranch for their rental horse rides. Depending on which trails you ride, you could see a beaver dam, pass through groves of aspen, or even ride to the Black Butte General Store for a soda or an ice cream bar. We recommend that you ride these trails primarily in the spring and fall, since in summer they have significant rental-horse traffic and get quite dusty. If you encounter a string of rental-horse riders, please move off the trail and allow them to pass safely.

The Ride: From Graham Corral, pick up the Metolius-Windigo Trail #99 on the east side of the campground and head toward the Metolius River/Sheep Springs. The Met-Win Trail is marked with yellow diamonds. (The "No Trespassing" signs you may see in this section refer to the private property the trail crosses, not to the trail itself.) After 1.3 miles, the trail runs along the edge of Glaze Meadow for 0.5 mile. When the Met-Win Trail veers away from the meadow to the right, take the trail that goes to the left along the meadow. You will now be on the Back Butte Stables' rental-horse trail network. All of the trails are easy. Don't miss the trip to the top of Gobblers Knob, which offers a stunning view of the Three Sisters and Glaze Meadow. Have fun exploring!

Debbie and Split at Glaze Meadow on the Black Butte Stables Trails, with the South and North Sisters in the background.

Fourmile Butte Loop

Trailhead: Start at Graham Corral Horse Camp
Length: 10 miles round trip
Elevation: 3,300 to 4,050 feet
Difficulty: Easy
Footing: Suitable for barefoot horses
Season: Early spring through late fall
Permits: Camping fee; no fee for day use
Facilities: Toilets, stock water, and corrals at the horse camp. No stock water on the trail.

Highlights: At one time, the summit of Fourmile Butte was used as a source of road cinders. Its excavated summit is treeless now, providing panoramic 360-degree views. Getting to the butte is a fun, easy ride on the Metolius-Windigo Trail and several forest roads. The Four-

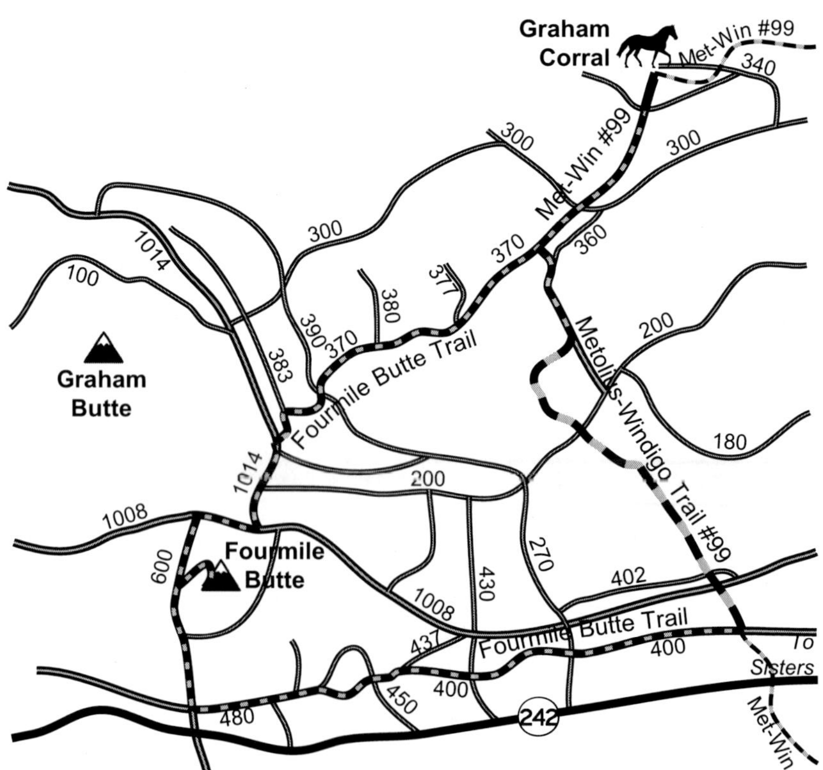

mile Butte Trail is signed with white diamonds on the trees, and the Met-Win Trail is signed with yellow diamonds.

The Ride: On the west side of Graham Corral, pick up the southbound Metolius-Windigo Trail #99 (heading toward Sisters Cow Camp/Three Creek Meadow). After 0.7 mile it crosses the red-cinder Road 300 and begins to run along Road 370. At the sign in 0.3 mile, the Met-Win veers left off Road 370, but you'll continue straight on Road 370 for 1.5 more miles. When you reach red-cinder Road 1014, turn left on it and ride 0.4 mile to the junction with Road 1008. Turn right on Road 1008, and in 0.4 mile turn left on Road 600, which will take you to up on the shoulder of Fourmile Butte. In 0.4 mile, take a hard left onto an unmarked dirt road that will take you to the top of the butte. After enjoying the view, come back down to Road 600 and turn left to ride down off the butte. After 0.5 mile, turn left on Road 480, which soon becomes Road 400. Ride 2.3 miles, then turn left on the Metolius-Windigo Trail and follow it 3 miles back to Graham Corral.

On top of Fourmile Butte, Pat and Tucker take in the view toward Sisters.

When you look to the west, Mt. Washington seems close enough to reach out and touch.

Green Ridge Trail

Trailhead: Start at the Green Ridge Trailhead
Length: Up to 18 miles round trip
Elevation: 3,800 to 4,800 feet
Difficulty: Moderate
Footing: Suitable for barefoot horses
Season: Early spring through late fall
Permits: None
Facilities: Parking for 3-4 horse trailers. No facilities at the trailhead. No stock water on the trail.

Highlights: Green Ridge is a fault-block ridge that runs north from Black Butte nearly to the Warm Springs Indian Reservation. The trail follows the crest of the ridge and offers great views of the Cascade

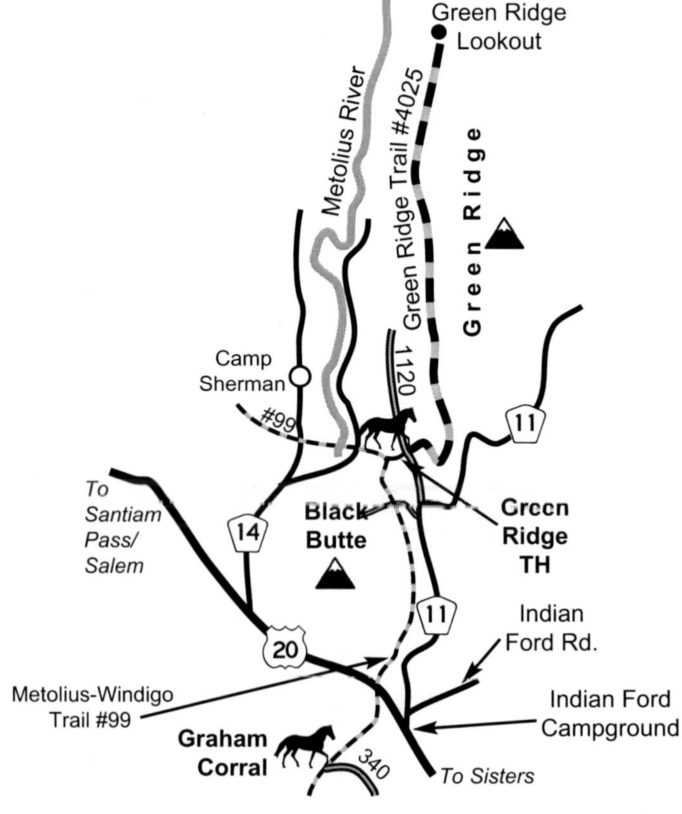

Lydia rides Shadow along the Green Ridge Trail, with Three Fingered Jack in the distance.

peaks and the Metolius Basin. The trail ends at the Green Ridge Lookout, which is available for overnight rental through the Forest Service. (Sorry, no horse facilities there.) Please respect the privacy of the guests who have rented the lookout.

Finding the Green Ridge Trailhead: From Sisters, take Hwy. 20 northwest for 6 miles. Turn right on Forest Road 11 near Indian Ford Campground. Drive north 4.2 miles and turn left on Road 1120 (about 0.5 mile past the turnoff to the Black Butte hiker trailhead), then go 0.9 mile to the parking area, which is little more than a dirt loop on your left. There is normally a sign on a post on the right side of the road that indicates where the trail begins, but last time we were there the sign was lying on the ground.

The Ride: The Green Ridge Trail #4025 climbs to the top of the ridge via several switchbacks and then follows the crest of the ridge for almost the entire distance. After the initial climb there is not much elevation change. The views of the Cascades are impressive, and on hot summer days, cool breezes waft up from the Metolius Basin below.

Metolius River

Trailhead: Start at Graham Corral Horse Camp
Length: 17 miles round trip
Elevation: 3,000 to 4,000 feet
Difficulty: Moderate
Footing: Suitable for barefoot horses
Season: Early spring through late fall
Permits: Camping fee; no fee for day use
Facilities: Toilets, stock water, and corrals at the horse camp. Stock water is available at the Metolius River.

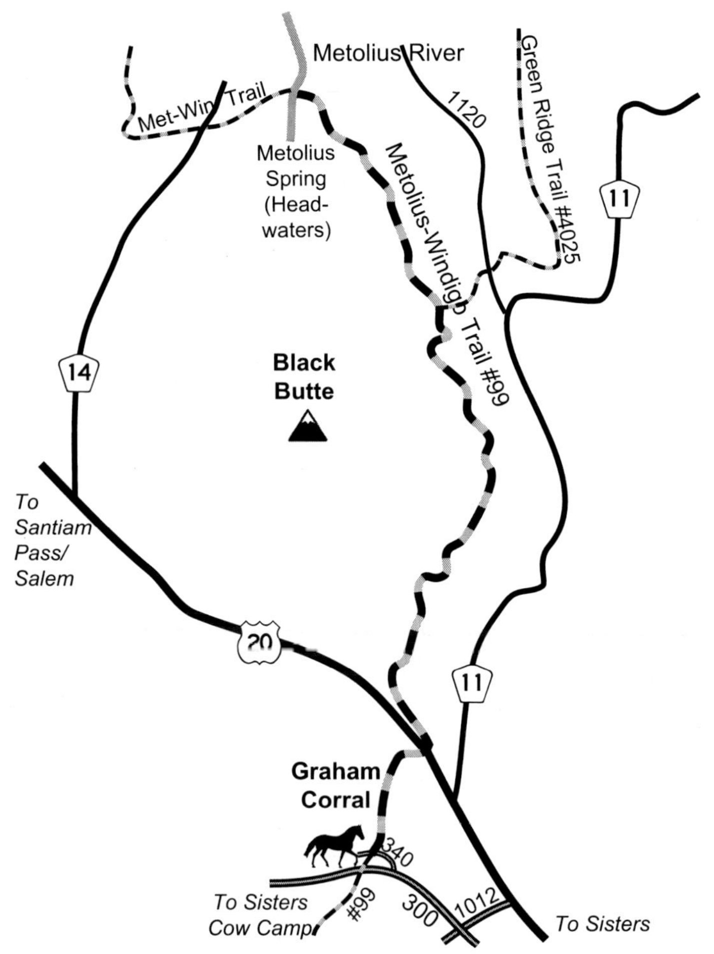

Suzanne on Marilyn and Judi on Padre, crossing the Metolius River.

Highlights: This section of the Metolius-Windigo Trail travels through a pleasant forest of ponderosa pines and incense cedars. On the lower slopes of Black Butte, an old fire scar offers open views to the east. You'll reach the Metolius River about 0.4 mile below its headwaters.

The Ride: Pick up the Metolius-Windigo Trail #99 on the east side of Graham Corral and head toward the Metolius River/Sheep Springs. (The "No Trespassing" signs you may see in this section refer to the private property the trail crosses, not to the trail itself.) Follow the trail northeast for 2 miles to a wooden bridge over Indian Ford Creek. Stay on the Met-Win and it will take you across Hwy. 20 and continue northward around the east side of Black Butte. The trail, which is clearly marked with yellow diamonds, eventually turns northwest and crosses the Metolius River not far from its headwaters, where the river springs out of the base of Black Butte at the astonishing rate of 50,000 gallons a minute. The Metolius is easy to ford here because it is fairly wide but not very deep, so if you like you can cross it and continue exploring the Met-Win Trail.

Sisters Cow Camp

Trailhead: Start at Graham Corral Horse Camp
Length: 13.5 miles round trip
Elevation: 3,250 to 3,550 feet
Difficulty: Easy
Footing: Suitable for barefoot horses
Season: Early spring through late fall
Permits: Camping fee; no fee for day use
Facilities: Toilets, stock water, and corrals at Graham Corral. Stock water in season at Sisters Cow Camp.

Highlights: This is a nice forested ride on the Metolius-Windigo Trail between Graham Corral and Sisters Cow Camp. The trail goes over

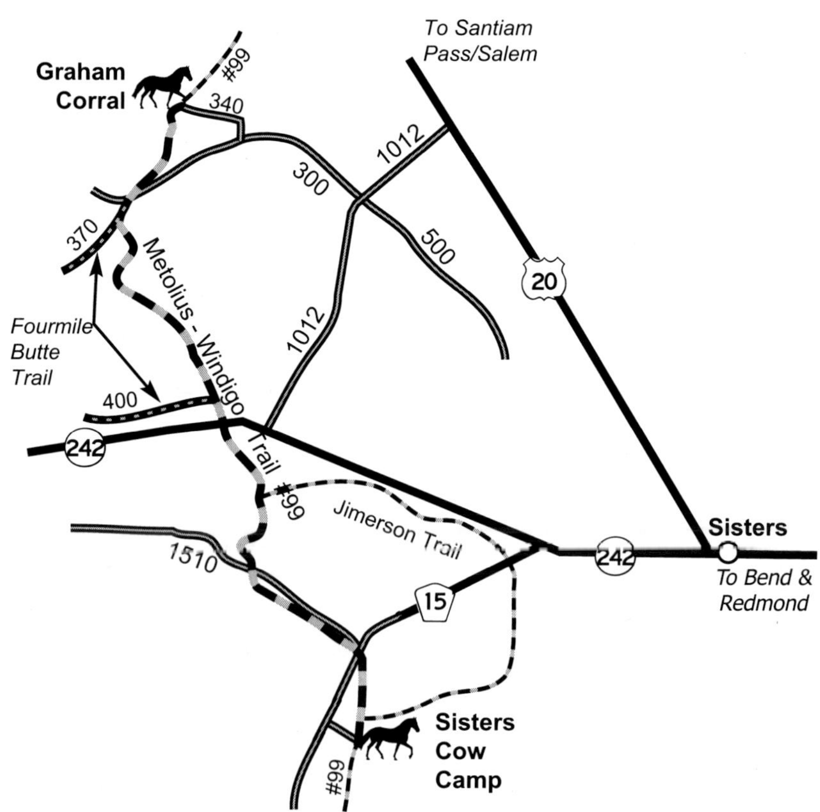

Whitney rides Dixie on the trail between Graham Corral and Sisters Cow Camp. The route is signed with yellow diamonds on the trees.

a small ridge that offers filtered mountain views through the trees and though an interesting basalt grotto.

The Ride: Pick up the Metolius-Windigo Trail #99 on the west side of Graham Corral and head toward Sisters Cow Camp/Three Creek Meadow. The route is clearly marked with yellow diamonds. In 1.0 mile, the Met-Win veers left and the Fourmile Butte Trail goes straight ahead. Turn left and go over a low ridge. Near the top of the ridge, look to the north and west to see the mountain views. About 1.8 miles beyond the ridge top, you'll pass a second junction with the Fourmile Butte Trail. About 0.1 mile later, the trail runs down into an interesting little grotto with rock outcroppings, old growth ponderosas, aspen, and plentiful grass. A short distance beyond the grotto, the trail crosses paved Hwy. 242. In 1.0 mile you'll pass the first junction with the Jimerson Trail. After another 0.8 miles the trail crosses Road 1510 and runs beside it for 1.1 miles, then it crosses gravel Road 15. In 0.5 mile you'll pass the second junction with the Jimerson Trail. Continue 0.1 mile to reach Sisters Cow Camp.

Sisters Tie Trail

Trailhead: Start at the Sisters Tie Trailhead or at Graham Corral Horse Camp

Length: 13 miles round trip from the Sisters Tie Trailhead to Indian Ford Campground, or 20 miles round trip to Sisters from Graham Corral

Elevation: 3,200 to 3,350 feet

Difficulty: Easy

Footing: Suitable for barefoot horses

Season: Early spring through late fall

Permits: Camping fee at Graham Corral; no fee for day use at Graham Corral or Sisters Tie Trailhead

Facilities: Toilets, stock water, and corrals at the horse camp. Stock water is available on the trail.

Highlights: The Sisters Tie Trail is a fun ride that links the town of Sisters with the Metolius-Windigo Trail. If you're camping at Graham

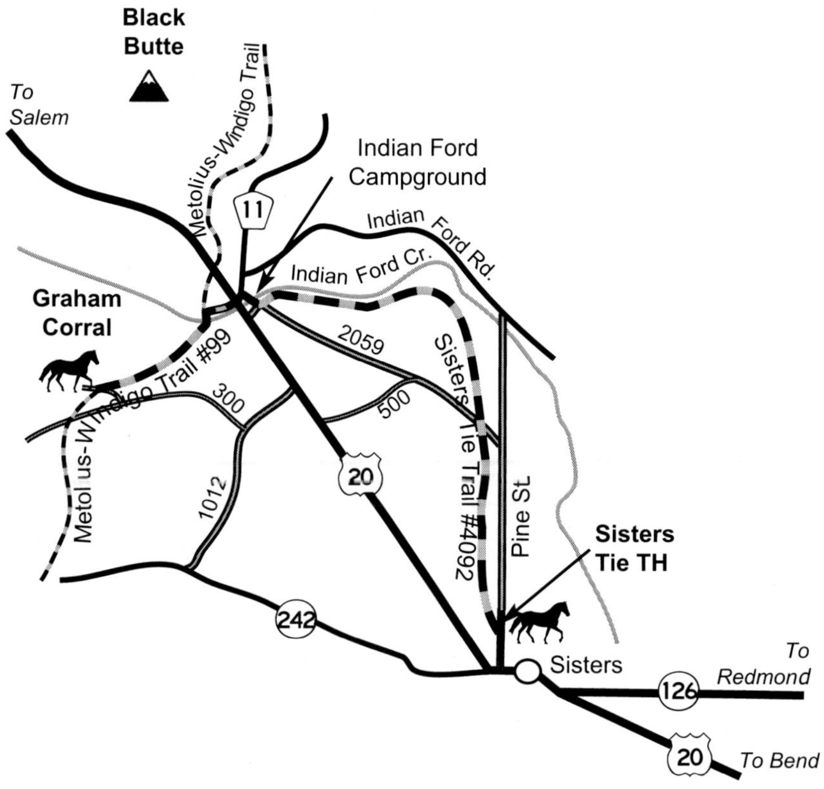

Lydia rides Shadow on the Sisters Tie Trail, headed to Indian Ford Campground.

Corral, you can ride to Sisters, though it's a rather long jaunt. Or you can ride this pleasant trail from its trailhead in Sisters.

The Ride: From the Sisters Tie Trailhead, the trail follows a combination of forest roads and single-tracks through pretty ponderosa pine forest. On the stretch beside Indian Ford Creek, watch for evidence of beaver activity. When you reach Indian Ford Campground, retrace your steps to return to Sisters. From Graham Corral, pick up the Metolius-Windigo Trail #99 on the east side of the camp and head toward the Metolius River/Sheep Springs. Follow the trail northeast for 2 miles to the bridge over Indian Ford Creek. About 200 feet after crossing the creek, leave the Met-Win Trail and turn hard right on a dirt road marked with Sisters Trails Alliance signs. Follow the Sisters Trails signs 0.6 mile to the intersection of Hwy. 20 and Road 11. Normally you will cross Hwy. 20 and ride along Road 11 a short distance, enter Indian Ford Campground, skirt the campsites, and cross Indian Ford Creek on the road bridge, then continue a short distance to reach the Sisters Tie Trail. However, as of our publication date the bridge is out and there is not a good place to ford the creek. You'll need to ride cross-country to Hwy. 20, cross the creek on the side of the highway, and ride cross-country back to pick up the Sisters Tie Trail. The bridge is slated to be replaced in 2018 or 2019.

Skylight Cave

Trailhead: Start at Graham Corral Horse Camp
Length: 12.5 miles round trip
Elevation: 3,300 to 4,100 feet
Difficulty: Moderate -- easy riding, but you'll need wayfinding skills, a Sisters Ranger District map, and a GPS or compass
Footing: Hoof protection recommended
Season: Early spring through late fall
Permits: Camping fee; no fee for day use
Facilities: Toilets, stock water, and corrals at the horse camp. No stock water on the trail.

Highlights: Skylight Cave doesn't look all that impressive from above -- it's just a hole in the ground with a ladder leading down into it. However, if you visit Skylight Cave at the right time of year you'll be treated to an amazing sight. Arrive on a May or June morning between 9:00 and 11:00, tie your horse, and go inside to see the sun streaming through the holes in the roof of the cave. You won't see this later in the day, or at any other time of year. Wow! Be sure to bring a warm jacket, sturdy shoes, and extra flashlights. The cave is

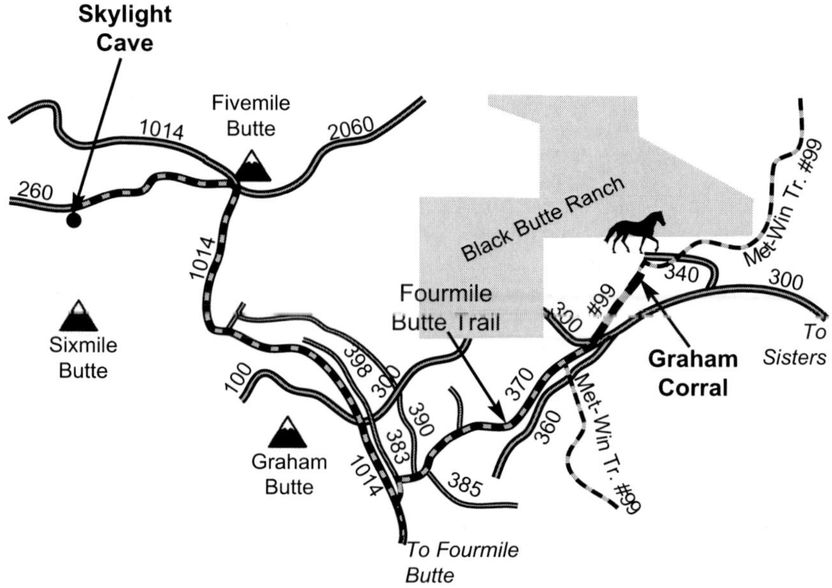

Connie enjoys the summer-morning light show at Skylight Cave.

closed from November 1st to April 15th to protect hibernating big-eared bats.

The Ride: On the west side of Graham Corral, pick up the southbound Metolius-Windigo Trail #99 (heading toward Cow Camp and Three Creek Meadow). After 0.7 mile, it crosses the red-cinder 300 Road and runs along Road 370. In 0.3 mile the Met-Win veers left off Road 370, but you'll continue straight on the Fourmile Butte Trail for 1.5 miles. When you reach red-cinder Road 1014, turn right off the Fourmile Butte Trail and ride along the road for 2.5 miles. (If you prefer dirt roads over gravel ones, you can ride part of this distance on closed Roads 383 and 398, located about 100 feet to the right of Road 1014.) At the base of Five Mile Butte (which has antennas on top), turn left on unsigned dirt Road 260 and ride 1.4 miles to Skylight Cave. The cave is located at the junction of Road 260 and another unsigned dirt road. Watch for a wooden Forest Service "Events" sign on the left, next to the cave entrance. Climb down the ladder into the cave and walk 200 feet east on the boulder-strewn floor to reach the skylights.

Upper Butte Loop

Trailhead: Start at Graham Corral Horse Camp, or at the entrance to Indian Ford Campground

Length: 20 miles round trip from Graham Corral, or 16 miles round trip from Indian Ford Campground

Elevation: 3,250 to 4,000 feet

Difficulty: Moderate

Footing: Hoof protection recommended

Season: Early spring through late fall

Permits: Camping fee; no fee for day use at Graham Corral or outside Indian Ford campground.

Facilities: Toilets, stock water, and corrals at Graham Corral. Parking for 2 trailers just outside the entrance to Indian Ford Campground. No stock water on the trail.

Highlights: The trail makes a loop completely around Black Butte and offers impressive mountain views through breaks in the trees.

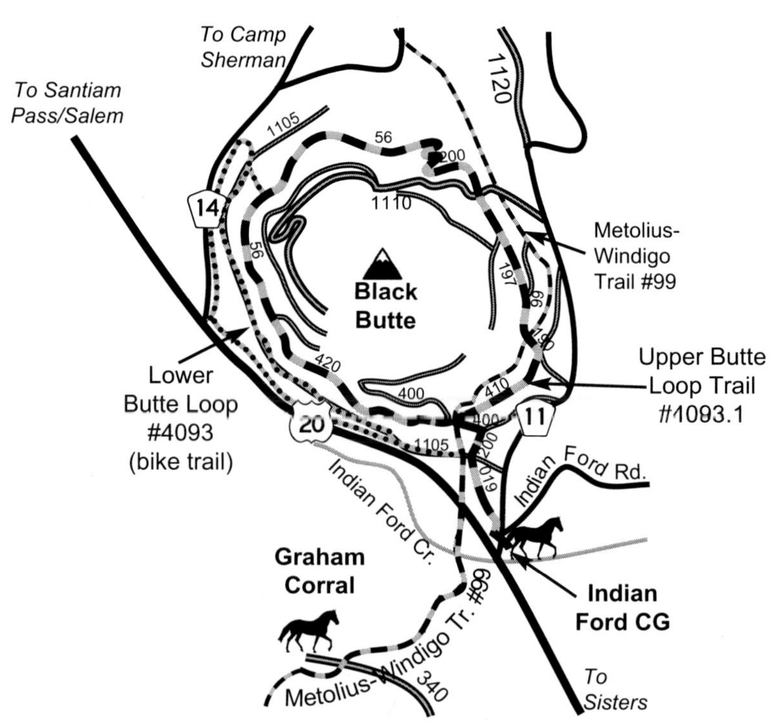

North and South Sister from the Upper Butte Loop Trail.

Finding Indian Ford Campground: From Sisters, drive northwest on Hwy. 20 for 6 miles. Turn right on Road 11, then turn right into Indian Ford Campground and park next to the kiosk outside the entrance.

The Ride: From Graham Corral, on the east side of the campground, pick up the northbound Metolius-Windigo Trail #99 (toward Metolius River/Sheep Springs). You'll cross Hwy. 20 in about 2.4 miles. Continue on the Met-Win for 0.7 mile to the junction of Roads 400, 410, and 420. Turn right on Road 410, following the sign indicating the Upper Butte Loop. From Indian Ford Campground, cross Road 11 and pick up the trail immediately across the street. The trail veers to the right, and in 0.1 mile it turns left on Road 019 and heads toward Black Butte. After 1.1 miles, veer left next to a 4x4 post and follow the trail 0.1 mile to the intersection of Roads 1105 and 200. Follow the sign to the right on Road 200, then in 0.1 mile turn left on Road 400, and in another 0.1 mile you'll see a sign indicating you've reached the loop part of the trail. Turn right on Road 410. All, follow the Upper Butte Loop trail signs. In several places the trail is somewhat overgrown, but it is discernable. The mountain views through the trees are impressive.

Watch for signs of beaver activity along Indian Ford Creek, on the Sisters Tie Trail.

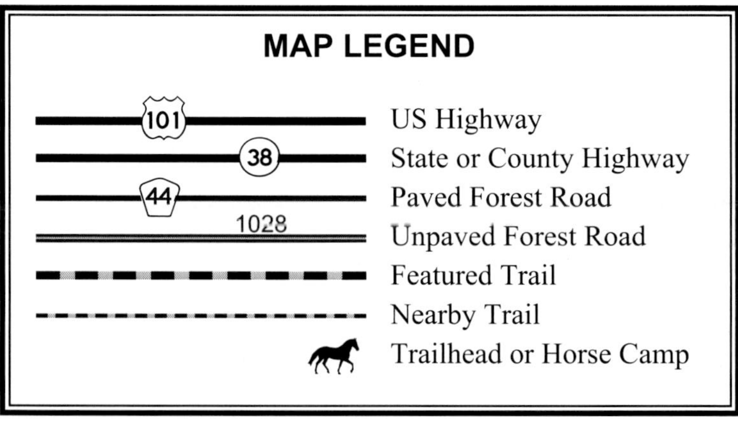

Horse Butte Area

Deschutes National Forest

The 70-mile Swamp Wells Trail System extends from the south end of Bend all the way south to Newberry Crater. Near the middle of the trail network, Swamp Wells Horse Camp offers overnight accommodations (see the Swamp Wells chapter for details), but you don't have to drive all the way to Swamp Wells to access the trails. Instead, you can park at the Horse Butte Trailhead, the Boyd Cave parking area, or a turnout beside the junction of China Hat Road and Road 1810. All three are conveniently located just south of Bend. They provide access to several moderate-length loops that are rideable nearly year round. The trails, which are signed with gray diamonds on the trees, run through ponderosa pine forest and across open grasslands. The terrain is gently rolling and dotted with volcanic cinder buttes, basalt outcroppings, and even a few lava caves. You can expect to see plenty of bikes on these trails, but there's little elevation change so they won't be going that fast, and the lines of sight are open so you can usually see them coming.

Debbie and Lydia ride Split and Shadow past a lava outcropping on the Arnold Ice Cave Trail.

Getting to the Trailheads

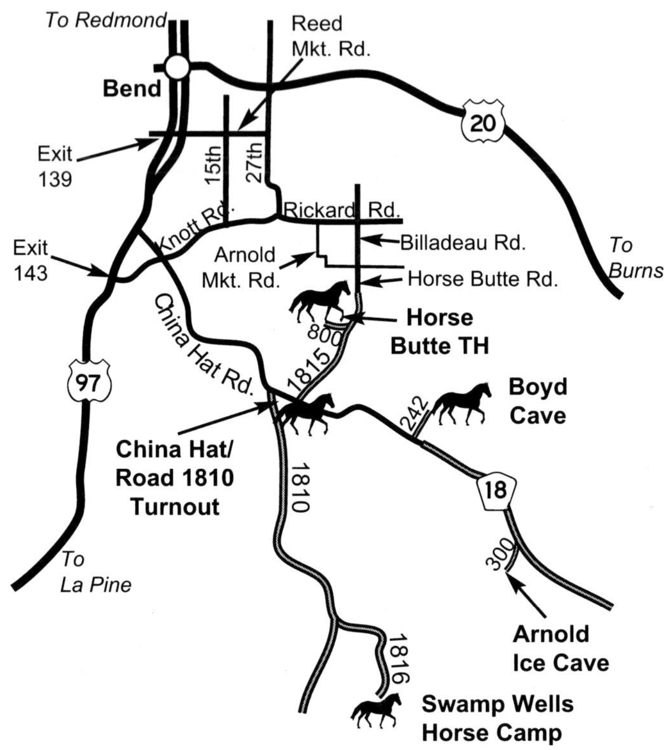

Horse Butte Area Trails

rail	Difficulty	Elevation	Round Trip
Arnold Ice Cave Loop	Moderate	4,200-4,800	11.5 miles
Bessie Butte	Moderate	4,000-4,800	7 miles
Coyote Trail Loop	Moderate	4,300-5,000	8 miles
Kelsey Butte	Moderate	4,200-5,000	12-16.5 miles
Skeleton Cave Loop	Moderate	3,900-4,300	11.5 miles

Horse Butte Area Trailheads

HORSE BUTTE TRAILHEAD

Directions: From Bend, drive south on Hwy. 97, take Exit 139 (Reed Market Road), and drive east on Reed Market Road for 2.3 miles. Turn right on 27th St., and in 2 miles turn left on Rickard Road. Continue 1.8 miles and turn right on Billadeau Rd. After 1 mile Billadeau becomes Horse Butte Rd., and after another mile it turns to gravel and becomes Road 1815. Drive 0.5 mile farther, then turn right on Road 800 and continue 0.3 mile to the trailhead.

Elevation: 4,000 feet

Facilities: Parking for 5-6 trailers

Permits: None

Season: Year round

Contact: Bend/Ft. Rock Ranger District, 541-383-5300

BOYD CAVE PARKING AREA

Directions: From Bend, drive south on Hwy. 97 and take Exit 143 (Baker Rd./Knott Rd.) Turn left on Knott Road and drive 1.3 miles. Turn right on China Hat Road and continue 8.2 miles, then turn left on Road 242. The parking loop at Boyd Cave is in 0.2 mile.

Elevation: 4,300 feet

Facilities: Parking for 3-4 trailers

Permits: None

Season: Year round

CHINA HAT/ROAD 1810 TURNOUT

Directions: From Bend, drive south on Hwy. 97 and take Exit 143 (Baker Rd./Knott Rd.) Turn left on Knott Road and continue 1.3 miles. Turn right on China Hat Road and go 4.6 miles. Turn left into a dirt turnout at the intersection of China Hat Road and Road 1810.

Elevation: 4,250 feet

Facilities: Parking for 1-3 trailers

Permits: None

Season: Year round

Arnold Ice Cave Loop

Trailhead: Start at the Boyd Cave parking area
Length: 11.5 miles round trip
Elevation: 4,200 to 4,800 feet
Difficulty: Moderate
Footing: Hoof protection recommended
Season: Early spring through late fall
Permits: None
Facilities: Parking for 3-4 trailers at Boyd Cave parking area. No stock water on the trail.

Highlights: This loop trail takes you to Arnold Ice Cave (which really does contain ice year round), Charcoal Cave, and several other collapsed lava tubes. You'll see interesting rock outcroppings along the way, and you can make a nice loop by following the 61-63 Tie

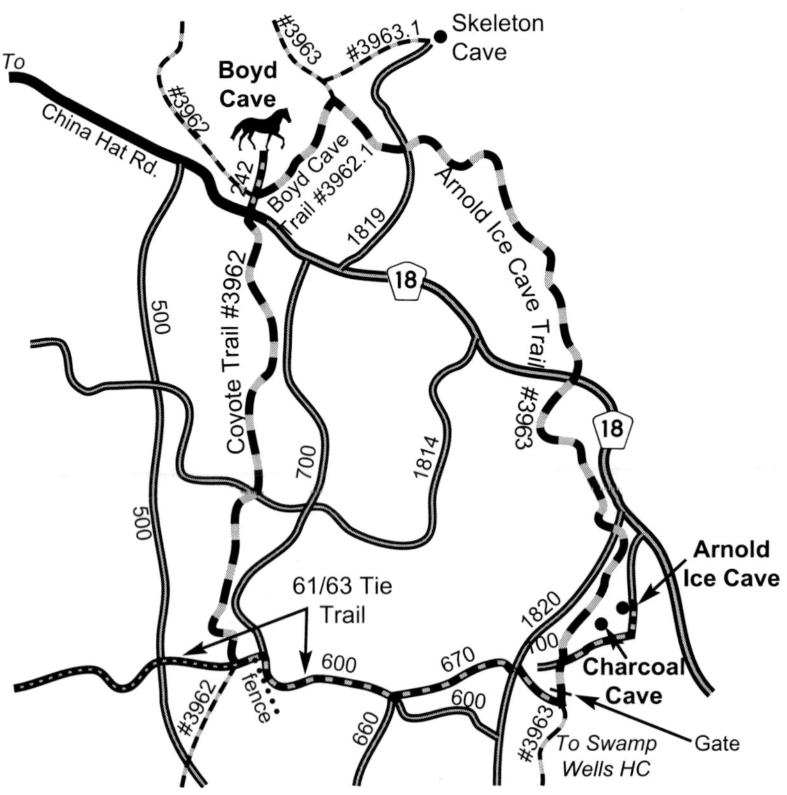

Trail to connect with the Coyote Trail for the return leg. The entire route is marked with gray diamonds.

The Ride: Ride on Road 242, the entrance road to Boyd Cave, back toward China Hat Road. Just before you reach China Hat Road, turn left on the Boyd Cave Trail #3962.1 and follow it 0.9 mile to the junction with the Arnold Ice Cave Trail #3963. Turn right toward Swamp Wells Horse Camp. In 2.5 miles the trail crosses China Hat Road, and 1.2 miles after that it crosses Road 1820, a red cinder road. Continue 0.7 mile to a junction sign that points left toward Arnold Ice Cave. Turn left here, and in 0.4 mile you'll pass Charcoal Cave, Arnold Ice Cave, and several other collapsed lava tubes. Then retrace your steps to the junction and turn left on the Arnold Ice Cave Trail. In 0.2 mile you'll reach a gate. Go through it and turn right on the dirt road that runs beside the fence. You are now on the 61/63 Tie Trail. Following the gray diamonds, ride 0.3 mile along the fence, up a hill, between some big rocks placed to block vehicle traffic, and past a couple of primitive campsites. When you reach red cinder Road 1820, turn left on it and immediately turn right on Road 670. Continue to follow the gray diamonds on the trees, and in 0.2 mile the road forks. Veer right on Road 600. In another 1.6 miles, you'll see trees that were planted in rows after a forest fire. There is a fence on your left, which ends in 0.3 mile. Turn left on the dirt road just past the end of the fence and follow it 0.2 mile. At the junction sign, turn right on the Coyote Trail #3962. Follow the Coyote Trail 3 miles back to Boyd Cave.

The Arnold Ice Cave Loop offers excellent views of Mt. Jefferson and other Cascades peaks.

Bessie Butte

Trailhead: Start at the Horse Butte Trailhead
Length: 7 miles round trip
Elevation: 4,000 to 4,800 feet
Difficulty: Moderate (steep climb to top of butte)
Footing: Suitable for barefoot horses
Season: Early spring through late fall
Permits: None
Facilities: Parking for 5-6 trailers at Horse Butte Trailhead. No stock water on the trail.

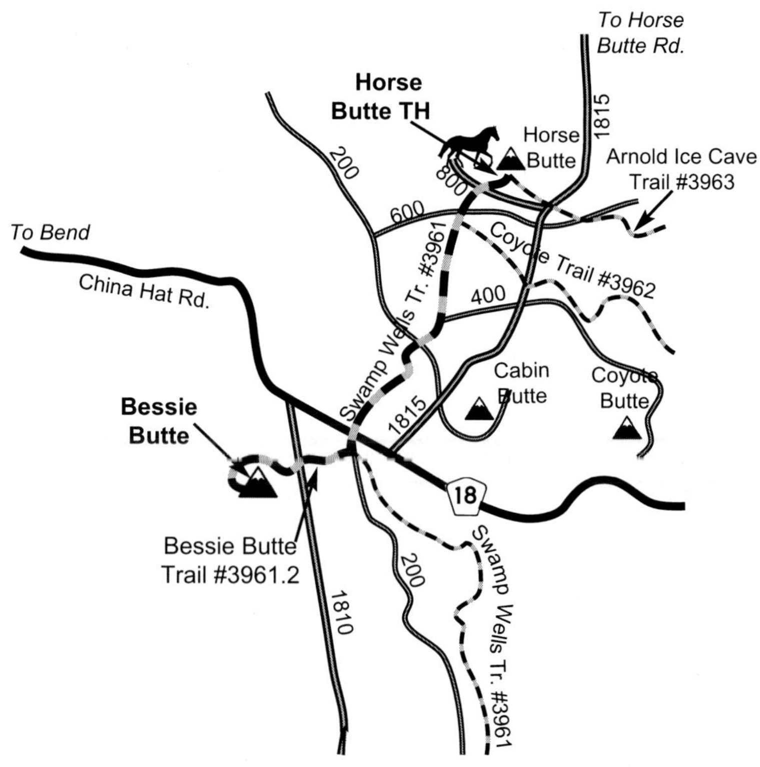

Debbie on Split, Lydia on Shadow, and Teresa on Kodie, enjoying the 360-degree view from the top of Bessie Butte.

Highlights: This ride travels through pretty ponderosa pine forest, then through a fire scar, then steeply uphill for 500 feet to the top of Bessie Butte. The summit offers a 360-degree panoramic view.

The Ride: Pick up the Swamp Wells Trail #3961 on the south side of the parking area. In 0.5 mile you'll reach a junction with the Coyote Trail #3962. Stay to the right and continue 1.8 miles to paved China Hat Road. Cross it, and in about 100 feet turn right on the Bessie Butte Trail #3961.2. You will shortly enter an area burned in 2003's 18 Fire, named after the Forest Service's road number for China Hat Road. In 0.4 mile you'll cross gravel Road 1810 and begin climbing the butte. The 18 Fire killed a lot of trees, but it also opened up some impressive vistas from the flanks of Bessie Butte. The trail gains 500 feet in 0.7 mile, but the expansive views from the summit are worth the climb.

Coyote Trail Loop

Trailhead: Start at the Boyd Cave parking area
Length: 8 miles round trip
Elevation: 4,300 to 5,000 feet
Difficulty: Moderate
Footing: Hoof protection recommended
Season: Early spring through late fall
Permits: None
Facilities: Parking for 3-4 trailers. No stock water on the trail.

Highlights: This pleasant trail is rideable almost year-round. Most of the route is forested, but there are a couple of spots where you'll find

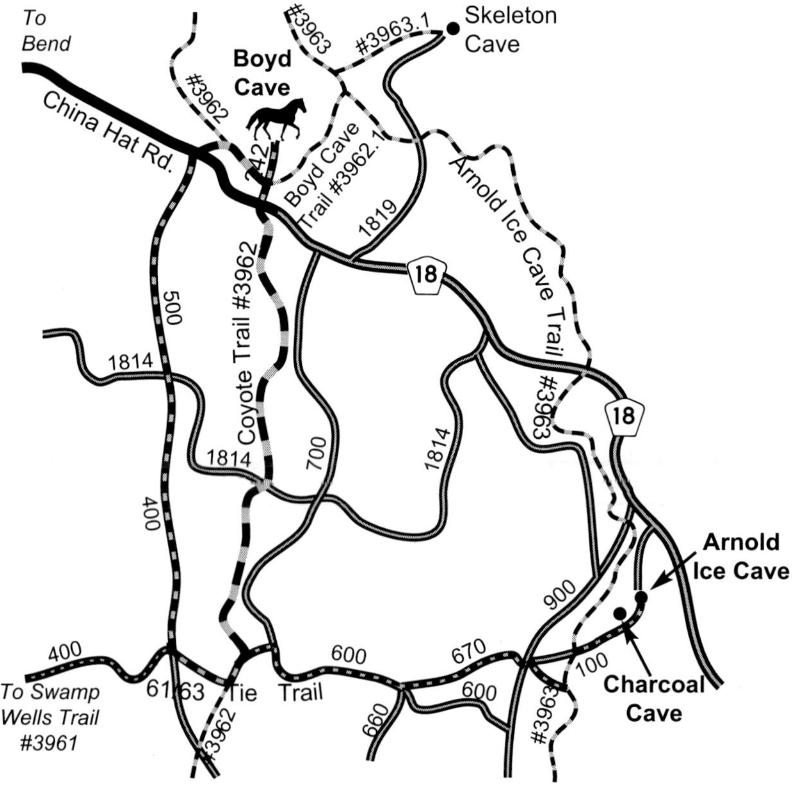

Debbie on Cowboy, Whitney on Dixie, and Connie on Diamond, enjoying a beautiful day on the Coyote Loop Trail.

nice views to the east. Spring, early summer, and fall are the best seasons, as the trail can be pretty dusty in summer.

The Ride: Ride south on Road 242, cross China Hat Road, and pick up the Coyote Trail #3962. The trail starts out on a dirt road, then veers left and becomes a single-track. About 1.8 mile after crossing China Hat Road, the trail crosses dirt Road 1814 and continues straight ahead. In another 1.2 miles the 61/63 Tie Trail goes off to the left on dirt Road 600, toward Trail 3963 and Arnold Ice Cave. Veer right and continue 0.3 mile to the next junction sign. Turn right on the 61/63 Tie Trail, toward the Swamp Wells Trail #3961. In 0.5 mile, turn right on dirt Road 400 and follow it 3.7 miles back to China Hat Road. (It becomes Road 500 on the north side of Road 1814.) Cross China Hat Road and ride cross-country to Trail #3962, then turn right on the trail and follow it back to the parking area.

Kelsey Butte

Trailhead:	Start at Horse Butte Trailhead or at an unofficial dirt turnout at the intersection of China Hat Road and Road 1810
Length:	12 miles round trip from the unofficial parking spot, or 16.5 miles round trip from Horse Butte Trailhead
Elevation:	4,200 to 5,000 feet
Difficulty:	Moderate
Footing:	Suitable for barefoot horses
Season:	Early spring through late fall
Permits:	None
Facilities:	Parking for 1-3 trailers at the China Hat/Road 1810 turnout, or for 5-6 trailers at Horse Butte Trailhead. No stock water on the trail.

Highlights: Be sure to ride this trail on a clear day, because the 180-degree views from the flank of Kelsey Butte are amazing. You'll see

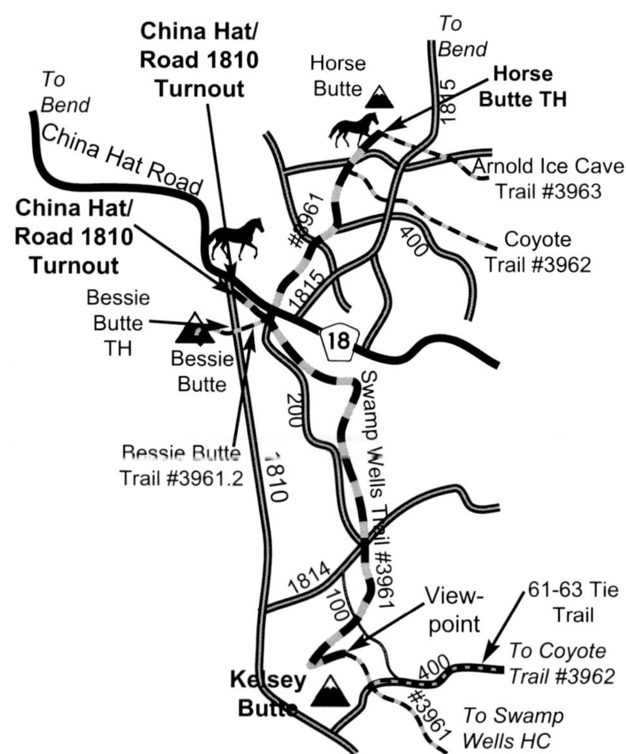

all of the Cascades from Broken Top to Mt. Hood, plus views to the north and east. The open ponderosa forest on the way to the butte is very pretty.

The Ride: From Horse Butte Trailhead, pick up the Swamp Wells Trail #3961 on the south side of the parking area. In 0.5 mile you'll reach a junction with the Coyote Trail #3962. Stay to the right and continue 1.8 miles to paved China Hat Road. Cross it, and in about 100 feet the Bessie Butte Trail #3961.2 goes off to the right. From the China Hat/Road 1810 Turnout, head southwest and ride cross-country beside China Hat Road for 0.5 mile, then turn right on the Swamp Wells Trail #3961. Almost immediately you'll come to the junction with the Bessie Butte Trail. All, continue straight ahead on the Swamp Wells Trail. For the next 5 miles the trail winds through open forest and gently rolling terrain, then it begins climbing Kelsey Butte through young ponderosas that were planted in rows after a forest fire. The trail angles up the flank of Kelsey Butte, taking you above the tree line and providing expansive views. Enjoy the sights, then retrace your steps to return to the trailhead.

Gillian rides Allegro on the flank of Kelsey Butte.
The Cascades are arrayed across the horizon behind them.

Skeleton Cave Loop

Trailhead: Start at Horse Butte Trailhead
Length: 11.5 miles round trip
Elevation: 3,900 to 4,300 feet
Difficulty: Moderate — heavy mountain bike use
Footing: Suitable for barefoot horses
Season: Nearly year-round
Permits: None
Facilities: Parking for 5-6 trailers at Horse Butte Trailhead. No stock water on the trail.

Highlights: This is an easy, low-elevation loop ride that goes through Ponderosa forest, past several large cinder buttes, and across broad expanses of grass and rabbitbrush punctuated with the charred remains of trees torched by the Skeleton Fire in 1996. Wildflowers can be plentiful in spring. This trail is very popular with mountain bike riders.

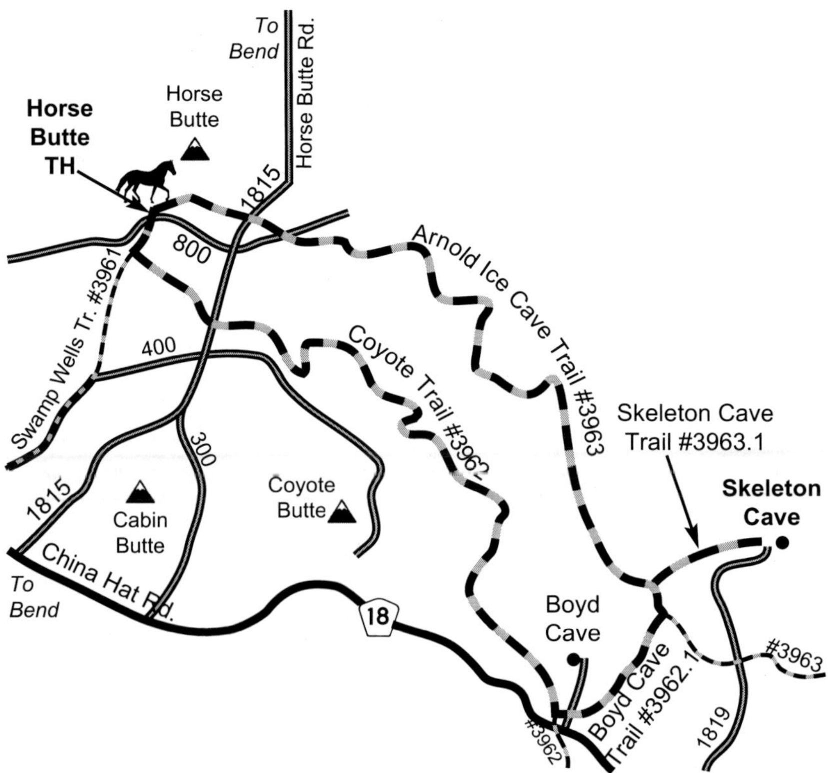

The Ride: Pick up Arnold Ice Cave Trail #3963 on the east side of the parking area. In the first mile, several user-created trails depart from Trail #3963, so follow the gray diamonds that mark all the trails in the Swamp Wells system. After 4.3 miles, you'll reach a junction where the trail crosses a dirt road and the Skeleton Cave Trail #3963.1 goes off at a hard left. Follow Trail #3963.1 and in 0.7 mile you'll reach Skeleton Cave, situated in a grove of large pines. This is a nice lunch spot. Note that Skeleton Cave is closed to the public to protect the cave from vandalism and to protect the habitat for the bats that hibernate here. Follow Trail #3963.1 back to the Arnold Ice Cave Trail and turn left, then in 0.1 mile turn right on Boyd Cave Trail #3962.1. Follow it 0.8 mile, then turn right on the Coyote Trail #3962. Continue 4.2 miles and turn right on the Swamp Wells Trail #3961. In 0.5 mile you'll arrive back at the trailhead.

Whitney on Dixie and Debbie on Split, gazing into the mouth of Skeleton Cave.

Gillian rides Allegro on the Swamp Wells Trail near Kelsey Butte.

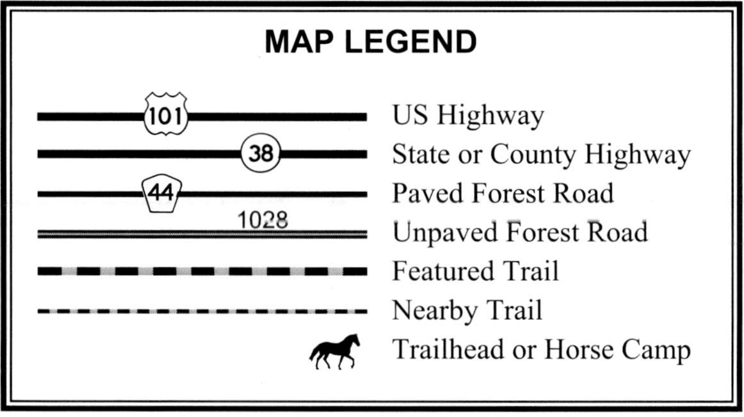

McKenzie Pass Area

Deschutes & Willamette National Forests

McKenzie Pass is located about 15 miles west of Sisters, on Highway 242. The trails in the area extend into the northern part of the Three Sisters Wilderness and the southern part of the Mt. Washington Wilderness. The trails near McKenzie Pass offer spectacular scenery, with panoramic views, beautiful forests, alpine lakes, lava flows, and mountain vistas — all the makings of a truly memorable ride.

Unfortunately, in late summer 2017, the Milli Fire burned through this area, affecting the Black Crater, Millican Crater, Scott Pass, and North Matthieu Lake Trails, as well as sections of the Pacific Crest Trail. When this book went to press, we had little information about how much damage the fire inflicted on the forest around these trails. Before you ride, we suggest you call the Forest Service to make sure the trails are passable.

South Matthieu Lake and North Sister.

McKenzie Pass Area

Directions: McKenzie Pass is located about 15 miles west of Sisters. The area trails are accessed from Hwy. 242. For directions, see "Finding the Trailhead" on the pages for each trail.

Elevation: 5,200 feet

Camping: Dispersed camping is permitted at Lava Camp Trailhead. Or you can camp at Whispering Pine Horse Camp or Sisters Cow Camp. See the Whispering Pine and Sisters Cow Camp chapters for more information.

Facilities: See "Facilities" on the pages for each trail

Permits: See "Permits" on the pages for each trail

Season: Summer through fall

Contact: For information about the Black Crater or Millican Crater/Matthieu Lakes trails, contact the Sisters Ranger District: 541-549-7700
For information about the Obsidian and Scott Mountain trails, contact the McKenzie Ranger District: 541-822-3381
For a Limited-Entry Permit for the Obsidian Loop, go to www.recreation.gov.

Riders head up over Opie Dilldock Pass on the Obsidian Loop.

Getting to McKenzie Pass

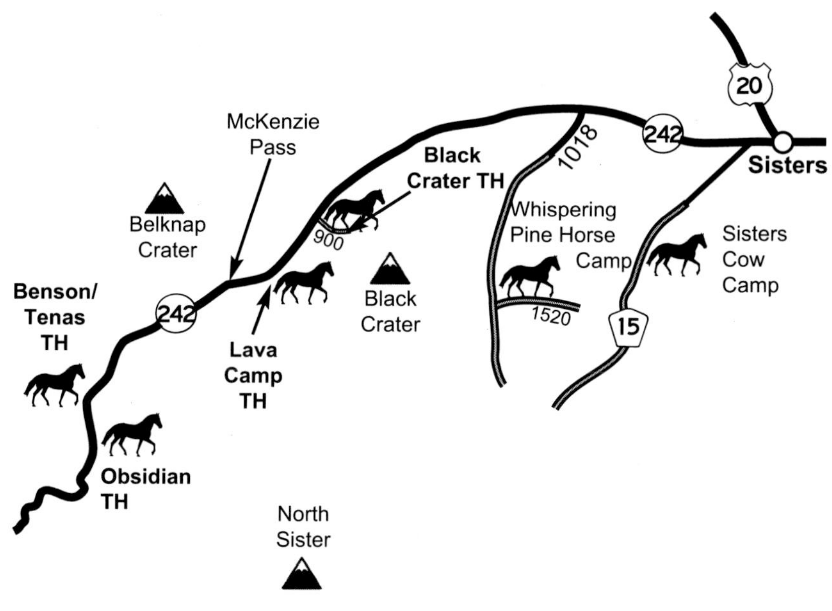

McKenzie Pass Area Trails

Trail	Difficulty	Elevation	Round Trip
Black Crater	Challenging	4,900-7,200	7.5 miles
Millican Crater/Matthieu Lks.	Moderate	5,200-6,100	10.5 miles
Obsidian Loop	Moderate	4,800-6,900	13-16 miles
Scott Mountain Loop	Moderate	4,800-6,100	8 miles

Black Crater

Trailhead: Start at the Black Crater Trailhead

Length: 7.5 miles round trip

Elevation: 4,900 to 7,200 feet

Difficulty: Challenging -- big elevation gain

Footing: Hoof protection recommended

Season: Summer through fall

Permits: None

Facilities: Parking for 2-3 trailers (possibly more on a weekday when there are fewer hiker cars). No water on the trail.

Highlights: On a scale of 1 to 10, the views from the summit of Black Crater rate a 15. They are arguably the best views from any horse trail in Central Oregon. On a clear day you can see Mt. Hood, Mt. Jefferson, Three Fingered Jack, and Mt. Washington to the north, and North Sister, South Sister, and Broken Top to the south. The trail gains 2,200 feet of elevation in 3.5 miles, though, so your horse will need to be in condition.

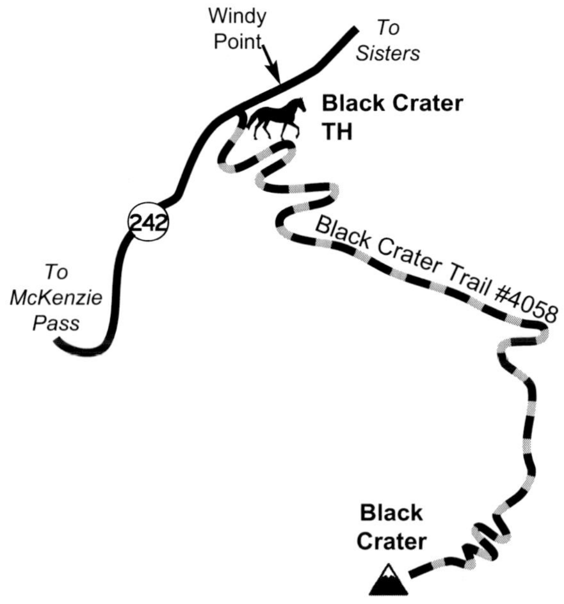

Lydia on Shadow and Whitney on Cody, admiring the view of Mt. Washington from the summit of Black Crater.

Finding the Black Crater Trailhead: From Sisters, go west on Hwy. 242 for 11 miles and turn left into the trailhead parking area, located about 0.5 mile past Windy Point.

The Ride: The Black Crater Trail #4058 departs from the south side of the trailhead, next to the kiosk. It climbs steadily, and as it nears the top the trail traverses open, cinder-strewn hillsides punctuated with wind-stunted trees. The cinder cone's summit is wide open, offering jaw-dropping 360-degree views. Note: We understand that the Black Crater Trail was severely damaged by the Milli Fire and will need extensive reconstruction and rerouting. Before you ride, please contact the Forest Service to get updated details on trail conditions and trail access.

Millican Crater/Matthieu Lks. Lp.

Trailhead: Start at Lava Camp Trailhead
Length: 10.5 miles round trip
Elevation: 5,200 to 6,100 feet
Difficulty: Moderate
Footing: Hoof protection recommended
Season: Summer through fall
Permits: None
Facilities: Toilet and 2 dispersed campsites at Lava Camp Trailhead. Stock water is available on the trail.

Highlights: This ride goes through dense forest, along a huge lava flow, over Scott Pass, and past the picturesque Matthieu Lakes. Scott Pass offers expansive views of lava flows and cinder cones. The 2017 Milli Fire burned through this area, but as this book went to press we had little information about the extent of the damage near the trails, so please contact the Forest Service for an update. Dogs must be on leash near Matthieu Lakes from July 15 to September 15.

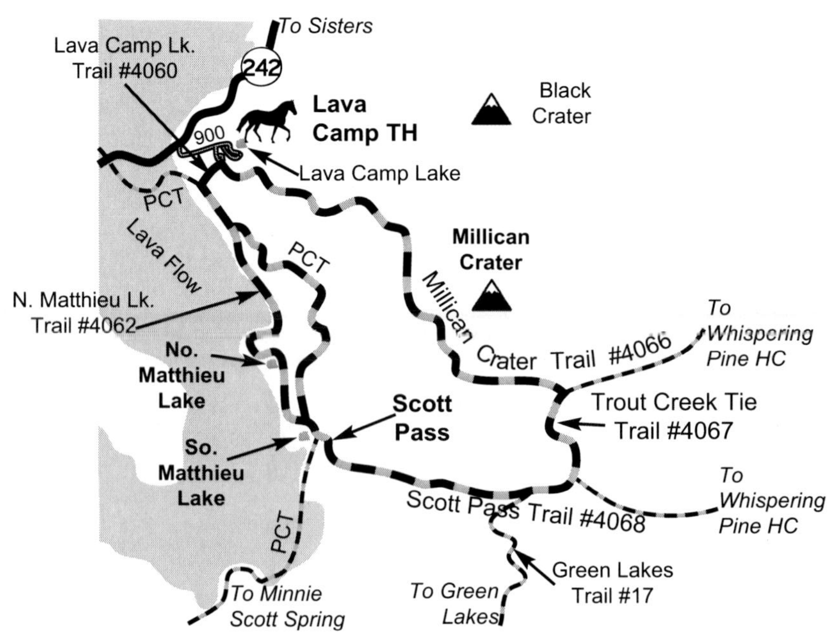

Finding Lava Camp Trailhead: Take Hwy. 242 (McKenzie Hwy.) west from Sisters for 14.5 miles and turn left on Road 900. Continue 0.4 mile to the equestrian parking area.

The Ride: On the south side of the parking area, pick up the trail on the left (the Millican Crater Trail #4066). In 3.5 miles, you'll reach the junction with the Trout Creek Tie Trail #4067. Turn right on the Tie Trail toward Scott Pass, and in 1.0 mile you'll reach the Scott Pass Trail #4068. Turn right toward Green Lakes and the PCT. After 0.4 mile, the Green Lakes Trail #17 goes off to the left. Stay right and continue 1.8 mile to Scott Pass, with its impressive views. After a short distance the trail intersects with the PCT. Turn right on the PCT and continue to South Matthieu Lake for a good view of North Sister over the lake. From here you can either stay on the PCT or go left on the North Matthieu Lake Trail #4062. Since the detour adds no distance and runs along an interesting lava flow, we recommend going to the left. The trail rejoins the PCT in 2 miles. In another 0.7 mile, veer right on the Lava Camp Lake Trail #4060 to return to the trailhead.

Lydia and Shadow relax on the shore of North Matthieu Lake.

Obsidian Loop

Trailhead: Start at the Obsidian Trailhead

Length: 13 miles round trip, or 16 miles if you detour to Obsidian Falls

Elevation: 4,800 to 6,900 feet

Difficulty: Moderate

Footing: Hoof protection recommended

Season: Summer through fall

Permits: A limited-use permit is required to ride this trail (see below). Northwest Forest Pass required for parking.

Facilities: Toilet, parking for many trailers. Stock water is available on the trail.

Highlights: Located in the shadow of North Sister, this scenic ride features soaring obsidian cliffs, lava moonscapes, immense cinder cones, sparkling springs, pretty meadows, and sweeping vistas. This is a fragile environment, so the Forest Service limits the number of riders, hikers, and backpackers in the area at any one time. To ride in this area, you must obtain a limited-entry permit. Go to www.recreation.gov to obtain a permit for the Obsidian Limited Entry Area.

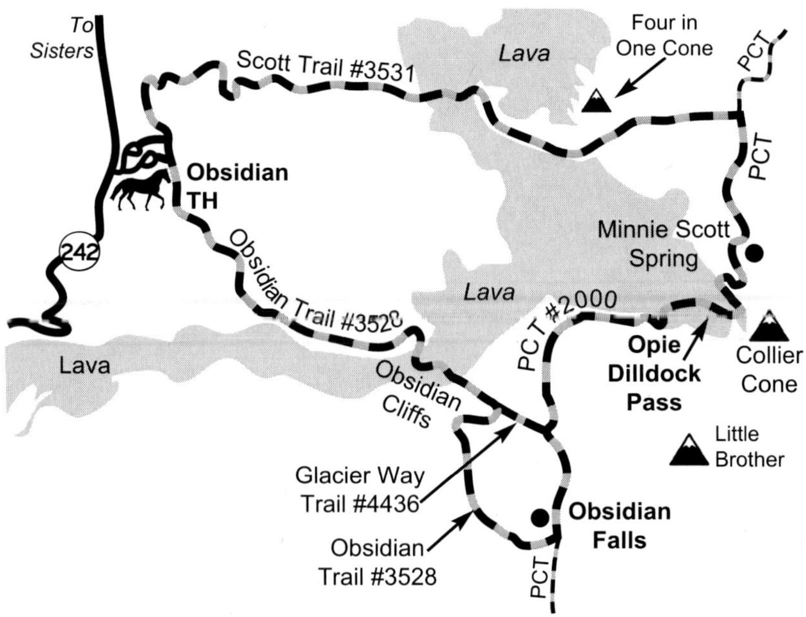

The fabulous Obsidian Loop lies at the foot of North Sister.

Finding the Obsidian Trailhead: Take Highway 242 west from Sisters for 22 miles and turn left into the Obsidian Trailhead. Note that only truck/trailer combinations less than 35 feet long are permitted over McKenzie Pass, so you'll need to use a 2-horse trailer to get there.

The Ride: Pick up the trail on the east side of the Obsidian Trailhead. At the first fork, go right on the Obsidian Trail #3528. After 3 miles you will see the Obsidian Cliffs, which tower over the forest and lava flows. The trail leads across the lava flow and back into the forest. Shortly afterward, the trail forks. The left fork (Glacier Way Trail #4436) will lead you to the Pacific Crest Trail in 0.6 mile. Or, for a very scenic 3-mile detour, turn right and continue on the Obsidian Trail toward Obsidian Falls. When the trail intersects with the PCT, turn left (north) and soon you will pass Obsidian Falls. Proceed on the PCT for 1 mile to the junction with the Glacier Way Trail. Stay to the right and continue on the PCT for 2 miles to Opie Dilldock Pass, where a series of switchbacks will take you over an avalanche of black and red lava that flowed down between two cliffs. Although each switchback is only a couple of horse-lengths long, each is comfortably wide, so while the elevation gain is significant, there are no steep drop offs. From the pass, continue about a mile past Minnie Scott Spring to the junction with the Scott Trail #3531. Turn left to return to the trailhead.

Scott Mountain Loop

Trailhead: Start at the Benson/Tenas Trailhead in the quarry next to Scott Lake Campground

Length: 8 miles round trip

Elevation: 4,800 to 6,100 feet

Difficulty: Moderate

Footing: Hoof protection recommended

Season: Summer through fall

Permits: Northwest Forest Pass required

Facilities: Toilet and parking for several horse trailers at the trailhead. Stock water is available on the trail.

Highlights: Scott Mountain's open summit offers phenomenal views of the Three Sisters, Mt. Washington, Three Fingered Jack, Mt. Jefferson, and Mt. Hood. The trail passes several pretty lakes and an interesting lava flow. It is a relatively easy ride except for a couple of steep switchbacks near the top of Scott Mountain.

Finding the Benson/Tenas Trailhead: From Sisters, drive west on Hwy. 242 for 20 miles. Turn right on Road 260 and proceed about a

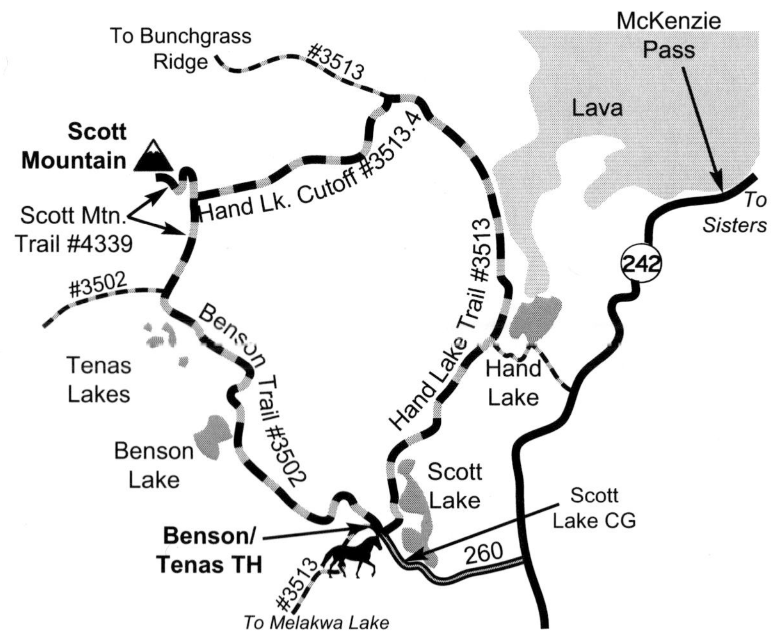

From the top of Scott Mountain, you feel like you could reach out and touch the Three Sisters.

mile to the old quarry at the end of the road, near Scott Lake Campground. Note that only truck/trailer combinations less than 35 feet long are permitted over McKenzie Pass, so you'll need to use a 2-horse trailer to get there.

The Ride: Take the Hand Lake Trail #3513 from the eastern edge of the parking area. The trail along the shore of Scott Lake may be a bit overgrown with grass, but if you bear left along the lake shore you can't miss the trail as it heads up into the timber. After 1.5 miles you'll reach Hand Lake, and for the next mile or so the trail travels along a lava flow. About 1.5 miles beyond Hand Lake, you'll come to a sign indicating that Bunchgrass Ridge is straight ahead. Turn left here on the unsigned Hand Lake Cutoff Trail #3513.4. Continue 1.5 miles and turn right on the Scott Mountain Trail #4339. Ascend another 0.5 mile (including several steep switchbacks) to reach the open, grassy summit with its dazzling views. To complete the loop, follow the Scott Mountain Trail down to the Benson Trail #3502 and turn left. The Tenas Lakes are 1.5 miles from the summit (2.5 miles from the trailhead), and Benson Lake is 2.5 miles from the summit (1.5 miles from the trailhead).

Whitney on Cody and Lydia on Shadow, admiring the view of the Three Sisters from the summit of Scott Mountain.

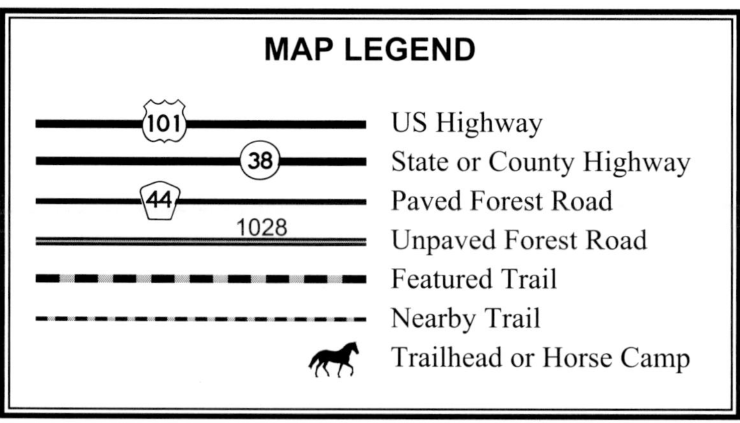

Metolius Basin

Deschutes National Forest

The Metolius Basin, located about 15 miles northwest of the town of Sisters, is bordered by Black Butte to the south, Green Ridge to the east, the Warm Springs Reservation to the north, and the high Cascades to the west. You can stay at Sheep Springs Horse Camp and ride the nearby trails, which are covered in the Sheep Springs Horse Camp chapter of this book. Or you can trailer to the interesting trails in this chapter, which range from easy riding near the tiny town of Camp Sherman to more strenuous excursions into the high Cascades and Mt. Jefferson Wilderness. The high-Cascades trails were affected by the 2003 B&B fire, so you'll see plenty of burned tree trunks as you ride, but the fire also opened up some impressive vistas.

Three Fingered Jack from the Rockpile Lake Trail.

Getting to the Metolius Basin

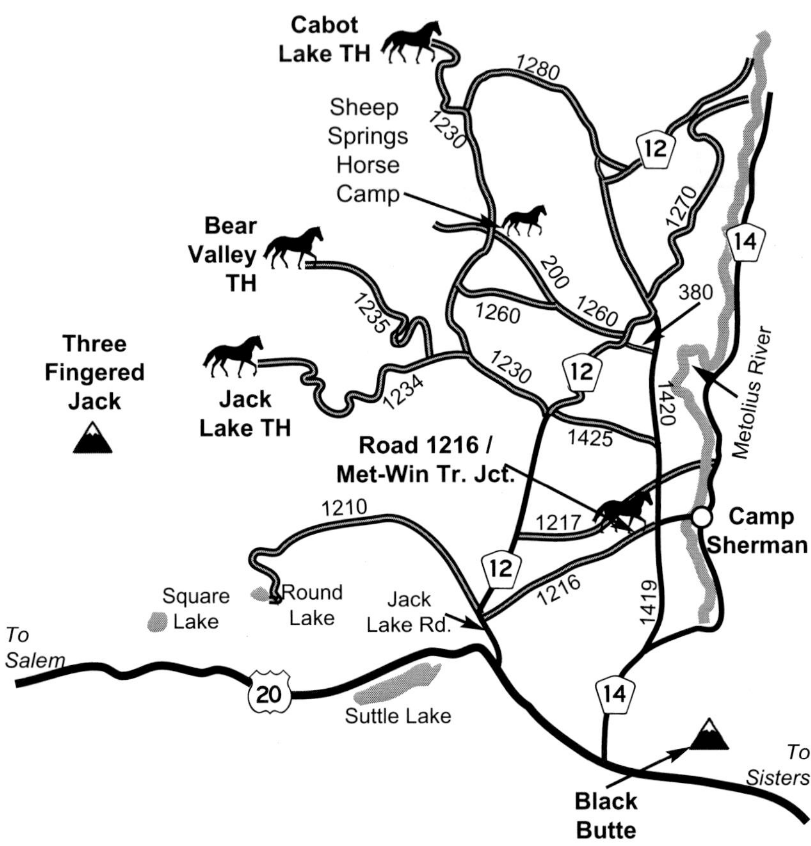

Metolius Basin Trails

Trail	Difficulty	Elevation	Round Trip
Cabot & Carl Lakes	Moderate+	4,600-5,500	4-10 miles
Camp Sherman Loop	Moderate	2,950-3,050	6 miles
Canyon Creek Meadows Lp.	Moderate	5,150-5,700	5-8 miles
Rockpile Lake	Moderate	4,150-6,300	11.5 miles

Metolius Basin Trailheads

BEAR VALLEY TRAILHEAD

Directions: From Sisters, drive northwest on Hwy. 20 for 12 miles and turn right on Jack Lake Road (Road 12). In 4 miles veer left on Road 1230. In another 1.5 miles, turn left on Road 1234, and 0.7 mile after that veer right on road 1235. In 4 miles you'll reach the trailhead.

More Info: Parking for 5-6 trailers, no amenities, no permit needed, season is summer through fall. Contact: Sisters Ranger District, 541-549-7700

CABOT LAKE TRAILHEAD

Directions: From Sisters, drive northwest on Hwy. 20 for 12 miles. Turn right on Jack Lake Road (Road 12) and continue 4.3 miles. Turn left on Road 1230 and drive 8.2 miles to the trailhead.

More Info: Parking for 2-3 trailers, no amenities, no permit needed, season is summer through fall. Contact: Sisters Ranger District, 541-549-7700

JACK LAKE TRAILHEAD

Directions: From Sisters, drive northwest on Hwy. 20 for 12 miles. Turn right on Jack Lake Road (Road 12). After 4 miles, turn left on Road 1230 and continue 1.5 miles. Turn left on Road 1234 and go 5 miles to the trailhead. The route is well signed. The last 3 miles of road are very steep and very rough. Four-wheel drive is a must.

More Info: Parking for 1-2 trailers, toilet, no permit needed, season is summer through fall. Contact: Sisters Ranger District, 541-549-7700

ROAD 1216 / METOLIUS-WINDIGO TRAIL JUNCTION

Directions: From Sisters, drive northwest on Hwy. 20 for 9.5 miles. Turn right on Road 14 (toward Camp Sherman). In 2.7 miles, Road 14 veers to the right. Continue straight ahead on Road 1419 and in another 2.2 miles turn left on Road 1216. Continue 0.5 mile and park on the side of the road where the Met-Win Trail crosses Road 1216. You can't turn around here, so after your ride follow Road 1216 to paved Road 12 and turn left to return to Hwy. 20.

More Info: Parking for 1-2 trailers, no amenities, no permit needed, season is spring through fall. Contact: Sisters Ranger District, 541-549-7700.

Cabot & Carl Lakes

Trailhead: Start at the Cabot Lake Trailhead

Length: 4 miles round trip to Cabot Lake, 10 miles round trip to Carl Lake

Elevation: 4,600 to 4,700 feet to Cabot Lake, or 4,600 to 5,500 feet to Carl Lake

Difficulty: Moderate to Cabot Lake, but challenging between Cabot and Carl Lakes (very rocky trail)

Footing: Hoof protection strongly recommended

Season: Summer through fall

Permits: None

Facilities: Parking for 2-3 rigs at the trailhead. Stock water is available on the trail.

Highlights: The Cabot Lake Trail is one of the few east-side Mt. Jefferson Wilderness Area trails that was not completely burned by the B&B fire in 2003. The terrain is fairly rugged and the trail is rocky, but the scenery is beautiful.

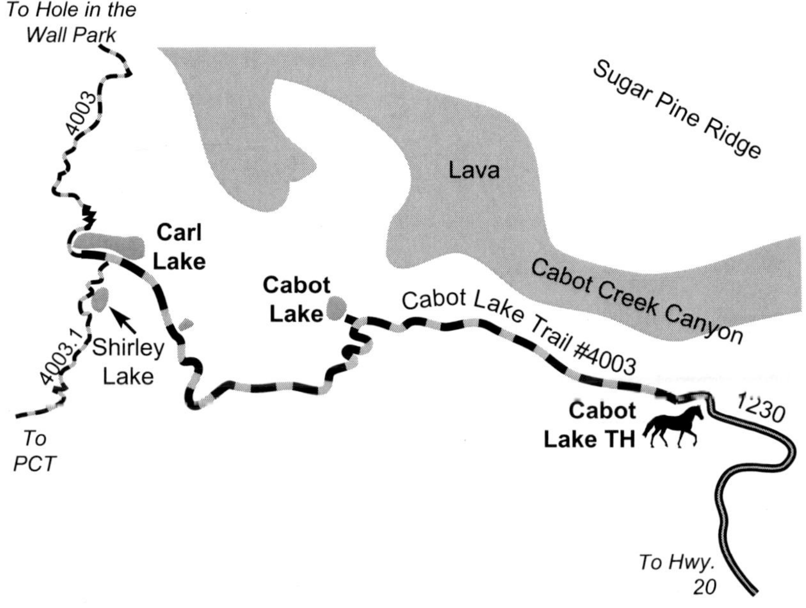

The Ride: The first mile of the Cabot Lake Trail #4003, which runs along a ridge above Cabot Creek Canyon, was badly burned by the B&B fire. While the fire's devastation is appalling, it opened up views of the lava flows in the canyon below, and of Mt. Jefferson looming over Sugar Pine Ridge. Next the trail enters an unburned area, and the contrast between the lovely live forest and the burned area is striking. Two miles from the parking area, the trail forks. Take the trail to the right and ride a short distance to Cabot Lake, or take the left fork and go 3 miles farther to Carl Lake. Both lakes are aquamarine gems cradled between rocky ridges, and both make excellent lunch spots. The trail is very rocky between Cabot Lake and Carl Lake. Downed trees in the burned area can be a problem, so before you do this ride, check with the Forest Service to make sure the trail has been cleared.

Riders and horses take a lunch break along the Cabot Lake Trail.

Camp Sherman Loop

Trailhead: Start at the junction of Road 1216 & the Metolius-Windigo Trail (not an official trailhead — park beside the road)

Length: 6 miles round trip

Elevation: 2,950 to 3,050 feet

Difficulty: Moderate -- creek and river crossings; some wayfinding skills required

Footing: Suitable for barefoot horses

Season: Early spring through late fall

Permits: None

Facilities: No facilities at the parking area. Stock water is available on the trail.

Highlights: This is a fun ride, with plenty of shade, little elevation change, and several refreshing creek crossings. Plus, you can get lunch, ice cream, or a cold drink at the Camp Sherman Store. However, the route involves some unsigned trails and some cross-country travel.

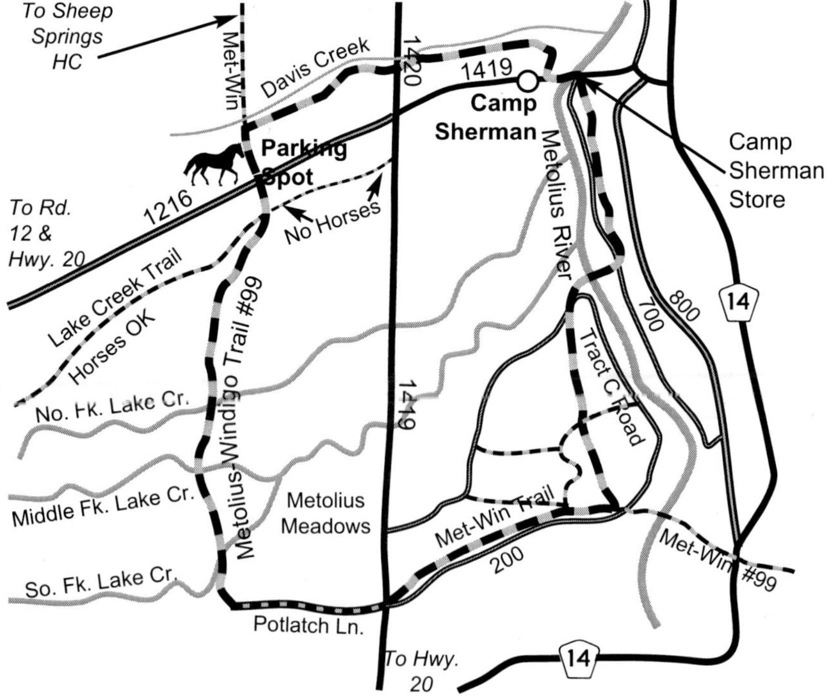

Laurie and Debbie ride Seeker and Split across the Metolius River on the Camp Sherman Loop.

The Ride: From your parking spot beside Road 1216, head south on the Metolius-Windigo Trail #99, which is signed with yellow diamonds. In the first 2 miles you'll cross the North, Middle, and South Forks of Lake Creek. Then the trail will take you around the perimeter of the Metolius Meadows subdivision and across paved Road 1419. Continue on the Metolius-Windigo Trail for 0.9 mile. After riding around the base of a 40-foot knoll, turn left on the first trail you come to. This trail is signed with blue diamonds on the trees. Follow this trail straight ahead, ignoring any trails that go off in either direction, for 0.7 mile. It will take you to the red cinder Tract C Road (named for the tract of summer homes along its length). Veer slightly right on the Tract C Road, then in 100 feet turn left at the address sign for Cabin 12921. This driveway turns into a single-track trail that runs behind the cabins and takes you to an easy crossing of the Metolius River. About 50 feet after crossing the river you'll reach Road 700. Turn left on it, and in 50 feet veer right on a single-track trail. The trail parallels Road 700 and the Metolius River as it runs past several clusters of summer homes. After about 0.6 mile, you'll reach the Camp Sherman Store. Tie your horses at the hitching rail behind the store and go inside to get a drink or a sandwich. Then lead your horse across the road bridge over the Metolius River and continue about 400 feet along the road. Directly across from the Kokanee Café, mount up again and turn right to ride around the big green gate that blocks the power line road. Follow this dirt road for 0.1 mile to a power sub-station. Turn left at the sub-station and follow the single-track/dirt road that goes to the left. In 0.5 mile, it will take you to paved Road 1419. Cross Road 1419 and ride cross-country. (The fringe of riparian vegetation along the bank of seasonal Davis Creek will be on your right, so just follow it.) In 0.6 mile, you'll reach the Metolius-Windigo Trail. Turn left on it and you'll arrive at your trailer in 0.2 mile.

Canyon Creek Meadows Loop

Trailhead: Start at Jack Lake Trailhead

Length: 5 miles round trip for Jack Lake Loop, 6.5 miles round trip if you ride to the base of Three Fingered Jack, 8 miles round trip if you ride to the base of Three Fingered Jack and to Wasco Lake

Elevation: 5,150 to 5,700 feet

Difficulty: Moderate

Footing: Suitable for barefoot horses

Season: Summer through early fall

Permits: Northwest Forest Pass required

Facilities: Toilet, parking for several trailers (depending on the number of hiker cars). Stock water is available on the trail.

Highlights: This is a delightful ride across manzanita-covered hillsides and through dense forest to the flower-filled Canyon Creek Meadows and then along Canyon Creek. Some of the trail was burned in the 2003 B&B fire, but fortunately the lovely meadows were untouched. The western end of the loop offers excellent views of Three Fingered Jack, and a short extension takes you nearly to the base of the

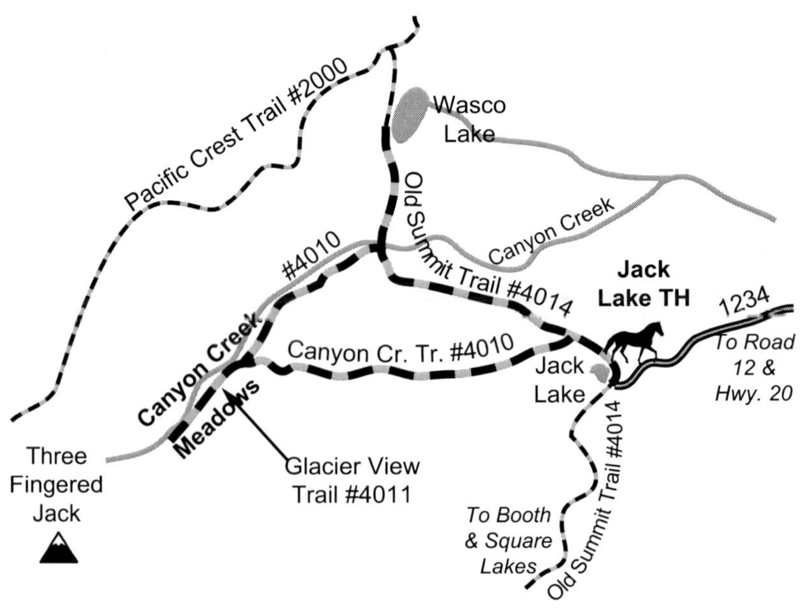

Riders pause on the extension trail that leads to the base of Three Fingered Jack.

mountain. If desired, you can also ride a 0.6 mile (one way) extension to Wasco Lake. Unfortunately, the road to the trailhead is very steep and rough. Four-wheel drive is a must! This trail is very popular, so it's best to ride it on a weekday.

The Ride: From the parking lot, pick up the trail going to the right past Jack Lake. After 0.5 mile, the trail forks. Go left on Canyon Creek Trail #4010. In another 1.7 miles you'll reach a junction. Turn left on the Glacier View Trail #4011 to reach Canyon Creek Meadows and good views of nearby Three Fingered Jack. You can ride about 0.7 mile one way, almost to the base of the peak. Then return to the junction and turn left to continue around the loop. The trail follows Canyon Creek for about a mile, after which the 0.6-mile extension to Wasco Lake on the Old Summit Trail turns left, crosses Canyon Creek, and heads north. If you don't want to go to Wasco Lake, don't cross the creek and the trail will return you to the Jack Lake Trailhead.

Rockpile Lake

Trailhead: Start at the Bear Valley Trailhead
Length: 11.5 miles round trip
Elevation: 4,150 to 6,300 feet
Difficulty: Moderate
Footing: Hoof protection recommended
Season: Summer through fall
Permits: None
Facilities: Parking for 4-6 trailers, but no other facilities. Stock water is available at Rockpile Lake.

Highlights: This trail links the north end of the Metolius-Windigo Trail to the Pacific Crest Trail at Rockpile Lake. It runs alternately through hemlock/fir forest and areas burned by the B&B fire in 2003. The forested areas are beautiful, and the burned areas offer panoramic views of the Metolius Basin, Black Butte, Three-Fingered Jack, Mt. Washington, North and Middle Sister, and Broken Top.

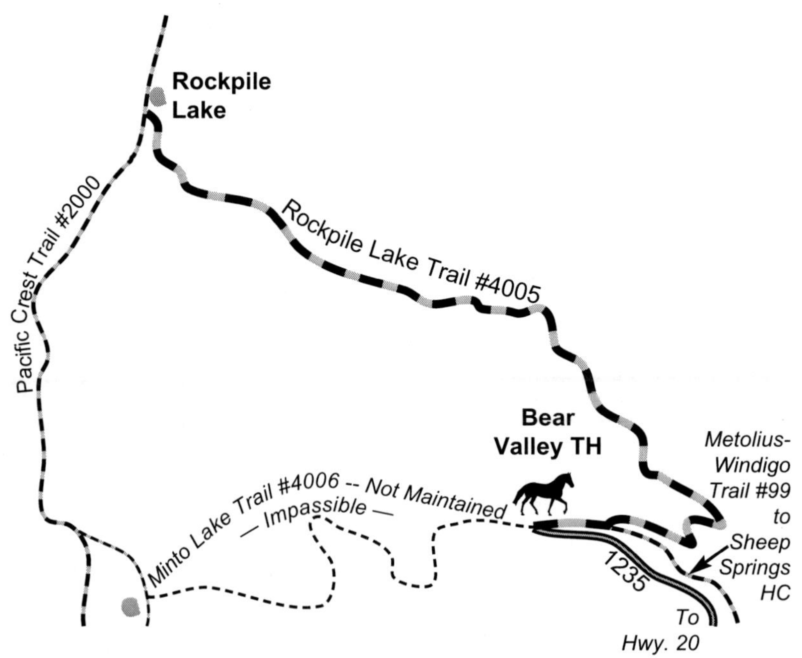

Frank, Doug, Sandy, Dave, Rhonda, Bob, and Kit are the volunteers who used cross-cut saws to clear the Rockpile Lake Trail of downed logs in 2011. They deserve our thanks for keeping this delightful trail accessible to horses.

The Ride: Pick up the Metolius-Windigo Trail #99 next to the kiosk on the west end of the parking area. Almost immediately there is a junction, but stay to the right because the trail to Minto Lake is not maintained and is impassible. After 0.3 mile, turn left onto the Rockpile Lake Trail #4005. It makes a couple of switchbacks, then heads up along the nose of a ridge. The trail climbs fairly steadily, but is otherwise not challenging. Rockpile Lake is a delight, and is the only source of stock water along the trail. Like the other nearby wilderness trails, fallen trees can completely block the trail, so before you go be sure to check with the Forest Service to find out if the trail has been cleared.

Connie on Moose and Lydia on Magic, riding through the Metolius Basin on the Camp Sherman Loop.

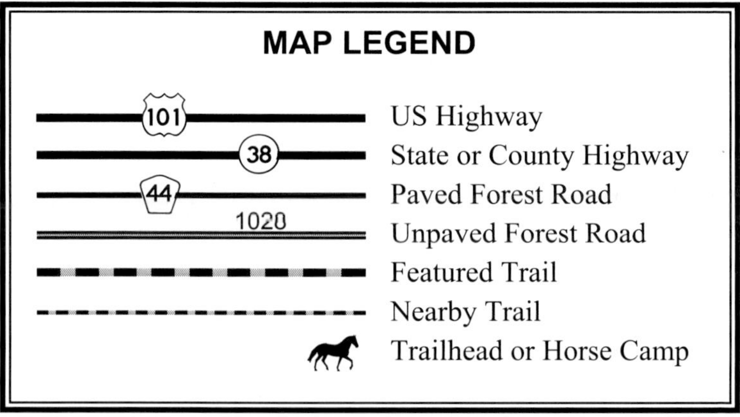

North Cascade Lakes Area

Deschutes National Forest

In the North Cascade Lakes area, you can do plenty of rides out of Quinn Meadow and Todd Creek Horse Camps. Some of the loop rides can also be accessed from nearby trailheads. These rides are covered in the Quinn Meadow and Todd Creek chapters. However, you are missing some real gems if you limit yourself to only the rides you can do from the horse camps. This chapter covers the day rides in the northern Cascade Lakes area that cannot easily be accessed from the horse camps. Because of this area's proximity to Bend, the more popular trails can be very crowded with hikers, especially on summer weekends. To address issues of overuse, the Forest Service is contemplating a permit system that will limit use to a certain number of visitors per day. Check the Deschutes National Forest website for updates on this proposal. Please keep your horse out of the lakes in this area, as backpackers use them for drinking water.

Lel and Whitney ride Jane and Dixie across Wickiup Plains, with South Sister in the background.

Getting to North Cascade Lakes

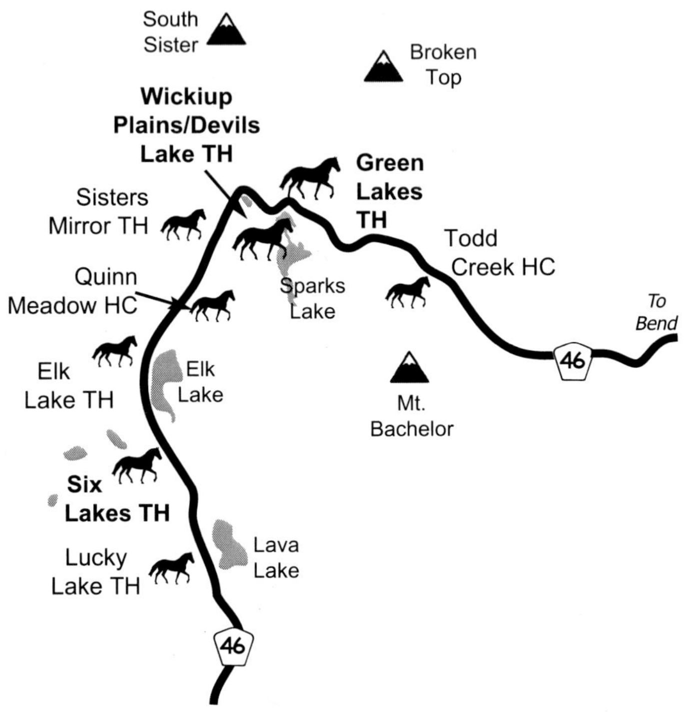

North Cascade Lakes Trails

Trail	Difficulty	Elevation	Round Trip
Green Lakes Loop	Moderate	5,450-6,500	9-12.5 miles
Mink Lake Basin	Moderate	4,000-5,700	17 miles
Moraine Lake	Moderate	5,400-6,700	7.5-10 miles
Senoj Lake	Moderate	4,900-5,600	9 miles
Wickiup Plains	Moderate	5,500-6,300	9-11 miles

North Cascade Lakes Trailheads

ALL

Directions: From Hwy. 97 in Bend, take Exit 138 (Colorado Ave.) and head west toward Mt. Bachelor. Follow the signs toward Mt. Bachelor and Century Drive, going through 3 roundabouts. Take the second exit from roundabouts 1 and 3, and take the third exit from roundabout 2. This will put you on Road 46 (Century Drive/Cascade Lakes Hwy.)

GREEN LAKES TRAILHEAD

Directions: Follow Road 46 for 26 miles. The trailhead is on the right side of the road.

Elevation: 5,450 feet

Facilities: Toilet. Parking for 1-2 trailers, though heavy use by hikers virtually guarantees that cars will park in the trailer spaces. It's best to arrive very early in the morning, and park so you can't be blocked in.

Permits: Northwest Forest Pass required

Season: Summer through fall

Contact: Bend/Ft. Rock Ranger District, 541-383-5300

SIX LAKES TRAILHEAD

Directions: Follow Road 46 for 34 miles. Just past the south end of Elk Lake, turn right into the trailhead parking area.

Elevation: 4,800 feet

Facilities: Toilet, plus parking for many trailers

Permits: None

Season: Summer through fall

Contact: Bend/Ft. Rock Ranger District, 541-383-5300

WICKIUP PLAINS/DEVILS LAKE TRAILHEAD

Directions: Follow Road 46 for 28 miles. The Wickiup Plains Trailhead is on the left side of the road, just past Devils Lake.

Elevation: 5,500 feet

Facilities: Toilet, hitching rails, and parking for many trailers

Permits: Northwest Forest Pass required

Season: Summer through fall

Contact: Bend/Ft. Rock Ranger District, 541-383-5300

Green Lakes Loop

Trailhead: Start at the Green Lakes Trailhead

Length: 12.5 miles round trip for the loop, or 9 miles up and back to Green Lakes on the Green Lakes Trail

Elevation: 5,450 to 6,500 feet

Difficulty: Moderate

Footing: Hoof protection recommended

Season: Summer through fall

Permits: Northwest Forest Pass required

Facilities: Toilet, hitching post, and parking for several trailers at the trailhead. Stock water is available on the trail.

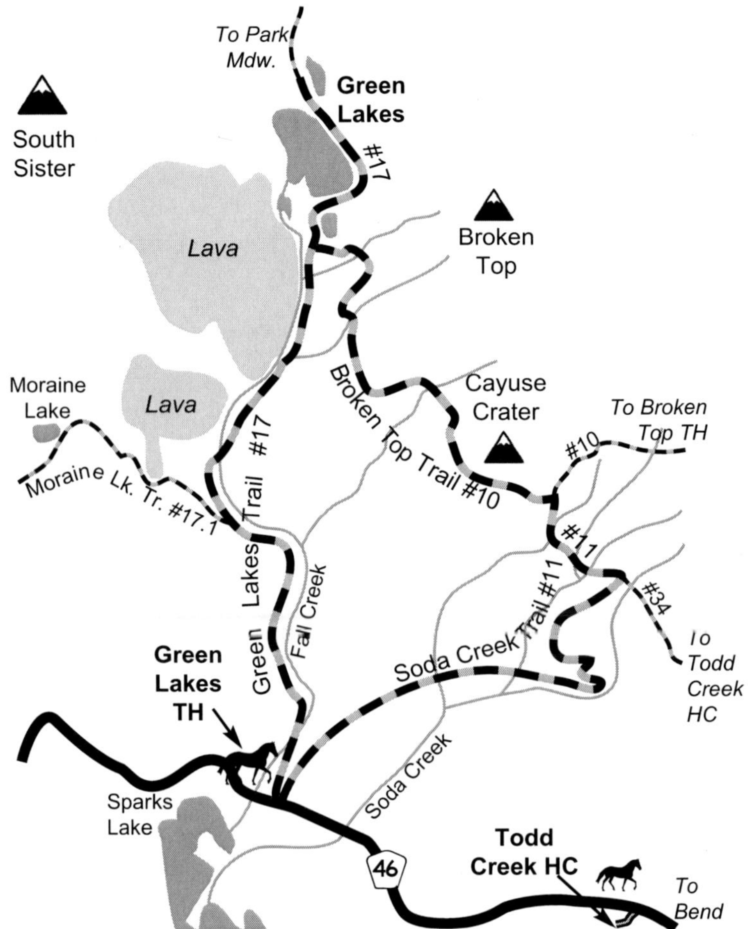

Nancy and Mesa take a break along the Green Lakes Trail. That's a waterfall behind them.

Highlights: This trail has it all. The Green Lakes are nestled between South Sister and Broken Top, with the mountains looming so close you can almost touch them. Add to this the waterfalls along Fall Creek and the enormous lava mesa on the flank of South Sister, and you have the makings of an unforgettable ride. The downside is that the Green Lakes Trail is one of the most popular hiking trails in Central Oregon. It's very crowded in summer and on weekends, so we recommend riding it on a weekday, after Labor Day. Dogs must be on leash on this trail from July 15 to September 15. Please keep your horse out of the lakes, as they are used for drinking water by backpackers.

The Ride: From the Green Lakes Trailhead, ride north on the Green Lakes Trail #17. It goes through fairly dense forest and along the bank of Fall Creek (aptly named, as it has many small waterfalls). In 2.1 miles you'll reach the junction with the Moraine Lake Trail #17.1. Stay to the right, and in 2.3 more miles you'll reach the Green Lakes, passing a massive lava flow from South Sister along the way. To make a loop back to the trailhead after visiting the lakes, return to the south end of the Green Lakes basin, turn left on the Broken Top Trail #10 and follow it 3 miles, then veer right on the Soda Creek Trail #11. In 0.9 mile, stay to the right at the junction with the Todd Trail #34, and follow the Soda Creek Trail 3.9 miles back to the trailhead. The return part of the loop is less heavily forested (and less heavily used) than the Green Lakes Trail, and offers some nice views to the south.

Mink Lake Basin

Trailhead:	Start at the Six Lakes Trailhead
Length:	17 miles round trip to Mink Lake, or 19.5 miles if you circle Mink Lake
Elevation:	4,800 to 5,700 feet
Difficulty:	Moderate
Footing:	Hoof protection recommended
Season:	Summer through fall
Permits:	None
Facilities:	Toilet and parking for many trailers at Six Lakes Trailhead. Stock water is available on the trail.

Highlights: The Mink Lake Basin is on the west side of the Cascades, so the forest there is quite different than the east-side forest near Doris and Blow Lakes. In the basin, the undergrowth beneath the old-growth trees is lush and green, and if you throw a rock in any direction it will probably land in a lake. Please keep your horse out of the lakes, as they are used for drinking water by backpackers. Mosquitoes can be fierce early in the season.

The Ride: Several lollipop-style loop rides are possible in the Mink Lake Basin. To begin any of the loops, go west 3.4 miles on the Six Lakes Trail #14, passing Blow Lake and Doris Lake along the way. At

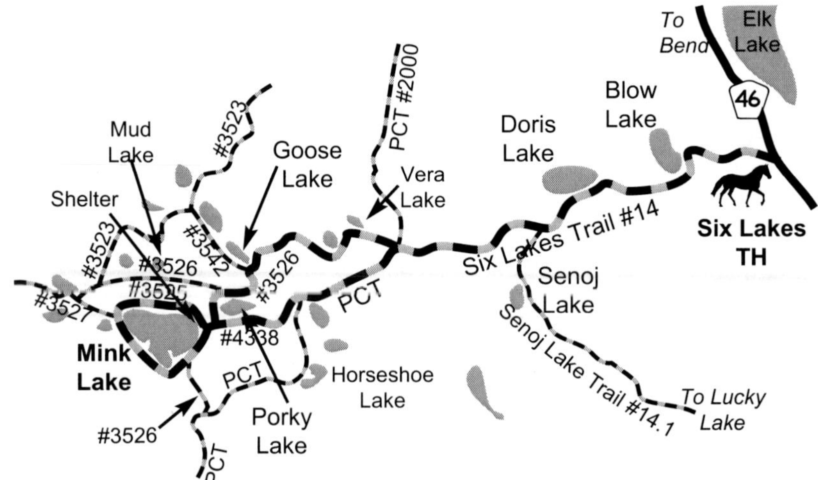

the junction with the Senoj Lake Trail #14.1, stay to the right, toward the PCT. Continue 2 miles, then turn left on the Pacific Crest Trail #2000 toward Horseshoe Lake. To make the loop to Mink Lake, follow the PCT southwest for 1.4 miles. At this point an unmarked spur trail goes off to the left. Stay to the right and in 100 feet turn right on the Porky Lake Trail #4338 toward Porky Lake. In 1.1 miles you'll reach a junction where Mink Lake is straight ahead and Goose Lake is to the right. Go straight and in 0.2 mile you'll reach Mink Lake. At the lake shore, take the Lakeside Trail #3525 to the right a short distance to find a dilapidated forest shelter and a good spot to water your horses. To return to the trailhead, go back to the last junction and turn left toward Goose Lake. In 0.3 mile, turn right on the Mink Lake Trail #3526, again toward Goose Lake. In another mile you'll reach Goose Lake and the junction with the Goose Lake Trail #3542. Veer right on the Mink Lake Trail toward Vera Lake. In 2.2 miles you'll be back at the PCT. Cross it and continue straight ahead on the Six Lakes Trail to return to the trailhead. Other loops in the basin are possible, so go exploring!

Mona on Eclipse and Linda on Brumby, relaxing on the shore of Mink Lake.

Moraine Lake

Trailhead: Start at either the Green Lakes Trailhead or the Wickiup Plains/Devils Lake Trailhead

Length: 10 miles round trip from Wickiup Plains/Devils Lake Trailhead, or 7.5 miles round trip from Green Lakes Trailhead

Elevation: 5,400 to 6,700 feet

Difficulty: Moderate

Footing: Hoof protection recommended

Season: Summer through fall

Permits: Northwest Forest Pass required

Facilities: Toilets and parking for several trailers at either trailhead. Stock water is available on the trail.

Highlights: As its name would suggest, Moraine Lake is located at the foot of a glacial moraine, a pile of dirt and rock deposited by a long-ago glacier. The sparse vegetation on the hills around the lake contrasts sharply with the beautiful alpine forest you ride through to get

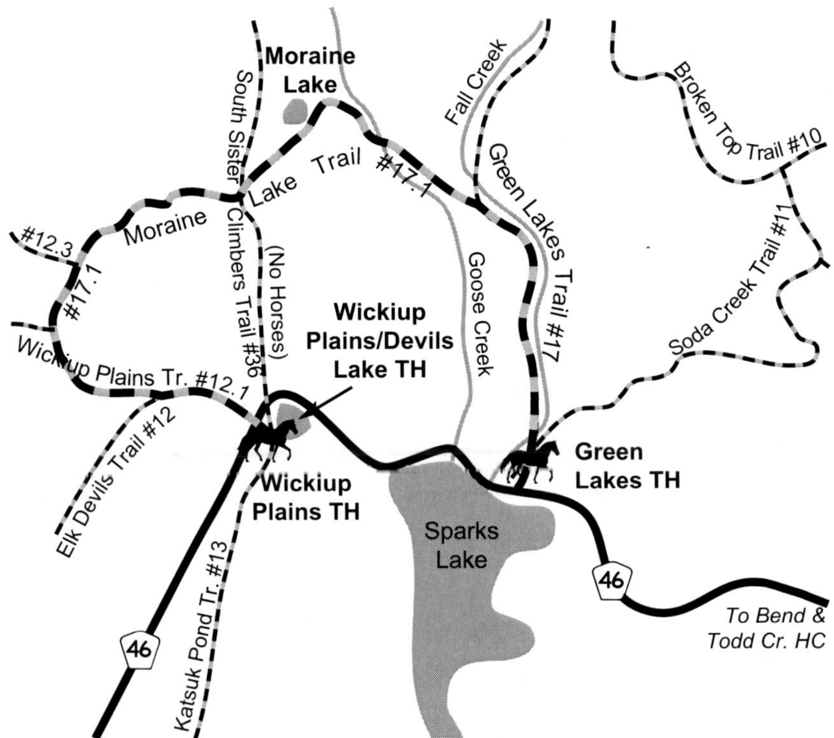

there. Please keep your horse out of the lake, as it is a source of drinking water for many backpackers. Dogs must be on leash on this trail from July 15 to September 15.

The Ride: From the Green Lakes Trailhead, pick up the Green Lakes Trail #17 and follow it along beautiful Fall Creek for 2.1 miles. At the junction with the Moraine Lake Trail #17.1, turn left and ride about 1.5 mile farther to reach Moraine Lake. From the Wickiup Plains/Devils Lake Trailhead, pick up the Wickiup Plains Trail #12.1 and ride it 0.9 mile. At the junction with the Elk-Devils Trail #12, stay to the right. Continue another mile and turn right on the Moraine Lake Trail #17.1. In 0.5 mile, go right at the junction with the LeConte Crater Trail #12.3. In another mile you'll cross the South Sister Climbers Trail #36, and a mile after that you'll reach Moraine Lake. For a fun 9-mile variation on this ride, you can drop off a trailer at the Green Lakes Trailhead, drive another trailer the 2 miles to the Wickiup Plains Trailhead, then ride the Wickiup Plains/Moraine Lake Trails up and the Green Lakes trail down to retrieve the dropped trailer.

Whitney on Luke, Mona on Eclipse, and Lydia on Shadow, on a pretty fall day at Moraine Lake.

Senoj Lake

Trailhead: Start at the Six Lakes Trailhead

Length: 9 miles round trip to Senoj Lake, or 5.5 miles round trip to Doris Lake, or 2.6 miles round trip to Blow Lake

Elevation: 4,900 to 5,600 feet to Senoj Lake. Doris Lake is at 5,300 feet, and Blow Lake is at 5,100 feet

Difficulty: Moderate

Footing: Hoof protection recommended

Season: Summer through fall

Permits: None

Facilities: Toilet, hitching post, and parking for many trailers at the trailhead. Stock water is available on the trail.

Highlights: Senoj Lake was named in honor of someone named Jones -- spelled backward. This is a nice ride on a forested trail that runs past Blow Lake and Doris Lake and ends on the grassy shore of Senoj Lake.

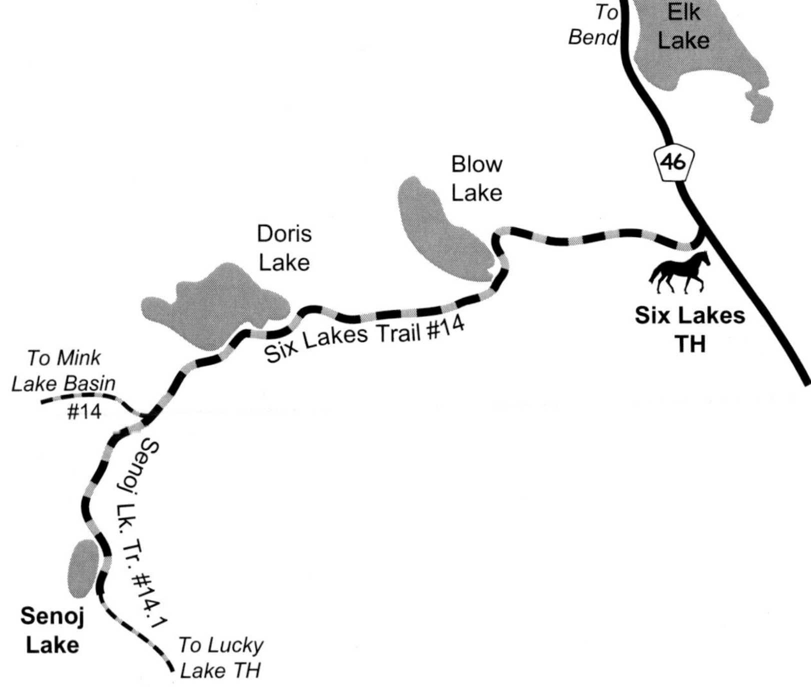

The Ride: Pick up the Six Lakes Trail #14 on the west side of the trailhead. It winds through the forest and reaches Blow Lake in 1.3 miles. After another 1.4 miles, Doris Lake appears. Both lakes are worth a detour, and both are good destinations for short, easy rides. About 0.6 mile beyond Doris Lake, turn left on the Senoj Lake Trail #14.1. In another mile you'll reach Senoj Lake. Its grassy banks are an inviting spot for lunch, for both you and your horse. Retrace your steps to return to the trailhead.

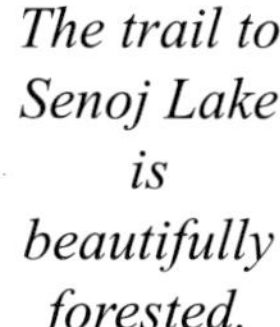

The trail to Senoj Lake is beautifully forested.

Debbie and Mel relax at Senoj Lake.

Wickiup Plains

Trailhead: Start at Wickiup Plains/Devils Lake Trailhead
Length: 9 miles round trip to the end of Wickiup Plains, or 11 miles round trip to Mesa Creek
Elevation: 5,500 to 6,300 feet
Difficulty: Moderate
Footing: Hoof protection recommended
Season: Summer through fall
Permits: Northwest Forest Pass required
Facilities: Toilets, hitching posts, plenty of parking for trailers. No water is available on the trail unless you continue to Mesa Creek.

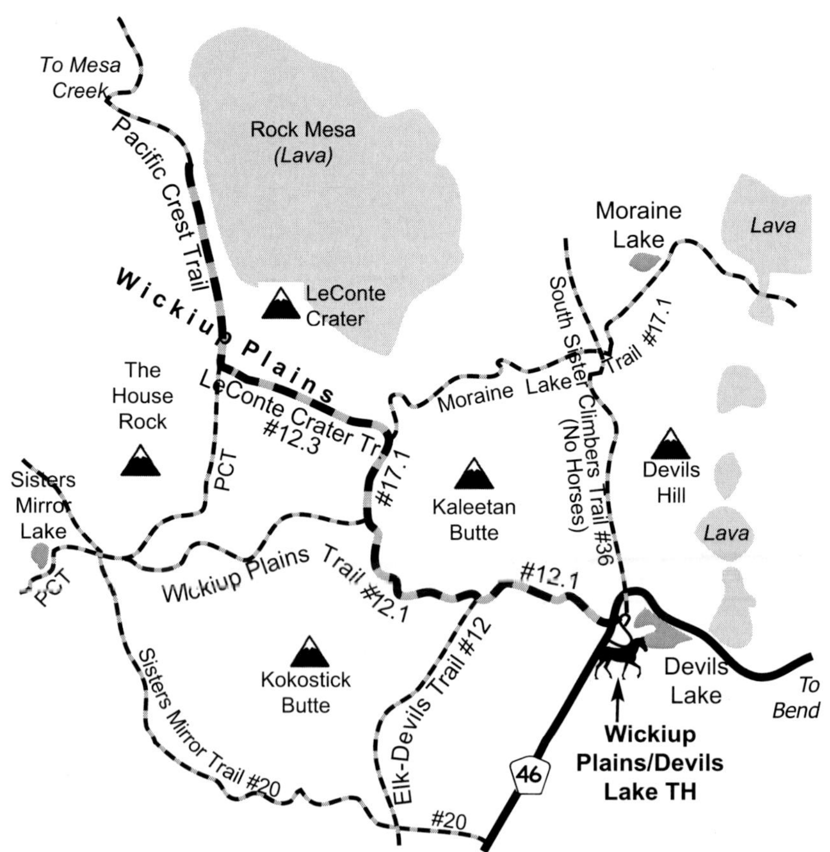

Connie and Lydia ride Jane and Shadow across Wickiup Plains, with South Sister in the background.

Highlights: Wickiup Plains is an ancient ash flow that lies at the base of Rock Mesa and LeConte Crater, south and a little west of South Sister. Its gravelly surface and sparse vegetation contrast sharply with the surrounding forest, plus it offers spectacular views of South Sister. The trail includes beautiful stands of old-growth trees. On the Wickiup Plains, please stay on the trail to protect this fragile ecosystem. Dogs must be on leash July 15-September 15 at on the Moraine Lake and Sisters Mirror Trails.

The Ride: Pick up the Wickup Plains Trail #12.1 from the horse trailer parking area. After 0.9 mile, stay to the right at the junction with the Elk-Devils Trail, and in another mile veer right on the Moraine Lake Trail #17.1. Follow it 0.5 mile, then turn left toward Wickiup Plains on the LeConte Crater Trail #12.3. Ride across the plains, and after 1.4 miles the trail intersects with the Pacific Crest Trail. Turn right on the PCT and continue another 1.3 miles across the plains. Once you reach the forest at the north end of Wickiup Plains, you can continue on the PCT another mile to Mesa Creek to water your horses before returning to the trailhead.

Suzanne rides Marilyn on the shore of the largest of the Green Lakes, with Broken Top in the background.

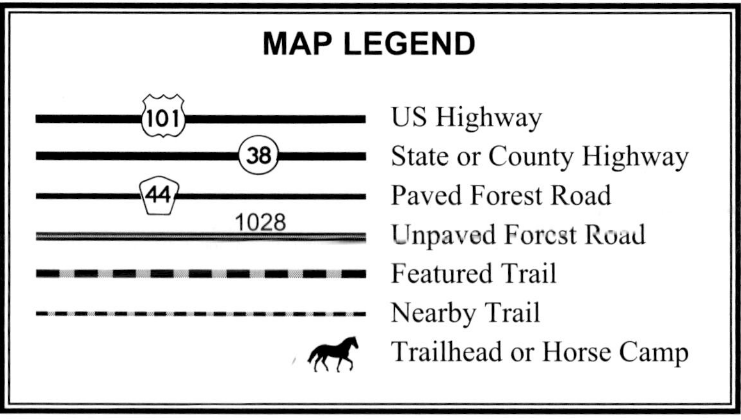

Oregon Badlands Wilderness

Bureau of Land Management

Located in the high desert just 15 miles east of Bend, the Oregon Badlands Wilderness Area features fascinating lava outcroppings, and ancient junipers (including some over 1,000 years old). Nearly all the trails follow old dirt roads. The footing is sandy volcanic ash and pumice, so the riding is excellent in the winter and spring, but can be dusty in summer. Please stay on the trails to avoid damaging this fragile ecosystem.

The Badlands were formed by an ancient volcanic vent that slowly oozed lava. The outer layers of lava cooled as they flowed, and were pushed up by the hotter lava below to form pressure ridges like Badlands Rock, Flatiron Rock, and the other basalt outcroppings you'll see along the trails.

A gnarled old juniper grows out of a lava flow in the Badlands.

Oregon Badlands Wilderness

Directions: The Oregon Badlands Wilderness Area is located about 15 miles east of Bend, off Hwy. 20. Four Badlands trailheads are large enough accommodate horse trailers. For directions, see "Finding the Trailhead" on the pages for each ride.

Elevation: 3,600 feet

Camping No camping facilities, but primitive camping is permitted anywhere other than at trailheads. (The nearest horse camps are Sisters Cow Camp and Cyrus Horse Camp. See these chapters for details.) Only certified weed-free hay may be used in the Oregon Badlands.

Facilities: Parking availability varies at each trailhead -- see "Facilities" on the pages for each trail

Permits: None

Season: Year-round

Contact: BLM, Prineville District, 541-416-6700

Connie and Diamond examine a deep fissure in a lava outcropping beside the trail.

Getting to the Oregon Badlands

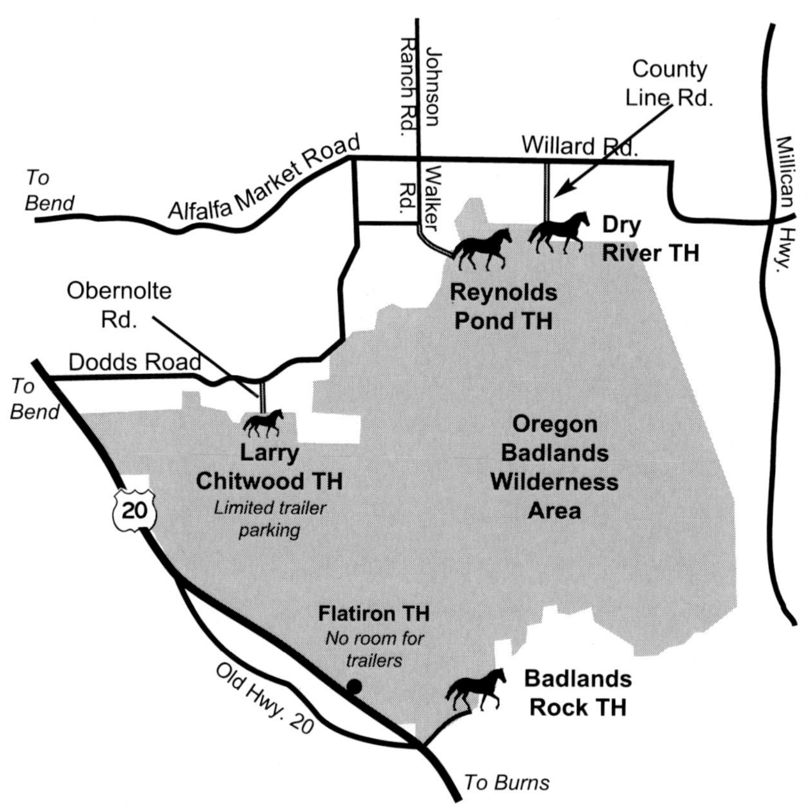

Oregon Badlands Wilderness Trails

Trail	Difficulty	Elevation	Round Trip
Badlands Rock/Dry River Lp.	Easy	3,450-3,600	12.5 miles
Badlands/Flatiron Rocks Lp.	Easy	3,550-3,775	8-11.5 miles
Black Lava Trail	Moderate	3,375-3,500	9.5-12 miles
Dry River Loop	Easy	3,350-3,500	9.5 miles
Larry Chitwood Loops	Easy	3,450-3,600	6-11 miles
Tumulus/Black Lava Loop	Moderate	3,300-3,450	8.3 miles
Tumulus Trail	Moderate	3,375-3,550	13.5-20 miles

Badlands Rock/Dry River Loop

Trailhead: Start at the Badlands Rock Trailhead
Length: 12.5 miles round trip
Elevation: 3,450 to 3,600 feet
Difficulty: Easy
Footing: Suitable for barefoot horses
Season: Year-round
Permits: None
Facilities: Parking for 6-8 trailers at the trailhead. No stock water on the trail.

Highlights: The focal point of the Badlands Rock Trail is Badlands Rock itself, a large volcanic pressure ridge covered with fissures and rifts. Along the Badlands Rock Trail you'll also see small and

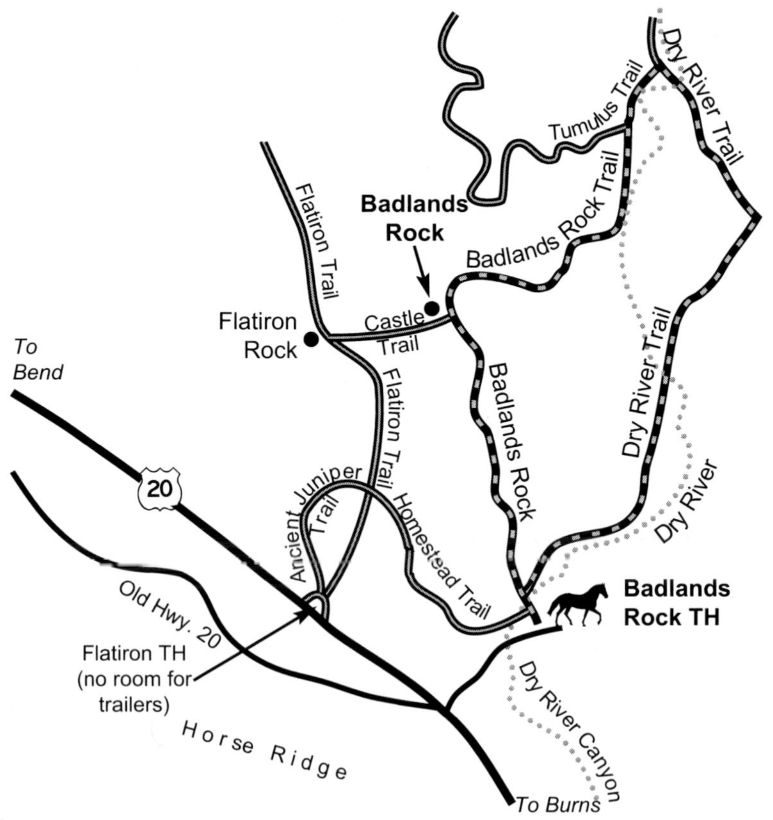

medium-sized pressure ridges. The Dry River Trail follows a dry river bed through terrain that is fairly open, with lots of sagebrush, old junipers, and mountain views. Combining the two trails makes a good loop.

Finding the Badlands Rock Trailhead: From Bend, drive east on Hwy. 20. Just before the 18-mile marker, turn left on a paved road marked by an Oregon Badlands sign. Follow it 1 mile and turn left into the Badlands Rock Trailhead parking area.

Ride: The Badlands Rock Trail goes north from the trailhead, following an old dirt road. In 0.3 mile, the Homestead Trail goes off to the left. Shortly after, the Dry River Trail goes to the right. This is your return route, so stay to the left on the Badlands Rock Trail. In another 2.7 miles, the Castle Trail goes to the left and the trail passes Badlands Rock. Veer right to stay on the Badlands Rock Trail. You'll find some interesting lava outcroppings in the area beyond Badlands Rock, including rocks with fissures large enough to ride through. About 3.3 miles past Badlands Rock, the trail intersects with the Tumulus Trail. Turn right and follow the Tumulus Trail 0.6 mile to the Dry River Trail. Turn right again, and follow the Dry River Trail back to its junction with the Badlands Rock Trail, about 5.3 miles. Turn left and continue 0.3 mile to return to the trailhead.

Debbie on Split, Whitney on Dixie, and Diana on Mel, ambling down the Dry River Trail.

Badlands Rock/Flatiron Rock Loop

Trailhead: Start at the Badlands Rock Trailhead

Length: 8 miles round trip to Badlands Rock and Flatiron Rock, or 11.5 miles if you include the Ancient Juniper Trail loop

Elevation: 3,550 to 3,650 feet for the shorter loop; 3,550 to 3,775 feet for the longer loop

Difficulty: Easy

Footing: Suitable for barefoot horses

Season: Year-round

Permits: None

Facilities: Parking for 6-8 rigs at the trailhead. No stock water on the trail.

Highlights: This fascinating loop goes past three of the most prominent rock formations in the Badlands: Badlands Rock, Castle Rock, and Flatiron Rock. Both Castle Rock and Flatiron Rock have deep

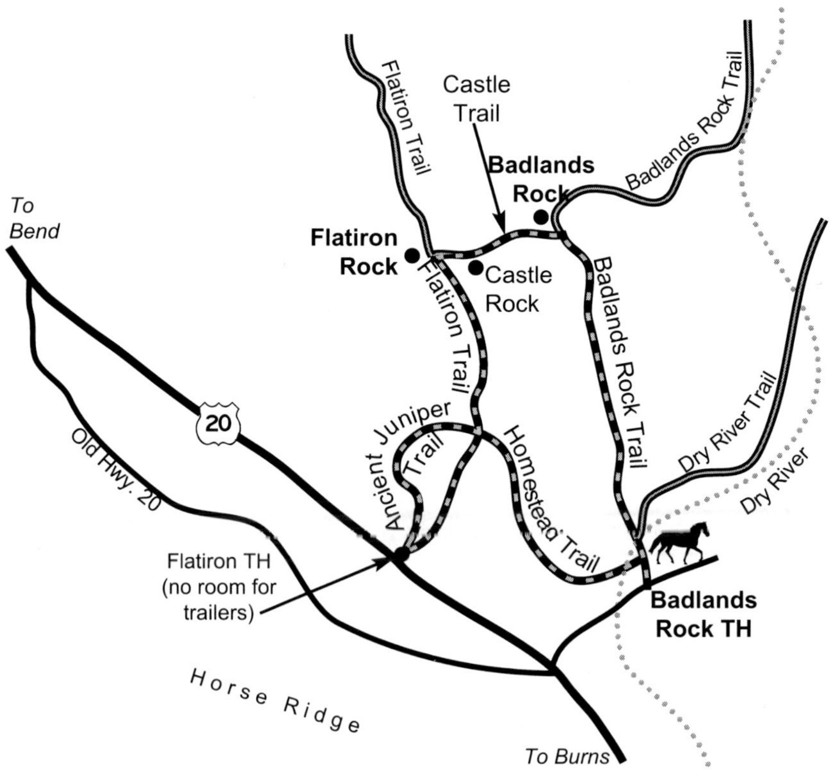

Suzanne rides Skipper past Badlands Rock.

fissures at the top that you can walk through on foot, so tie your horses at the base and climb up to have a look--it's worth it. If you want to extend your ride you can add a detour along the Ancient Juniper Trail, which offers slightly elevated views of the Badlands.

Finding the Badlands Rock Trailhead: From Bend, drive east on Hwy. 20. Just before the 18-mile marker, turn left on a paved road marked by an Oregon Badlands sign. Follow it 1 mile and turn left into the Badlands Rock Trailhead parking area.

The Ride: The Badlands Rock Trail goes north from the trailhead, following an old dirt road. In 0.3 mile the Homestead Trail goes off to the left. Continue on the Badlands Rock Trail for another 2.7 miles to Badlands Rock, a large mound of fractured basalt. Turn left on the Castle Trail and ride 0.7 mile to Castle Rock, then 0.4 mile farther to Flatiron Rock. Turn left on the Flatiron Trail and follow it 1.5 miles to the junction with the Homestead Trail. Here you can do a loop detour on the Ancient Juniper Trail to add 3.3 miles to your journey, or you can head back to the trailhead by veering left and riding 2.1 miles on the Homestead Trail. When the Homestead Trail intersects with the Badlands Rock Trail, turn right to return to the trailhead.

Black Lava Trail

Trailhead: Start at the Reynolds Pond Trailhead

Length: 9.5 miles round trip to the historic corral, or 12 miles round trip to the junction with the Mazama Ash Trail

Elevation: 3,375 to 3,500 feet

Difficulty: Moderate because of the horse step-overs next to the canal gates

Footing: Hoof protection recommended

Season: Year-round

Permits: None

Facilities: Parking for many trailers at Reynolds Pond Trailhead. Stock water is available on the trail during irrigation season.

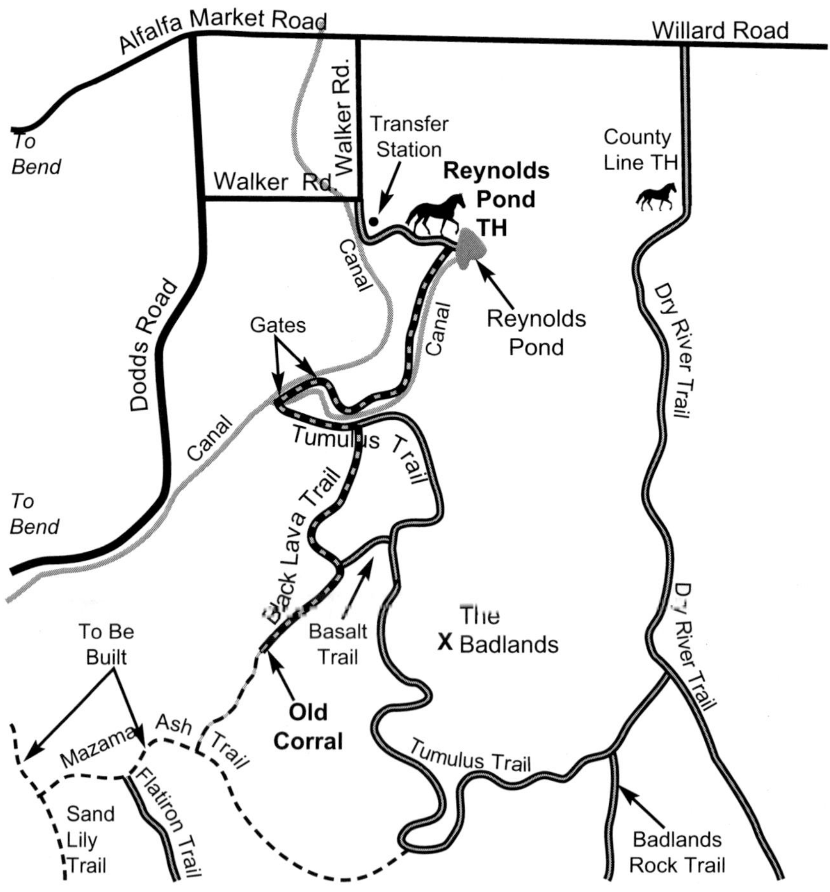

Debbie and Split check out a historic corral built into the rocks.

Highlights: The Black Lava trail goes through an area with many small to mid-sized lava outcroppings. Many are deeply fissured and fractured, with hardy juniper trees growing out of the rocks. About 4.8 miles from the trailhead you'll see an old corral that is cleverly built into a basalt outcropping. Plans call for the trail to be extended to meet the yet-to-be-built Mazama Ash Trail.

Finding the Reynolds Pond Trailhead: From Bend, drive east on Hwy. 20 for 4.7 miles. Turn left on Powell Butte Highway, and at the roundabout in 0.9 mile, take the first right onto Alfalfa Market Road. Follow it 9.4 miles to Walker Road and turn right. In 1 mile, Walker Road makes a 90-degree turn to the right. Go straight, and in 0.2 mile you'll pass the entrance to the transfer station. About 200 feet later, veer left and drive over the cattle guard. Continue 0.6 mile to the trailhead.

The Ride: From the Reynolds Pond Trailhead, pick up the dirt road that runs south along the irrigation canal. Ride the canal road for 1.9 miles, go through the horse step-over next to a gate, and continue 0.3 mile to a second gate and horse step-over. Cross the bridge over the canal, turn left, and ride back along the canal on the Tumulus Trail. In 0.5 mile, turn right on the Black Lava Trail. In 1.3 miles you'll reach the junction with the Basalt Trail. Stay to the right on the Black Lava Trail, and in 0.7 mile you'll come to an interesting old corral used many years ago for rounding up stock. Sometime soon, the trail will be extended to meet the Mazama Ash Trail in another 1.3 mile.

Dry River Loop

Trailhead: Start at the Dry River Trailhead
Length: 9.5 miles round trip
Elevation: 3,350 to 3,500 feet
Difficulty: Easy
Footing: Suitable for barefoot horses
Season: Year-round
Permits: None
Facilities: Parking for 3-4 trailers. No stock water on the trail.

Highlights: The Dry River Trail section of this loop features a mile-long basalt ridge, plus views of Mt. Jefferson, the Three Sisters, and Broken Top. The Sand Trail (no longer an official trail, but you can still ride it) features old-growth junipers, sagebrush, bunch grass, and

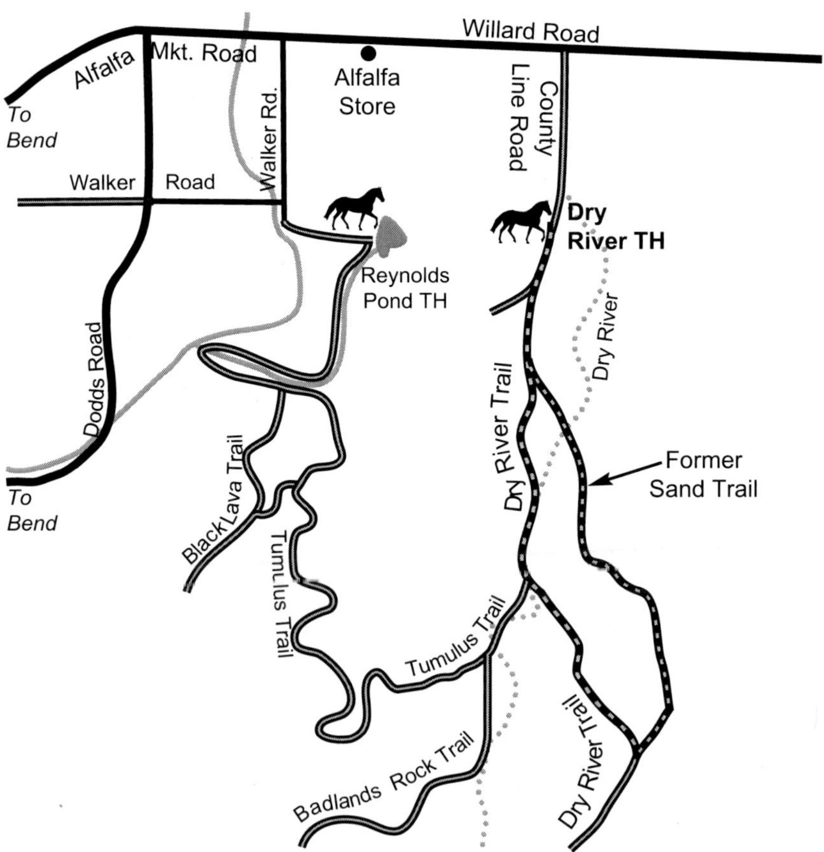

very sandy footing. You'll want to ride this loop clockwise so you are facing the Dry River Trail's mountain views on your way back to the trailhead.

Finding the Dry River Trailhead: From Bend, drive east on Hwy. 20 for 4.7 miles. Turn left on Powell Butte Highway. At the roundabout in 0.9 mile, take the first right onto Alfalfa Market Road. In 9.4 miles, at the junction with Walker Road, the road name changes to Willard Road. In 2 more miles, turn right on County Line Road. The trailhead is on the right in 1 mile. Additional trailer parking is available just past the main parking area.

The Ride: Ride out on the gravel road that runs south from the trailhead. At the trail sign in 0.7 mile, veer left off the gravel road onto the Dry River Trail. In 0.8 mile, veer left again on a dirt road. This road used to be called the Sand Trail, and while it is no longer an official trail, the road is maintained for use by a livestock permittee, so you can ride it. Follow it for 3.3 miles, then turn right on the Dry River Trail. For the next mile or so you'll enjoy very nice mountain views as you ride beside a long basalt ridge. In 1.9 miles, the Tumulus Trail goes off to the left. In another 2.1 miles, you'll rejoin the gravel road that leads back to the trailhead.

Debbie and Split admire a juniper growing out of the rocks on the Dry River Trail.

Larry Chitwood Loops

Trailhead: Start at the Larry Chitwood Trailhead

Length: 6 miles around the East Loop, 7 miles around the West Loop, 7.5 miles around the perimeter, or 11 miles around both loops in a figure eight.

Elevation: 3,450 to 3,600 feet

Difficulty: Easy

Footing: Suitable for barefoot horses

Season: Year-round

Permits: None

Facilities: The parking area is too small for trailers, but you can turn around by backing into the trailhead, then parking on the side of Obernolte Road. No stock water on the trail.

Highlights: This is an easy, relaxing ride that lacks the impressive lava outcroppings of some of the other Badlands trails, but it runs past many gnarled, ancient junipers. You can tell which junipers are old by

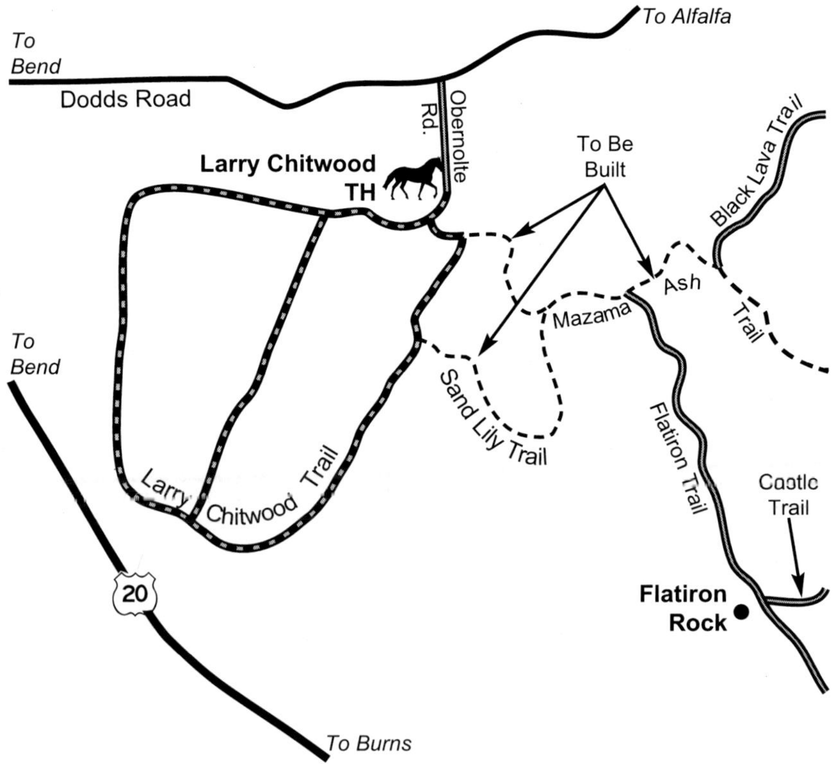

Debbie and Split enjoy a leisurely amble past an ancient juniper on the Larry Chitwood Loops.

looking at their tops: younger junipers have pointed tops, and the older ones are rounded. Like all the other Badlands trails, the Obernolte Loops are suitable for green horses and inexperienced riders.

Finding the Larry Chitwood Trailhead: From Bend, drive east on Hwy. 20 for 8.6 miles. Turn left on Dodds Road and continue 3.3 miles. Turn right on Obernolte Road and drive 0.5 mile to the trailhead. The parking area is too small for horse trailers, so turn around and park on the side of Obernolte Rd.

The Ride: Go through the trailhead gate and ride 0.3 mile to the junction with the loop trails. You can ride these loops in a variety of ways, doing the east loop, the west loop, the perimeter, or both loops in a sort of sideways figure eight (riding the center leg twice). The far eastern leg is a bit rocky, but the rest of the trails are not. The Sand Lily Trail and Mazama Ash Trails are in the works, but as of our publication date they had not yet been built. Hopefully, by the time you read this the trails will exist on the ground, not just on the BLM map.

Tumulus/Black Lava Loop

Trailhead: Start at Reynolds Pond Trailhead
Length: 8.3 miles round trip
Elevation: 3,300 to 3,450 feet
Difficulty: Moderate because of the horse step-overs next to the canal gates
Footing: Hoof protection recommended
Season: Year-round
Permits: None
Facilities: Parking for many trailers at Reynolds Pond Trailhead. Stock water is available on the trail during irrigation season.

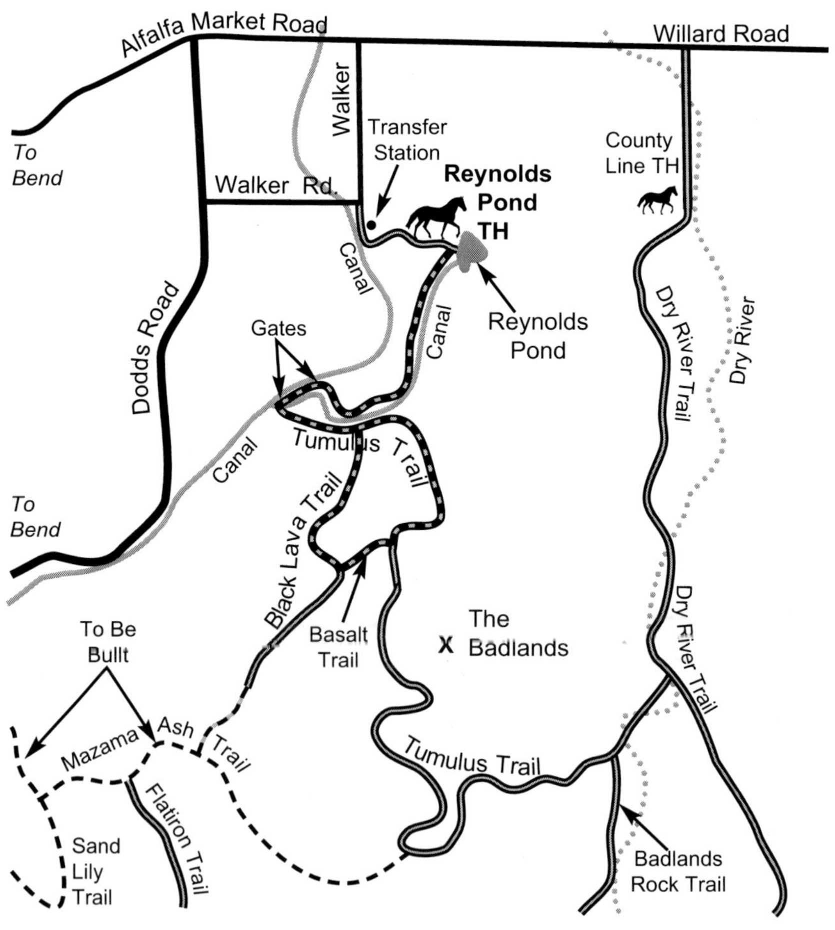

You'll marvel at the fascinating lava outcroppings along the Black Lava and Tumulus Trails.

Highlights: This is a fun lollipop loop that follows an irrigation canal. The loop segment showcases interesting basalt outcroppings.

Finding the Reynolds Pond Trailhead: From Bend, drive east on Hwy. 20 for 4.7 miles. Turn left on Powell Butte Highway, and in 0.9 mile turn right on Alfalfa Market Road. Follow it 9.4 miles to Walker Road and turn right. In 1 mile, Walker Road makes a 90-degree turn to the right. Go straight, and in 0.2 mile you'll pass the entrance to the transfer station. About 200 feet later, veer left and drive over the cattle guard. Continue 0.6 mile to the trailhead.

The Ride: From Reynolds Pond Trailhead, pick up the dirt road that runs south along the irrigation canal. Ride the canal road for 1.9 miles, go through the horse step-over next to a gate, and continue 0.3 mile to a second gate and horse step-over. Cross the bridge over the canal, turn left and ride back along the canal on the Tumulus Trail for 0.5 mile. At the signed junction with the Black Lava Trail, turn right and follow it 1.3 miles, then turn right on the Basalt Trail. In another 0.6 mile, turn right again on the Tumulus Trail. In 1.5 miles, you'll pass the junction with the Black Lava Trail, and in another 0.5 mile you'll recross the canal. Retrace your steps to return to the trailhead.

Tumulus Trail

Trailhead: Start at Reynolds Pond Trailhead

Length: 13.5 miles round trip to interesting rock outcroppings, or 20 miles round trip to the Dry River Trail

Elevation: 3,375 to 3,550 feet

Difficulty: Moderate because of the horse step-overs next to the canal gates

Footing: Hoof protection recommended

Season: Year-round

Permits: None

Facilities: Parking for many trailers at Reynolds Pond Trailhead. Stock water is available on the trail during irrigation season.

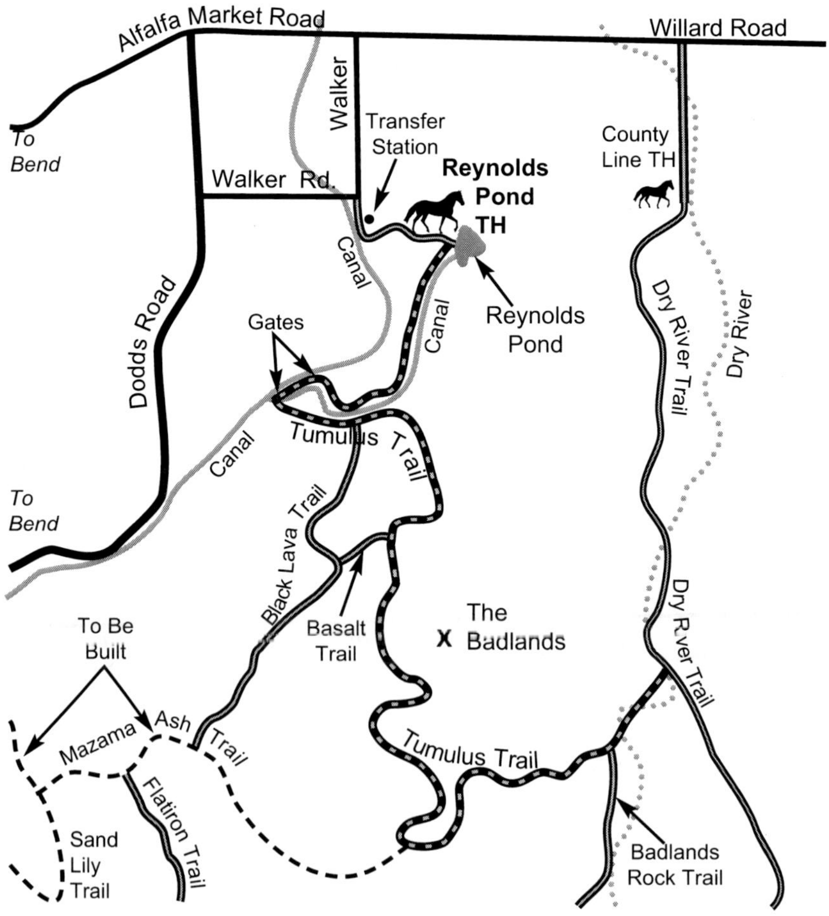

The horse step-overs next to the canal gates allow horses and hikers to pass, but keep out motor vehicles.

The Tumulus Trail features hundreds of cracked and fissured basalt outcroppings.

Highlights: The fascinating basalt outcroppings you'll see along this trail qualify it as the most scenic ride in the Badlands.

Finding the Reynolds Pond Trailhead: From Bend, drive east on Hwy. 20 for 4.7 miles. Turn left on Powell Butte Highway, and in 0.9 mile turn right on Alfalfa Market Road. Follow it 9.4 miles to Walker Road and turn right. In 1 mile, Walker Road makes a 90-degree turn to the right. Go straight, and in 0.2 mile you'll pass the entrance to the transfer station. About 200 feet later, veer left and drive over the cattle guard. Continue 0.6 mile to the trailhead.

The Ride: From Reynolds Pond Trailhead, pick up the dirt road that runs south along the irrigation canal. Ride the canal road for 1.9 miles, go through the horse step-over next to a gate, and continue 0.3 mile to a second gate and horse step-over. Cross the bridge over the canal, turn left and ride back along the canal on the Tumulus Trail for 0.5 mile to the signed junction with the Black Lava Trail. Continue straight on the Tumulus Trail. In 1.5 miles, the Basalt Trail goes off to the right. In another 2.5 miles, you'll reach "The Badlands," an area of huge basalt outcroppings. Some of the outcroppings are split by deep rifts, and some feature small caves. You'll also find many ancient junipers along the trail.

Jane enjoys a sunny spring day on the Dry River Trail.

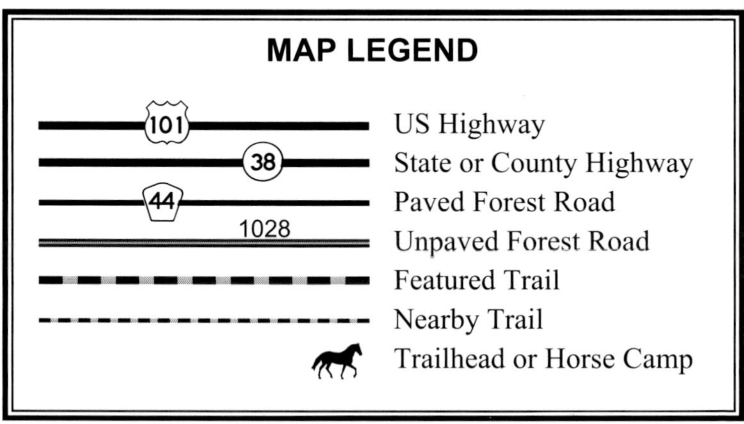

Peterson Ridge

Deschutes National Forest

Located just southeast of the town of Sisters, Peterson Ridge offers over 20 miles of easy horse trails with spectacular views of the Cascades. Peterson Ridge is very popular with mountain bike riders, but the mountain bike trails are completely separate from the horse trails. Please don't ride the bike trails, as horse hooves tear up the trail tread and ruin the riding experience for the bicyclists. Members of the mountain bike community helped build the horse trail system, so please be neighborly and respect the integrity of their trails. Also, note that this trail system utilizes many forest roads. The road number signs aren't always present, but you can easily find your way by following the white trailblazer diamonds on the trees. If you would like to camp nearby, Sisters Cow Camp and Graham Corral are only a short distance away.

Dottie and Hope, at the Eagle Rock Two Viewpoint

Getting to Peterson Ridge

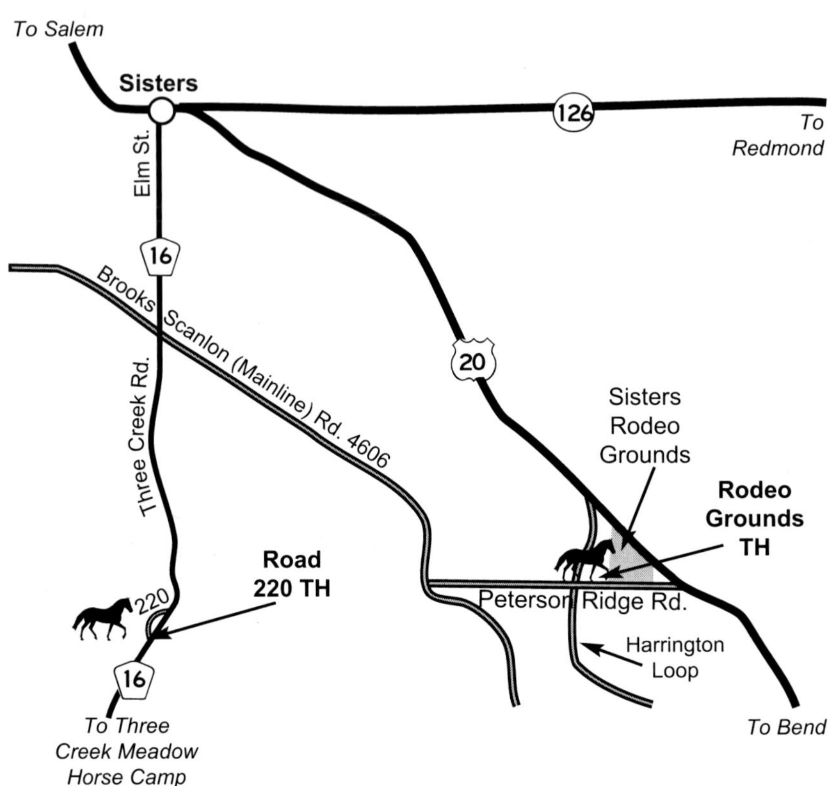

Peterson Ridge Area Trails

Trail	Difficulty	Elevation	Round Trip
Lazy Z Loop	Easy	3,250-3,550	7.5 miles
Peterson Ridge Horse Trail	Easy	3,250-3,800	7-12 miles
Road 16 to Whychus Creek	Moderate	3,400-3,900	10 miles
Rodeo Grnds to Whychus Cr.	Easy	3,200-3,400	8.5 miles
Rodeo Short Loop	Easy	3,200-3,300	4.5 miles

Rodeo Grounds Trailhead

Directions: On Hwy. 20, drive 4.5 miles southeast from Sisters or 16.5 miles northwest from Bend and turn west on Peterson Ridge Road. Continue 0.5 mile to the parking area just past the southwest corner of the Sisters Rodeo grounds.

Elevation: 3,250 feet

Facilities: Parking for 5-6 trailers

Camping: The closest horse camps are Sisters Cow Camp and Graham Corral. See these chapters for more details.

Permits: None

Season: Year-round

Contact: Sisters Ranger District, 541-549-7700

Tex looks out at the view of the Sisters from the Met-Win to Rodeo Grounds Trail, near Whychus Creek.

Ann on Spook and Dottie on Hope, riding along the Peterson Ridge Horse Trail, with North Sister behind them.

Lazy Z Loop

Trailhead: Start at the Rodeo Grounds Trailhead
Length: 7.5 miles round trip
Elevation: 3,250 to 3,550 feet
Difficulty: Easy -- two water crossings during irrigation season
Footing: Suitable for barefoot horses
Season: Early spring through late fall
Permits: None
Facilities: Parking for 5-6 trailers at the rodeo grounds. Stock water is available on the trail only during the summer irrigation season.

Highlights: This is an easy trail that runs on a combination of forest roads and single-track trails. The route is clearly marked with white di-

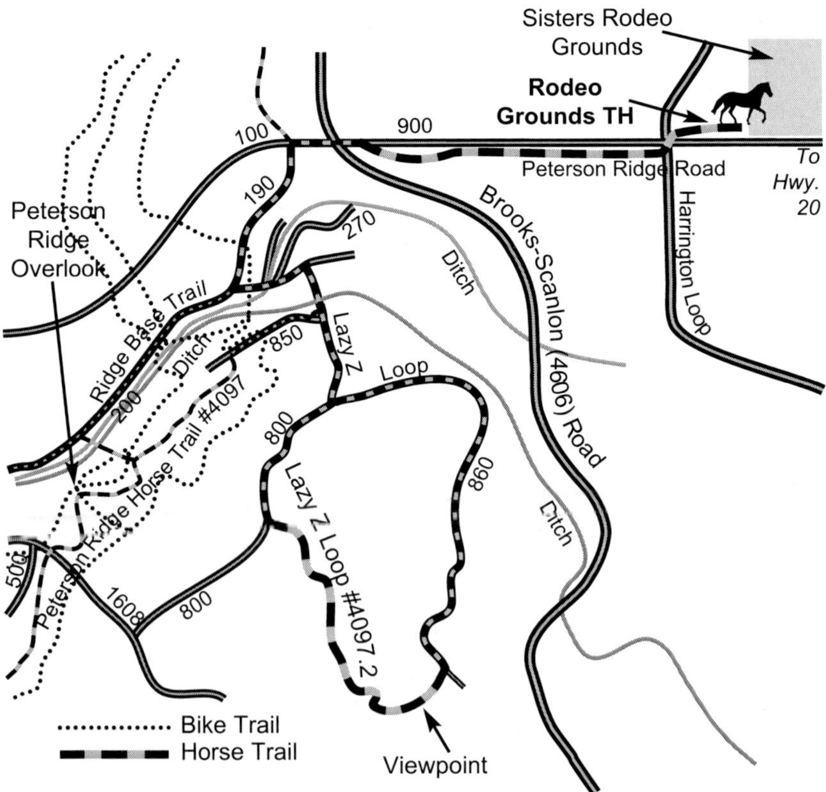

amond trailblazers on the trees. When you reach the south end of the loop you'll have a splendid view of the Three Sisters and Broken Top.

The Ride: From the kiosk at the Rodeo Grounds Trailhead, pick up the Peterson Ridge Horse Trail #4097 heading west. In 0.2 mile the trail crosses Harrington Loop and continues to the left of Road 900. After another mile you'll cross the red cinder Brooks-Scanlon Mainline Road 4606. Continue straight on Road 100, and in 200 feet turn left at the junction sign, onto Road 190. In 0.5 mile, make a sharp left at the next junction sign and ride up onto Peterson Ridge. Near the top of the hill, the trail veers right and crosses an irrigation ditch. In another 0.2 mile you'll reach another irrigation ditch. At the junction just beyond the ditch, go straight ahead on the Lazy Z Trail #4097.2 In 0.5 mile, you'll reach the loop portion of the trail. Turn right onto the loop, ride 0.5 mile, and then veer left onto a single-track trail. Follow it 0.7 mile to the edge of the ridge, near a rock outcropping where you'll have a great view of the Three Sisters and Broken Top. Continue 0.2 mile to Road 860 and veer left, then ride 1.4 miles to where you entered the loop. Turn right and retrace your steps to the trailhead.

Whitney and Dixie enjoy the view from the Lazy Z Loop.

Peterson Ridge Horse Trail

Trailhead: Start at the Rodeo Grounds Trailhead

Length: 7 miles round trip to the Peterson Ridge Overlook, 10.5 miles round trip to the Eagle Rock 2 viewpoint, or 12 miles round trip to the Peak View viewpoint

Elevation: 3,250 to 3,800 feet

Difficulty: Easy -- two water crossings during irrigation season

Footing: Suitable for barefoot horses

Season: Early spring through late fall

Permits: None

Facilities: Parking for 5-6 trailers. Stock water is available on the trail only during the summer irrigation season.

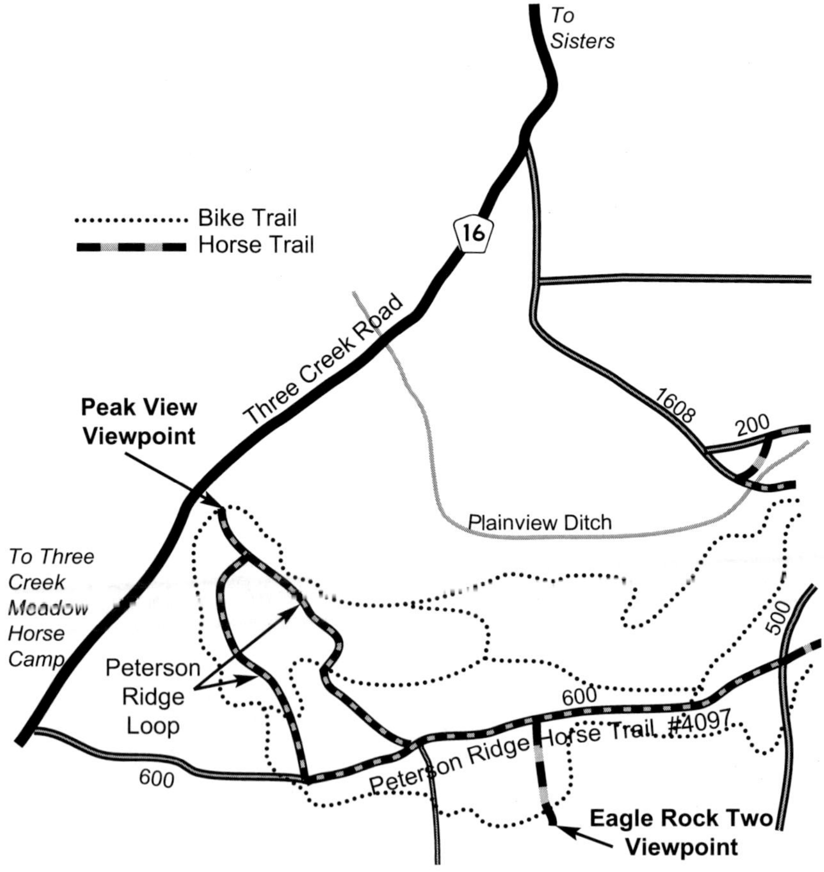

Highlights: This easy trail follows the Peterson Ridge Horse Trail through open ponderosa pine forest, offering several viewpoints along the way that provide splendid views of the Cascades. The trail runs on both dirt roads and single-track, with the route clearly signed with white trailblazer diamonds on the trees. Diamonds that are tilted to one side indicate that the trail makes a turn.

The Ride: From the kiosk at the Rodeo Grounds Trailhead, pick up the Peterson Ridge Horse Trail #4097 heading west. In 0.2 mile the trail crosses Harrington Loop and continues to the left of Road 900. After another mile you'll cross the red cinder Brooks-Scanlon Road 4606. Continue straight on Road 100, and in 200 feet turn left at the junction sign, onto Road 190. In 0.5 mile, make a sharp left at the next junction sign and ride up onto Peterson Ridge. *(continued on next page)*

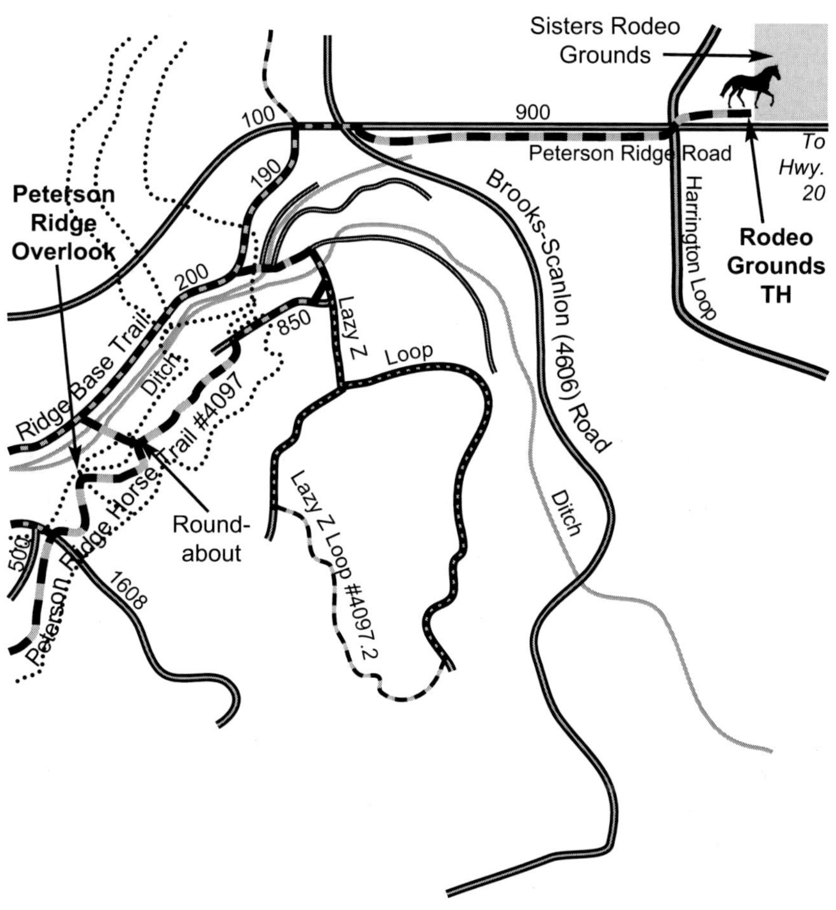

Peterson Ridge Trail (continued)

Near the top of the hill, the trail veers right and crosses an irrigation ditch. In another 0.2 mile you'll reach another irrigation ditch. Just past the ditch, at the junction with the Lazy Z Trail, turn right on a single track trail that soon veers onto Road 850. In 0.3 mile, the trail makes a sharp left onto a single-track trail. After 0.4 mile, you'll reach the Roundabout, an intersection where two bike trails meet right next to the horse trail. If you turn right here, a spur trail will take you across the bike trails and down the hill to the Ridge Base Trail. Instead, stay to the left, and in 0.3 mile you'll reach a hitching rail and picnic table at the Peterson Ridge Overlook, your first viewpoint.

Continue another 0.3 mile to red cinder Road 1608. If you turn right here, you can follow Road 1608 down off the ridge and across both irrigation canals, then veer right on the Ridge Base Trail, a single track that takes you to Road 200 and along it back toward the Rodeo Grounds Trailhead. To continue on the Peterson Ridge Horse Trail, go straight, and in another 0.5 mile the trail crosses Road 500 and continues along

Debbie and Split at the Peak View Viewpoint, with Mt. Jefferson and Black Butte in the background.

Debbie on Split, enjoying the view of the Three Sisters from the Eagle Rock Two Viewpoint.

Road 600. After about 0.7 mile you'll start to see ponderosas growing in rows. (They were planted by machine after the Peterson Burn.) In another 0.6 mile, turn left at the junction sign and ride 0.3 mile to the Eagle Rock Two viewpoint. You'll have an excellent view of the Three Sisters from this rock pinnacle.

Return to Road 600 and continue west another 0.4 mile to reach the Peterson Ridge Loop. The east leg of the loop goes to the right immediately after a forest road veers off Road 600 to the left. Continue straight ahead on Road 600 for 0.3 mile to reach the west leg of the loop, and turn right at the sign that points to Peterson Ridge Loop. In 0.8 mile, the west leg joins the east leg of the loop. Turn left and continue 0.2 mile to the Peak View Viewpoint, then follow the east leg of the loop back to Road 600.

To return to the trailhead, retrace your steps back to Road 1608. From there you can either continue the way you came, or vary your ride by turning left on Road 1608 and picking up the Ridge Base Trail.

Road 16 to Whychus Creek

Trailhead: Start at the Road 220 Trailhead. You can also reach this trail from the Rodeo Grounds Trailhead.

Length: 10 miles round trip from Road 220, or 19.5 miles round trip from the Rodeo Grounds Trailhead

Elevation: 3,400 to 3,900 feet from the Road 220 Trailhead

Difficulty: Moderate -- crossing Whychus Creek may be challenging during spring runoff

Footing: Suitable for barefoot horses

Season: Late spring through late fall

Permits: None

Facilities: Parking for 2-3 trailers on Road 220, or 5-6 trailers at the rodeo grounds. Stock water is available on the trail.

Highlights: This is a terrific out-and-back ride that roughly parallels Whychus Creek. It showcases the canyon carved by the creek, some interesting rock formations, and the Three Sisters.

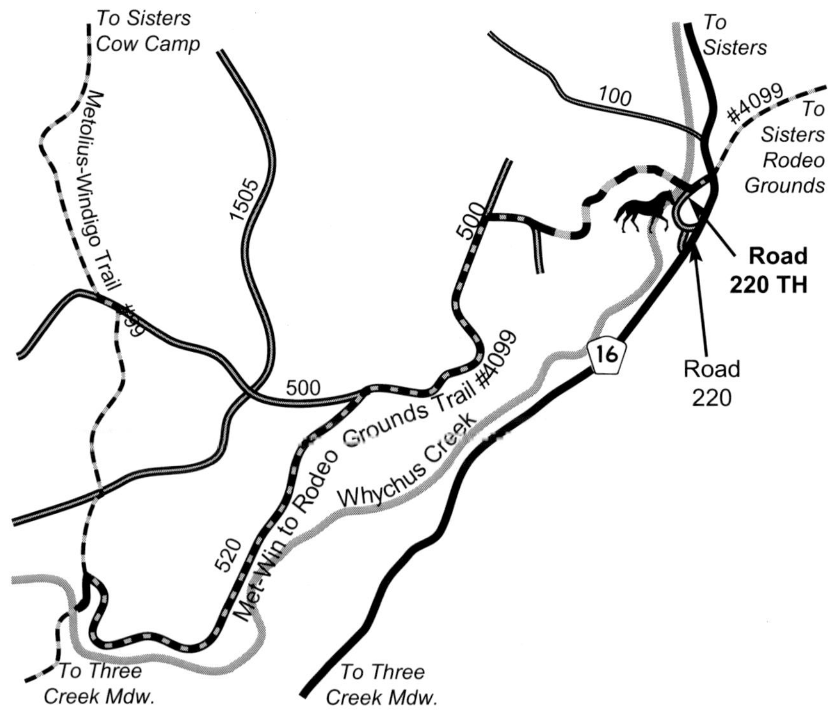

Linda and Beamer on the Met-Win to Rodeo Grounds Trail, on the way to Whychus Creek.

Finding the Road 220 Trailhead: You can follow this trail from the Sisters Rodeo grounds, but it's a long ride. You can make it a shorter ride by parking on Road 220, near a primitive campground just off Road 16. From Sisters, go south on Elm St., which becomes Road 16/Three Creeks Road. Just past the 3-mile marker, turn right on the second Road 220 and park on it. When you leave, just drive straight ahead to return to Road 16. (If you choose to start at the Sisters Rodeo Grounds instead, follow the directions for the Rodeo Grounds to Whychus Creek Trail on the following pages.)

The Ride: From Road 220, ride down the hill into a primitive campground on the bank of Whychus Creek. Near the north end of the campground, look for the Sisters Trails Alliance signs that will lead you to the Whychus Creek ford and the Met-Win to Rodeo Grounds Trail #4099. The entire trail is marked with Sisters Trails signs. Cross Whychus Creek and follow the trail up the hill. After about 1.5 miles, the trail veers left onto Road 500, then it veers left again on Road 520. In this section the trail runs along the canyon rim above Whychus Creek. After 3.1 miles, you'll reach the Metolius-Windigo Trail. Turn left on the Met-Win, and in 0.2 mile it will take you to Whychus Creek, where you can water your horses. If you continue north on the Met-Win from here, you'll reach Sisters Cow Camp in 5 miles.

Rodeo Grounds to Whychus Creek

Trailhead: Start at the Rodeo Grounds Trailhead
Length: 8.5 miles round trip
Elevation: 3,200 to 3,400 feet
Difficulty: Easy
Footing: Suitable for barefoot horses
Season: Early spring through late fall
Permits: None
Facilities: Parking for 5-6 trailers. Stock water is available on the trail.

Highlights: This ride is a fun, relaxing ride that follows the Met-Win to Rodeo Grounds Trail through open ponderosa pine forest to the bank of Whychus Creek. (The trail fords the creek and continues to the spot where the Metolius-Windigo Trail crosses Whychus Creek. See the pages for the Road 16 to Whychus Creek Trail for more information.)

The Ride: From the kiosk at the Rodeo Grounds Trailhead, head north on the Met-Win to Rodeo Grounds Trail #4099, which follows a dirt road and is signed with white trailblazer diamonds on the trees. In 0.3

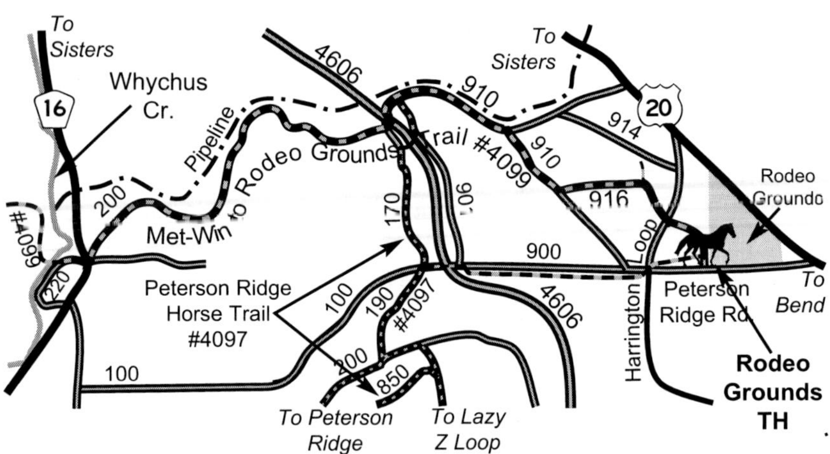

mile, you'll cross Harrington Loop, a well-traveled gravel road. The trail becomes a single track and continues 0.3 mile to dirt Road 916. (Watch for the white diamonds, as an unsigned user trail continues straight ahead.) Turn left on Road 916 and continue 0.4 mile, then turn right on Road 910. After about 0.3 mile, you'll be riding beside a buried pipeline on your left. In 0.9 mile you'll see a sign on the left indicating the route to the Lazy Z Loop and Peterson Ridge. Continue straight, toward Whychus Creek. About 0.1 mile beyond the sign you'll reach the red cinder Road 4606 (Brooks Scanlon Mainline Road). Veer left on it for 200 feet, then turn right and follow the white diamonds up a little hill. The trail veers right, then left onto an unsigned dirt road. Follow it for 2 miles. You'll again be traveling beside the buried pipeline. When you reach paved Road 16 (Three Creek Road), cross it and continue straight ahead on Road 220 to Whychus Creek. After watering your horse at the creek, retrace your steps to return to the Rodeo Grounds Trailhead.

Dixie and Split pause for a refreshing drink at Whychus Creek.

Rodeo Short Loop

Trailhead: Start at the Rodeo Grounds Trailhead
Length: 4.5 miles round trip
Elevation: 3,200 to 3,300 feet
Difficulty: Easy
Footing: Suitable for barefoot horses
Season: Early spring through late fall
Permits: None
Facilities: Parking for 5-6 trailers. No stock water on the trail.

Highlights: This is a nice, easy loop for riding a green horse, or for those times when you can only do a short ride but still want a pleasant forest experience.

The Ride: From the kiosk at the Rodeo Grounds Trailhead, pick up the Met-Win to Rodeo Grounds Trail #4099, which follows a dirt road northwest and is marked with white trailblazer diamonds on the trees. In 0.3 mile you'll cross Harrington Loop, a well-traveled gravel road.

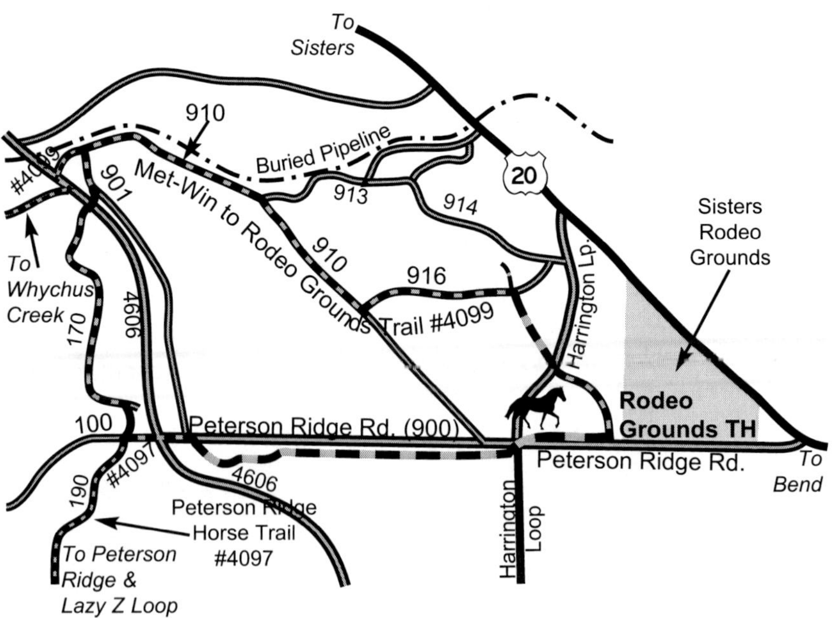

Tex moves out along the Rodeo Short Loop.

The trail becomes a single track and continues 0.3 mile to dirt Road 916. (Watch for the white diamonds—an unsigned user trail continues straight ahead.) Turn left on Road 916 and continue 0.4 mile, then turn right on Road 910. After about 0.3 mile, you'll be riding beside a buried pipeline on your left. In 0.9 mile, turn left at the sign indicating the route to the Lazy Z Loop and Peterson Ridge. It will soon take you across Road 4606 (the red cinder Brooks-Scanlon Road) and up a small hill. At the crest of the hill, the trail veers to the left and follows Road 170 for 0.6 mile. Then the trail goes up another small hill and in 0.1 mile it reaches Road 100. If you go straight, you'll be on Road 190 and on your way to Peterson Ridge. Instead, turn left on Road 100 and follow it 0.1 mile. Cross Road 4606 and continue straight on Peterson Ridge Road for 300 feet. Veer right on the single-track trail and follow it 1 mile to Harrington Loop. Cross Harrington Loop and Peterson Ridge Road, pick up the single-track trail on the northeast corner, and follow it 0.2 mile to the trailhead.

Linda rides Beamer across Whychus Creek, on the Met-Win to Rodeo Grounds Trail.

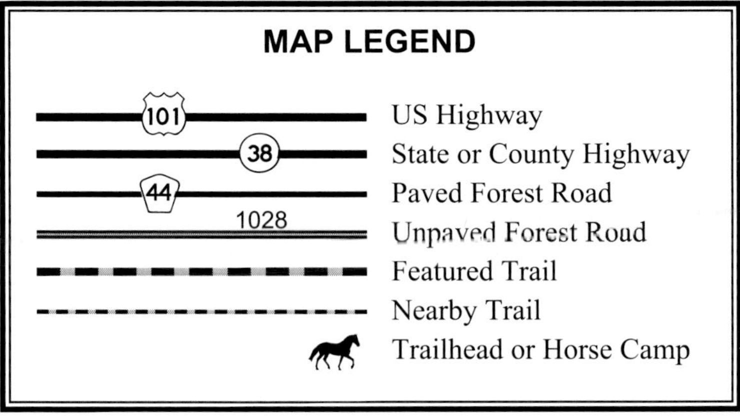

Pole Creek Trailhead

Deschutes National Forest

Pole Creek Trailhead, at the base of North Sister near the town of Sisters, is the jumping-off point for backpackers and horse packers doing multi-day treks around the Three Sisters. It also provides access to some beautiful day rides at the north end of the Three Sisters Wilderness. Perhaps because you have to drive 10 miles on a dusty, washboard dirt road to reach Pole Creek Trailhead, the north end of the Three Sisters Wilderness provides more solitude and, well, wildness, than the more easily-accessible Three Sisters Wilderness trails off Hwy. 46 near Mt. Bachelor. This area's scenic views are breathtaking, and the trails are a delight, so it's definitely worth the drive to get here. The nearest horse camp is Sisters Cow Camp, about 8 miles away. (See the Sisters Cow Camp chapter for details.)

Lydia and Shadow near Camp Lake.

Getting to Pole Creek Trailhead

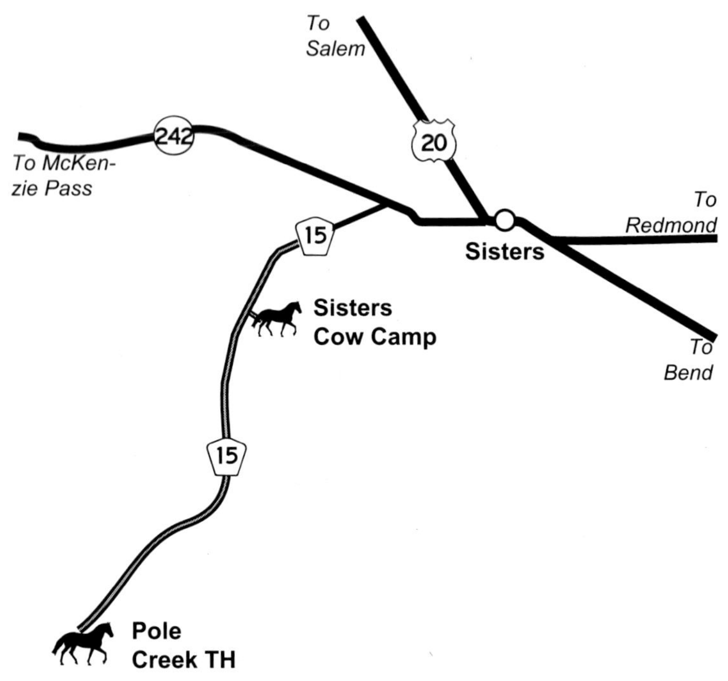

Pole Creek Area Trails

Trail	Difficulty	Elevation	Round Trip
Camp Lake	Challenging	5,300-7,000	13 miles
Demaris Lake	Challenging	5,300-6,400	11 miles
Park Meadow	Moderate	5,300-6,200	12 miles

Pole Creek Trailhead

Directions: Take Hwy. 242 west from Sisters for 1.5 miles, turn left on Road 15, and follow it for 10.5 miles. Pole Creek Trailhead is very popular with hikers doing multi-day hiking trips around the Sisters, so be sure to turn your trailer around when you arrive, and park where you cannot be blocked in by hiker cars.

Elevation: 5,300 feet

Camping: The closest horse camp is at Sisters Cow Camp. See the Sisters Cow Camp chapter for more details.

Facilities: Vault toilet, large parking area. Note that trailer parking may be limited by hiker cars, so be sure to turn around and park facing out so you can't be blocked in.

Permits: Northwest Forest Pass required

Season: Spring through late fall

Contact: Sisters Ranger District, 541-549-7700

Lydia rides Shadow on the Green Lakes Trail.

Camp Lake

Trailhead: Start at Pole Creek Trailhead

Length: 13 miles round trip

Elevation: 5,300 to 7,000 feet

Difficulty: Challenging -- trail is steep, rocky, and narrow near the end; challenging crossing of glacier-fed creek

Footing: Hoof protection recommended

Season: Late summer through early fall

Permits: Northwest Forest Pass required

Facilities: Toilet and parking for 2-3 trailers (depending on the number of parked hiker cars) at Pole Creek Trailhead. Stock water is available on the trail.

Highlights: This fabulous ride gives you a chance to see all Three Sisters up close. Much of the distance is a moderate climb through

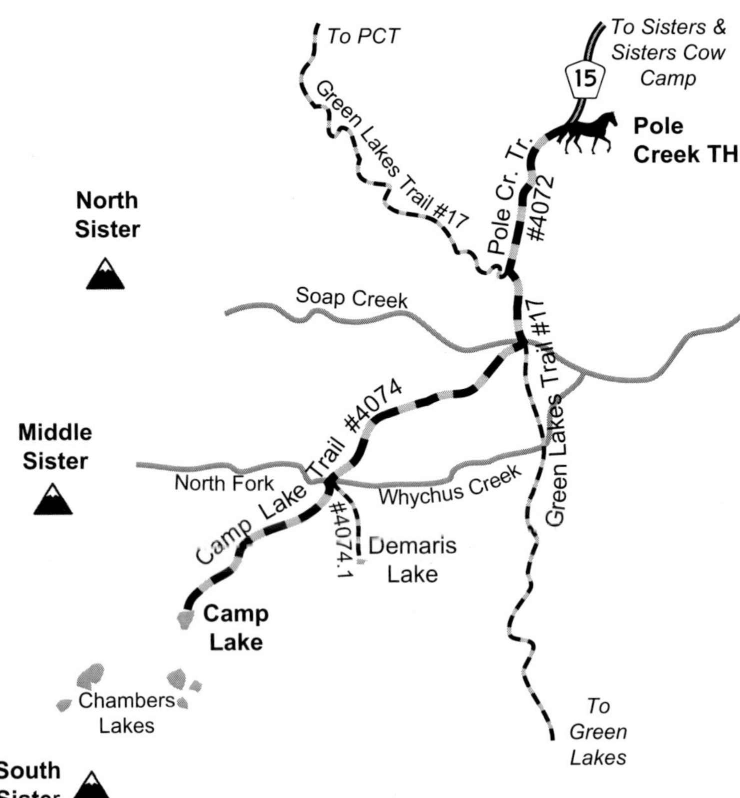

the forest. Midway through the ride you'll go through old growth forest punctuated by interesting rock outcroppings. As you near Camp Lake, the forest thins out and the trail gets steep, narrow, and rocky. You'll come out above timberline, where the Three Sisters seem close enough to touch. The views of Middle Sister's glaciers are impressive. In some years, you may not be able to reach Camp Lake because of lingering snowfields. Note that dogs must be on leash near Camp Lake from July 15 to September 15.

The Ride: Ride south from the trailhead on the Pole Creek Trail #4072 for 1.5 miles. At the first junction, veer left on the Green Lakes Trail #17. Continue 0.7 mile, and after crossing Soap Creek turn right toward the Chambers Lakes on the Camp Lake Trail #4074. After 2.5 miles you'll cross the fast-flowing, glacier-fed North Fork of Whychus Creek (you can't see the bottom because of the glacial silt in the water) and come to the junction with the Demaris Lake Trail #4074.1. Keep right and continue 2 miles to Camp Lake.

Lydia and Shadow check out the view of North Sister on the trail to Camp Lake.

Demaris Lake

Trailhead: Start at the Pole Creek Trailhead

Length: 11 miles round trip

Elevation: 5,300 to 6,400 feet

Difficulty: Challenging -- glacier-fed stream crossing can be challenging early in the season

Footing: Hoof protection recommended

Season: Summer through early fall

Permits: Northwest Forest Pass required

Facilities: Toilet and parking for 2-3 trailers (depending on the number of parked hiker cars) at Pole Creek Trailhead. Stock water is available on the trail.

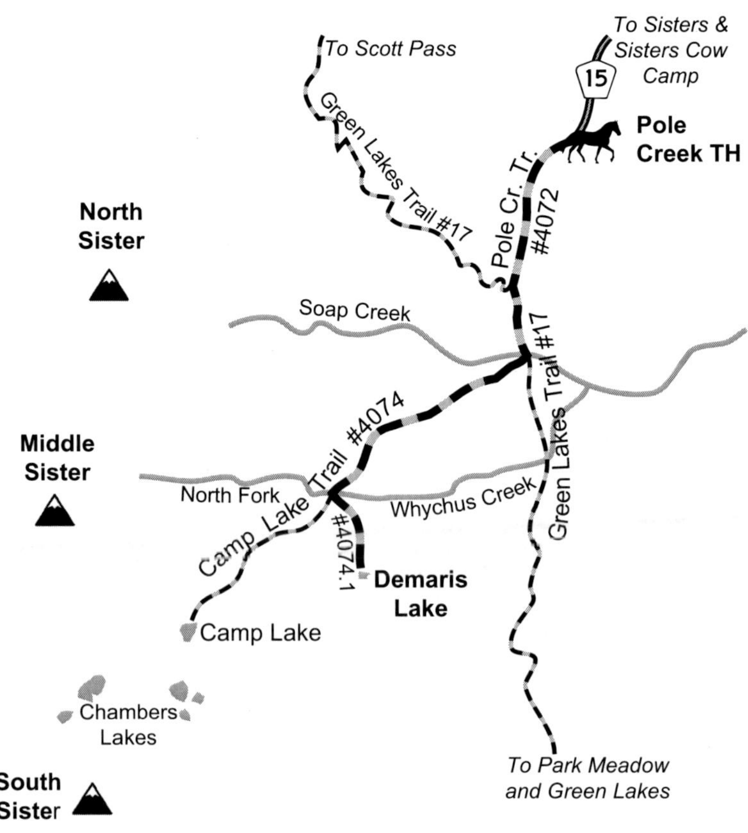

North Sister is reflected in the calm surface of Demaris Lake.

Highlights: At several points this forested trail offers filtered views of the Three Sisters and Broken Top. As you approach the North Fork of Whychus Creek you'll ride through stands of old-growth trees and past interesting rock outcroppings. When you reach the lake, tie your horse in the trees and hike to the left along the east side of the lake (the trail is not suitable for horses) for a view of the Three Sisters.

The Ride: Ride south from the trailhead on the Pole Creek Trail #4072 for 1.5 miles. At the first junction, veer left on the Green Lakes Trail #17. Continue 0.7 mile, and after crossing Soap Creek turn right toward the Chambers Lakes on the Camp Lake Trail #4074. After 2.5 miles you'll cross the fast-flowing, glacier-fed North Fork of Whychus Creek (you can't see the bottom because of the glacial silt in the water) and come to the junction with the Demaris Lake Trail #4074.1. Turn left and continue 0.7 mile to Demaris Lake.

Park Meadow

Trailhead: Start at Pole Creek Trailhead
Length: 12 miles round trip
Elevation: 5,300 to 6,200 feet
Difficulty: Moderate -- crossing Whychus Creek in early summer can be challenging if the water level is high
Footing: Hoof protection recommended
Season: Summer through fall
Permits: Northwest Forest Pass required
Facilities: Toilet and parking for 2-3 trailers (depending on the number of parked hiker cars) at Pole Creek Trailhead. Stock water is available on the trail.

Highlights: Most people ride to the beautiful Park Meadow using the trail that originates near Three Creek Meadow Horse Camp. The route

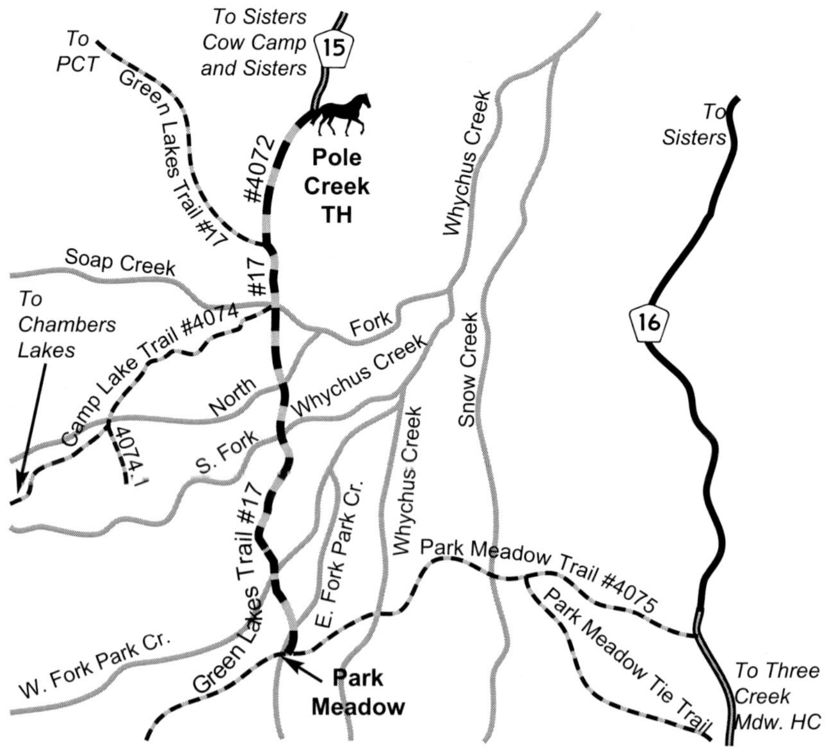

described here is more difficult, with more elevation change and a potentially challenging crossing of Whychus Creek if you ride early in the season. But the views and solitude on this lightly-travelled trail are ample rewards for the extra exertion.

The Ride: From the trailhead, ride south on the Pole Creek Trail #4072 for 1.5 mile. At the first junction, veer left on the Green Lakes Trail #17 and continue 0.7 mile. Just across Soap Creek, the Camp Lake Trail #4074 goes off to the right. Stay to the left, and in 0.8 mile you'll cross the North Fork of Whychus Creek. About 0.6 mile after that you'll cross the South Fork of Whychus Creek. The trail then climbs a steep ridge and enters an area burned several years ago by a forest fire. Be sure to look behind you and take in the views. About 0.8 mile after crossing the South Fork of Whychus Creek you'll pass a tiny unnamed lake, and 1.5 miles after that the trail reaches Park Meadow.

Riders cross Park Meadow, in the shadow of Broken Top.

Riders cross Park Meadow on the Green Lakes Trail, with South Sister in the background.

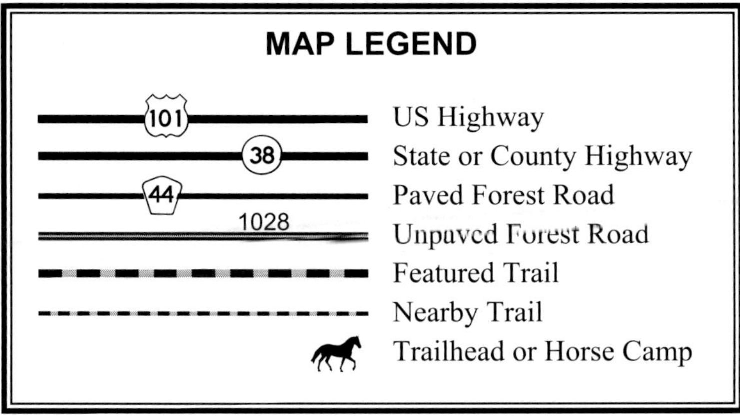

Quinn Meadow Horse Camp

Deschutes & Willamette National Forests

Quinn Meadow Horse Camp is a horseback rider's paradise. The views in this part of the Cascade Lakes area can be breathtaking, with mountain peaks soaring above pristine lakes, jagged lava flows next to verdant forests, and sparkling streams flowing through lush meadows. Whether you base your riding out of Quinn Meadow Horse Camp (camping only, no day-use parking) or take day rides from the nearby trailheads (see the North Cascade Lakes chapter for trailhead directions and more details), there are almost endless opportunities for loop rides on the region's network of intersecting trails. Be aware that the Metolius-Windigo Trail near here is popular with mountain bike riders. And please keep your horses out of the lakes, as they are the source of drinking water for backpackers.

South Sister reflected in Sisters Mirror Lake.

Getting to Quinn Meadow

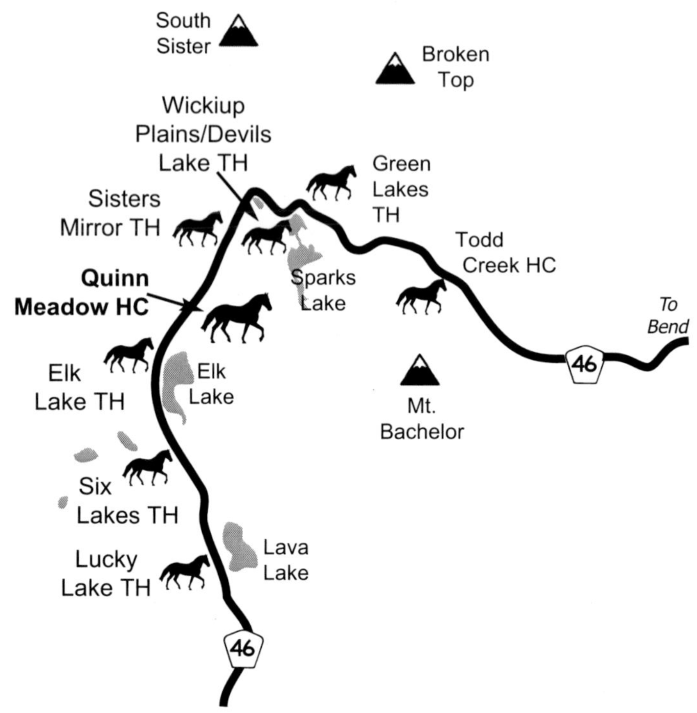

Quinn Meadow Area Trails

Trail	Difficulty	Elevation	Round Trip
Appaloosa/Quinn Cr. Lp.	Moderate	5,000-5,450	7 miles
Elk-Devils/Katsuk Pond Lp.	Moderate	5,100-5,700	9.5 miles
Elk Lake	Easy	4,900-5,200	6 miles
Horse Lake Loop	Moderate	4,950-5,300	9-15 miles
Lava Lake	Moderate	4,800-5,100	15-18 miles
Quinn Springs Loop	Moderate	5,050-5,150	2.2 miles
Sink Creek Loop	Moderate	5,050-5,450	5.5 miles
Sisters Mirror/Koosah Lp.	Moderate	5,000-6,500	13-14 miles
Sisters Mirror/Wickiup Lp.	Moderate	5,500-6,300	13-14.5 miles
Sparks Lake/Todd Creek	Moderate	5,000-6,100	6-13 miles
Wickiup Plains Loop	Moderate	5,100-6,300	9-16 miles

Quinn Meadow Horse Camp

Directions: From Hwy. 97 in Bend, take Exit 138 (Colorado Ave.) and head west. Follow the signs toward Mt. Bachelor and Century Drive, going through 3 roundabouts. Take the second exit from roundabouts 1 and 3, and take the third exit from roundabout 2. This will put you on Road 46 (Century Drive/Cascade Lakes Hwy.) Continue for 30 miles and turn left into the horse camp.

Elevation: 5,100 feet

Campsites: 25 sites with 2- or 4-horse corrals. 20 sites are back-in, 5 are pull-through. All sites have fire pits and picnic tables, and most have room for 2 vehicles.

Facilities: Toilets, manure bin, potable water from a hand pump, garbage dumpsters. Camp host. No day-use parking at Quinn Meadow Horse Camp — use nearby trailheads instead.

Permits: Camping fee. Advance reservations required.

Season: Summer through fall

Contact: Bend/Ft. Rock Ranger District (Deschutes National Forest): 541-383-4000
Concessionaire: 541-338-7869, www.hoodoo.com
Reservations: www.recreation.gov or call 877-444-6777

Ruger mugs for the camera at Quinn Meadow Horse Camp.

Appaloosa/Quinn Creek Loop

Trailhead: Start at Quinn Meadow Horse Camp
Length: 7 miles round trip, or 8 miles if you detour to Sparks Lake
Elevation: 5,000 to 5,450 feet
Difficulty: Moderate -- water crossings, steep switchbacks on the Quinn Creek Trail, plus mountain bike traffic on the Metolius-Windigo Trail
Footing: Hoof protection recommended
Season: Summer through fall
Permits: Camping fee. No day-use parking at Quinn Meadow.
Facilities: Toilets, potable water, and manure bins at the horse camp. Stock water is available on the trail.

Highlights: This is a delightful ride that offers tree-filtered views of South Sister, Mt. Bachelor, and Hosmer Lake. It runs along Quinn Creek at the beginning and end of the ride, and goes through several different types of forest along the way. The switchbacks on the Quinn

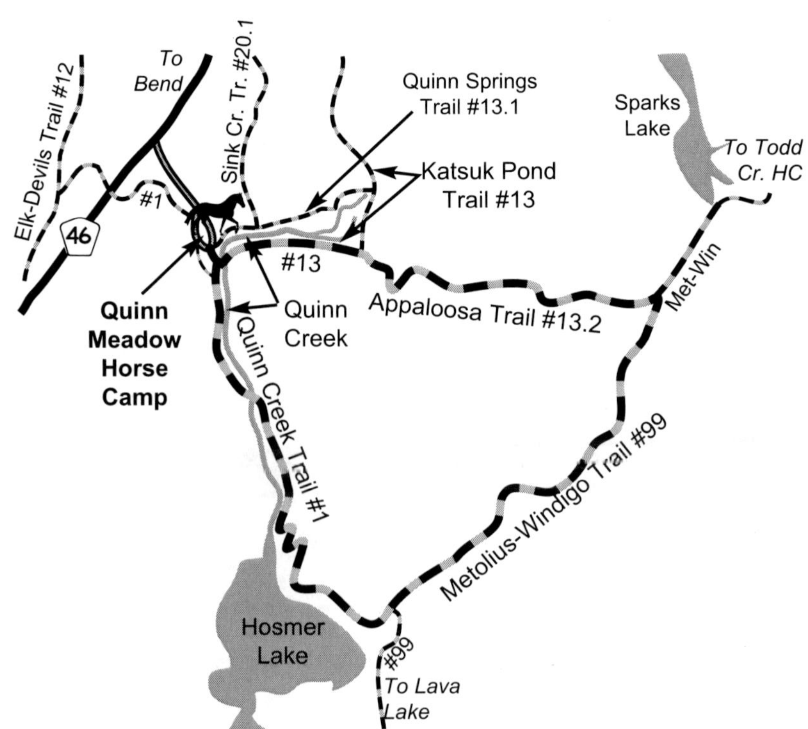

Ruger enjoys a drink from Quinn Creek, next to the trail.

Creek Trail going down toward Hosmer Lake are steep and rocky, but manageable.

The Ride: Pick up the Katsuk Pond Trail #13 next to campsite 15. In 300 feet, veer left and cross Quinn Creek to stay on the Katsuk Pond Trail. The trail runs beside the creek for 0.8 mile, and in this stretch you'll get some filtered views of South Sister. At the next trail junction, veer right on the Appaloosa Trail #13.2. Follow it up some gentle switchbacks and over a low ridge, where you'll have some views of Mt. Bachelor. After 1.6 miles, you'll come to the Metolius-Windigo Trail #99. Turn right toward Lava Lake. The trail runs gently downhill for 2.3 miles. At the next junction, the Met-Win jogs to the left and the Quinn Creek Trail #1 goes straight ahead. Go straight, and as the trail runs along the ridge above Hosmer Lake you'll get filtered views of the lake below you. Then the trail makes a series of steep switchbacks that take you to the bank of Quinn Creek, near where it flows into Hosmer Lake. About 1.2 miles after turning onto the Quinn Creek Trail, you'll come to a small waterfall and a bridge over the creek. Ford the creek (the bridge isn't safe for horses) and continue 1 mile to return to the horse camp.

Bonus Ride to Sparks Lake: You can detour 0.5 mile one way to visit the shore of Sparks Lake by turning left on the Metolius-Windigo Trail from the Appaloosa Trail. Ride 0.5 mile, then turn left on an unsigned trail. The lake is ahead in 0.1 mile.

Elk-Devils/Katsuk Pond Loop

Trailhead: Start at either Quinn Meadow Horse Camp or the Wickiup Plains/Devils Lake Trailhead

Length: 9.5 miles round trip

Elevation: 5,100 to 5,700 feet

Difficulty: Moderate — creek crossings, some rocky stretches

Footing: Hoof protection recommended

Season: Summer through fall

Permits: Northwest Forest Pass required at Wickiup Plains/Devils Lake Trailhead. Camping fee at Quinn Meadow.

Facilities: Toilet and plenty of trailer parking at Wickiup Plains Trailhead. Camping facilities at Quinn Meadow. Stock water is available on the trail.

Highlights: The trail runs primarily through lodgepole pine and mountain hemlock forest. On the east side of Road 46, the Katsuk Pond Trail passes fascinating lava outcroppings and the delightful

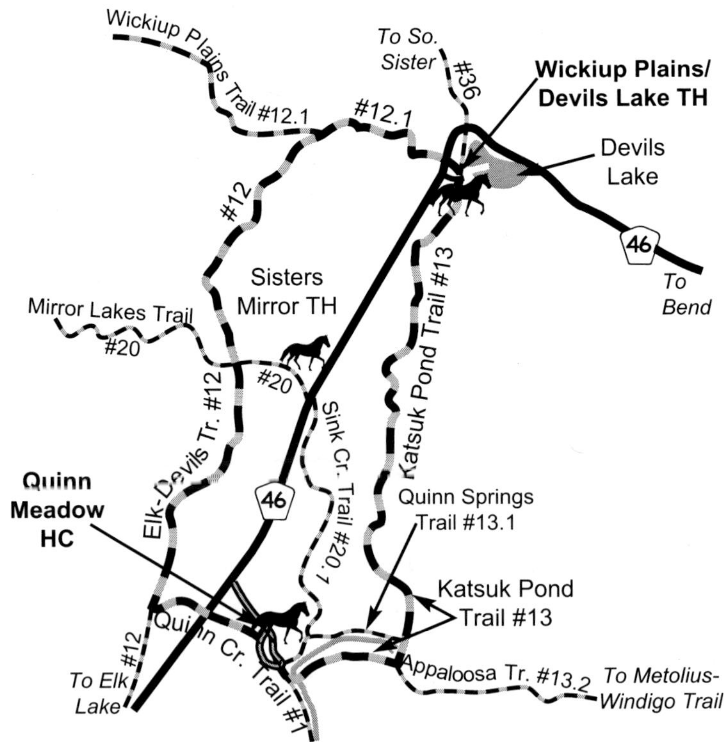

springs that create Quinn Creek. On the west side of the highway, the Elk-Devils Trail follows the track of an old wagon road.

Finding the Wickiup Plains/Devils Lake Trailhead: From Bend, drive west on Road 46 (the Cascade Lakes Hwy.) for 28 miles. Just past Devils Lake, turn left into the trailhead.

The Ride: From Quinn Meadow, pick up the Quinn Creek Trail #1 next to campsite #1. Follow it 0.5 mile to the underpass under Road 46, then another 0.4 mile to the Elk-Devils Trail #12. Turn right on the Elk-Devils Trail toward Devils Lake. You'll cross the Mirror Lakes Trail in 1.6 miles. Continue another 1.7 miles, and at the junction with the Wickiup Plains Trail #12.1, stay to the right. Continue 0.9 mile to the Wickiup Plains/Devils Lake Trailhead. From Wickiup Plains/Devils Lake Trailhead, cross Road 46 and take the Katsuk Pond Trail #13 south toward Quinn Meadow Horse Camp. Interesting lava outcroppings are dotted all along this portion of the trail. After 3.2 miles, the Quinn Springs Trail #13.1 goes off to the right. It will take you to Quinn Meadow in 1.2 miles. Or, for an easier route you can stay to the left and continue 0.2 mile to the next junction, then veer right on the Katsuk Pond Trail and continue 0.8 mile to Quinn Meadow.

Lydia rides Shadow through a lava outcropping on the Katsuk Pond Trail.

Elk Lake

Trailhead: Start at Quinn Meadow Horse Camp
Length: 6 miles round trip
Elevation: 4,900 to 5,200 feet
Difficulty: Easy
Footing: Hoof protection recommended
Season: Summer through fall
Permits: Camping fee at Quinn Meadow. Northwest Forest Pass required at Elk Lake Trailhead.
Facilities: Toilets, potable water, and manure bins at the horse camp. Stock water is available on the trail.

Highlights: While you're camping at Quinn Meadow, it's a short jaunt down the Elk-Devils trail to get lunch, dinner, or ice cream at Elk Lake Lodge on the shore of beautiful Elk Lake.

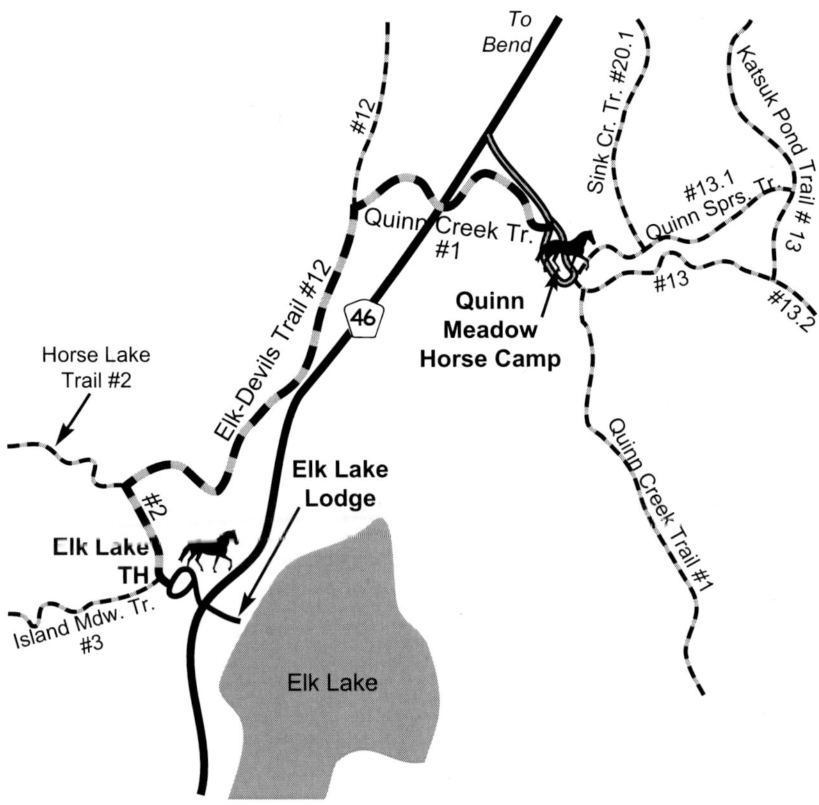

Diana and Mo lead the group down the Elk-Devils Trail.

The Ride: From Quinn Meadow, pick up the Quinn Creek Trail #1 next to campsite #1. In 0.5 mile it will take you to the underpass under Road 46, and in another 0.4 mile you'll reach the Elk-Devils Trail #12. Turn left toward Elk Lake, and in 1.5 mile you'll reach the junction with the Horse Lake Trail #2. Turn left, and in 0.3 mile you'll reach the trailhead. Ride down the trailhead entrance road, cross Road 46, and continue about 0.1 mile to Elk Lake Lodge. Tie your horses in the trees behind the lodge, take in the view, and enjoy a relaxing meal. Life is good!

Elk Lake Lodge has a pretty view of Mt. Bachelor and the lake, and the burgers are good, too.

Horse Lake Loop

Trailhead: Start at Quinn Meadow Horse Camp or the Elk Lake Trailhead

Length: 9 miles round trip from Elk Lake Trailhead, or 15 miles round trip from Quinn Meadow

Elevation: 4,950 to 5,300 feet

Difficulty: Moderate

Footing: Hoof protection recommended

Season: Summer through fall

Permits: Northwest Forest Pass required at Elk Lake Trailhead. Camping fee at Quinn Meadow.

Facilities: Camping facilities at Quinn Meadow. Toilet and parking for several trailers at Elk Lake Trailhead. Stock water is available on the trail.

Highlights: This is a very nice ride over forested terrain, and Horse Lake is a pretty destination. The large meadow just east of Horse Lake makes a good picnic spot. The lakes in this area are heavily used by backpackers for drinking water, so please keep your horse out of the lakes.

Finding the Elk Lake Trailhead: From Bend, drive west on Road 46 (the Cascade Lakes Hwy.) for 32.5 miles and turn right into the trailhead, directly across from the entrance to Elk Lake Lodge.

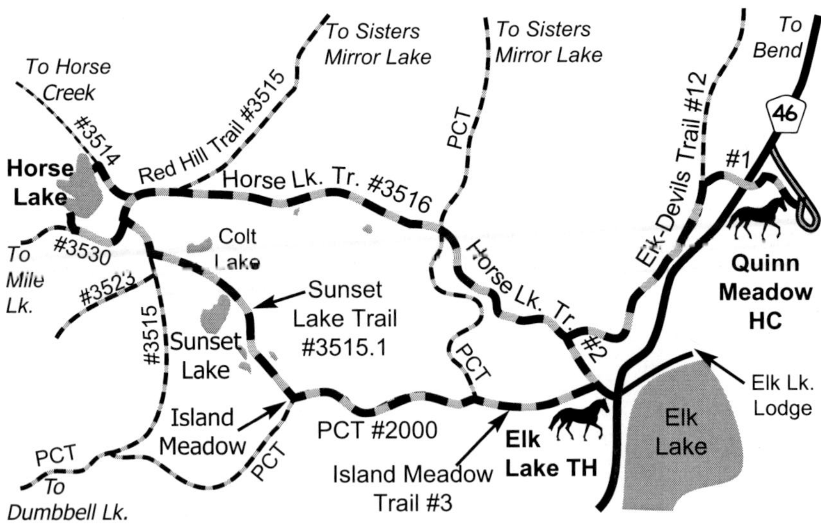

The Ride: From Quinn Meadow Horse Camp, pick up the Quinn Creek Trail #1 near campsite 1, ride 0.9 mile (crossing under the highway) and turn left on the Elk-Devils Trail #12. Continue 1.5 miles to the junction with the Horse Lake Trail #2. Turn right on the Horse Lake Trail. From Elk Lake Trailhead, pick up the Horse Lake Trail #2 on the west side of the parking area. In 0.3 mile, the Elk-Devils Trail #12 to Quinn Meadow goes off to the right. Stay left. All, in another 1.2 miles, the trail crosses the PCT and the trail number changes to #3516 because you've entered the Willamette National Forest. Continue straight for 2.0 miles more, at which point you'll turn left on the Red Hill Trail #3515. In another 0.2 mile, turn right on the Horse Creek Trail #3514. Follow it 0.5 mile, then turn left on an unsigned trail that will take you to the shore of Horse Lake. After enjoying the view, return to the Red Hill Trail #3515 and turn right. In 0.2 mile, veer to the right on the Park Trail #3530. In 0.5 mile, an unsigned spur trail on the right will again take you to the shore of Horse Lake. After that, retrace your steps to the junction of Trails #3530 and #3515. Turn right on Trail #3515, and in 0.2 mile turn left on the Sunset Lake Trail #3515.1. After 1.4 miles you'll reach Island Meadow. Turn left at the junction with the Pacific Crest Trail #2000 and follow it 1.4 miles, then veer right on the Island Meadow Trail #3 to return to the Horse Lake Trail. Turn right to go to Elk Lake Trailhead, or left to return to Quinn Meadow.

Eli and Dottie and ride Dakota and Hope on the Horse Lake Loop.

Lava Lake

Trailhead: Start at Quinn Meadow Horse Camp or the Lucky Lake Trailhead

Length: 15 miles round trip from Quinn Meadow to Lava Lake, or 18 miles round trip from Lucky Lake Trailhead to Quinn

Elevation: 4,800 to 5,100 feet

Difficulty: Moderate — this stretch of the Metolius-Windigo Trail is popular with mountain bike riders

Footing: Hoof protection recommended

Season: Summer through fall

Permits: Camping fee at Quinn Meadow. No fee at Lucky Lake.

Facilities: Camping facilities at Quinn Meadow. Toilet and parking for 4-5 trailers at Lucky Lake Trailhead. Stock water is available on the trail.

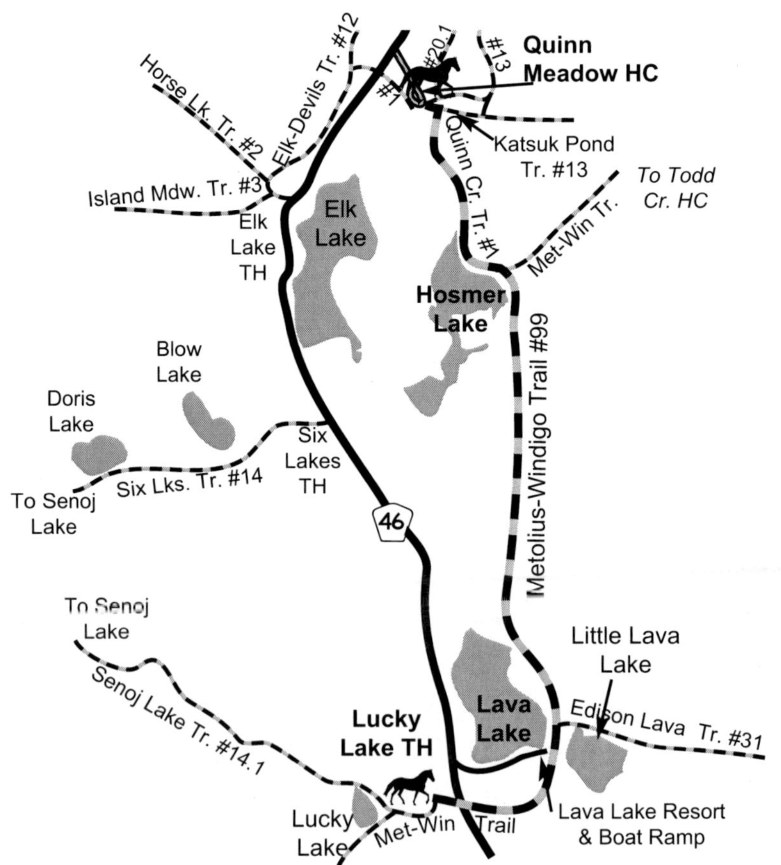

Suzanne rides Mick along the shore of Lava Lake.

Highlights: This section of the Met-Win Trail runs though lodgepole pine forest and past both Hosmer Lake and Lava Lake. You'll encounter interesting lava outcroppings near the south end of Hosmer Lake. Watch for mountain bike riders on this trail.

Finding the Lucky Lake Trailhead: From Bend, take Road 46 (the Cascade Lakes Hwy.) west for 38.5 miles and turn right into the trailhead.

The Ride: From Quinn Meadow Horse Camp, pick up the Katsuk Pond Trail #13 next to campsite 15, and in 300 feet veer right on the Quinn Creek Trail #1. Ride along the creek and up some steep switchbacks, and in 2.2 miles turn right on the Metolius-Windigo Trail. Ride it for 5 miles to Lucky Lake. From Lucky Lake Trailhead, cross Road 46 and pick up the Metolius-Windigo Trail #99 toward Lava Lake. The trail travels 1.5 miles, passing Lava Lake Campground and Little Lava Lake. Then it runs along the shore of Lava Lake for 1.5 miles. Once the trail leaves Lava Lake, it travels through mostly-lodgepole forest for 3.5 miles. For the last mile or so it parallels the shore of Hosmer Lake some distance away, with filtered views of the lake through the trees. Turn left at the junction with the Quinn Creek Trail #1 and continue about 2.2 miles to Quinn Meadow.

Quinn Springs Loop

Trailhead: Start at Quinn Meadow Horse Camp
Length: 2.2 miles round trip
Elevation: 5,050 to 5,150 feet
Difficulty: Moderate
Footing: Hoof protection recommended
Season: Summer through fall
Permits: Camping fee. No day-use parking at Quinn Meadow.
Facilities: Toilet, potable water, and manure bins at the horse camp. Stock water is available on the trail.

Highlights: This is an amazing little loop. It's short but unique, and so scenic you must make the time to ride it. The trail runs along both sides of Quinn Creek, encircling the springs that feed this crystal-clear stream. Along the trail you'll ride through lodgepole pine forest and stark lava outcroppings. The contrasts are striking.

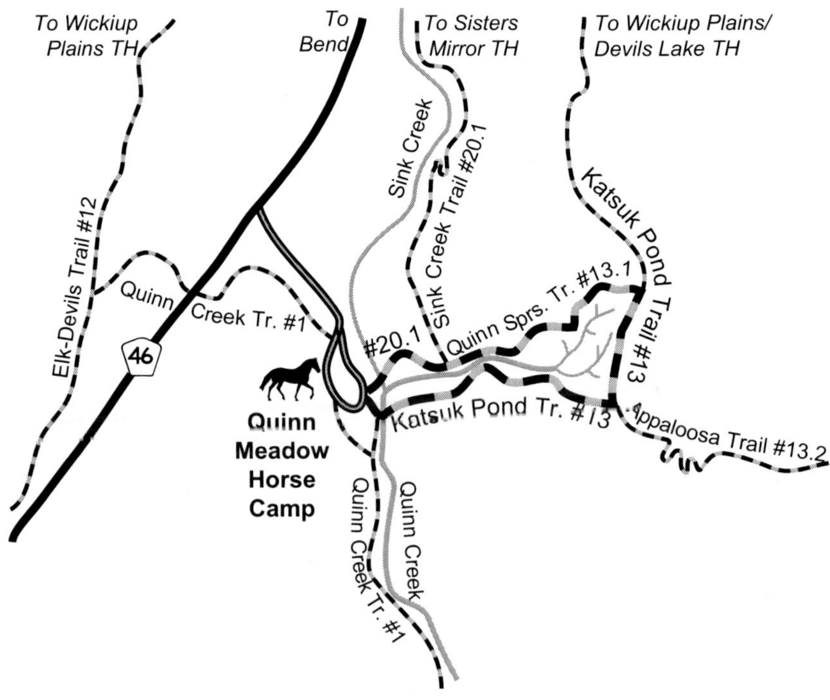

The Ride: Pick up the Sink Creek Trail #20.1, which departs next to campsite #15. Cross the creek and follow the trail for 0.3 mile. At the trail junction, veer to the right on the Quinn Springs Trail #13.1. In 0.8 mile, turn right again on the Katsuk Pond Trail #13, and 0.2 mile later turn right again to stay on the Katsuk Pond Trail. After 0.8 mile you'll ford Quinn Creek and reach the junction with the Quinn Creek Trail #1 in a meadow. Veer right to return to Quinn Meadow in 0.1 mile.

Mt. Bachelor is visible above sparkling Quinn Creek.

Robert and Ruger make their way through a lava flow on the Quinn Springs Trail.

Sink Creek Loop

Trailhead: Start at Quinn Meadow Horse Camp
Length: 5.5 miles round trip
Elevation: 5,050 to 5,450 feet
Difficulty: Moderate
Footing: Hoof protection recommended
Permits: Camping fee at Quinn Meadow.
Facilities: Camping facilities at Quinn Meadow. Stock water is available on the trail.

Highlights: The Elk-Devils Trail runs along an old wagon road through mixed conifer forest, including some old-growth areas. The Sink Creek Trail runs past some impressive lava flows and in places follows Sink Creek, which earns its name by flowing underground

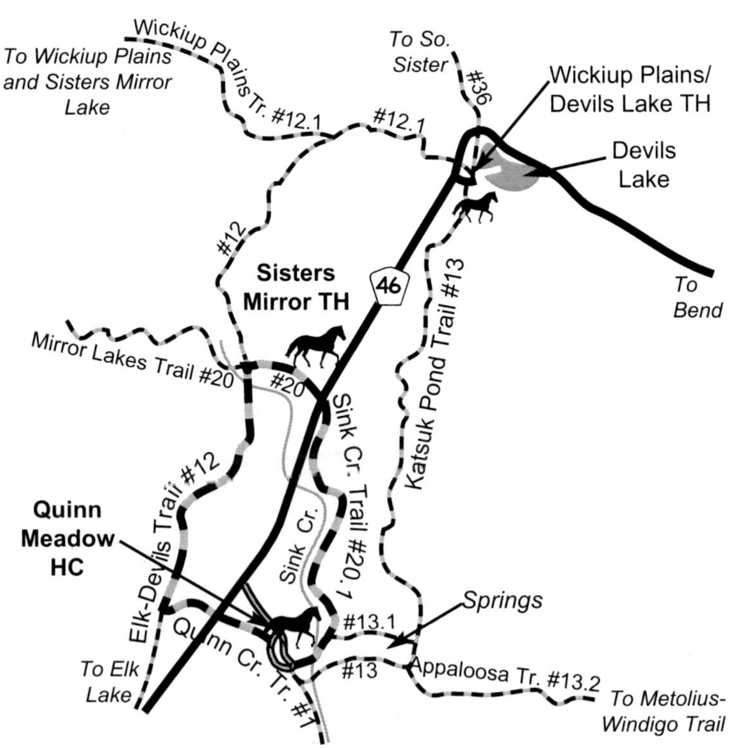

most of the way. Look for the stretches of green vegetation to indicate the creek's course.

The Ride: Pick up the Quinn Creek Trail #1 near campsite 1. In 0.5 mile you'll reach the underpass under Road 46, and 0.4 mile later you'll reach the Elk-Devils Trail #12. Turn right toward Devils Lake. In 1.5 miles the trail crosses Sink Creek, and 0.1 mile later you'll come to the junction with the Mirror Lakes Trail #20. Turn right toward the Sisters Mirror Trailhead, and in 0.5 mile you'll arrive at the trailhead. Cross Road 46 and pick up the Sink Creek Trail #20.1. Ride it 1.7 miles. At the junction with the Quinn Springs Trail #13.1, turn right toward Quinn Meadow. In 0.4 mile you'll reach the horse camp.

Ray on Moose and Connie on Diamond, traveling through the forest on the Sink Creek Loop.

Sisters Mirror/Koosah Mtn. Loop

Trailhead: Start at Quinn Meadow Horse Camp or Elk Lake Trailhead

Length: 13 miles round trip from Elk Lake Trailhead, or 14 miles round trip from Quinn Meadow

Elevation: 5,000 to 6,500 feet

Difficulty: Moderate -- creek crossings and a couple of short but steep side hills to traverse

Footing: Hoof protection recommended

Season: Summer through fall

Permits: Northwest Forest Pass required at Elk Lake. Camping fee at Quinn Meadow.

Facilities: Toilets at the trailheads. Elk Lake has a large parking area. Camping facilities at Quinn Meadow. Stock water is available on the trail.

Highlights: Sisters Mirror Lake is a pretty lunch spot, and the summit of Koosah Mountain offers excellent views of South Sister, Mt.

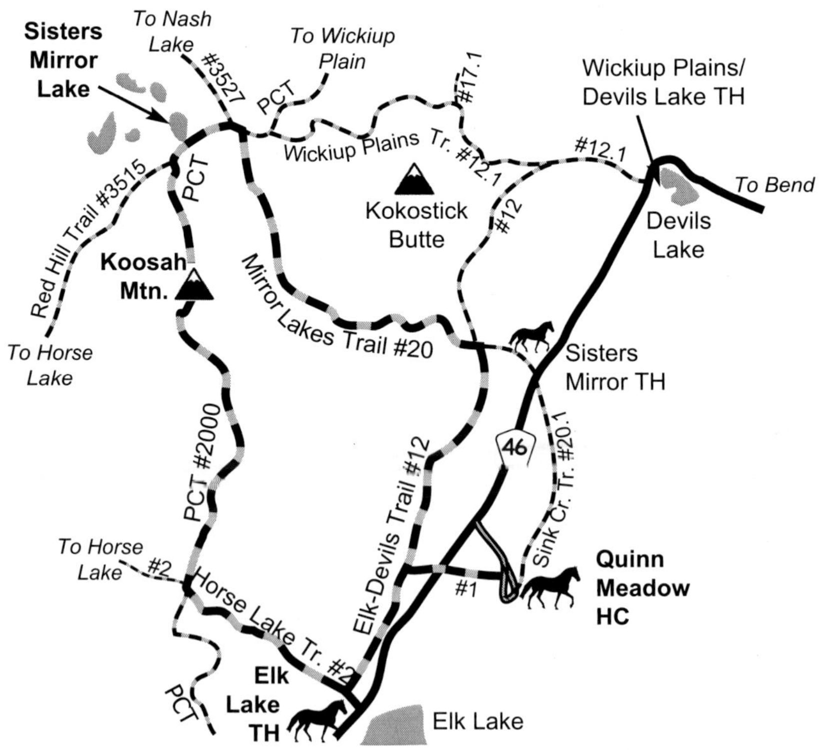

Debbie on Cowboy and Lydia on Shadow, traveling over Koosah Mountain. That's South Sister behind them.

Bachelor, and Broken Top. Dogs must be on leash on this trail, July 15-September 15.

Finding the Elk Lake Trailhead: From Bend, drive west on Road 46 (the Cascade Lakes Hwy.) for 32.5 miles. The trailhead is on the right.

The Ride: From Quinn Meadow Horse Camp, pick up the Quinn Creek Trail #1 near campsite 1 and ride it 0.9 mile, through the tunnel under Road 46, to the Elk-Devils Trail #12. Turn right, ride 1.5 miles, and turn left on the Mirror Lakes Trail #20. From Elk Lake Trailhead, pick up the Elk-Devils Trail #12 and in 0.3 mile veer right on it. Ride 3.1 miles and turn left on the Mirror Lakes Trail #20. All, ride west on the Mirror Lakes Trail #20. In 3.2 miles, you'll reach the Pacific Crest Trail #2000. Turn left and ride 0.3 mile to Sisters Mirror Lake or one of the other nearby lakes for a good lunch stop. Continue south on the PCT for 1.5 miles to the top of Koosah Mountain, which offers nice views of nearby peaks and the surrounding forest. Ride the PCT another 3 miles to the Horse Lake Trail #2, then turn left and ride 1.5 miles to the Elk-Devils Trail #12. Go straight ahead to reach the Elk Lake Trailhead, or turn left, ride about 1.6 miles, and turn right to go back to Quinn Meadow.

Sisters Mirror/Wickiup Plains Loop

Trailhead: Start at Quinn Meadow Horse Camp or Wickiup Plains/Devils Lake Trailhead

Length: 13 miles round trip from Wickiup Plains/Devils Lake Trailhead, or 14.5 miles round trip from Quinn Meadow

Elevation: 5,500 to 6,300 feet

Difficulty: Moderate

Footing: Hoof protection recommended

Season: Summer through fall

Permits: Northwest Forest Pass required at Wickiup Plains/Devils Lake. Camping fee at Quinn Meadow.

Facilities: Toilets at the trailheads. Wickiup Plains has a large trailer parking area. Camping facilities at Quinn Meadow. Stock water is available on the trail.

Highlights: This loop near the base of South Sister is a great way to take in both Sisters Mirror Lake and Wickiup Plain. On a calm day, South Sister is beautifully reflected in Sisters Mirror Lake. The open

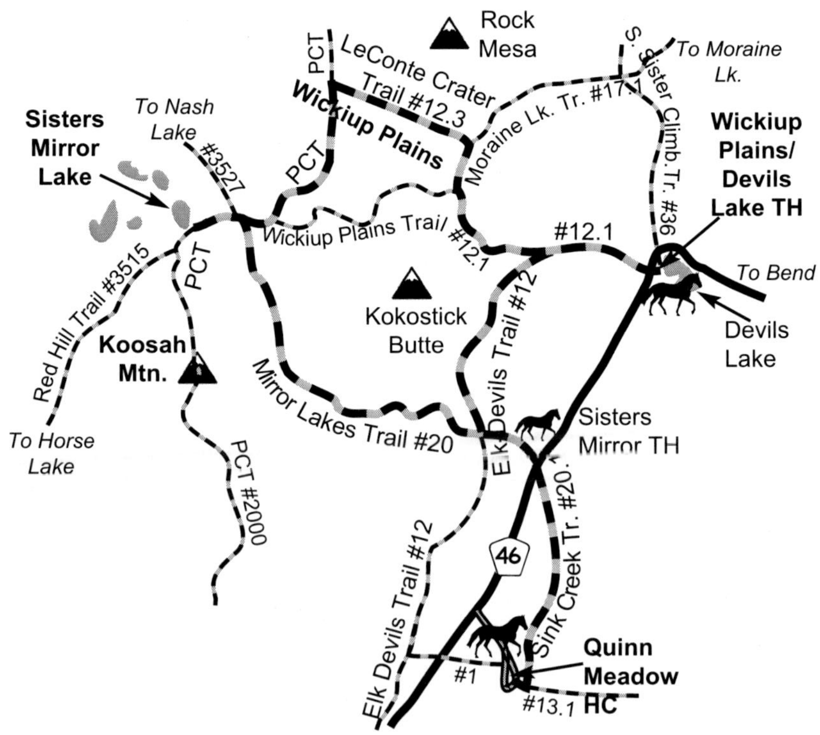

Linda and Beamer on the LeConte Crater Trail, with South Sister in the background.

expanse of Wickiup Plain is a stark contrast to the forest that surrounds it. Please ride single file on the plain to avoid damaging the fragile vegetation. Dogs must be on leash on this trail, July 15-September 15.

Finding the Wickiup Plains/Devils Lake Trailhead: From Bend, drive west on Road 46 (the Cascade Lakes Hwy.) for 28 miles. The trailhead is on the left.

The Ride: <u>From Wickiup Plains/Devils Lake Trailhead</u>, pick up the Wickiup Plains Trail #12.1 and ride it 0.9 mile. Turn left on the Elk-Devils Trail #12, and continue 1.7 miles, then turn right on the Mirror Lakes Trail #20. <u>From Quinn Meadow Horse Camp</u>, pick up the Sink Creek Trail #20.1 next to campsite 15 and ride it 2.1 miles to the Sisters Mirror Trailhead. Follow the Mirror Lakes Trail #20 for 0.5 mile. <u>All</u>, ride west on the Mirror Lakes Trail #20 for 3.2 miles. Turn left on the PCT and make a 0.3 mile detour to Sisters Mirror Lake. Return to the junction with the Mirror Lakes Trail and continue on the PCT 0.3 mile. At the junction with the Wickiup Plains Trail #12.1, stay to the left on the PCT and continue 1.7 more miles, crossing Wickiup Plain. At the next junction, turn right on the LeConte Crater Trail #12.3. In 1.4 mile, turn right at the junction with the Moraine Lake Trail #17.1. After 0.5 mile, veer left on the Wickiup Plains Trail #12.1 and follow it for a mile. To return to Wickiup Plains/Devils Lake Trailhead, continue straight ahead on the Wickiup Plains Trail. To return to Quinn Meadow, turn right on the Elk-Devils Trail. In 1.7 miles turn left on the Mirror Lakes Trail to reach Sisters Mirror Trailhead. Cross Road 46 and follow the Sink Creek Trail back to the horse camp.

Sparks Lake/Todd Creek

Trailhead: Start at Quinn Meadow Horse Camp

Length: 6 miles round trip to Sparks Lake or 13 miles round trip to Todd Creek Horse Camp

Elevation: 5,000 to 6,100 feet

Difficulty: Moderate

Footing: Hoof protection recommended

Season: Summer through fall

Permits: Camping fee. No day-use parking at Quinn Meadow.

Facilities: Horse camping facilities at Quinn Meadow. Toilet and stock water at Todd Creek. Stock water is available on the trail.

Highlights: This is a mostly-forested ride that connects the two horse camps in the area with Sparks Lake. Along the way you'll enjoy views

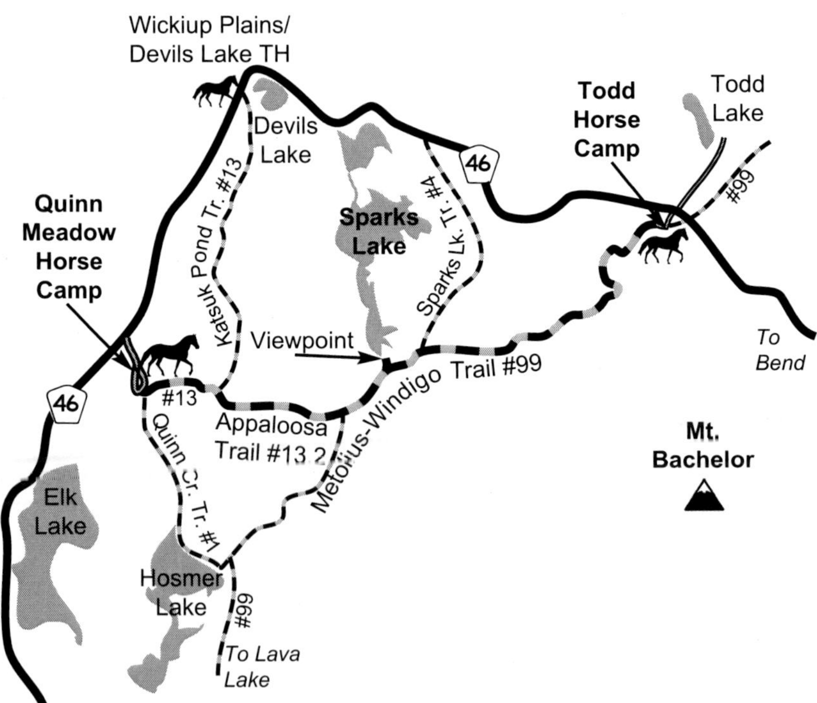

of South Sister, Mt. Bachelor, and Sparks Lake. The shore of Sparks Lake is a beautiful place for lunch. You are likely to encounter mountain bikes on this stretch of the Met-Win Trail.

The Ride: Pick up the Katsuk Pond Trail #13 next to campsite 15. In 300 feet, veer left to stay on the Katsuk Pond Trail and cross Quinn Creek. The trail runs beside Quinn Creek for 0.8 mile and offers glimpses of South Sister. At the junction, veer right on the Appaloosa Trail #13.2 and follow it up some switchbacks and over a low ridge. Watch for filtered views of Mt. Bachelor. After 1.6 miles you'll come to the Metolius-Windigo Trail #99. Turn left, and in 0.5 mile you'll reach a short spur trail that will take you to the shore of Sparks Lake in 0.1 mile. To continue to Todd Creek, stay on the Metolius-Windigo Trail. About 0.5 mile past Sparks Lake, the Sparks Lake Trail #4 goes off to the left. Stay right on the Met-Win, and in 3.5 miles you'll reach Todd Creek Horse Camp. In this last section you'll have more views of Mt. Bachelor. It's pretty much uphill all the way from Quinn to Todd Creek, and interestingly enough, it's downhill all the way back.

Kayakers ply the waters of Sparks Lake, with South Sister in the background.

Wickiup Plains Loop

Trailhead: Start at Quinn Meadow Horse Camp or the Wickiup Plains/Devils Lake Trailhead

Length: 16 miles round trip from Quinn Meadow, or 9 miles round trip from Wickiup Plains/Devils Lake Trailhead

Elevation: 5,100 to 6,300 from Quinn Meadow, or 5,500 to 6,300 feet from Wickiup Plains/Devils Lake Trailhead

Difficulty: Moderate

Footing: Hoof protection recommended

Season: Summer through fall

Permits: Camping fee at Quinn Meadow. Northwest Forest Pass required at Wickiup Plains/Devils Lake Trailhead.

Facilities: Horse camping facilities at Quinn Meadow. Toilet and plenty of trailer parking at Wickiup Plains/Devils Lake Trailhead. Stock water is available on the trail.

Highlights: Wickiup Plains, a huge pumice plain at the base of South Sister, offers expansive views of the surrounding peaks, contrasting

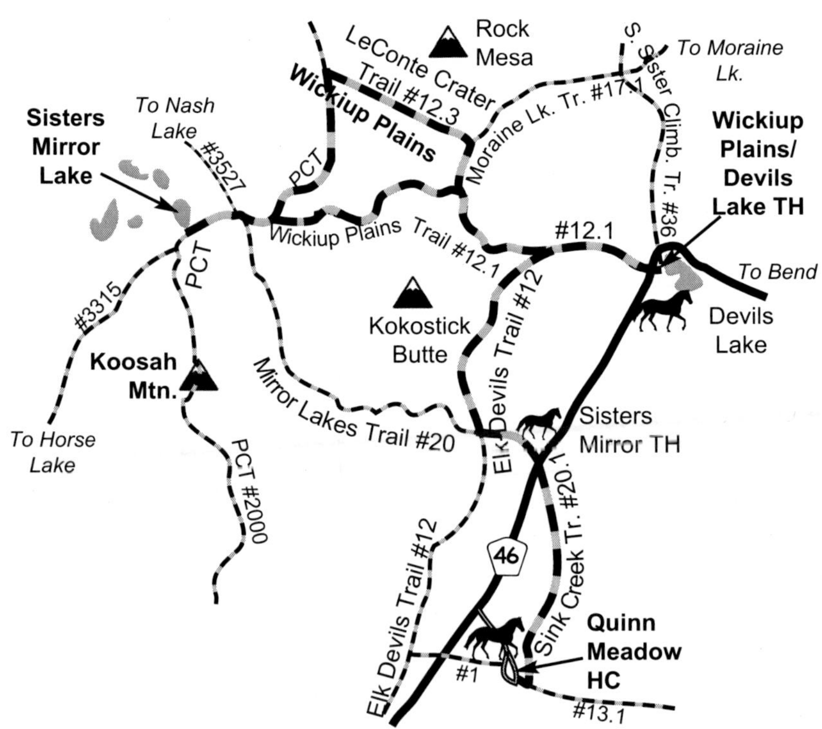

Lel and Whitney ride Jane and Dixie across Wickiup Plains, in front of Rock Mesa and South Sister.

sharply with the dense forest you ride through to reach it. Please ride horses single file on the plains to avoid damaging the fragile vegetation. If desired, you can detour 1.2 miles round trip to reach Sisters Mirror Lake. Dogs must be on leash on this trail, July 15-September 15.

The Ride: From Quinn Meadow Horse Camp, pick up the Sink Creek Trail #20.1 next to campsite 15 and follow it 2.1 miles to the Sisters Mirror Trailhead. Cross Road 46 and follow the Mirror Lakes Trail #20. In 0.5 mile, turn right on the Elk-Devils Trail #12. Continue 1.7 miles and veer left on the Wickiup Plains Trail #12.1. From Wickiup Plains/Devils Lake Trailhead, pick up the Wickiup Plains Trail #12.1 and ride west for 0.9 mile. At the junction with the Elk-Devils Trail, stay right. All, stay on the Wickiup Plains Trail for 2.7 miles, then turn right on the Pacific Crest Trail. (If desired you can turn left and detour 0.6 mile each way to Sisters Mirror Lake, then return to this junction.) Ride north on the PCT and in 1.7 miles it will take you to Wickiup Plains and the LeConte Crater Trail #12.3. Turn right here and ride past the Rock Mesa lava flow at the base of South Sister. In 1.4 miles turn right on the Moraine Lake Trail #17.1. In 0.5 mile, turn left on the Wickiup Plains Trail and follow it 0.9 mile. Continue straight on the Wickiup Plains Trail to return to the Wickiup Plains Trailhead, or turn left on the Elk-Devils Trail to return to Quinn Meadow or the Sisters Mirror Trailhead.

Robert and Ruger, on the Quinn Creek Trail near Quinn Meadow Horse Camp.

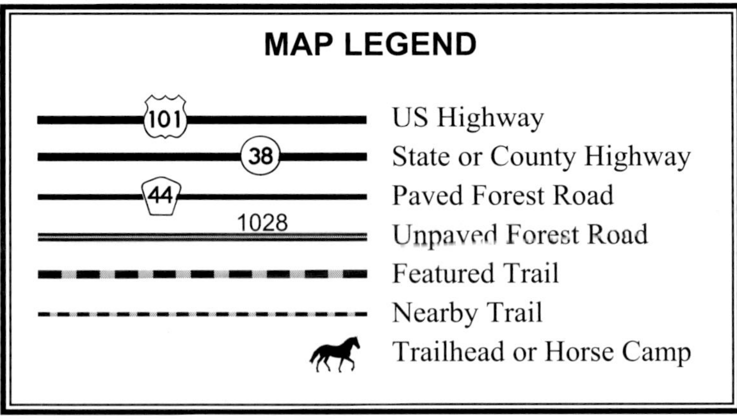

Santiam Pass Area

Deschutes National Forest

The trails near Santiam Pass provide access to the southern Mt. Jefferson and northern Mt. Washington Wildernesses. Most of these trails, which you can easily reach from Hwy. 20, go through the area burned in the 90,000-acre B&B fire in 2003. You'll see thousands of burned trees as you ride, but the fire also opened up tremendous mountain views that you wouldn't otherwise have. And it's interesting to watch the forest grow back year by year: dense undergrowth, wildflowers, and young trees now cover the area that in 2004 was nothing but gray ash and blackened tree trunks.

If you want to camp nearby, Sheep Springs Horse Camp is not far away. See the Sheep Springs chapter for more information.

The trails near Santiam Pass provide amazing mountain views.

Santiam Pass Area

Directions: Santiam Pass is located about 20 miles northwest of Sisters, on Hwy. 20. For directions to the nearby trailheads, see "Finding the Trailhead" on the pages for each trail.

Elevation: 4,800 feet

Camping: The nearest horse camping facilities are at Sheep Springs Horse Camp. See the Sheep Springs chapter for more information.

Facilities: See "Facilities" on the pages for each trail

Permits: See "Permits" on the pages for each trail

Season: Summer through fall

Contact: For information about the Old Summit and Square/Round Lake Trails, contact the Sisters Ranger District: 541-549-7700
For information about the Patjens Lake Trail, contact the McKenzie Ranger District: 541-822-3381
For information about the Santiam Lake Trail contact the Detroit Ranger District: 503-854-3366

Santiam Pass Trails

Trail	Difficulty	Elevation	Round Trip
Old Summit Trail	Moderate	4,750-5,400	15 miles
Patjens Lake Loop	Moderate	4,400-4,800	6 miles
Santiam Lake	Moderate	4,850-5,450	12 miles
Square & Round Lakes	Moderate	4,300-5,000	9.5 miles

Getting to Santiam Pass Trailheads

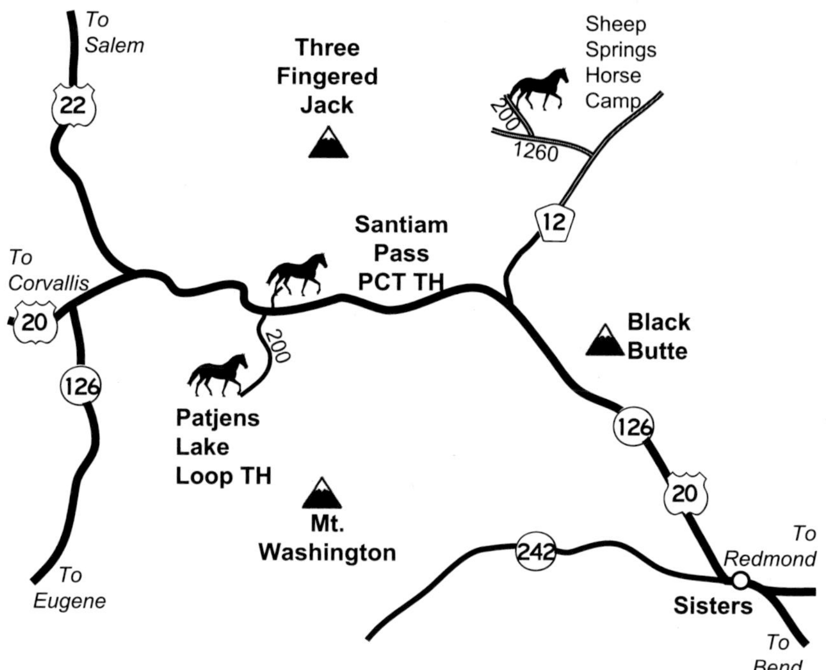

Debbie rides Split beneath Three Fingered Jack on the Santiam Lake Trail.

Old Summit Trail

Trailhead: Start at the Santiam Pass Trailhead for the Pacific Crest Trail

Length: 15 miles round trip

Elevation: 4,750 to 5,400 feet

Difficulty: Moderate

Footing: Hoof protection recommended

Season: Summer through fall

Permits: Northwest Forest Pass required

Facilities: Toilet, hitching posts, parking for several trailers. Stock water is available on the trail.

Highlights: The Old Summit Trail used to be a beautifully forested ride across a shoulder of Three Fingered Jack, but the 2003 B&B fire changed all that. On the entire 7.5-mile trail, you won't see more than a couple hundred full-size living trees. The underbrush is back,

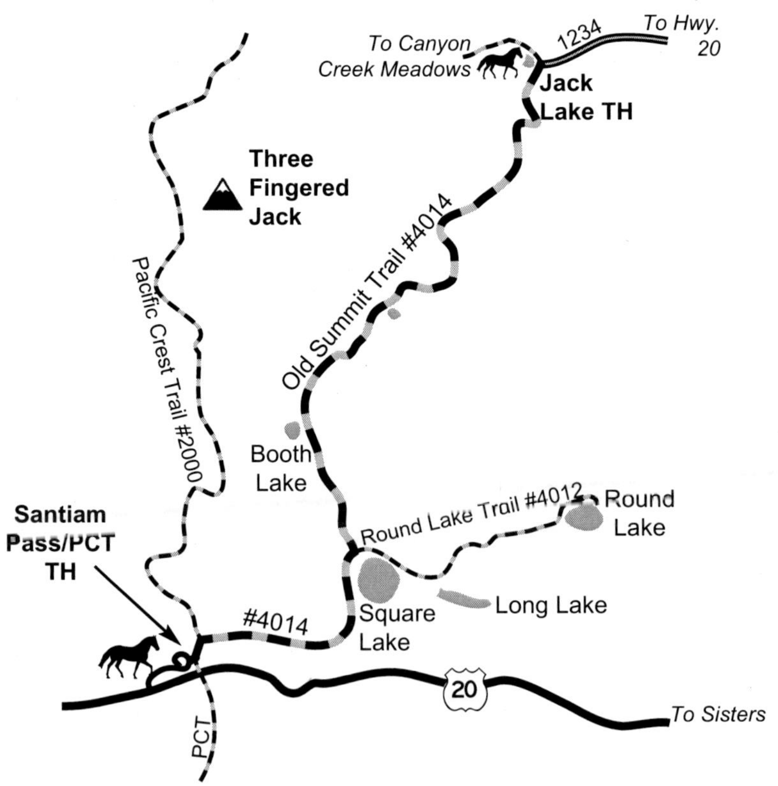

though, and young trees are flourishing. Silvery tree trunks now frame views of Mt. Washington, the North and Middle Sisters, Broken Top, Black Crater, Black Butte, and Three Fingered Jack.

Finding the Santiam Pass PCT Trailhead: From Sisters, drive northwest on Hwy. 20 for 19 miles. Turn right at the Santiam Pass trailhead for the Pacific Crest Trail (PCT), and drive 0.4 mile to the parking area.

The Ride: Pick up the trail next to the kiosk on the east side of the parking loop and turn left on the PCT. After 0.2 mile, turn right on the Old Summit Trail #4014 (aka the Summit Lakes Trail) toward Square Lake and Jack Lake. In 2 miles you'll come to Square Lake. Ride along the lake for 0.2 mile and turn left at the junction with the Round Lake Trail #4012. About 1.5 miles later, you'll pass Booth Lake. Continue another 3.8 miles to reach Jack Lake. Retrace your steps to return to the trailhead.

Three Fingered Jack is reflected in a tiny unnamed lake along the trail.

Through the trees burned in the B&B fire, you'll get great views of North & Middle Sister and Mt. Washington.

Patjens Lakes Loop

Trailhead: Start at Patjens Lake Trailhead
Length: 6 miles round trip
Elevation: 4,400 to 4,800 feet
Difficulty: Moderate
Footing: Hoof protection recommended
Season: Summer through fall
Permits: None
Facilities: Toilet and potable water at nearby Big Lake Campground. Parking for 2-3 trailers at the trailhead. Stock water is available on the trail.

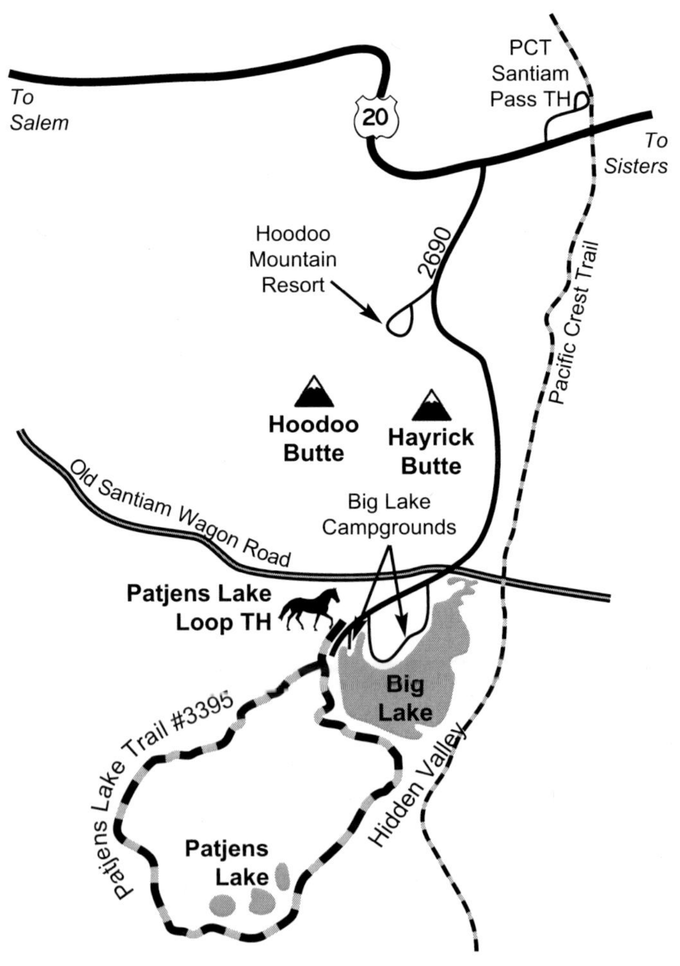

Connie on Princess, Lydia on Shadow, and Teresa on Jane, at the Patjens Lakes.

Highlights: This is a fun forested loop ride that provides good views of Big Lake and the tiny Patjens Lakes. In late June and early July it features more blooming bear grass than any other trail in Central Oregon.

Finding the Patjens Lake Loop Trailhead: From Sisters, drive northwest on Highway 20 for 19 miles. At Santiam Pass, turn left on Road 2690 toward Hoodoo Ski Area and Big Lake. Continue toward Big Lake for 3.7 miles. Drive past the first Big Lake campground and park in the trailhead parking area on the right, just outside the second campground.

The Ride: Head south from the trailhead. The trail forks after about 0.3 mile. Take the left fork, which follows the shore of Big Lake and goes through Hidden Valley, turns west and passes Patjens Lake, then loops north over a ridge and back to the trailhead. The bear grass is at its most beautiful in late June and early July. Unfortunately, that's when the mosquitoes are hungriest, and both Bug Lake -- oops, I mean Big Lake -- and Patjens Lake produce a bumper crop of them. Be sure to slather yourself and your horse with mosquito repellent if riding early in the season.

Santiam Lake

Trailhead: Start at the Santiam Pass Trailhead for the Pacific Crest Trail

Length: 12 miles round trip

Elevation: 4,850 to 5,450 feet

Difficulty: Moderate

Footing: Hoof protection recommended

Season: Summer through fall

Permits: Northwest Forest Pass required

Facilities: Toilet, hitching rails, and parking for several trailers. Stock water is available on the trail.

Highlights: This absolute gem of a ride is mostly on the west side of the Cascades, so technically speaking it may not be in Central Oregon. But it starts in Central Oregon, so that counts, right? The trail takes you through the area burned by the B&B fire, with impressive

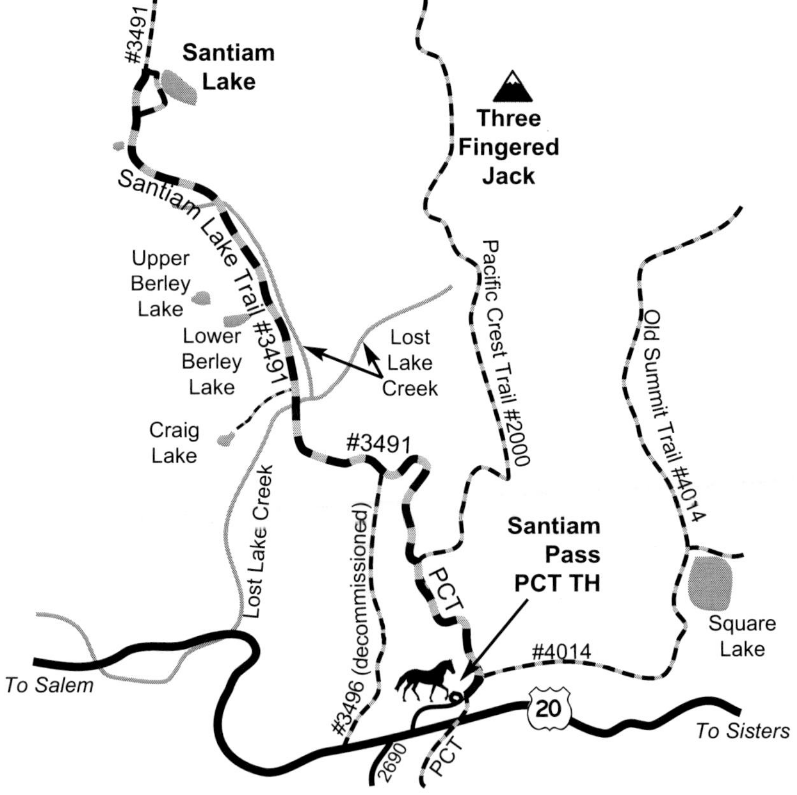

views of the Cascade peaks to the south. Next it goes through dense fir and hemlock forest to the shore of beautiful Santiam Lake. Be sure to do this ride on a clear day, because the reflection of Three Fingered Jack in the lake is stunning.

Finding the Santiam Pass PCT Trailhead: From Sisters, drive northwest on Hwy. 20 for 19 miles. Turn right at the Santiam Pass Trailhead for the Pacific Crest Trail (PCT), and drive 0.4 mile to the parking area.

The Ride: Pick up the trail next to the kiosk on the east end of the parking loop, and turn left on the PCT. In 0.2 mile, the Old Summit Trail #4014 goes off to the right. Stay to the left on the PCT, and in 1 mile turn left on the Santiam Lake Trail #3491 toward Santiam Lake. In another mile you'll reach the unsigned junction with the decommissioned Trail #3496. Veer right to stay on Trail #3491. In about 0.5 mile an unsigned user trail goes off to the left to Craig Lake. Stay to the right, and for the next 2 miles you'll ride beside Lost Lake Creek (dry in late summer). Not long after leaving the creek, you'll see a pretty little unnamed lake on the left. Ride 0.3 mile farther and watch for an unsigned trail on the right that will take you downhill to Santiam Lake. (The lake is not visible from the main trail.) Walk along the lake shore, and you'll find several other spur trails that will return you to the Santiam Lake Trail. Turn left to return to the trailhead.

Three Fingered Jack reflected in Santiam Lake.

Square and Round Lakes

Trailhead: Start at the Santiam Pass Trailhead for the Pacific Crest Trail
Length: 9.5 miles round trip
Elevation: 4,300 to 5,000 feet
Difficulty: Moderate
Footing: Suitable for barefoot horses
Season: Summer through fall
Permits: Northwest Forest Pass required
Facilities: Toilet, hitching rails, and parking for several trailers. Stock water is available on the trail.

Highlights: The Round Lake Trail follows the Old Summit Trail to Square Lake, then branches off to Round Lake. The entire ride is within the area burned by the B&B fire in 2003. While the black and silver skeletons of the burned trees remain, the forest is regenerating. Underbrush is plentiful, and juvenile lodgepole pines are growing. Plus, the trail now offers mountain views that were formerly obscured by the forest.

Finding the Santiam Pass PCT Trailhead: From Sisters, drive northwest about 19 miles on Highway 20. Turn right at the Santiam Pass Trailhead for the Pacific Crest Trail (PCT), and drive 0.4 mile to the parking area.

The Ride: Pick up the trail next to the kiosk on the east end of the parking loop and turn left on the PCT. In 0.2 mile, turn right on the

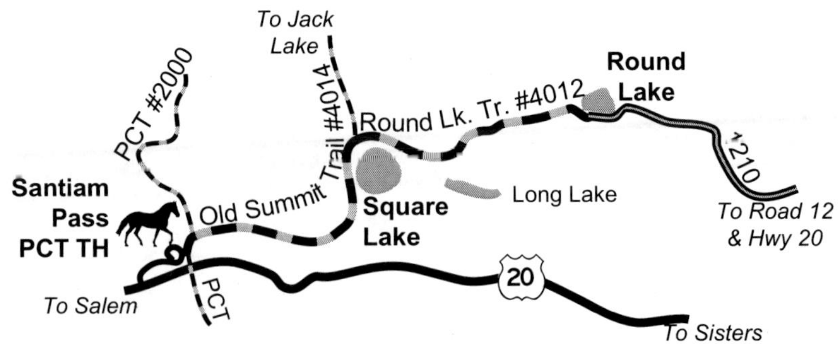

Suzanne and Skipper travel past Square Lake.

Old Summit Trail #4014 (aka the Summit Lakes Trail). In another 2 miles you'll reach Square Lake. After following the lake shore for 0.2 mile, the Old Summit Trail turns left and heads toward Jack Lake, while the Round Lake Trail #4012 goes straight ahead. Go straight, and in 0.1 mile you'll reach a good place to take your horse down to Square Lake for a drink. Continue on the trail for 2 more miles to reach Round Lake. The trail ends at the hiker trailhead at Round Lake, at the end of Road 1210. Unfortunately, there isn't a trail to the shore of Round Lake.

Suzanne rides Skipper through the silvery tree trunks along the trail.

Debbie and Split at Santiam Lake,
with Broken Top in the background.

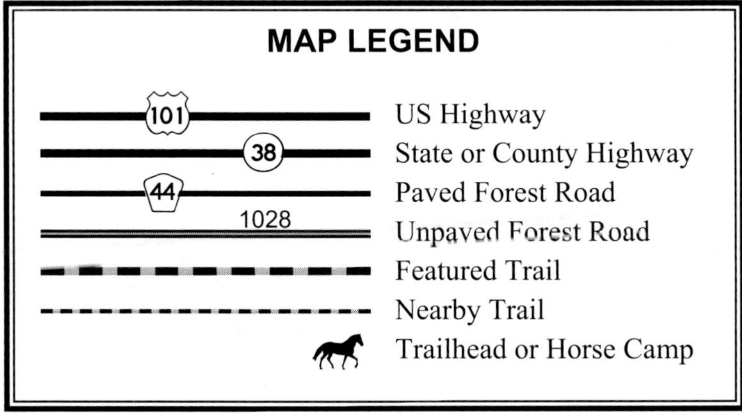

Sheep Springs Horse Camp

Deschutes National Forest

Sheep Springs Horse Camp lies in the Metolius Basin northwest of Sisters, a park-like area flanked by Mt. Jefferson to the north, Black Butte to the south, Green Ridge to the east, and Three Fingered Jack to the west. From Sheep Springs Horse Camp, you can ride several fun loops that run on the Metolius-Windigo Trail (which runs the entire length of the Deschutes National Forest and is signed with yellow trail-blazer diamonds on the trees), nearby forest roads, and a couple of other trails. Several trails in this chapter travel through areas torched by the B&B fire, opening up impressive mountain views that the forest once hid.

The Metolius Basin chapter of this book covers other nearby trails that are accessible from trailheads located a few miles from Sheep Springs.

Gayla and Jane on Dusty and Champ, enjoying the view of Broken Top, on the trail near Sheep Springs Horse Camp.

Getting to Sheep Springs

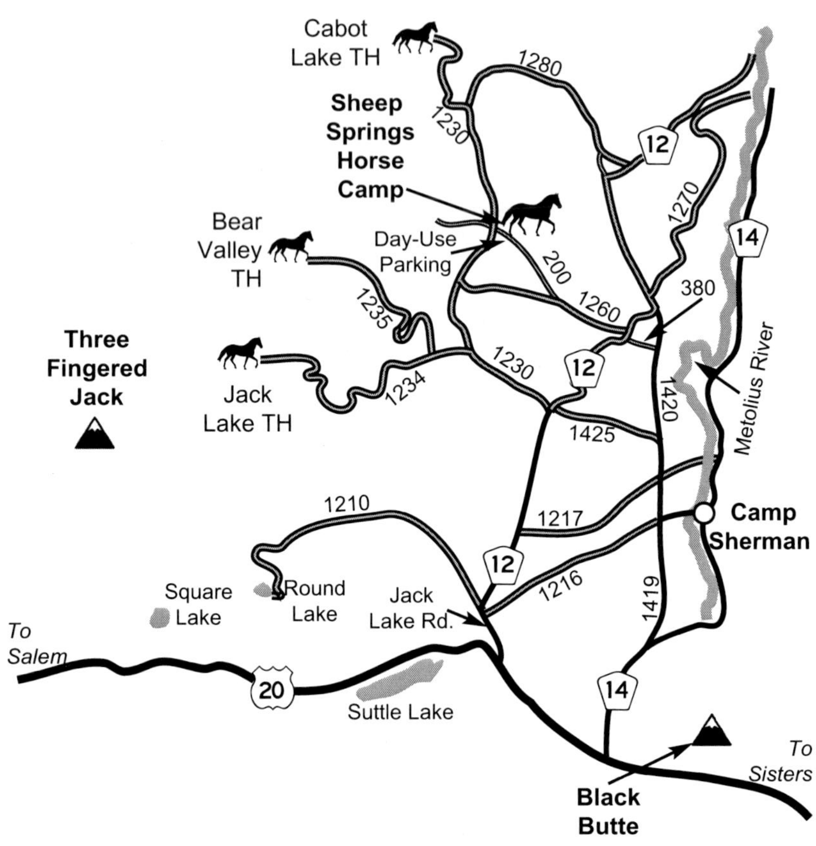

Sheep Springs Area Trails

Trail	Difficulty	Elevation	Round Trip
Bear Valley	Moderate	3,100-4,200	10 miles
Brush Creek Loop	Easy	2,900-3,200	6 miles
Camp Loops	Easy	3,150-3,500	1-3 miles
Camp Sherman	Moderate	2,950-3,300	17 miles
Head of Jack Creek	Moderate	3,000-3,200	11 miles
Metolius River Loop	Moderate	2,900-3,250	9.5 miles
Shovel Loop	Moderate	3,000-3,600	7 miles

Sheep Springs Horse Camp

Directions: From Sisters, drive northwest on Hwy. 20 for 12 miles. Turn right on Jack Lake Road (Road 12) and continue for 6.8 miles, then turn left on Road 1260. Drive about 1.0 mile, turn right on Road 200, and continue another 1.4 miles to the horse camp. The route is well signed. Day riders can park in an unofficial turnout along Road 200, on the left about 0.3 mile before the horse camp.

Elevation: 3,200 feet

Campsites: 11 sites with 4-horse log corrals. A couple are pull-through; the rest are back-in. Most sites have room for 2 vehicles.

Facilities: Vault toilet, manure bins, potable water, garbage cans. All sites have fire pits and picnic tables.

Permits: Camping fee. Reservations required. No fee if you park at the turnout on the left, 0.3 miles before the horse camp.

Season: May to October

Contact: Sisters Ranger District: 541-549-7700
Concessionaire: 541-338-786
Reservations: 877-444-6777 or www.recreation.gov.

Sheep Springs Horse Camp has log corrals that are nicely shaded by huge firs and ponderosas.

Bear Valley

Trailhead: Start at Sheep Springs Horse Camp
Length: 10 miles round trip
Elevation: 3,100 to 4,200 feet
Difficulty: Moderate
Footing: Hoof protection recommended
Season: Summer through fall
Permits: Camping fee at Sheep Springs. No fee to park at the turnout beside Road 200 about 0.3 mile before Sheep Springs.
Facilities: Toilets, potable water, and manure bins at the horse camp. Parking for 3-4 trailers at the turnout beside Road 200. Stock water is available on the trail.

Highlights: This ride follows the Metolius-Windigo Trail from Sheep Springs Horse Camp to the Bear Valley Trailhead, the jumping-off point for the Rockpile Lake Trail (covered in the Metolius Basin chapter). The trail runs in and out of the area burned by the B&B fire, and the contrast between the shade of the unburned forest and the sunny, brushy burned areas is remarkable. You will enjoy filtered views of the mountains along the way.

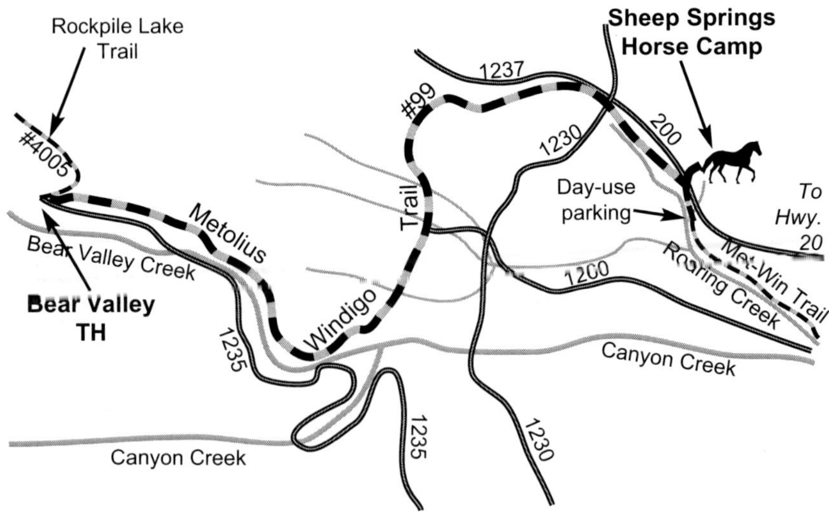

The Ride: Pick up the Metolius-Windigo Trail #99 directly across Road 200 from the entrance to the camp. Ride about 100 feet and veer right on the Met-Win. The trail is marked with yellow diamonds. The last 2 miles of the trail traverse a ridge above Bear Valley Creek on an old roadbed. Some of the trail goes through forest and grassy meadows, and some goes through burned areas with little shade but nice views of the mountains, the Metolius Basin, and Green Ridge.

Connie and Moose travel through the burned area on the way to Bear Valley Trailhead.

Jane follows the Metolius-Windigo Trail through a forested area unscathed by the fire.

Brush Creek Loop

Trailhead: Start at Sheep Springs Horse Camp

Length: 6 miles round trip

Elevation: 2,900 to 3,200 feet

Difficulty: Easy

Footing: Hoof protection suggested

Season: Summer through fall

Permits: Camping fee at Sheep Springs. No fee to park at the turnout beside Road 200 about 0.3 mile before Sheep Springs.

Facilities: Toilets, potable water, and manure bins at the horse camp. Parking for 3-4 trailers at the turnout beside Road 200. Stock water is available on the trail.

Highlights: This ride follows dirt roads and user-created trails outbound along Brush Creek, and then follows the Metolius-Windigo Trail beside Canyon Creek and Roaring Creek for the homeward leg of the loop. Most of the ride runs through open ponderosa pine forest carpeted in grass and seasonal wildflowers. There's plenty of shade,

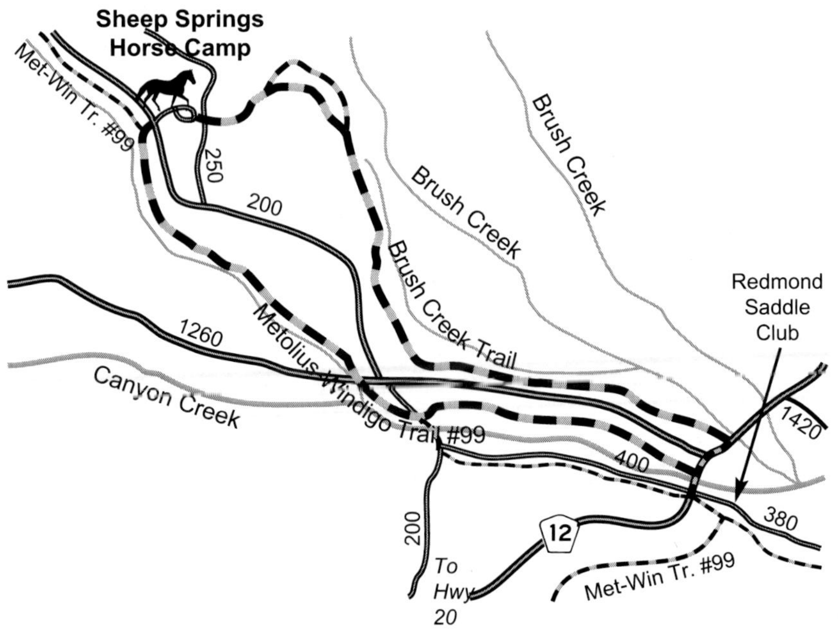

Judi on Tray, Diana on Tommy, and Suzanne on Skipper, heading out on the trail along Brush Creek.

and you'll have multiple opportunities to water your horse along the way.

The Ride: Pick up the trail heading east out of Sheep Springs Horse Camp, between sites 8 and 9. It crosses Road 250, and after 0.4 mile, you can either go up a low hill or skirt around the base of it. If you go up on the hill, be sure to look behind you and to your left for good views of Mt. Jefferson and Three Fingered Jack. In another 0.3 mile, the trail comes down the hill and veers to the right on an old forest road that soon becomes a single-track. For the next 2 miles, the trail parallels a tributary of Brush Creek, and later, the creek itself. You can't miss the thick brush and young trees along the boggy shore of the creek — quite a contrast with the open ponderosa forest you're traveling through. After you've traveled along the creek for about a mile, you'll be riding on the north side of red cinder Road 1260. After a mile, the Brush Creek Trail ends at Road 12. Turn right here and ride along or beside Road 12 for 0.2 mile. Just before Road 12 crosses the bridge over Canyon Creek, turn right on the Metolius-Windigo Trail. Follow the Met-Win for 3 miles back to the horse camp.

Camp Loops

Trailhead: Start at Sheep Springs Horse Camp

Length: 1.0 mile round trip for South Loop; 1.4 mile round trip for Middle Loop; 3.2 miles round trip for North Loop

Elevation: 3,150 to 3,200 feet for South Loop; 3,200 to 3,300 feet for Middle Loop; 3,200 to 3,500 feet for North Loop

Difficulty: Easy

Footing: Hoof protection recommended on the North Loop

Season: Spring through late fall

Permits: Camping fee at Sheep Springs. No fee to park at the turnout beside Road 200 about 0.3 mile before Sheep Springs.

Facilities: Toilets, potable water, and manure bins at the horse camp. Parking for 3-4 trailers at the turnout beside Road 200. No stock water on the trail.

Highlights: If you'd like to do some fun road rides not far from camp, you have 3 easy loops to choose from. The middle and south loops

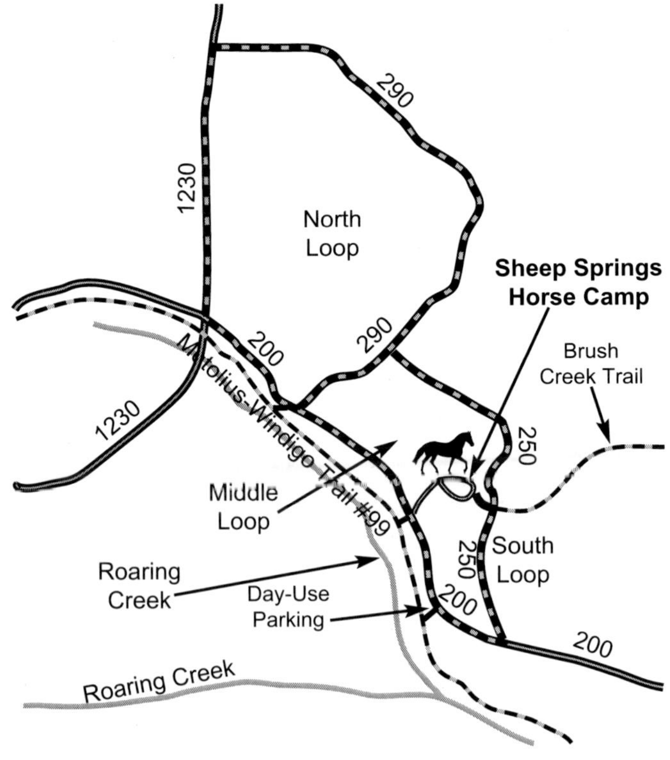

simply circle around the ends of the camp, and you can vary the routes depending on whether you ride the Metolius-Windigo Trail or simply follow Road 200. The northern loop is longer, rockier, and follows a rougher and more overgrown road, but it offers amazing views of Mt. Jefferson, Three Fingered Jack, Mt. Washington, Broken Top, the Three Sisters, Black Butte, and Green Ridge.

The Ride: All Loops, pick up the trail that leads east out of camp between sites 8 and 9. Ride 200 feet to the intersection with Road 250. South Loop: turn right on Road 250 and follow it 0.3 mile to Road 200. Turn right on Road 200, and either follow it 0.4 mile back to the horse camp, or ride the road for 0.2 mile, then veer left at the day-use parking area and follow the Met-Win back to camp. Middle Loop: turn left on Road 250 and ride 0.5 mile to Road 290. Turn left and continue 0.3 mile, then turn left on Road 200 to return to the horse camp. Or, turn right on Road 200 and in 500 feet turn left to pick up the Met-Win to return to the camp. North Loop: turn left on Road 250 and ride 0.5 mile to Road 290. Turn right and follow Road 290 for 1.1 miles. It goes through the area burned by the B&B Fire, which opened up amazing views of the surrounding mountains. When Road 290 intersects with the wide red cinder Road 1230, turn left on it and ride 0.7 mile. Turn left on Road 200 and follow it 0.6 mile to the horse camp, or continue straight ahead on Road 1230 for 200 feet more, then turn left on the Met-Win to return to camp.

Laurie and Diana ride Jonny and Tommy on the North Loop, with Mt. Jefferson on the horizon.

Camp Sherman

Trailhead: Start at Sheep Springs Horse Camp
Length: 17 miles round trip
Elevation: 2,950 to 3,300 feet
Difficulty: Moderate — several water crossings
Footing: Suitable for barefoot horses
Season: Spring through late fall
Permits: Camping fee at Sheep Springs. No fee to park at the turnout beside Road 200 about 0.3 mile before Sheep Springs.
Facilities: Toilets, potable water, and manure bins at the horse camp. Parking for 3-4 trailers at the turnout beside Road 200. Stock water is available on the trail.

Highlights: This section of the Metolius-Windigo Trail explores the park-like forest, meadows, and creeks of the beautiful Metolius Basin.

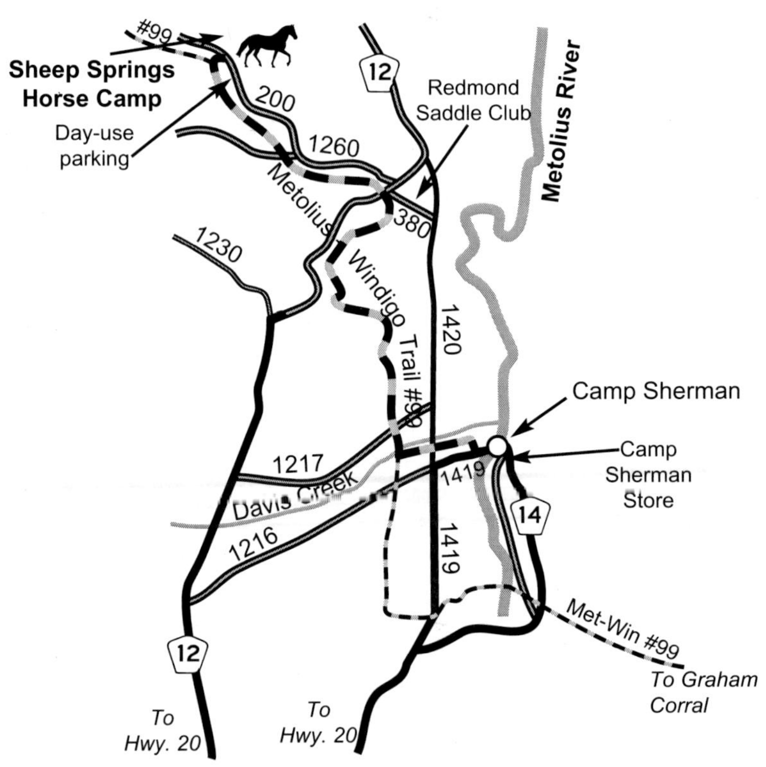

torrent of water out of a hillside, instantly creating a good-sized creek. Along the way to the headwaters, you'll experience the grandeur of the open ponderosa pine forest that covers the Metolius Basin. On a hot summer day, the smell of the pines is intoxicating.

The Ride: From Sheep Springs Horse Camp, ride out to Road 200, cross it, and veer left on the Metolius-Windigo Trail. Follow it beside Roaring Creek for 1.4 miles, cross Road 1260, and continue 0.4 mile. After you pass a couple of dispersed campsites on your right, turn right off the Met-Win Trail and cross Canyon Creek. Follow the trail away from the creek, and when it forks in 200 feet, veer right on Road 200. Follow it 1.2 miles. When you begin traveling along the dense stand of fir trees on your left that mark the bank of Jack Creek, the road will go through a dry wash carved by a seasonal creek. Immediately veer left off the road, and in 50 feet turn right on the trail that runs beside Jack Creek. Note this spot, so you can find it on your return. Continue 0.6 mile, cross Road 1230 next to the bridge, and for the next 0.5 mile you'll be riding past Jack Creek Campground. At the far end of the campground, pick up the Head of Jack Creek Trail #4016 and ride 1.3 miles to the Jack Creek headwaters. Surely, if fairy folk exist, some of them live in this special place. Retrace your steps to return to Sheep Springs.

Ann on Comfort and Tony on Raven, riding beneath the huge ponderosas and Douglas-firs near the headwaters of Jack Creek.

Metolius River Loop

Trailhead: Start at Sheep Springs Horse Camp
Length: 9.5 miles round trip
Elevation: 2,900 to 3,250 feet
Difficulty: Moderate
Footing: Hoof protection suggested
Season: Summer through fall
Permits: Camping fee at Sheep Springs. No fee to park at the turnout beside Road 200 about 0.3 mile before Sheep Springs.
Facilities: Toilets, potable water, and manure bins at the horse camp. Parking for 3-4 trailers at the turnout beside Road 200. Stock water is available on the trail.

Highlights: You have several options for doing this ride, depending on whether you choose to follow the Metolius-Windigo Trail, the Brush Creek Trail, or the trail beside Road 400. Regardless of the route you choose, you'll follow the bank of pretty Canyon Creek to its confluence with the Metolius River, ride along the river for awhile, then loop back to Sheep Springs.

The Ride: Brush Creek Route: Pick up the trail heading east between campsites 8 and 9, and follow the trail 2.9 miles to its end at Road 12. Turn right and ride beside Road 12 for 0.2 mile. Cross Canyon Creek on the Road 12 bridge, then turn left on Road 380 and immediately

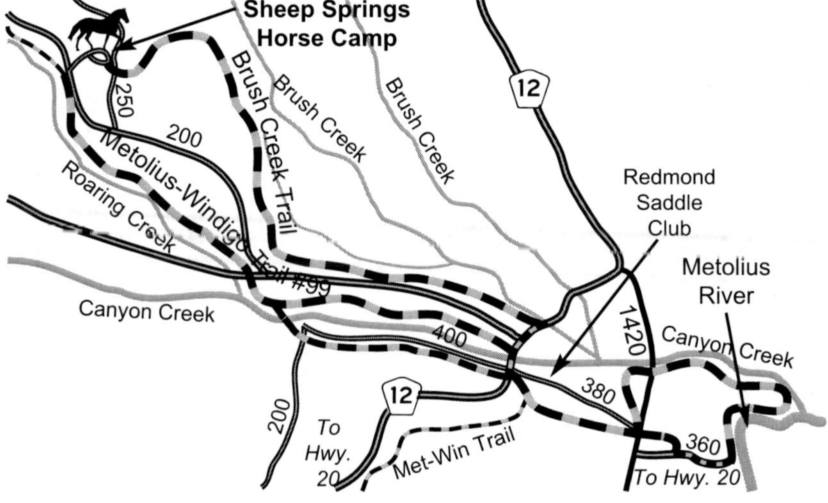

Merriane and Hoot saunter along the Metolius River.

veer right on the Metolius-Windigo Trail. <u>Metolius-Windigo Route:</u> Go out Sheep Springs' main entrance, cross Road 200, and veer left on the Met-Win Trail. Follow it for 2.7 miles. Cross Canyon Creek on the Road 12 bridge, then turn left on Road 380 and pick up the Met-Win again on the right. <u>Road 400 Route:</u> Go out Sheep Springs' main entrance, cross Road 200, and veer left on the Met-Win Trail. Follow it for 1.7 miles. Turn right off the Met-Win, ford Canyon Creek, and veer left to pick up the trail to the right of Road 400. Continue 1.0 mile, cross Road 12, go straight on Road 380, then immediately veer right on the Met-Win Trail. <u>All Routes:</u> Ride the Met-Win for 0.2 mile, heading up a hill. At the top, the Met-Win makes a sharp right turn. Instead, you'll turn left on an unsigned trail, and follow it for 0.5 mile. Just before you reach paved Road 1420, turn left on an unsigned trail, cross Road 380, and on the northwest corner of Roads 1420 and 380, pick up an unsigned single-track. Follow it 0.4 mile, cross Road 1420, and ride along the bank of Canyon Creek. In 0.8 mile, you'll reach the creek's confluence with the Metolius River. The trail veers right and follows the river 0.4 mile, to a picnic table. Continue on Road 360 for 0.3 mile, then veer right on an unsigned single-track. It will take you across Road 1420 and back to the junction with the Met-Win at the top of the hill. Veer right on the Met-Win, and when you reach Road 12, take the return route of your choice.

Shovel Loop

Trailhead: Start at Sheep Springs Horse Camp

Length: 7 miles round trip

Elevation: 3,000 to 3,600 feet

Difficulty: Moderate

Footing: Hoof protection recommended

Season: Summer through fall

Permits: Camping fee at Sheep Springs. No fee to park at the turnout beside Road 200 about 0.3 mile before Sheep Springs.

Facilities: Toilets, potable water, and manure bins at the horse camp. Parking for 3-4 trailers at the turnout beside Road 200. Stock water is available on the trail.

Highlights: This scenic ride got its name several years ago when a fellow rider found a camping shovel while riding this route. It was a nice shovel, so she picked it up to carry it home. After several more miles, her horse noticed the shovel for the first time, spooked hard, and dumped the rider. Her friends couldn't stop laughing, and it's been called the Shovel Loop ever since. The loop follows the Metolius-Windigo Trail, then veers off it and follows forest roads through beau-

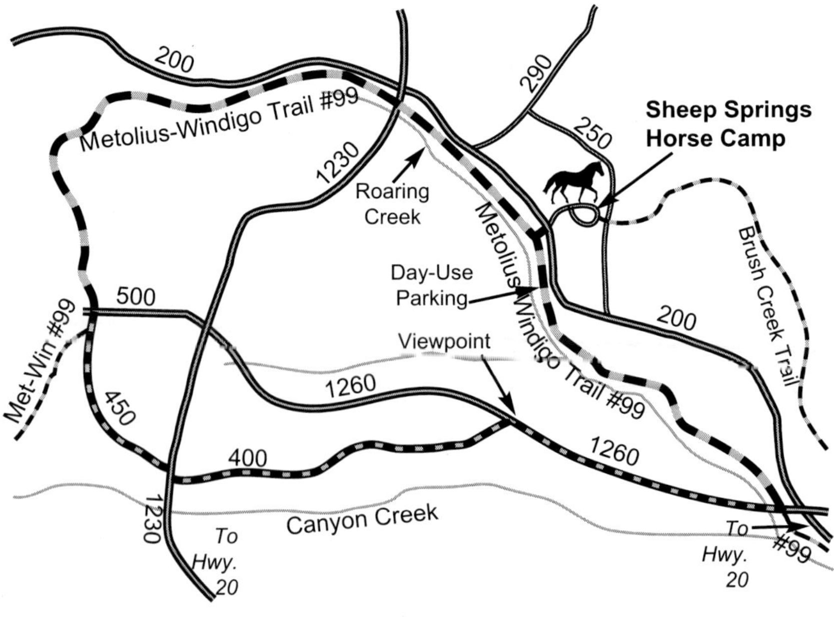

Diana, Suzanne, and Judi, on Tommy, Skipper, and Tray, taking a break in a meadow along the Shovel Loop, with Mt. Jefferson in the background.

tiful forest and past grassy meadows before hooking back into the Met-Win to return to camp. Don't miss the Kodak-moment view of Mt. Jefferson from the meadow beside Road 1260.

The Ride: Ride out the entrance to Sheep Springs, cross Road 200, and turn right on the Metolius-Windigo Trail. Follow it for 2.5 miles. The Met-Win crosses gravel Road 500 (notice the rock barricade across the end of the road on your right) and starts down Road 450, then immediately veers off the road to the right, but you'll go straight ahead and follow Road 450 for 0.7 mile. When the road ends at a junction with gravel Road 1230, jog to the right and immediately turn left on Road 400. It takes you through an impressive corridor of firs and tamaracks as it parallels Canyon Creek. In 1.1 mile, Road 400 ends at Road 1260. You'll turn right on Road 1260, but first ride straight ahead out into the meadow for a good view of Mt. Jefferson. Return to Road 1260 and follow it 0.9 mile. Immediately after the road crosses Roaring Creek, turn right on the Metolius-Windigo Trail. In 1.1 miles you'll pass the day-use parking area, and 0.3 mile after that you'll turn right off the Met-Win, across from the entrance to the horse camp.

Diana on Tommy and Laurie on Jonny,
on one of the Camp Loops near Sheep Springs.

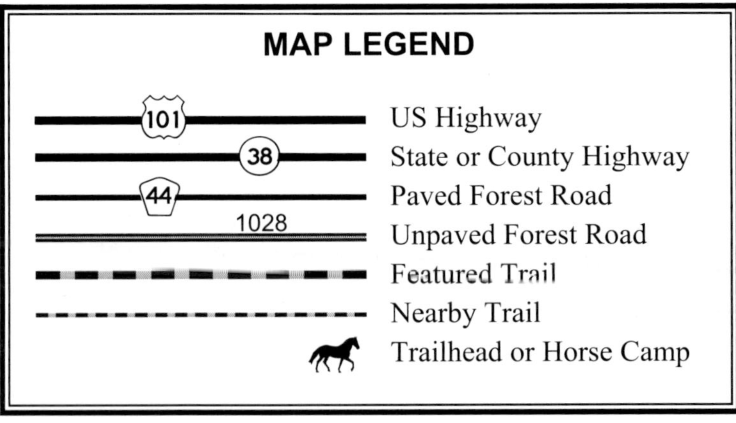

Sisters Cow Camp

Deschutes National Forest

Sisters Cow Camp, near the town of Sisters, is the gateway to wonderful low- to mid-elevation riding. Some trails offer mountain views, while others are primarily in beautiful ponderosa pine forest. The historic Sisters Cow Camp, which at one time was used by ranchers to gather cows to take them off their summer range, features a vintage storage shed, large corrals, and a loading chute to remind us of its original purpose. Nowadays, Sisters Cow Camp is a popular camping area and trailhead for horseback riders. You can ride here nearly year round, and the camping is free.

Katherine, Debbie, and Suzi ride a forest road near Sisters Cow Camp, with Mt. Jefferson in the background.

Getting to Sisters Cow Camp

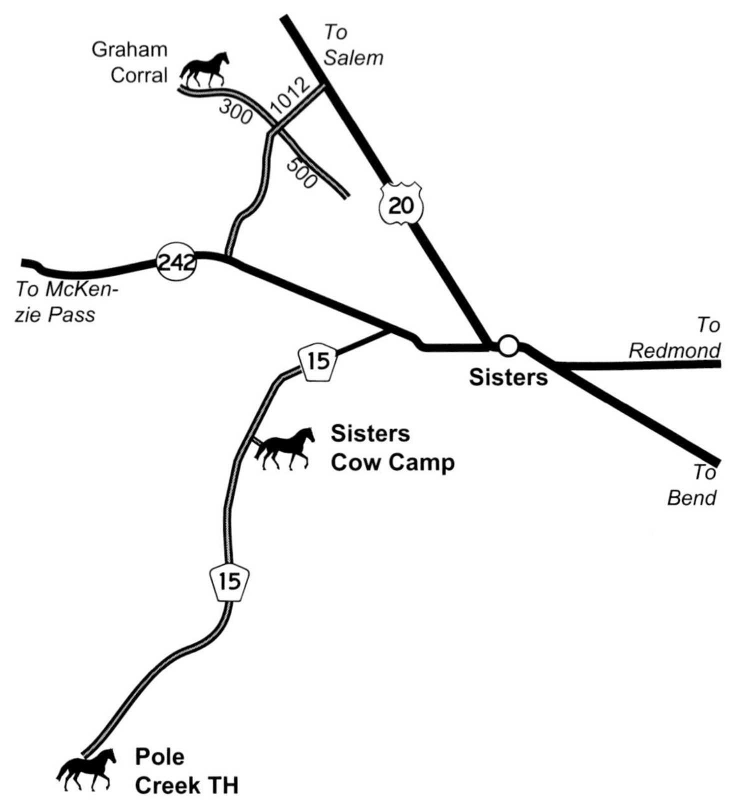

Sisters Cow Camp Trails

Trail	Difficulty	Elevation	Round Trip
Cow Camp to Sisters	Moderate	3,200-3,400	8 miles
Graham Corral	Easy	3,250-3,550	13.5 miles
Jimerson Loop	Easy	3,300-3,500	7.5 miles
Marquis Loop	Moderate	3,400-4,250	9.5-12 miles
Pole Cr. & Whychus Cr.	Moderate	3,400-3,900	7-10 miles

Sisters Cow Camp

Directions: From Sisters, drive west 1.5 miles on Hwy. 242 and turn left on Road 15, toward Pole Creek Trailhead. Continue 2.5 miles, then turn left toward Sisters Cow Camp. (The sign is on the right side of the road.) Drive 0.4 mile to reach the camp.

Elevation: 3,300 feet

Campsites: 5 campsites with fire pits and picnic tables. Level parking areas. Four large corrals in the center of camp, plus trees for highlining.

Facilities: Vault toilet, stock water in season, manure bin. Plenty of parking for day-riders.

Permits: No fee for camping or day use

Season: Spring through late fall

Contact: Sisters Ranger District, 541-549-7700

The four large corrals at Sisters Cow Camp can hold many horses.

Cow Camp to Sisters

Trailhead: Start at Sisters Cow Camp
Length: 8 miles round trip
Elevation: 3,200 to 3,400 feet
Difficulty: Moderate - some riding in traffic
Footing: Suitable for barefoot horses
Season: Early spring through late fall
Permits: None
Facilities: Toilet, stock water in season, and plenty of trailer parking at the horse camp. No stock water on the trail.

Highlights: This route links Sisters Cow Camp with the town of Sisters. The last mile of the ride runs along the side of Hwy. 242. The road shoulder is very wide so unless your horse is afraid of traffic this should not be a problem. Once you arrive in town, you can get an excellent burger or ice cream at the Sno Cap Drive-In.

The Ride: From Sisters Cow Camp, pick up the Metolius-Windigo Trail #99 on the north side of the camp and follow it 0.1 mile. At the junction with the Jimerson Trail, turn right. Follow the Jimerson Trail (signed with white diamonds on the trees) for 1.2 miles. When the trail crosses gravel Road 100, the horse trail to the Crossroads subdivision goes left along the road. Go straight, and in 0.6 mile the trail veers left

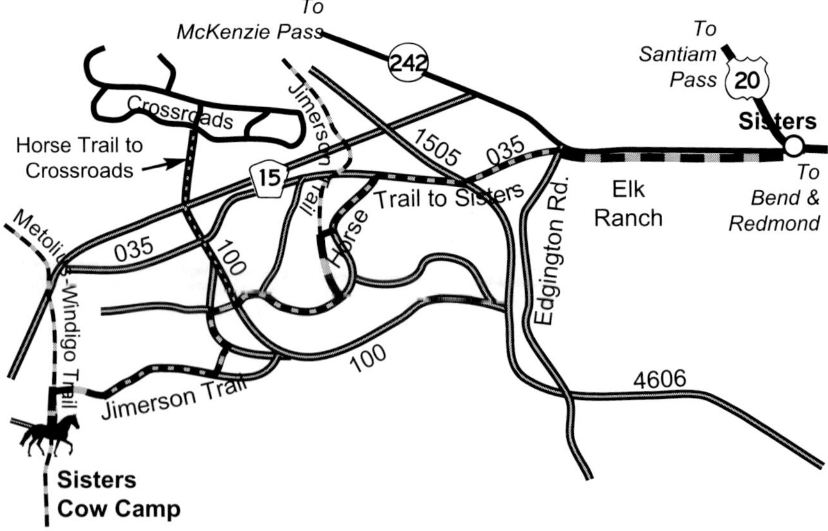

Jane cruises along the trail to Sisters.

You can ride from Cow Camp to Sisters and get a delicious burger or milkshake at the Snow Cap Drive-In.

off the road onto a single track. In another 0.3 mile you'll reach the junction sign indicating the Horse Trail to Sisters. Turn right here, and in 100 feet turn left on the dirt road. Follow it 0.3 mile and veer right on Road 035. In 0.3 mile you'll cross gravel Road 1505, which runs beside a power line. Continue 0.4 mile to the intersection of Road 035, Edgington Road, and Hwy. 242. Veer right and ride beside Hwy. 242 for 0.9 mile to Hwy. 20 in Sisters. Hwy. 20 is very busy, so from here you'll want to lead your horse. If you head to the right, in 2 blocks you'll arrive at the Sno Cap Drive-In. Across Pine St. from the Sno Cap, you'll find a stand of trees in front of the Sisters Ranger Station. You can tie your horses there while you enjoy lunch.

Graham Corral

Trailhead: Start at Sisters Cow Camp
Length: 13.5 miles round trip
Elevation: 3,250 to 3,550 feet
Difficulty: Easy
Footing: Suitable for barefoot horses
Season: Early spring through late fall
Permits: None
Facilities: Toilet, stock water in season, corrals, and plenty of trailer parking at Sisters Cow Camp. Toilet, potable water and corrals at Graham Corral.

Highlights: This is a nice forested ride on the segment of the Metolius-Windigo Trail that runs between Sisters Cow Camp and Graham Corral. The trail goes over a small ridge that offers nice moun-

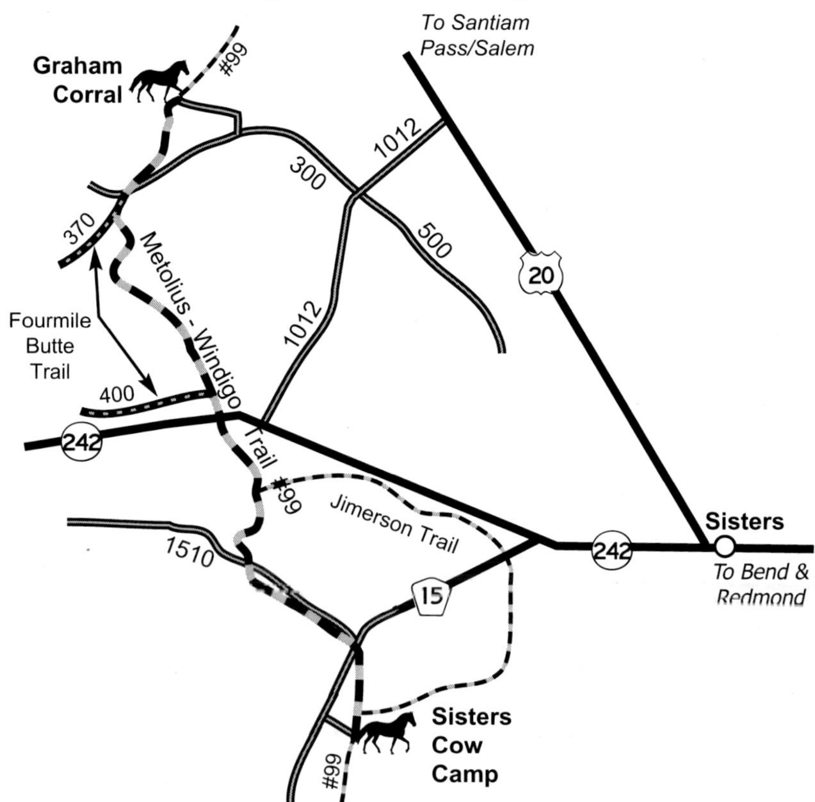

tain views through the trees. With its low elevation and easy terrain, this is a good springtime ride for getting your horse in shape for the summer riding season.

The Ride: Pick up the Metolius-Windigo Trail #99 on the north edge of Sisters Cow Camp and head north. Part of the route is on single-track trail and part is on old forest roads. The way is clearly marked with yellow diamonds. In 0.1 mile, the Jimerson Trail goes off to the right. Go straight, and in 0.5 mile you'll cross gravel Road 15 and the trail will run beside Road 1510 for 1.1 miles. Then it crosses Road 1510, and in another 0.8 mile you'll pass the second junction with the Jimerson Trail. In 1.0 mile later, you'll cross Hwy. 242. A short distance beyond the highway, the trail drops into a small grotto with interesting rock outcroppings, lots of grass, and old growth ponderosas. Not far after that, the Fourmile Butte Trail goes to the left. In another 1.8 miles, the trail goes over a low ridge that offers nice mountain views to the west. After descending from the ridge, you'll reach the second Fourmile Butte junction. Veer right here, and in 1.0 mile you'll reach Graham Corral.

Connie on Diamond, Lydia on Shadow, and Debbie on Mel, on the way to Graham Corral.

Jimerson Loop

Trailhead: Start at Sisters Cow Camp
Length: 7.5 miles round trip
Elevation: 3,300 to 3,500 feet
Difficulty: Easy
Footing: Suitable for barefoot horses
Season: Early spring through late fall
Permits: None
Facilities: Toilet, stock water in season, and plenty of trailer parking at the horse camp. No stock water on the trail.

Highlights: The Jimerson Trail was named in honor of Don and Gerry Jimerson, who for decades have led volunteer efforts to maintain Sisters Cow Camp and about 20 miles of the Metolius-Windigo Trail. The Jimerson Trail loops out from the Metolius-Windigo Trail following a mixture of single-track trails and dirt forest roads, and is suitable for green horses and riders.

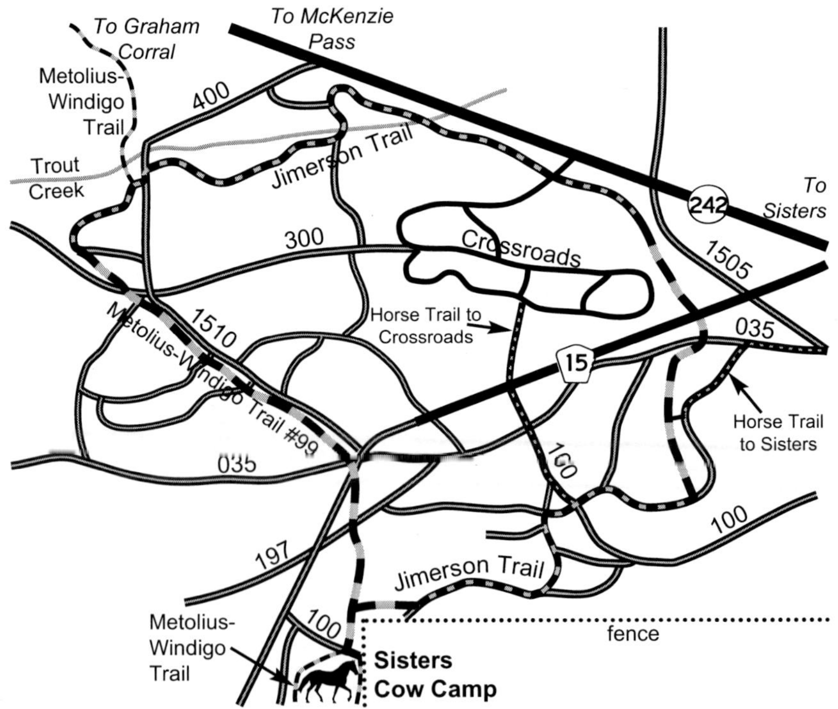

Suzanne, Paige, and Wendy ride Marilyn, Ricky, and Lacey along the Jimerson Trail

The Ride: From Sisters Cow Camp, pick up the Metolius-Windigo Trail #99 on the north side of camp and follow it 0.1 mile. At the junction with the Jimerson Trail, turn right. Follow the Jimerson Trail (signed with white diamonds on the trees) for 1.9 miles, and when the Horse Trail to Sisters goes off to the right, go straight. In another 0.5 mile the trail crosses paved Road 15 and begins skirting around the Crossroads subdivision. In 0.8 mile it crosses the paved entrance road to Crossroads. About 0.7 mile after that, the trail crosses Trout Creek (which is usually dry in the summer), then in 0.4 mile it crosses it a second time. In 0.7 mile, the trail crosses wide gravel Road 400, and 0.1 mile after that it intersects with the Metolius-Windigo Trail. Turn left on the Met-Win and follow the yellow diamonds on the trees for 1.7 miles to where it crosses gravel Road 15. About 0.5 mile later, you'll pass the junction where you turned onto the Jimerson Trail. Go straight, and in 0.1 mile you'll arrive back at Sisters Cow Camp.

Marquis Loop

Trailhead: Start at Sisters Cow Camp

Length: 9.5 miles or 12 miles round trip

Elevation: 3,400 to 4,250 feet

Difficulty: Moderate -- most of this ride is on unsigned trails and forest roads, so a Sisters Ranger District map and a GPS will be helpful

Footing: Hoof protection recommended

Season: Early spring through late fall

Permits: None

Facilities: Toilet, stock water in season, corrals, and plenty of trailer parking at Sisters Cow Camp

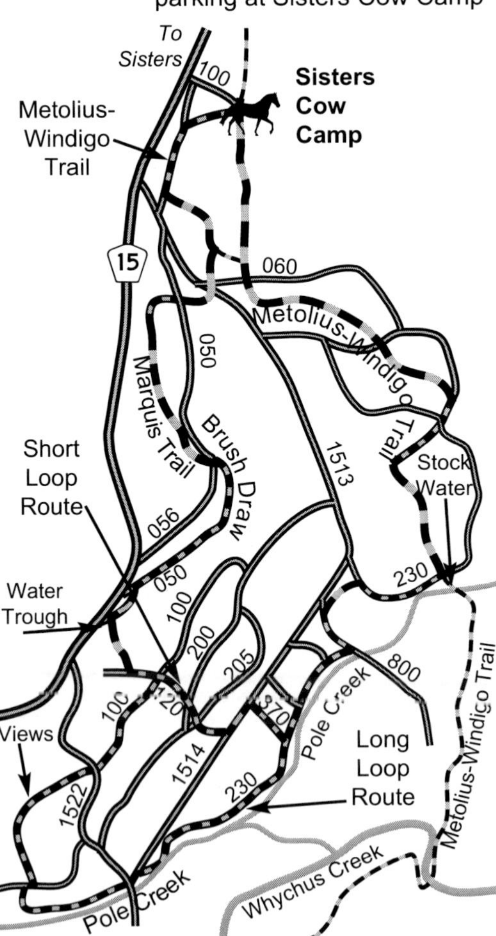

Highlights: Pat and Rhonda Marquis created this fun loop for Oregon Equestrian Trails' annual fund-raising ride for St. Jude's Children's Hospital. You can ride either a long loop or a shorter one. Both loops travel along the bank of pretty Pole Creek, and the long loop offers good views of the Three Sisters. The 2017 Milli Fire burned through this area, but as this book went to press we had little information about the extent of the damage near the trails, so please contact the Forest Service for an update.

The Ride: Pick up the Metolius-Windigo

Trail just west of the entrance to the horse camp. Follow the yellow diamonds for one mile, then as the trail goes up a low hill, veer right on the unsigned single-track Marquis Trail. In 0.5 mile, the trail crosses red cinder Road 050 and begins traveling along a dirt road. Using a combination of single-track trail and forest roads (including Road 050), the Marquis Trail takes you up through Brush Draw to a large dispersed campsite with a water trough in it. After watering your horse, backtrack a short distance and turn right on a trail that takes you up a steep hill, then along overgrown Road 120. At the junction of Roads 120 and 100, you can go straight if you want to do the short loop. To do the longer loop, turn right on Road 100. In 0.6 mile the road intersects gravel Road 1522. The forest on the other side of Road 1522 was burned in the 2012 Pole Creek Fire. Jog to your right on Road 1522, and in 100 feet turn left on a red cinder road. From here the mountain views are good, and they get better as you travel up the hill. After 0.4 mile, turn left on an overgrown dirt road and follow it downhill for 0.5 mile, then turn left again on the dirt road that parallels Pole Creek. In 0.6 mile you'll cross gravel Road 1522 again, go straight on Road 1514 for a short distance, then veer right on Road 230, which again parallels Pole Creek. In about 0.7 mile, Road 370 and the Marquis Short Loop come in on the left. Continue riding along the creek for 0.9 mile to a T-junction with Road 800 near where it crosses Pole Creek. Turn left here, and in 0.3 mile turn right on a single track that will take you to Road 230. Go right, and you'll soon be traveling along the creek again. In 0.5 mile you'll reach the Metolius-Windigo Trail. Detour to the right to a good horse-watering spot, then head north on the Met-Win and follow the yellow diamonds 3.2 miles back to camp.

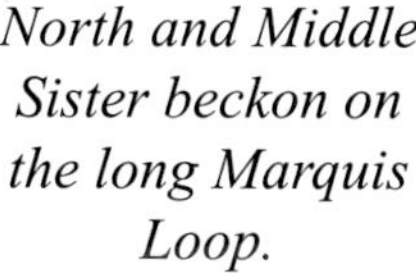

North and Middle Sister beckon on the long Marquis Loop.

Pole Creek and Whychus Creek

Trailhead: Start at Sisters Cow Camp

Length: 7 miles round trip to Pole Creek, or 10 miles round trip to Whychus Creek

Elevation: 3,400 to 3,900 feet

Difficulty: Moderate

Footing: Hoof protection recommended

Season: Late spring through fall

Permits: None

Facilities: Toilet, stock water in season, and plenty of trailer parking at the horse camp. No stock water on the trail.

Highlights: This trail travels mostly through ponderosa forest, and has little elevation change after climbing the hillside immediately south of Cow Camp. The treeless hillside above the camp has wonderful views of Mt. Jefferson, Mt. Washington, and the Three Sisters.

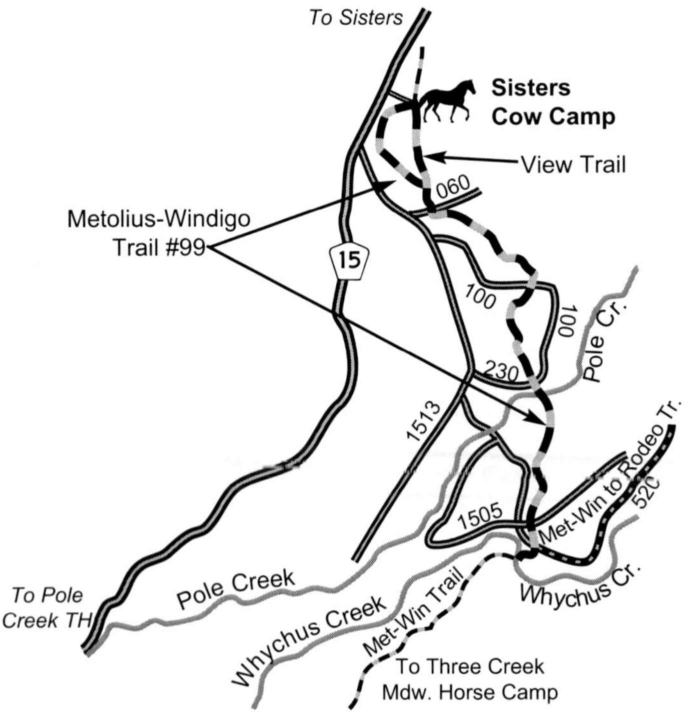

Suzi on Frosti, Debbie on Cowboy, and Katherine on Mel, enjoying the mountain views on the Met-Win Trail not far from Cow Camp.

The Ride: You can pick up the southbound Metolius-Windigo Trail #99 on the west side of Cow Camp. Instead, we suggest departing on the unsigned trail that begins on the south side of the campground near the fence. After climbing the treeless ridge, be sure to look behind you at the panoramic views of the Cascades. The trail then enters the forest and continues with little elevation gain. About 0.8 mile from camp, the trail you're on joins the Met-Win Trail. After another 0.4 mile, the Met-Win (marked with yellow diamonds) crosses gravel Road 060, and 2.4 miles farther it reaches Pole Creek. Cross the bridge, and in a mile the trail crosses gravel Road 1505. About 0.5 mile after that you'll cross Road 520, and 0.2 mile later you'll descend into the canyon carved by Whychus Creek. The entire route is clearly signed with yellow diamonds on the trees. On your return trip, you can make a bit of a loop back to camp by veering left on the Metolius-Windigo Trail about 0.1 mile after crossing Road 060 and following the Met-Win back to Cow Camp.

Whitney on Dixie and Debbie on Split, on the trail near Sisters Cow Camp. Mt. Washington and Mt. Jefferson are in the background.

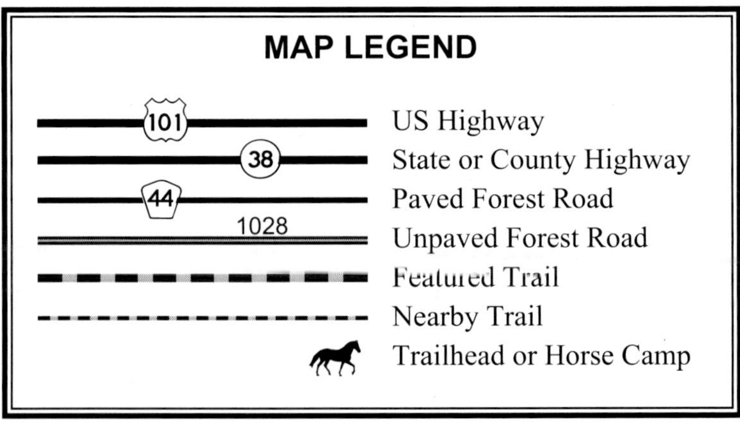

Swamp Wells Horse Camp

Deschutes National Forest

The Swamp Wells/Horse Butte trail system is huge, with well over 70 miles of fabulous trails. While the Horse Butte Trailhead is the primary access point for the northern trails and loops on this system (see the Horse Butte chapter for details), Swamp Wells Horse Camp is the gateway to the southern trails and loops. Swamp Wells and Horse Butte are connected by three long trails that roughly parallel one another. The 61/63 Tie Trail intersects with all three trails midway along their length, allowing you to create several moderate-length loops. In addition, the Swamp Wells Trail continues south from Swamp Wells all the way to Newberry Crater. All trails are signed with gray diamond trailblazers on the trees. The trails are forested with ponderosa and lodgepole pines, and the gently rolling terrain is dotted with volcanic cinder buttes, basalt outcroppings, and, in a few areas, lava caves.

Diana and Mo overlook the gaping mouth of Charcoal Cave, on the Arnold Ice Cave/Coyote Loop.

Getting to Swamp Wells Horse Camp

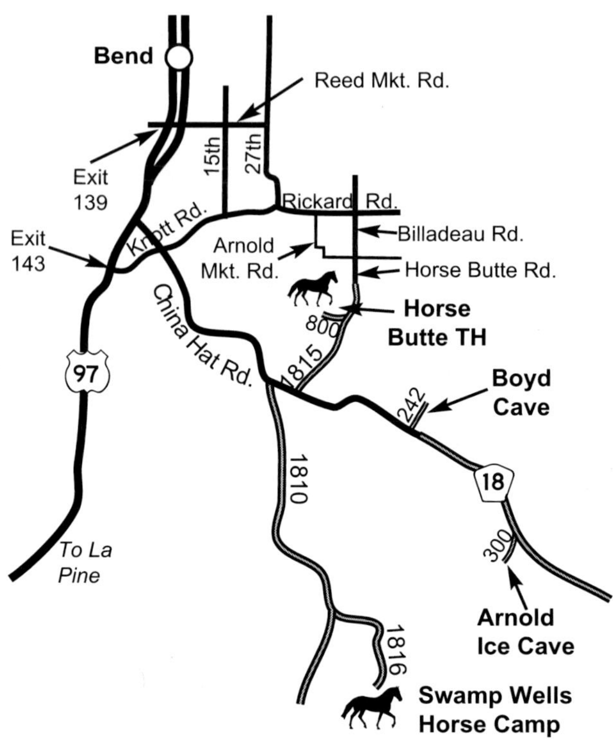

Swamp Wells Trails

Trail	Difficulty	Elevation	Round Trip
Arnold Ice Cave/Coyote Lp.	Moderate	4,500-5,750	13 miles
Fuzztail Butte Loop	Moderate	5,300-5,750	4.5 miles
Newberry Crater	Moderate	5,700-7,600	11.5-21 miles
Swamp Wells/Coyote Lp.	Moderate	4,800-5,500	12.5 miles

Swamp Wells Horse Camp

Directions: From Bend, drive south on Hwy. 97 and take Exit 143 (Baker Rd./Knott Rd.) Turn left on Knott Road and continue 1.4 miles. Turn right on China Hat Road and go 4.6 miles, then turn right on Road 1810. After 5.7 miles, turn left on Road 1816 and follow the signs 2.7 miles to the horse camp.

Elevation: 5,400 feet

Campsites: 5 sites, each with 4-horse metal corrals. All sites are level, gravelled, and back-in. Two sites have room for two vehicles. There are no gates on the corrals, so bring a rope to create your own stall gate.

Facilities: Vault toilet, manure bin, and a handicapped-accessible mounting ramp. While you may find water in a nearby wildlife guzzler in spring and early summer, it's pretty murky. We recommend bringing your own drinking and stock water. All sites have fire pits and picnic tables. The day-use area holds 10+ trailers.

Permits: None

Season: May through October

Contact: Bend/Ft. Rock Ranger District, 541-383-5300

Cheyenne and Lizzie relax in the corrals at Swamp Wells Horse Camp.

Arnold Ice Cave/Coyote Loop

Trailhead: Start at Swamp Wells Horse Camp
Length: 13 miles round trip
Elevation: 4,500 to 5,750 feet
Difficulty: Moderate
Footing: Suitable for barefoot horses
Season: Late spring through fall
Permits: None
Facilities: Toilet, manure bin, and plenty of trailer parking. You may find stock water at the horse camp through early summer. No stock water on the trail.

Highlights: This delightful forest trail meanders between Swamp Wells and Arnold Ice Cave, using the 61/63 Tie Trail to connect the Arnold Ice Cave and Coyote Trails to make a loop.

The Ride: Pick up the Arnold Ice Cave Trail #3963 on the southeast edge of the horse camp. In 3.2 miles, you'll cross Road 1820 next to

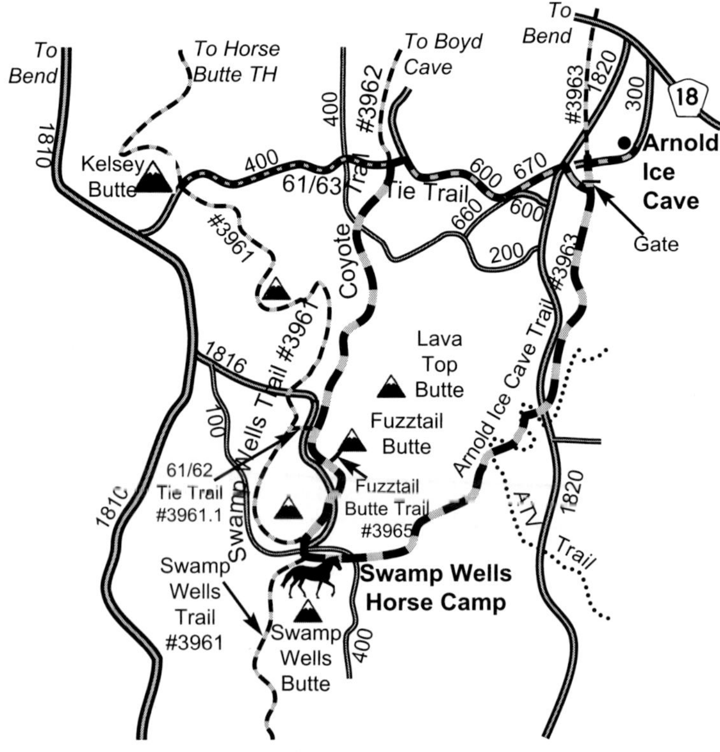

Lydia rides Shadow along the Arnold Ice Cave Trail between Swamp Wells and Arnold Ice Cave.

a cattle guard and go through a fence. In this general area you'll cross an ATV trail several times, and you'll notice a previously-burned area to the right that is now covered with young ponderosas. After another 2.5 miles, you'll reach a gate in a fence. If you want to see Arnold Ice Cave, Charcoal Cave, and several other collapsed lava tubes, go through the gate and ride 0.2 mile farther. At the junction sign, turn right on a dirt road and follow the gray diamonds to the caves and the Arnold Ice Cave parking area. Then retrace your steps to the gate, go through it, and turn right on the dirt road that runs beside the fence. You are now on the 61/63 Tie Trail. Continue about 0.3 mile along the fence, up a hill, between some big rocks placed to block vehicle traffic, and past a couple of primitive campsites. When you reach red cinder Road 1820, turn left on it and immediately turn right on Road 670. Continue to follow the gray diamonds on the trees, and in 0.2 mile the road forks. Veer right on Road 600. In another 1.6 miles, you'll see trees that were planted in rows after a forest fire. There is a fence on your left, and in 0.3 mile the fence ends. Turn left on the dirt road just past the end of the fence and follow it 0.2 mile, then turn left on the Coyote Trail #3962. In 3 miles you'll pass the 61/62 Tie Trail #3961.1, then the Fuzztail Butte Trail #3965, and 0.8 mile later you'll arrive at Swamp Wells.

Fuzztail Butte Loop

Trailhead: Start at Swamp Wells Horse Camp

Length: 4.5 miles round trip

Elevation: 5,300 to 5,750 feet

Difficulty: Moderate, but the trail to the summit of Fuzztail Butte is steep, rocky, and somewhat overgrown

Footing: Hoof protection recommended

Season: Late spring through fall

Permits: None

Facilities: Toilet, manure bin, and plenty of trailer parking. You may find stock water at the horse camp through early summer. No stock water on the trail.

Highlights: This is a short, pleasant loop trail that takes you to the top of Fuzztail Butte. The Fuzztail Butte trail is steep, gaining 300

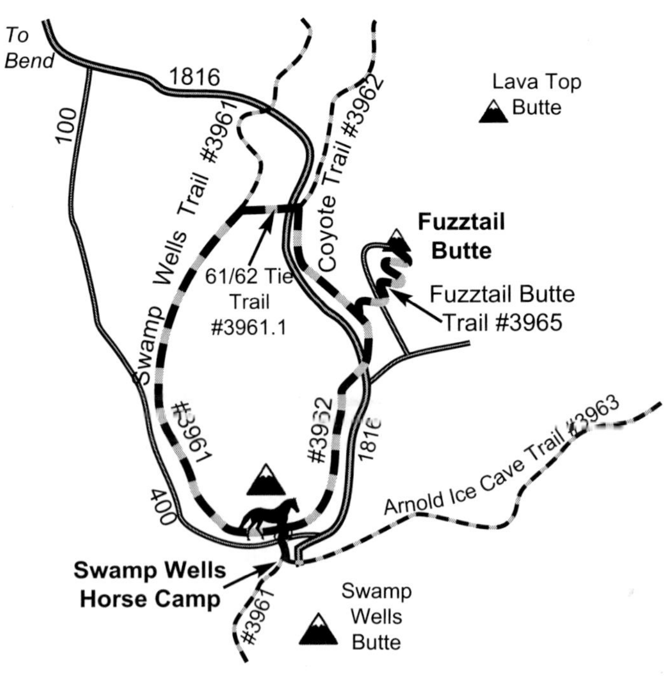

feet of elevation in 0.5 mile, but riders who persevere will be rewarded with a 360-degree view from the summit.

The Ride: At the horse camp, pick up the trail that runs behind the corrals and follow it north (to the right if you are standing in the campground road facing the campsites). At the junction in 0.2 mile, veer right on the Coyote Trail #3962. In 0.6 mile the trail crosses Road 1816, and 0.2 mile later the Fuzztail Butte Trail #3965 goes to the right. Follow it, and in 0.2 mile it crosses a dirt road and takes you to the top of the butte. You can either turn left on the road and take it to the top (easier), or stay on the trail and take the switchbacks (more challenging). After enjoying the tremendous views, return to the Coyote Trail #3962 and turn right. In 0.6 mile you'll reach the 61/62 Tie Trail #3961.1. Turn left on it, and in 0.2 mile turn left on the Swamp Wells Trail #3961. Follow it 1.8 miles back to the horse camp.

Lydia and Shadow take in the view from the summit of Fuzztail Butte.

Newberry Crater

Trailhead: Start at Swamp Wells Horse Camp or at the junction of Roads 9710 and 9735

Length: 21 miles round trip from Swamp Wells Horse Camp, or 11.5 miles round trip from the Road 9710 / 9735 junction

Elevation: 5,700 to 7,600 feet from Swamp Wells, or 6,000 to 7,600 feet from the Road 9710 / 9735 junction

Difficulty: Moderate

Footing: Hoof protection recommended

Season: Summer through fall

Permits: None

Facilities: Parking for one trailer at the Road 9710/9735 junction. Swamp Wells has a vault toilet, manure bin, plenty of trailer parking, and may have stock water until early summer. No stock water on the trail.

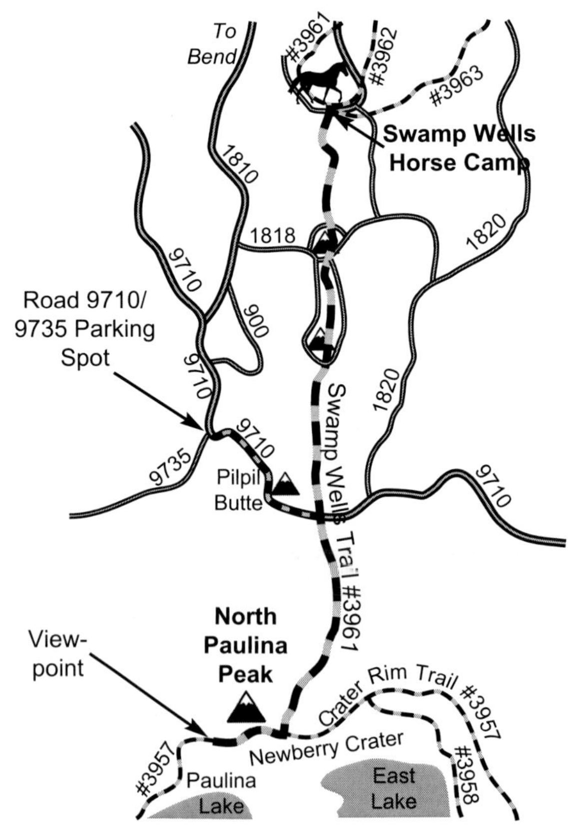

Highlights: This interesting trail showcases some of the volcanic forces that shaped this area, running through mostly-lodgepole forest, over and around cinder buttes, and past a lava flow to the Crater Rim Trail at Newberry Crater. If you don't want to do a 21-mile ride, you can drive part of the way there and still enjoy the most scenic part of the trail.

Finding the Road 9710 / 9735 Parking Spot: From Bend, drive south on Hwy. 97. Take Exit 143 (Baker Rd./Knott Rd.) and turn left on Knott Road. In 1.4 miles, turn right on China Hat Road. Continue 4.6 miles, then turn right on Road 1810. When the road ends in 10.9 miles, turn left on Road 9710. In 1.4 miles, Road 9735 comes in on the right. Turn around here and park beside the road.

The Ride: From Swamp Wells Horse Camp: on the southeast side of the camp, pick up the Swamp Wells Trail #3961 and ride south. In 2.6 miles you'll ride over a cinder butte, crossing cinder Road 1818. About 1.5 miles later you'll go over another cinder butte, and 2.6 miles after that you'll reach dirt Road 9710. From the Road 9710 / 9735 Junction: ride east on Road 9710 for 2.2 miles. At the sign, turn right on the Swamp Wells Trail #3961. All: In 4.5 miles the trail goes through a cinder canyon, crosses a pumice plain and runs along a lava flow. In 1.3 miles after that, it comes out at the Crater Rim Trail #3957 at Newberry Crater. To reach an excellent viewpoint, turn right on the Crater Rim Trail and ride 0.5 mile farther.

Mona and Roi head to the rim of Newberry Crater.

Swamp Wells/Coyote Loop

Trailhead: Start at Swamp Wells Horse Camp
Length: 12.5 miles round trip
Elevation: 4,800 to 5,500 feet
Difficulty: Moderate
Footing: Suitable for barefoot horses
Season: Late spring through fall
Permits: None
Facilities: Toilet, manure bin, and plenty of trailer parking. You may find stock water at the horse camp through early summer. No stock water on the trail.

Highlights: This pleasant loop trail features interesting basalt outcroppings, several volcanic buttes, and open ponderosa pine and lodgepole forest.

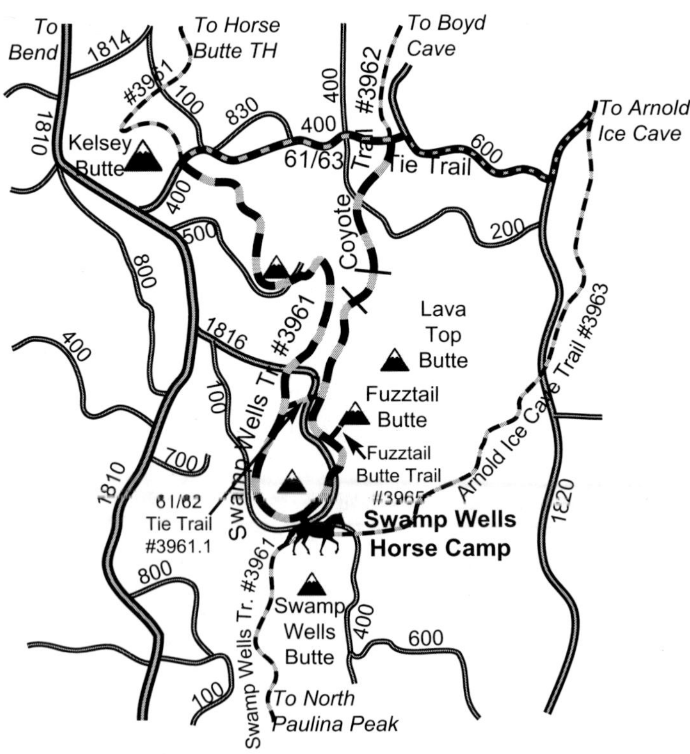

The Ride: From Swamp Wells Horse Camp, pick up the trail that runs behind the corrals and follow it north (to the right if you are standing in the campground road facing the campsites). At the junction in 0.2 mile, veer left on the Swamp Wells Trail #3961. The trail circles the butte, and in 1.5 miles the 61/62 Tie Trail #3961.1 goes off to the right. Stay left, and in another 2 miles the trail climbs the flank of an unnamed butte and partially circles it. Two miles after that, the Swamp Wells Trail crosses Road 400 at the base of Kelsey Butte. Turn right and follow Road 400 (the 61/63 Tie Trail, signed with gray diamonds on the trees). In 0.1 mile, Road 400 makes a 90-degree turn to the right. Follow it downhill, and at the bottom the road makes another 90-degree turn to the right. Again, follow it. In 1.7 miles you'll go through a gate in a fence. In another 0.5 mile, turn right on the Coyote Trail #3962. In 0.5 mile, you'll go through another gate across the trail. About 2.2 miles after that, you'll pass the 61/62 Tie Trail on your right. Then 0.2 mile later, the Fuzztail Butte Trail #3965 goes to the left. Continue straight, and in 0.6 mile you'll arrive at the junction with the Swamp Wells Trail. Turn left to return to the horse camp.

Mona rides Roi along the Swamp Wells Trail.

Mark and Janice ride Sonny and Baron through an interesting grotto on the Swamp Wells/Coyote Loop.

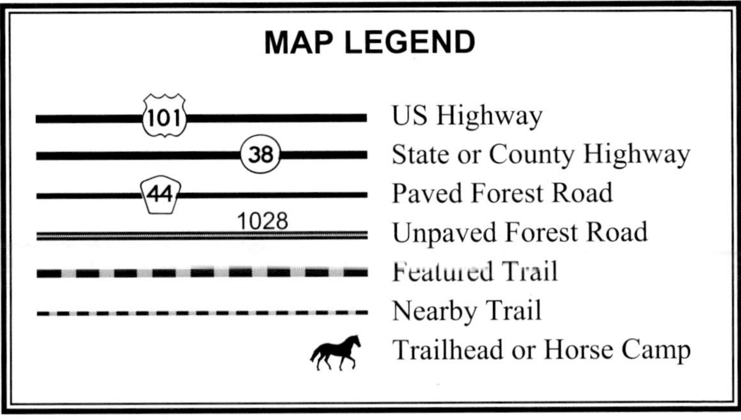

Three Creek Meadow Horse Camp

Deschutes National Forest

The Three Creek Meadow area is a study in contrasts. Some of the surrounding trails were severely burned in the Pole Creek Fire, so they travel through a stark landscape of burned trees, with views of the Three Sisters through the blackened trunks. Other trails run through unburned areas that feature pretty forest, creeks, and meadows filled with wildflowers. No matter which trails you choose, however, you'll be impressed. From Three Creek Meadow Horse Camp you can ride to Tam McArthur Rim, Three Creek Lake, Park Meadow, or Golden Lake, and see spectacular scenery framed by the Three Sisters and Broken Top. Fun Fact: The area's lakes, meadow, and campgrounds take their names from nearby Three Creek. There aren't three creeks, there is only one creek, and its name is Three Creek because it originates from three small tributaries.

Tam McArthur Rim towers above the Three Creek Meadow area.

Getting to the Three Creek Area

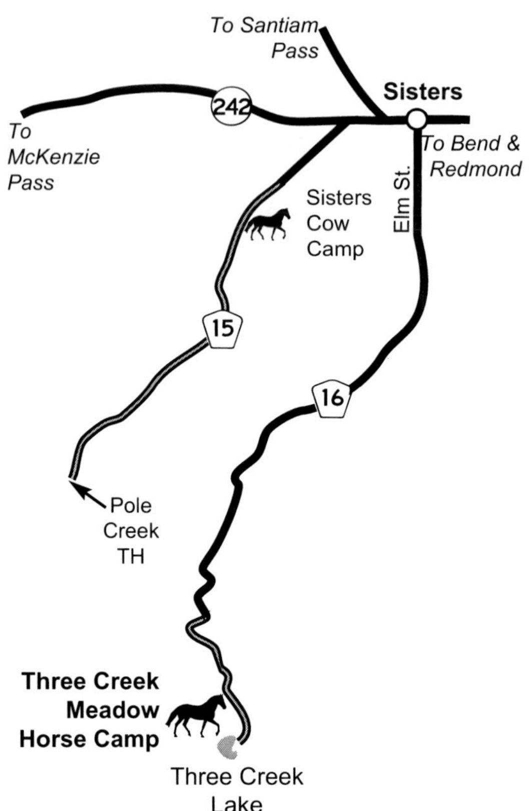

Three Creek Area Trails

Trail	Difficulty	Elevation	Round Trip
Golden Lake	Moderate	6,000-6,850	15.5 miles
Park Meadow	Moderate	6,000-6,850	12 miles
Tam McArthur Rim	Moderate	6,400-7,750	16.5 miles
Three Creek Lake Loop	Moderate	6,350-6,700	4 miles

Three Creek Meadow Horse Camp

Directions: In Sisters, turn south on Elm Street, which becomes Three Creek Road/Road 16. Drive 15 miles to the campground. Skip the first entrance, which leads to the family campsites. Instead, drive 0.2 mile farther and turn right into the campground's equestrian entrance. The day-use parking area is in 500 feet, and the horse camp is 500 feet after that. The campground loop on the right has more room for large trailers than the loop on the left.

Elevation: 6,350 feet

Campsites: 9 sites, each with a 4-horse corral. Most sites are back-in. Most sites have room for 2 vehicles if you park carefully. All sites have fire pits and picnic tables.

Facilities: Vault toilet, manure bin, garbage cans, day-use parking area. Stock water but no potable water.

Permits: Camping fee. No fee for day-use parking.

Season: Summer through fall

Contact: Sisters Ranger District: 541-549-7700
Hoodoo Recreation (Concessionaire): 541-338-7869, www.hoodoo.com

All of the Three Creek Meadow sites have 4-horse corrals.

Golden Lake

Trailhead: Start at Three Creek Meadow Horse Camp

Length: 15.5 miles round trip

Elevation: 6,000 to 6,850 feet

Difficulty: Moderate -- creek crossings; part of the route is on an unsigned trail

Footing: Hoof protection recommended

Season: Summer through fall

Permits: Camping fee. No fee for day-use parking.

Facilities: Toilet, stock water, and manure bin at the horse camp. Parking for 4-5 trailers in the day-use area. Stock water is available on the trail.

Highlights: The spur trail to Golden Lake isn't an official trail, so it doesn't have a sign pointing the way. But with a little wayfinding skill you can get to this beautiful spot. Please keep your horse out of the lake, as it is used by backpackers for drinking water. Dogs must be on leash near Golden Lake, July 15-September 15.

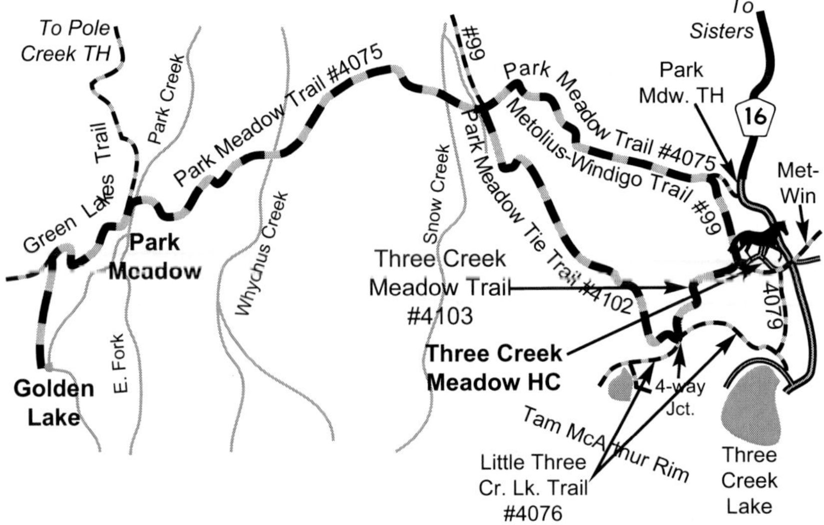

The Ride: Follow the directions to Park Meadow on the next page. Where the Park Meadow Trail #4075 intersects the Green Lakes Trail #17 in Park Meadow, veer left toward Green Lakes. The trail heads up along a ridge. After 0.8 mile, you'll reach an unsigned trail that goes off to the left. Follow this trail, and in 0.9 mile you'll reach Golden Lake. The middle of the lake is blue, but the perimeter is a beautiful golden color. The lake is situated with Broken Top on one side and South Sister on the other. The best place to water your horse is downstream from the lake's outlet.

Riders head to Golden Lake, with Broken Top towering above them.

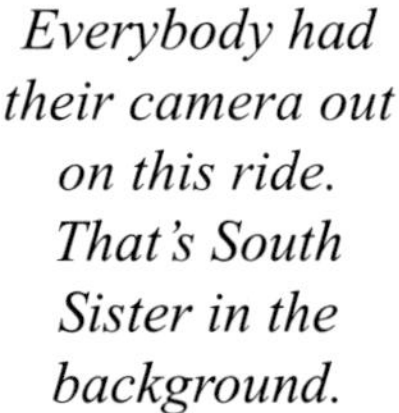

Everybody had their camera out on this ride. That's South Sister in the background.

Park Meadow

Trailhead: Start at Three Creek Meadow Horse Camp

Length: 12 miles round trip

Elevation: 6,000 to 6,850 feet

Difficulty: Moderate -- creek crossings

Footing: Hoof protection recommended

Season: Summer through fall

Permits: Camping fee. No fee for day-use parking.

Facilities: Toilet, stock water, and manure bin at the horse camp. Parking for 4-5 trailers in the day-use area. Stock water is available on the trail.

Highlights: Park Meadow is a lush green meadow nestled on the north side of Broken Top and South Sister. Several miles of the trail travel through the area devastated by the 2012 Pole Creek Fire, so you'll see plenty of burned trees. But then you'll leave the fire scar and enjoy shady forest and pretty meadows. Seasonal wildflowers abound, and the mountain views are splendid. If you want to extend your ride, you can continue on to Green Lakes (see below) or to Golden Lake.

The Ride: There are two ways to reach the Park Meadow Trail from Three Creek Meadow Campground. We suggest this lollipop loop

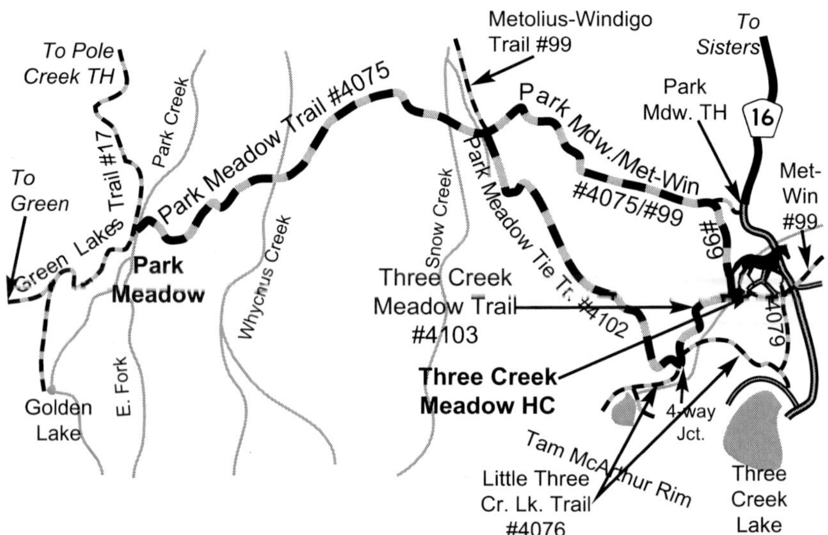

Broken Top towers above Park Meadow.

route: Pick up the trail between campsites 12 and 13. In 100 yards, veer right on the Metolius-Windigo Trail #99, which is marked with yellow diamonds and wooden signs with horseshoes on them. In 0.7 mile, the Met-Win Trail veers left onto the Park Meadow Trail #4075. For the next 1.8 miles, the two trails share the same tread, then the Met-Win splits off to the right. Stay left on the Park Meadow Trail and continue 3 miles to reach Park Meadow. To return, ride the Park Meadow Trail for 3 miles, then at the junction where the Met-Win Trail goes to the left, turn right on the Park Meadow Tie Trail #4102. As the trail gains elevation, be sure to look behind you at the mountain views. Ride 2.4 miles, and when you reach the 4-way junction, turn left on the Three Creek Meadow Trail #4103 to return to the horse camp.

Green Lakes Extension: If you aren't ready to head home after enjoying Park Meadow, you can continue another 3 miles (one way) on the Green Lakes Trail #17 to the spectacular Green Lakes on the southern side of Broken Top and South Sister. The elevation gain is about 900 feet from Park Meadow to the pass, and then the trail descends 600 feet to the lakes. The trail passes between Broken Top and South Sister, which loom so close you'll feel like you could reach out and touch them.

Tam McArthur Rim

Trailhead: Start at Three Creek Meadow Horse Camp
Length: 16.5 miles round trip
Elevation: 6,400 to 7,750 feet
Difficulty: Moderate
Footing: Hoof protection recommended
Season: Summer through fall
Permits: Camping fee. No fee for day-use parking.
Facilities: Toilet, stock water, and manure bin at the horse camp. Parking for 4-5 trailers in the day-use area. Stock water is available on the trail in season.

Highlights: Horseback riders and hikers used to share a short, steep, rocky, and crowded trail to Tam McArthur Rim. A few years ago the Forest Service created a new trail for horses. The new route is easier and safer for horses, though it's quite a bit longer than the hiker trail.

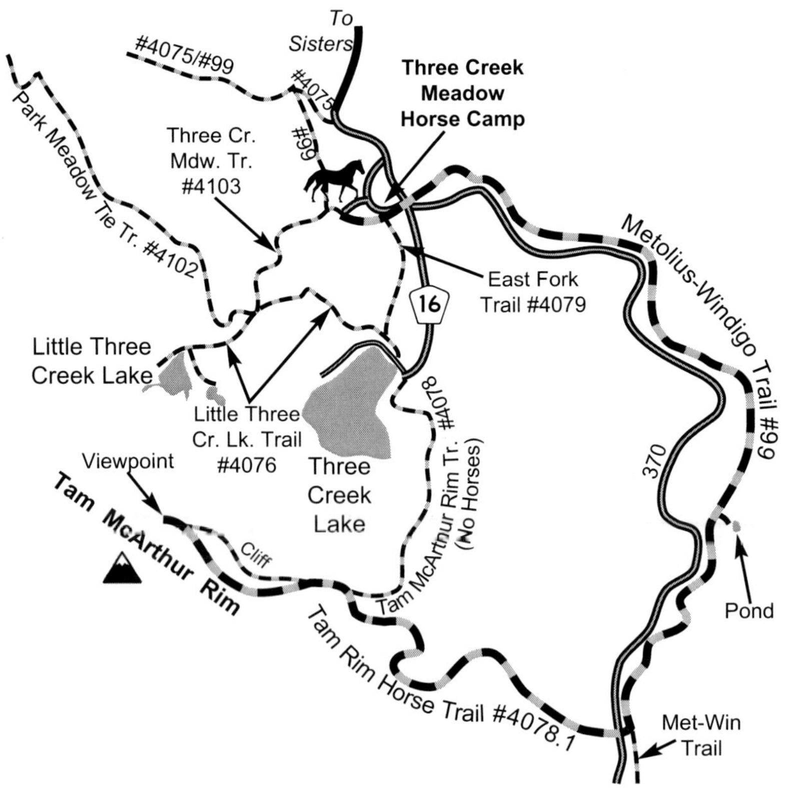

Whitney rides Dixie along the rim trail, taking in the great view.

The views from the rim are breathtaking. You can see the Three Creek Lakes 1,000 feet below, plus Broken Top, the Three Sisters, Mt. Washington, Three Fingered Jack, Mt. Jefferson, and Mt. Hood. Stunning!

The Ride: Pick up the trail between campsites 12 and 13 and ride about 200 feet. Just before the trail sign at the edge of the meadow, turn left on the Metolius-Windigo Trail #99. In 0.3 mile, the trail passes the day-use parking area and runs for about 0.1 mile down the entrance road for the horse camp. Cross Road 16 and continue on the Met-Win Trail for 3.2 miles. You'll see a rock cairn on the left side of the trail. Turn left here and ride down the hill and through the trees to a small seasonal pond, the only source of stock water along the trail. After watering your horse, return to the Met-Win Trail and ride 1.4 miles farther to the junction with the Tam Rim Horse Trail #4078.1. Turn right on the horse trail, which crosses Road 370 and then follows an old, eroded forest road for 2.1 miles. Where the horse trail intersects with the Tam Rim hiker trail (#4078), turn left and ride 1.1 miles to the summit. Near the top, the trail splits in several places, allowing access to the edge of the rim and the 1,000-foot sheer drop to the lakes below. We suggest tying your horses and walking to the rim to enjoy the panorama.

Three Creek Lakes Loop

Trailhead: Start at Three Creek Meadow Horse Camp
Length: 4 miles round trip
Elevation: 6,350 to 6,700 feet
Difficulty: Moderate
Footing: Hoof protection recommended
Season: Summer through fall
Permits: Camping fee. No fee for day-use parking.
Facilities: Toilet, stock water, and manure bin at the horse camp. Parking for 4-5 trailers in the day-use area. Stock water is available on the trail.

Highlights: This ride features creeks, wildflowers, meadows, lakes, and forest. The terrain is quite varied, and the footing is good except for a couple of rocky spots. You'll pass both Three Creek Lake and

Little Three Creek Lake, nestled at the base of Tam McArthur Rim. Wildflowers grow in abundance along the creeks, and several stream crossings provide opportunities to water the horses.

The Ride: Pick up the trail between campsites 12 and 13 and ride about 200 feet. Just before the trail sign at the edge of the meadow, turn right on the Metolius-Windigo Trail. In 0.1 mile, turn left on the Three Creek Meadow Trail #4103. In another 0.8 mile, you'll reach a 4-way junction. Go straight on the Little Three Creek Lake Trail #4076, and in 0.2 mile you'll reach Little Three Creek Lake. The trail to the right along the lake continues 0.2 mile before ending in a rocky area. The trail to the left goes over to another small lake and ends on the far side of it. After enjoying the lakes and the view of Tam McArthur Rim, return to the 4-way junction. This time, turn right on the Little Three Creek Lake Trail and follow it 0.9 mile to Three Creek Lake. Horses are not allowed in the lake or on the beach of Three Creek Lake, so enjoy the view of the lake and then turn left on the East Fork Trail #4079. Follow it 0.6 mile to return to the horse camp.

Jane gazes at Tam McArthur Rim across Little Three Creek Lake.

Veronica rides Harmony across Park Meadow, with South Sister in the background.

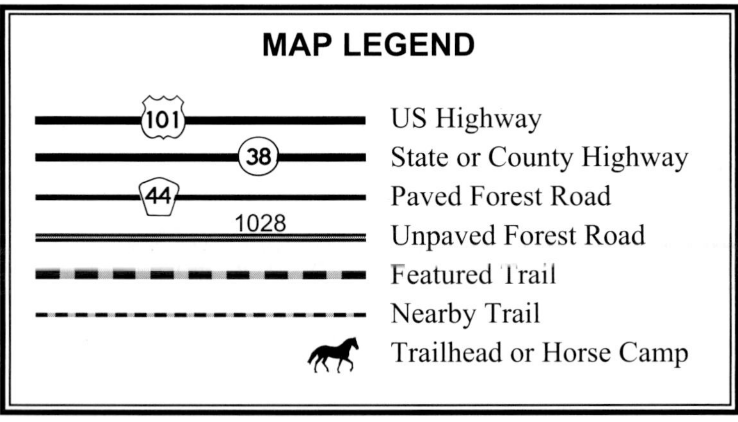

Todd Creek Horse Camp

Broken Top Area

Deschutes National Forest

Located less than 25 miles west of Bend, the trails that lie between Broken Top and Mt. Bachelor feature close-up mountain views, alpine lakes, beautiful wildflowers in season, and stretches of old-growth forest. Todd Creek Horse Camp doubles as a trailhead and overnight horse camp, and provides access to excellent high country riding in the Three Sisters Wilderness. Be aware that the Broken Top, Todd, and Green Lakes Trails are very popular with hikers. Dogs are required to be on leash on these trails. In addition, the Metolius-Windigo Trail in this area is heavily used by mountain bike riders. For more information about additional day-use trails in the area, see the North Cascade Lakes chapter.

Debbie on Split and Whitney on Dixie, on the Broken Top Trail with Broken Top behind them.

Getting to Todd Creek Horse Camp

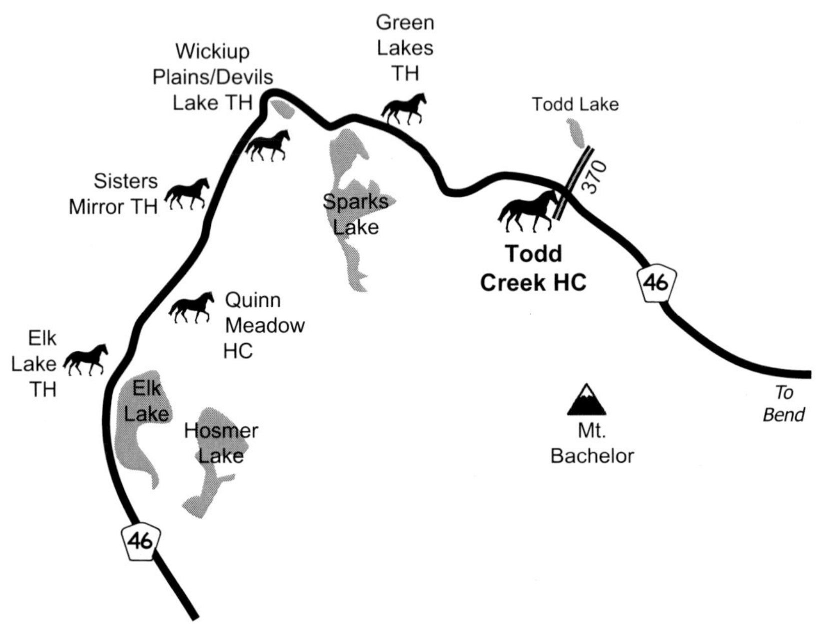

Todd Creek Trails

Trail	Difficulty	Elevation	Round Trip
Broken Top Loop	Moderate	6,100-7,200	13 miles
Green Lakes .	Moderate	6,100-6,800	15 miles
Sparks & Hosmer Lakes	Moderate	6,100-5,450	9-14 miles
Sparks Lake & Quinn Mdw.	Moderate	6,100-5,100	9-15 miles

Todd Creek Horse Camp

Directions: From Hwy. 97 in Bend, take Exit 138 (Colorado Ave.) and head west. Follow the signs toward Mt. Bachelor and Century Drive, going through 3 roundabouts. Take the second exit from roundabouts 1 and 3, and the third exit from roundabout 2. This will put you on Road 46 (Century Drive/Cascade Lakes Hwy.) Continue for 23 miles and turn left into the horse camp. The entrance is directly across the highway from the sign for Todd Lake.

Elevation: 6,200 feet

Campsites: 7 sites, each with 2- or 4-horse metal corrals, picnic tables, and fire rings. Easy parking for two trailers at each site. Todd Creek also has day-use parking for 5-6 trailers.

Facilities: Toilet, manure bins. Stock water is available from a hand pump and from nearby Todd Creek.

Permits: Northwest Forest Pass required for camping. No fee for day use.

Season: June through October

Contact: Bend/Ft. Rock Ranger District, 541-383-4000

The sun rises on Mt. Bachelor, seen from the parking area at Todd Creek Horse Camp.

Tex hangs out in her corral at Todd Creek.

Broken Top Loop

Trailhead: Start at Todd Creek Horse Camp
Length: 13 miles round trip
Elevation: 6,100 to 7,200 feet
Difficulty: Moderate -- stream crossings, a few moderately steep side slopes, and the Metolius-Windigo Trail segment is popular with mountain bike riders
Footing: Hoof protection recommended
Season: Summer through fall
Permits: Northwest Forest Pass required for camping; no fee for day use
Facilities: Toilets, stock water, manure bins, and a large parking area at the horse camp. Stock water is available on the trail.

Highlights: The trail goes through beautiful forest, along sunlit meadows, and across a broad pumice plain. It offers a close-up look at

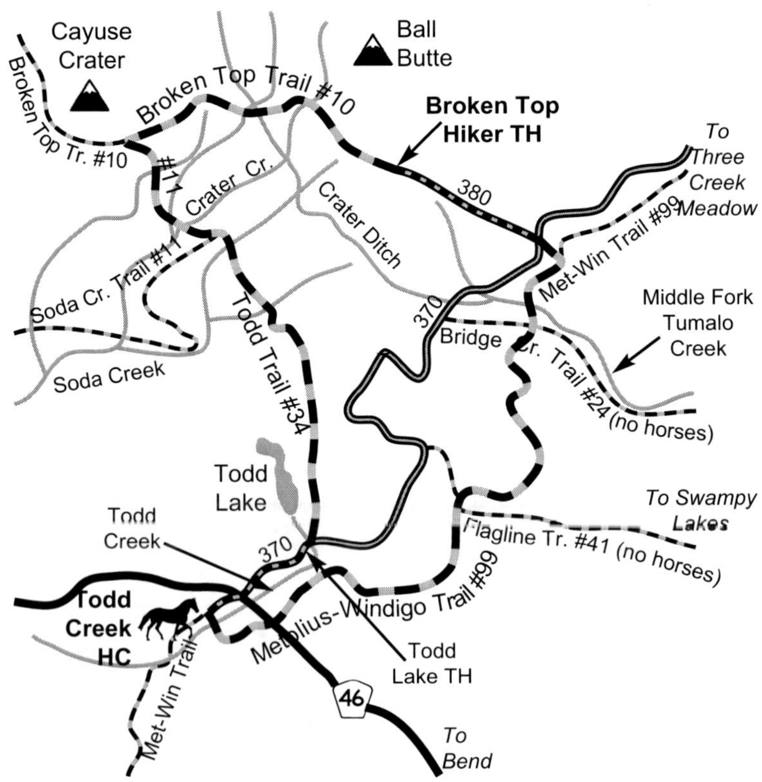

craggy Broken Top, plus views of Mt. Bachelor and Sparks Lake. You'll pass Todd Lake, but horses are not permitted at the lake. About a month after the snow melts, the creekside wildflowers on this ride are dazzling. Please keep your horse on the trail in this fragile alpine environment. Dogs must be on leash on this trail. This stretch of the Met-Win is frequently used by mountain bike riders.

The Ride: From Todd Creek Horse Camp, cross Todd Creek and pick up the northbound Metolius-Windigo Trail #99, which crosses Road 46 in 0.7 mile. For the next 4 miles, this trail is very popular with mountain bike riders. About 1.8 miles after crossing the road, the Flagline Trail #41 to goes off to the right to Swampy Lakes Sno-Park, and in 0.1 mile it goes off to the left to Road 370. In another 1.7 miles, the Bridge Creek Trail #24 crosses the Met-Win Trail. (Note the sign for the City of Bend Watershed.) Continue straight for 0.6 mile and turn left at the next junction, toward the Broken Top Trailhead. In 0.2 mile, cross Road 370 and pick up Road 380. Ride it 1.3 miles to the Broken Top Trailhead. Continue on the Broken Top Trail #10 for 2.2 miles, during which you'll have wonderful views of Broken Top and Mt. Bachelor, and you'll cross the man-made Crater Creek Ditch. When you reach the junction with the Soda Creek Trail #11, turn left. In 0.9 mile, veer left on the Todd Trail #34, and in 2.4 miles you'll reach the hiker trailhead at Todd Lake. Turn right and ride beside Road 370 to return to the horse camp.

Riders pass the Broken Top crater on the Broken Top Trail.

Green Lakes

Trailhead: Start at Todd Creek Horse Camp
Length: 15 miles round trip
Elevation: 6,100 to 6,800 feet
Difficulty: Moderate
Footing: Hoof protection recommended
Season: Summer through fall
Permits: Northwest Forest Pass required for camping; no fee for day use
Facilities: Toilets, stock water, manure bins, and a large parking area at the horse camp. Stock water is available on the trail.

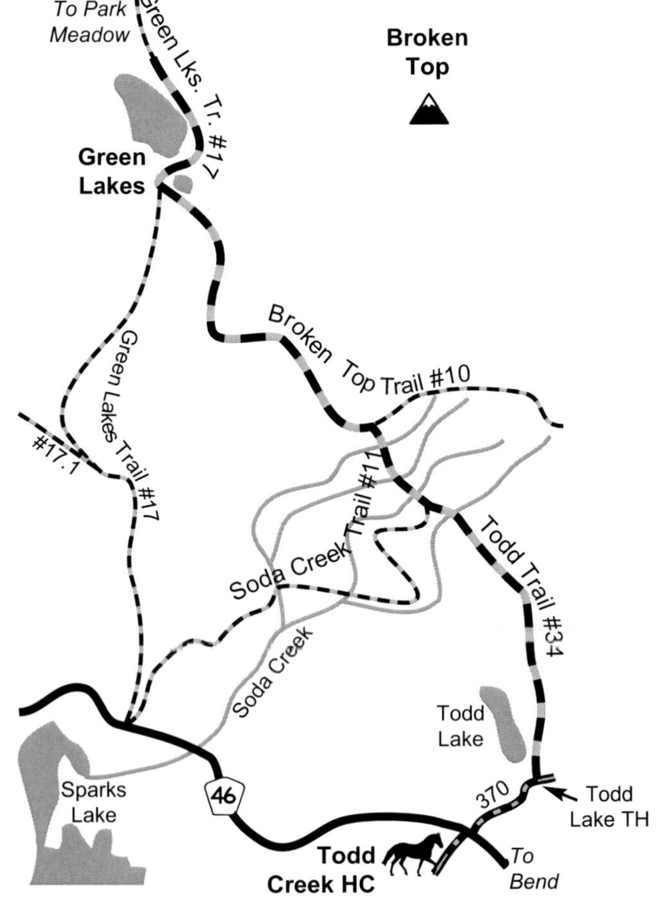

Highlights: Although this trail is a little less scenic than the Green Lakes Trail along Fall Creek, the Green Lakes themselves are just as impressive. And there are good reasons to take this route: (1) if you are camping at Todd Creek you can ride to Green Lakes without having to trailer out, (2) Todd Creek has more parking for day riders than the Green Lakes Trailhead, and (3) you'll encounter far fewer hikers on this route than on the Green Lakes Trail. Dogs must be on leash on this trail, July 15 to September 15. Please keep your horse out of the lakes, as they are used for drinking water by backpackers.

The Ride: From Todd Creek Horse Camp, ride out of the campground to Road 46, cross it, and continue for 0.6 mile along the side of Road 370 toward Todd Lake. Pick up the Todd Trail #34 and follow it 2.4 miles to the junction with the Soda Creek Trail #11. Veer right on the Soda Creek Trail. In late July/early August you'll see beautiful wildflower displays along the banks of the Soda Creek tributaries. After 0.9 mile, turn left on the Broken Top Trail #10 and follow it 3 miles to the southern-most Green Lake. Veer right on the Green Lakes Trail #17 to reach the larger Green Lake. The views of Broken Top and South Sister are impressive.

South Sister reflected in the largest of the Green Lakes.

Sparks & Hosmer Lakes

Trailhead: Start at Todd Creek Horse Camp

Length: 9 miles round trip to Sparks Lake, or 14 miles round trip to Hosmer Lake

Elevation: 6,100 to 5,450 feet to Sparks Lake, or 6,100 to 5,100 feet to Hosmer Lake

Difficulty: Moderate

Footing: Hoof protection recommended

Season: Summer through fall

Permits: Northwest Forest Pass required for camping; no fee for day use

Facilities: Toilets, stock water, manure bins, and a large parking area at the horse camp. Stock water is available on the trail.

Highlights: This trail runs from Todd Creek Horse Camp to Sparks Lake and Hosmer Lake. Most of the trail is forested, but you'll have filtered views of Mt. Bachelor and South Sister at several points along the trail. While at Sparks Lake, tie your horse and walk along the

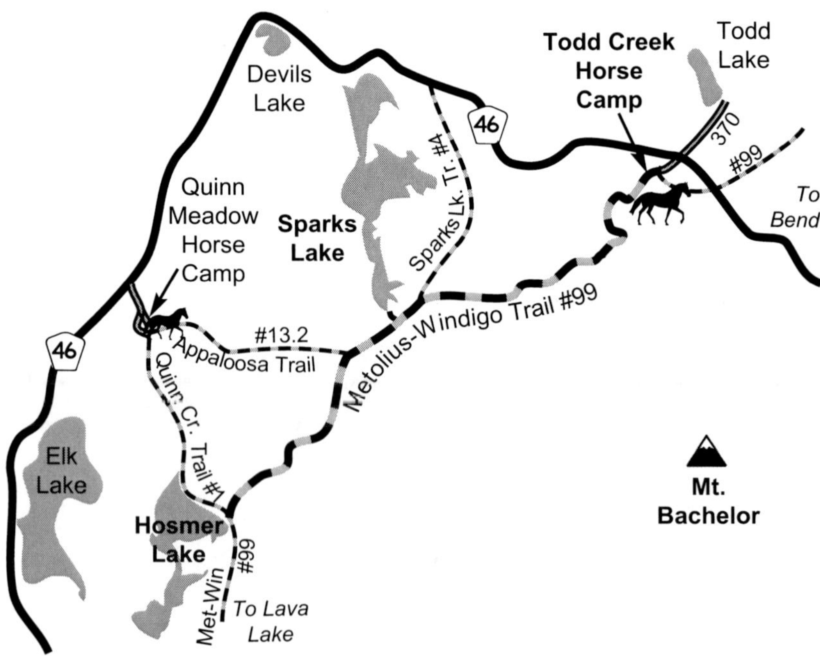

South Sister from Sparks Lake.

shore in either direction to get a marvelous view of South Sister. Hosmer Lake is a bit of a disappointment, because neither the Quinn Creek Trail nor the Met-Win Trail offer more than filtered views of the lake. You also can't get close enough to the lake to give your horse a drink. This stretch of the Met-Win is popular with mountain bike riders, so keep an eye out.

The Ride: At the green gate on the south side of the horse camp, pick up the southbound Metolius-Windigo Trail #99. For the first 0.6 mile, the trail follows the dirt road as it runs through a cinder quarry. Then it crosses Todd Creek and becomes a single-track trail through the forest. After 3.3 miles, the Sparks Lake Trail #4 goes to the right. Stay to the left, and in 0.4 mile you'll reach the unsigned trail on the right that leads to the shore of Sparks Lake in 0.1 mile. After enjoying the lake and the view of South Sister, return to the Met-Win Trail. In 0.5 mile, the Appaloosa Trail #13.2 to Quinn Meadow goes off to the right. Continue left toward Lava Lake for 2.2 miles, to the junction with the Quinn Creek Trail #1. If you turn right on the Quinn Creek Trail and ride a short distance, you can leave the trail, ride to the edge of the ridge you're on, and see Hosmer Lake below you. Retrace your steps to return to Todd Creek.

Sparks Lake & Quinn Meadow

Trailhead: Start at Todd Creek Horse Camp

Length: 9 miles round trip to Sparks Lake, or 15 miles round trip to Quinn Meadow

Elevation: 6,100 to 5,450 feet for Sparks Lake, or 6,100 to 5,100 feet to Quinn Meadow

Difficulty: Moderate

Footing: Hoof protection recommended

Season: Summer through fall

Permits: Northwest Forest Pass required for camping; no fee for day use

Facilities: Plenty of parking for horse trailers at Todd Creek. Toilets and stock water at both horse camps. Stock water is available on the trail.

Highlights: This is a mostly-forested ride that connects Sparks Lake with the two horse camps in the area. The trail is a steady downhill trek, with some switchbacks to ease the steeper sections. The first 2.5 miles out of Todd Creek Horse Camp run through shady hemlock for-

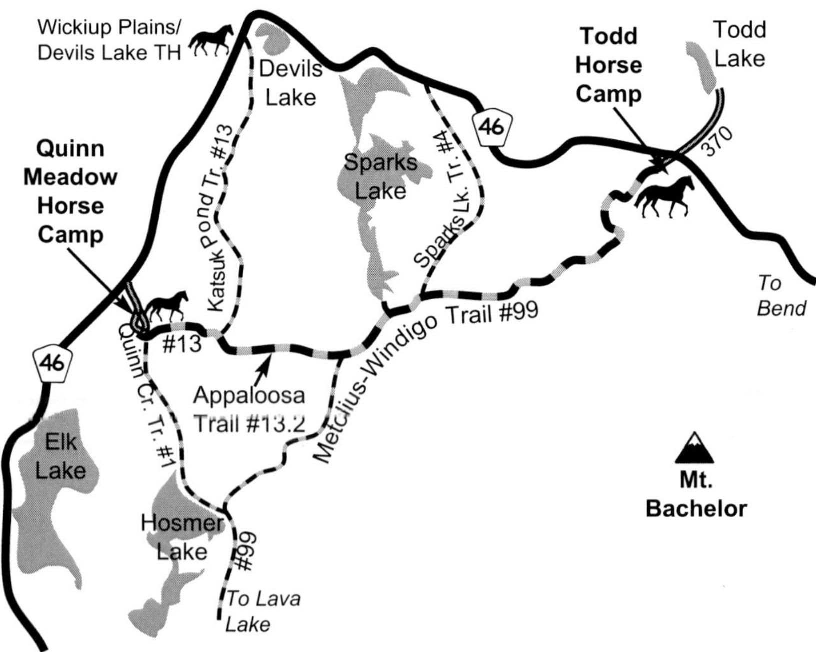

est. After that, the forest is mostly lodgepole pines. This stretch of the Met-Win is popular with mountain bike riders, so keep an eye out.

The Ride: Go through the green gate on the south end of the horse camp and follow the dirt road that is the Metolius-Windigo Trail #99 southbound. It runs through an old quarry, and after 0.6 mile it crosses Todd Creek on a bridge and becomes a single-track. As you switchback down the lower flank of Mt. Bachelor, you'll have good close-up views of the mountain and catch glimpses of South Sister through the trees. About 3.3 miles after crossing Todd Creek, you'll come to the junction with the Sparks Lake Trail #4. Stay to the left on the Met-Win Trail, and in 0.5 mile you'll come to an unsigned trail on the right that leads to Sparks Lake in a couple hundred yards. The shore of Sparks Lake is a nice spot for lunch. Be sure to walk along the shore to get the best view of South Sister across the lake. Return to the Met-Win and turn right. In 0.5 mile, turn right on the Appaloosa Trail #13.2. In 1.6 miles, you'll reach the junction with the Katsuk Pond Trail #13. Veer left, and in 0.8 mile you'll reach Quinn Meadow Horse Camp.

Ruger enjoys a refreshing drink at Sparks Lake.

Robert and Ruger travel through an impressive lava pressure ridge on the Metolius-Windigo Trail near Sparks Lake.

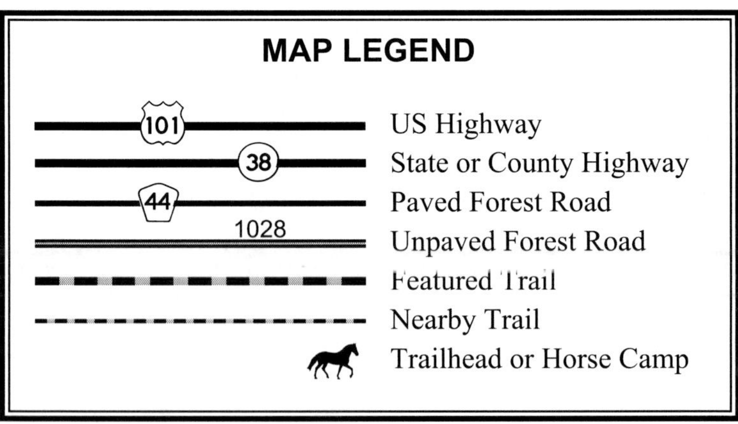

Tumalo Reservoir

Private Forest, Tumalo Irrig. Dist, BLM, Natl. Forest

The riding around Tumalo Reservoir is easy and scenic, with a surprising amount of variety. This area features excellent mountain views, water (a reservoir, a spring, and a creek), a large sagebrush flat, aspen stands, ponderosa pine forest, and a recent fire scar. The area also is a patchwork of public and private land. Tumalo Irrigation District owns the land around the reservoir. The forested area between the Brooks-Scanlon Road and the reservoir is National Forest. The areas southeast and north of the reservoir are BLM land. And most of the land west of the Brooks-Scanlon Road is private forestland. All of these landowners allow public access to their lands, much to the delight of equestrian trail riders. So saddle up, and go exploring!

Lydia and Connie ride Magic and Moose near Tumalo Reservoir, accompanied by Joylynn, the dog.

Tumalo Reservoir

Directions: Drive northwest from Bend on Hwy. 20 to Tumalo. Turn left on Bailey Rd. Drive to the top of the hill, and Bailey Rd. soon becomes Tumalo Reservoir Road. Follow it 3.7 miles. Just before the road bends sharply to the right and goes over a narrow bridge, turn left into the dirt parking area. You'll see a sign here indicating the spot is a school bus turnaround.

Elevation: 3,500 feet

Camping: The closest horse camp is Sisters Cow Camp. See the Sisters Cow Camp chapter for details.

Facilities: Parking for 10+ trailers. Stock water is available during irrigation season.

Permits: None

Season: Open year-round, but trails may be icy in winter

Note: The parking area is on private Tumalo Irrigation District Land. Please respect the permission they have granted for to equestrians for parking and access. Take your manure home with you, and keep your horse out of the reservoir.

Teresa rides Jane on the trail to Bull Spring.

Getting to Tumalo Reservoir

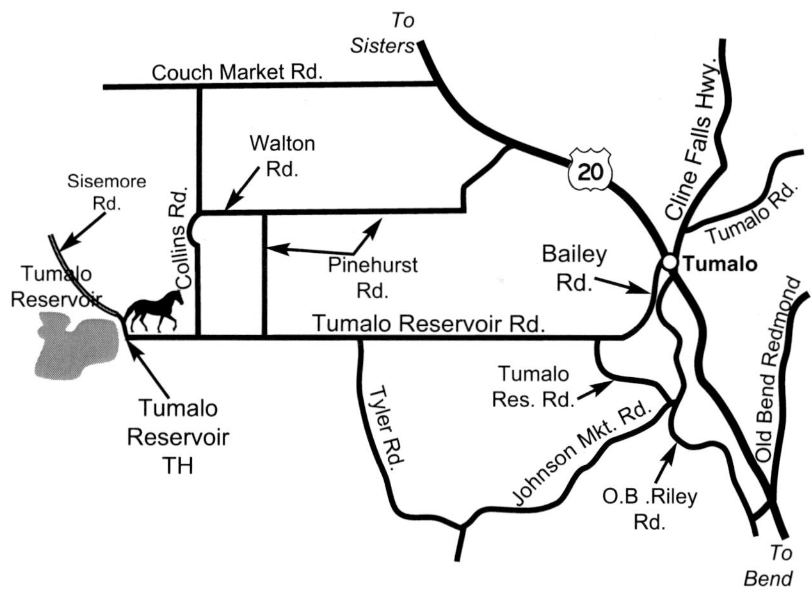

Tumalo Reservoir Area Trails

Trail	Difficulty	Elevation	Round Trip
Bull Spring Loops	Easy	3,500-3,800	7+ miles
Canals Area	Easy	3,500-3,600	Varies
Reservoir Area & Bull Flat	Easy	3,500-3,600	Varies
Skyline Gorge Loop	Moderate	3,500-4,000	12 miles

Bull Spring Loops

Trailhead: Start at the Tumalo Reservoir Trailhead
Length: 7+ miles round trip, depending on route taken
Elevation: 3,500 to 3,800 feet
Difficulty: Easy
Footing: Suitable for barefoot horses
Season: Nearly year-round
Permits: None
Facilities: Plenty of trailer parking. Stock water is available on the trail.

Highlights: Bull Spring is an interesting destination. The riding is easy, and there's a lot to see along the way. The ride travels past Tumalo Reservoir, through ponderosa pine forest, along tiny Bull Creek, and into the area burned by the 2014 Two Bulls Fire. The burned area should eventually be replanted, but for now you'll be traveling for

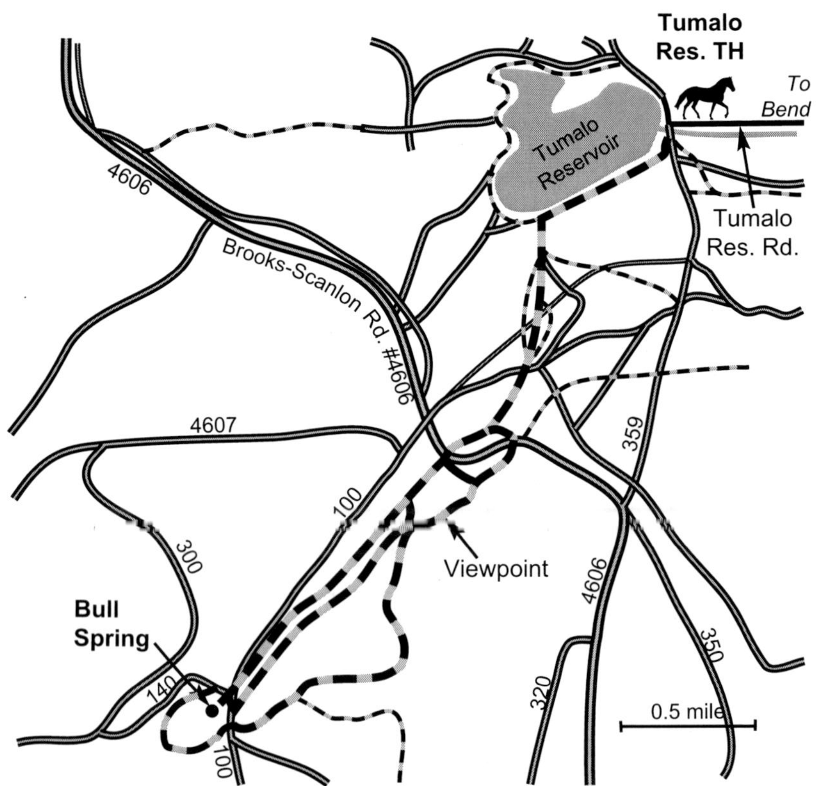

about a mile through charred trees and brushy areas. The fire and subsequent salvage logging operations have opened up some panoramic views. You can get to Bull Spring several ways, but the route described below is probably the easiest to follow. You can vary your return by following one of the other partial-loop routes.

The Ride: From the parking area at the end of Tumalo Reservoir Road, head south and ride across the bridge over the irrigation canal. Turn right and ride down the hill toward the reservoir. As you ride along the southern edge of the reservoir, you'll see a large field on your left. At the end of the field, about 0.7 mile from the trailhead, veer left and pick up the trail that runs up the hill. At the top of the hill, take the trail heading south, ignoring the less-distinct trails that go off to either side. This trail will take you to the Brooks-Scanlon Road (Road 4606) about 1.2 miles from the reservoir. Cross Road 4606 and pick up the trail again on the other side. The trail now runs beside Bull Creek, which may be dry by the time it reaches this area. But notice all the aspens here--the creek is flowing underground. In another 1.3 miles you'll reach Bull Spring. If you head to the right, you can make a short, interesting loop up onto the hillside above the spring. To return to the trailhead, you can pick up the trail that follows the east bank of Bull Creek, or you can jog a little south on Road 100 and pick up another trail that loops out and eventually rejoins the east bank trail.

Jane walks through the forest on the way to Bull Spring.

Canals Area

Trailhead: Start at the parking area at the end of Tumalo Reservoir Road

Length: Varies by route taken

Elevation: 3,500 to 3,600 feet

Difficulty: Easy, though some wayfinding skills are needed

Footing: Suitable for barefoot horses

Season: Nearly year-round

Permits: None

Facilities: Plenty of trailer parking. Stock water is available on the trail during irrigation season.

Highlights: The area southeast of Tumalo Reservoir is crisscrossed with old logging roads and trails and is a fun place to spend the day exploring. BLM has thinned the trees in this area and mowed the un-

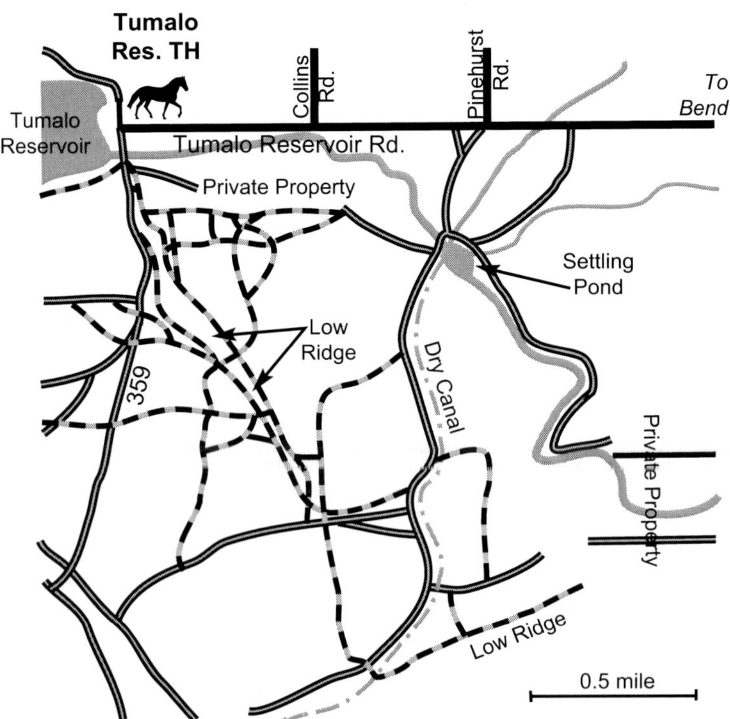

Debbie and Mel pause to enjoy a view of the canal.

derbrush to reduce the wildfire danger for nearby homes and improve the health of the remaining trees. In places, the forest now seems rather sparse. But because it's fairly open, it's easy to keep yourself oriented. And it will be interesting to see how the thinned forest changes in the coming years.

The Ride: From the parking area at the end of Tumalo Reservoir Road, head south and ride across the bridge over the irrigation canal. Pick up the single-track trail on your left, near the private driveway. It will take you up onto a low ridge. From here, you can head east to reach the settling pond, ride along the canal (to a private property boundary), or explore the single-track trails that lace the area. Or, instead of riding up onto the ridge, you can travel along the base of it via another single-track that departs from Road 359 on the left about 0.3 mile from the trailhead. Several trails connect the trails above the ridge with those below it. The canals, private-property fences, and the low ridge are all good landmarks to help you keep your bearings as you ride. Have fun exploring!

Reservoir Area & Bull Flat

Trailhead: Start at the parking area at the end of Tumalo Reservoir Road

Length: Varies by route taken

Elevation: 3,500 to 3,600 feet

Difficulty: Easy

Footing: Suitable for barefoot horses

Season: Nearly year-round

Permits: None

Facilities: Plenty of trailer parking Stock water is available near the reservoir during irrigation season.

Highlights: Tumalo Irrigation District allows equestrians to ride all around the reservoir, as long as we stay away from and out of the water. We can also ride across Bull Flat, an open sagebrush plain bordered by Sisemore Road on the east and the Brooks-Scanlon Road

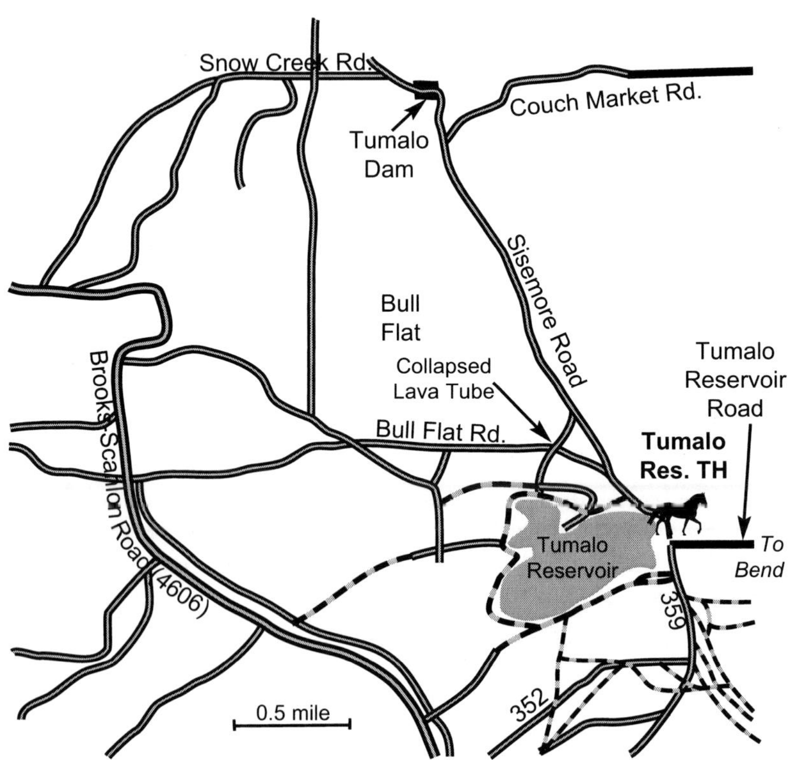

Debbie and Mel enjoy a winter ride on Bull Flat Road, with North and Middle Sister in the background.

(Road 4606) on the west. The mountain views from Bull Flat are excellent, and you can either ride the dirt roads or travel cross-country.

As you ride here, you'll see plenty of evidence of the area's history. In the early 1900s, a dam was built to provide the Tumalo area with irrigation water. Bull Flat was supposed to be covered by the water behind the reservoir. (On the north end of the flat, Sisemore Road travels across the old Tumalo Dam.) When the reservoir began filling, however, however, the weight of the stored water collapsed an underlying lava tube and most of the water drained away. Reportedly, you could hear the sucking sound for miles. You can see the collapsed lava tube on the north side of Bull Flat Road, near the southeast end of the flat.

The Ride: From the parking lot at the end of Tumalo Reservoir Road, you can circle the reservoir on a well-defined trail, or you can ride north on Sisemore Road to reach the dirt roads in the Bull Flat area. Saddle up and explore the pleasant, easy riding around Tumalo Reservoir.

Skyline Gorge Loop

Trailhead: Start at the parking area at the end of Tumalo Reservoir Road

Length: 12 miles round trip

Elevation: 3,500 to 4,000 feet

Difficulty: Moderate -- easy riding, but wayfinding skills, a Sisters Ranger District map, and a GPS will come in handy

Footing: Suitable for barefoot horses

Season: Nearly year-round

Permits: None

Facilities: Plenty of trailer parking. Stock water is available on the trail.

Highlights: This ride offers an interesting glimpse into the history of the area. For many years, the old Columbia Southern Canal brought water from Tumalo Creek to Tumalo Reservoir. For most of its length, the now-dry canal is about 3 feet deep. But in one section, the canal hit sandy soil and suddenly eroded to 75 feet deep. The resulting Sky-

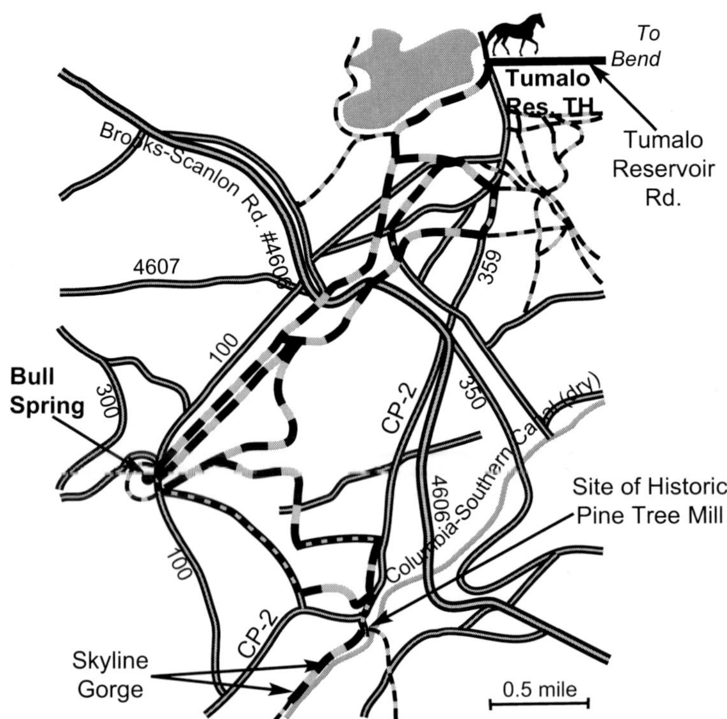

The old Columbia-Southern canal carved a surprisingly deep gorge not far from the historic Pine Tree Mill.

line Gorge is quite a sight. Just downstream from the gorge, you'll also see the remains of the historic Pine Tree Mill.

The Ride: Follow the directions to Bull Spring on the Bull Spring Loops pages. After watering your horse near the spring, turn right on Road 100, the dirt road you crossed as you entered the Bull Spring area. Follow it 0.1 mile and turn left on a single-track trail. In 0.3 mile, veer right on another single-track. It soon begins running on a forest road that will take you to the wide gravel Road CP-2. Turn right and follow the trail that parallels CP-2 for 0.5 mile. Cross Road CP-2 and turn left on a spur road that will take to you the site of the historic Pine Tree Mill and the big grassy depression that was once the mill's settling pond. Head to the right on the road/trail that runs along the settling pond, and you'll soon find yourself paralleling the old Columbia Southern Canal. The canal's ravine gets deeper as you go, and in 0.5 mile you'll come to the spot where the canal once cascaded in a waterfall down into the gorge. To return to the trailhead, retrace your steps to the Pine Tree Mill site, cross Road CP-2, and turn left on the single-track trail. Follow it 0.5 mile to a forest road. Turn right on it and follow it 0.9 mile back to the Bull Spring area. From here, you can select your favorite route back to the trailhead.

Diana rides Tommy along a forest road in the Canals area.

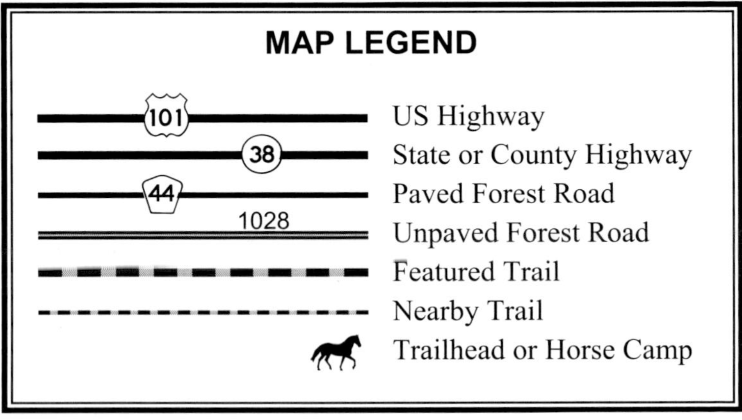

Western Ochocos

Ochoco National Forest

Located northeast of Prineville, the western side of the Ochoco National Forest is lower in elevation and gets less snow than the high Cascades. You can ride here in late spring, long before the Cascades are accessible. The trails in this area wind through beautiful ponderosa forest to fascinating geologic formations, to mountaintops with breathtaking vistas, or to historic mining sites. Some of the trails are pack routes that were once used to take supplies to mining camps or mountaintop fire lookouts. The only horse camp nearby is Dry Creek Horse Camp (see the Dry Creek chapter for more info), but you can dispersed camp anywhere in the forest except at trailheads. However, you can dispersed camp anywhere in the forest other than at trailheads, so look for opportunities to camp near your favorite trails, or trailer in for day rides. Either way, the Western Ochoco Mountains offer some wonderful trail riding opportunities.

Suzanne on Marilyn and Mona on Roi, at the Independent Mine.

Getting to Western Ochocos

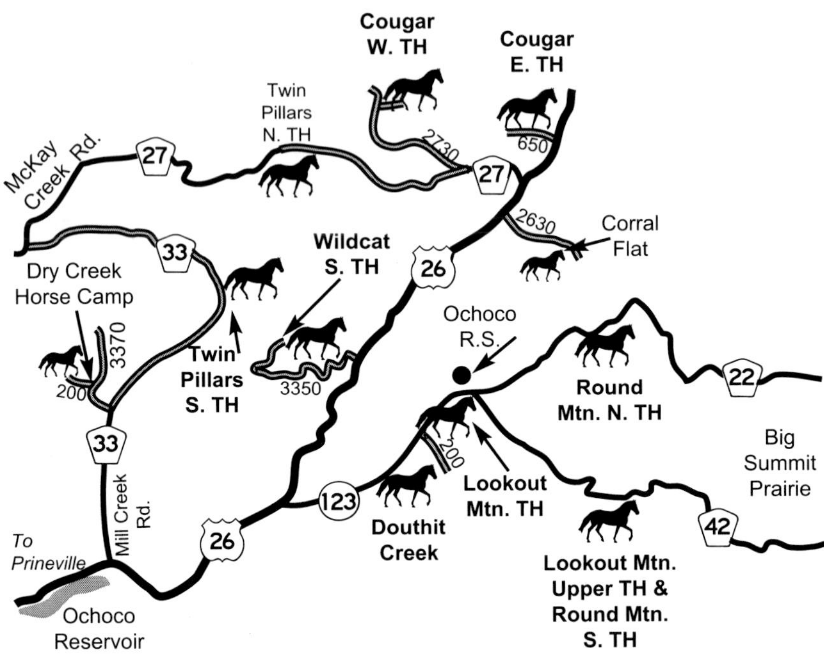

Western Ochoco Trails

Trail	Difficulty	Elevation	Round Trip
Cougar Creek Trail	Difficult	3,400-4,900	7-16 miles
Douthit Creek	Moderate	3,900-5,600	Varies
Independent Mine Loop	Moderate	5,400-7,000	7-10 miles
Lookout Mountain	Challenging	4,000-7,000	16 miles
Round Mountain North	Challenging	5,400-6,800	9 miles
Round Mountain South	Challenging	5,400-6,800	10 miles
Twin Pillars Trail	Moderate	3,800-5,400	7.5-17 miles
Wildcat Trail	Challenging	5,400-5,700	17 miles

Western Ochoco Trails

Connie and Moose enjoy the vista from the summit of Round Mountain.

Mona on Roi (front) and Suzanne on Marilyn, heading up the Lookout Mountain Trail.

Cougar Creek Trail

Trailhead: Start at the Cougar East or Cougar West Trailheads, or at the quarry just off Road 2730

Length: 16 miles round trip between the trailheads, or 9 miles round trip from the quarry to the West Trailhead, or 7 miles round trip from the East Trailhead to the quarry

Elevation: 3,400 to 4,900 feet from the quarry to the West Trailhead, or 4,200 to 4,900 from the quarry to the East Trailhead

Difficulty: Difficult — some traverses on steep side slopes, deteriorated tread in the aftermath of the Bailey Butte Fire

Footing: Hoof protection recommended

Season: Late spring through fall

Permits: None

Facilities: Parking for 2-3 trailers at the east trailhead, plenty of parking at the west trailhead and the quarry. Stock water is available on the trail.

Highlights: You can access this trail from trailheads on the east or west ends, or from the quarry on the flank of Cougar Butte. The trail west of the quarry follows a historic pack trail that was used from 1915 to 1922. It is more rugged and steep than the trail east of the quarry.

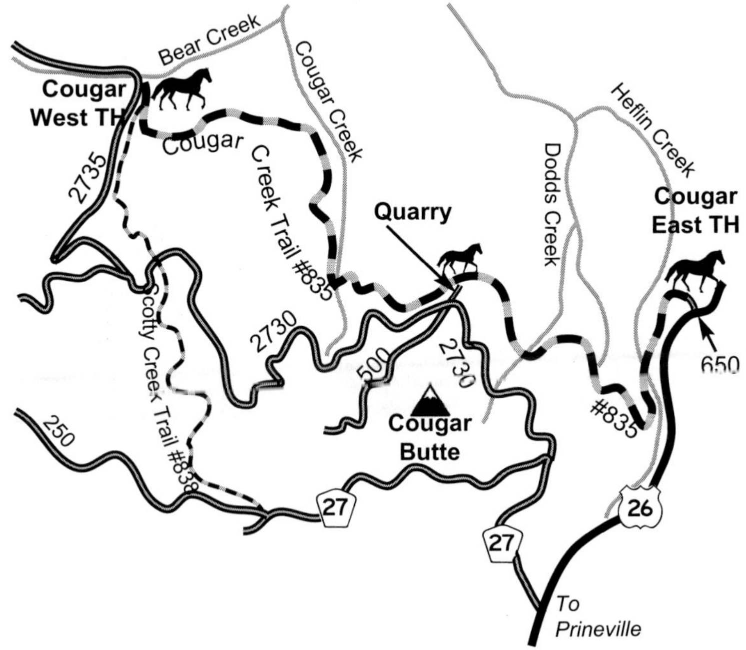

Connie rides Diamond across a steep ridge on the western part of the Cougar Creek Trail.

It is also traverses some very rocky and exposed slopes, and has more elevation gain and loss. Both segments cross pretty creeks and offer good vistas to the north. Parts of this trail were burned by the Bailey Butte Fire, so expect downed logs and eroded tread on the trail.

Finding the Cougar Trailheads: Cougar East Trailhead: Take Hwy. 26 east from Prineville for 27 miles (2 miles past the Ochoco Divide). At the 52-mile marker, turn left on Road 650 and continue 0.1 mile to the trailhead. Turn around in the grassy area beside Road 650. Cougar West Trailhead: Take Hwy. 26 east from Prineville for 25 miles and turn left on Road 27, about 0.4 mile past the Bandit Springs rest stop. Go 1.3 miles and turn right on Road 2730. Continue 6.5 miles, turn right on Road 2735, and drive 1.5 miles to the trailhead. Quarry: Follow the directions toward the Cougar West Trailhead above, but after driving 1.7 miles on Road 2730, turn right into the quarry.

The Ride: From the East Trailhead, the first mile is on an old dirt road that heads downhill almost parallel to the highway. There is a confusing junction about 1.5 miles from the trailhead where a sign indicates that the trail you came on and the trail straight ahead are the Cougar Creek Trail. It looks like you should continue straight, but instead turn right at the sign and continue following the trail marked with yellow diamonds. The trail crosses a meadow, climbs a ridge to the quarry, and then heads down to the west trailhead along a historic pack trail. This section of the trail drops down to Cougar Creek, traverses the steep ridge above Cougar Creek, then crosses very rocky, exposed slopes and descends steeply to the West Trailhead.

Douthit Creek

Trailhead:	Start at the Douthit Creek dispersed camp
Length:	Multiple rides are possible
Elevation:	3,900 to 5,600 feet
Difficulty:	Moderate -- easy riding, but wayfinding skills, a Prineville Ranger District map, and a GPS will come in handy
Footing:	Hoof protection recommended
Season:	Late spring through fall
Permits:	None
Facilities:	Parking for many rigs. Stock water is available on the trail.

Highlights: Douthit Creek isn't an official trailhead, but you'll find plenty of places to ride near this pleasant dispersed camping spot. Enjoy the area's lightly-traveled dirt roads, follow a trail, or head off cross-country. The terrain around Douthit Creek is beautiful and varied. The area is home to several herds of wild horses, so keep an eye out and you may spot some.

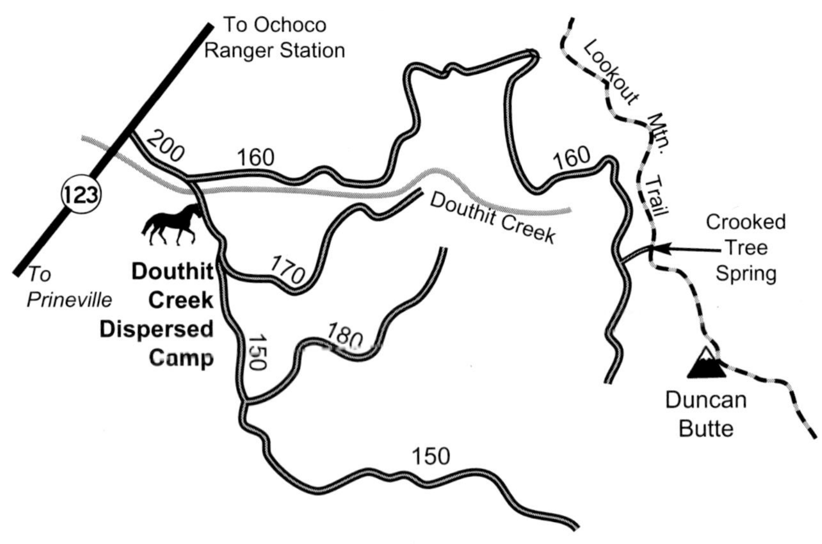

Finding the Douthit Creek Dispersed Camp: Take Hwy. 26 east from Prineville for 15 miles. Between the 34- and 35-mile markers, turn right on Hwy. 123 toward Walton Lake. Drive 6 miles and turn right on Road 200. After 0.4 mile, Road 160 splits off to the left and Road 200 becomes Road 150. Continue right on Road 150 for 0.1 mile to reach the camping/parking area.

The Ride: From the Douthit Creek dispersed camping area you can ride the forest roads, link up with the Lookout Mountain Trail, follow livestock trails, or ride cross-country through the forest and meadows that blanket the hillsides. Several bands of wild horses live here. If you want to see them, watch for the manure piles the horses use to mark their territory. When you find a pile with fresh manure on top, ride the surrounding forest and meadows looking for hoofprints. Chances are good some wild horses will be nearby. If you camp at Douthit Creek, there is even a chance that wild horses will come right into camp to check you out.

A band of wild horses hangs out in the shade near Douthit Creek.

Independent Mine Loop

Trailhead: Start at Lookout Mountain Upper Trailhead
Length: 7 to 10 miles round trip
Elevation: 5,400 to 7,000 feet
Difficulty: Moderate — trail is popular with mountain bike riders
Footing: Hoof protection recommended
Season: Summer through fall
Permits: None
Facilities: Parking for several trailers. Stock water is available on the trail.

Highlights: Three trails lead to the summit of Lookout Mountain, creating several options for making a loop. The trails run through dense forest at lower elevations and through flower-filled meadows near the top. On a clear day, the views from the mountaintop are breathtaking.

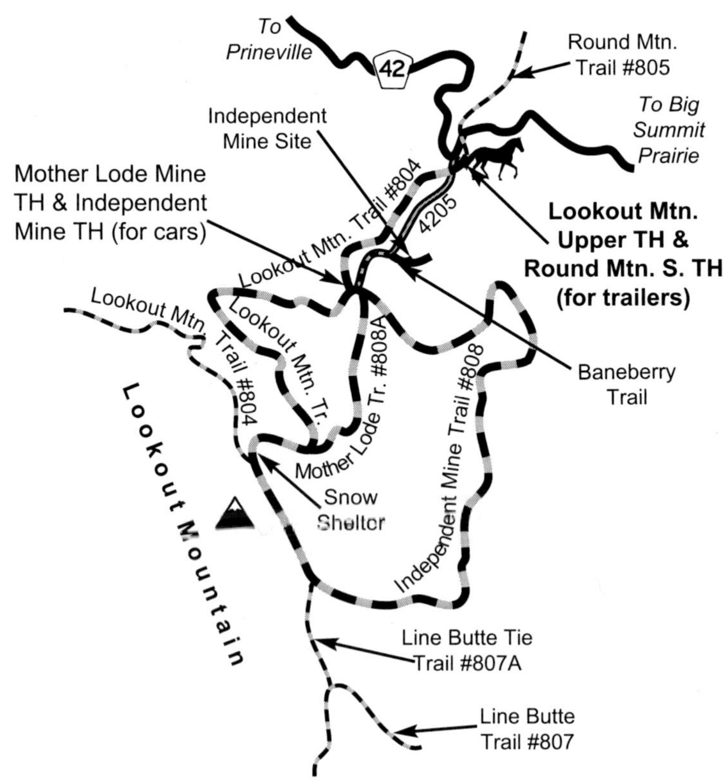

Be sure to take the short detour to the historic Independent Mine site. It's worthwhile.

Finding Lookout Mountain Upper Trailhead: Take Hwy. 26 east from Prineville for 15 miles. Between the 34- and 35-mile markers turn right on Hwy. 123 toward Walton Lake. Drive 8.5 miles, turn right on Road 42, continue 6.5 miles, and turn right to enter the trailer parking area just off the highway.

The Ride: The Lookout Mountain Trail departs near the kiosk at the entrance to the trailer parking area. It parallels Road 4205, and after a mile it leads to a car parking area and the Mother Lode Mine/Independent Mine Trailhead. Then it continues to the top of Lookout Mountain. From the car parking area to the summit, the Lookout Mountain Trail is 3 miles, the Mother Lode Mine Trail is 1.5 miles, and the Independent Mine Trail is 4 miles. You'll see evidence of mining activity along all three trails. When you return from your ride, if you'd like a close-up view of the abandoned buildings at the Independent Mine site, don't take the trail back to the trailhead. Instead, ride down Road 4205 and turn right at the sign for the Baneberry Trail, about 1/3 of the way between the car parking and trailer parking areas.

Along the trail, you'll see evidence of mining activity, including mine buildings and the entrance to an old mine shaft.

Lookout Mountain

Trailhead: Start at the Lookout Mountain Trailhead
Length: 16 miles round trip
Elevation: 4,000 to 7,000 feet
Difficulty: Challenging -- the trail is long and very rocky in places, with a big elevation gain and one harrowing drop-off beside the trail; trail is popular with mountain bike riders
Footing: Hoof protection recommended
Season: Summer through fall
Permits: None
Facilities: Parking for 2-3 trailers. Stock water is available on the trail.

Highlights: On a clear day, the summit of Lookout Mountain offers panoramic views of the Cascades, Big Summit Prairie, and the surrounding Ochocos. Wildflowers bloom in profusion in late spring and early summer, and wild horses inhabit the surrounding area.

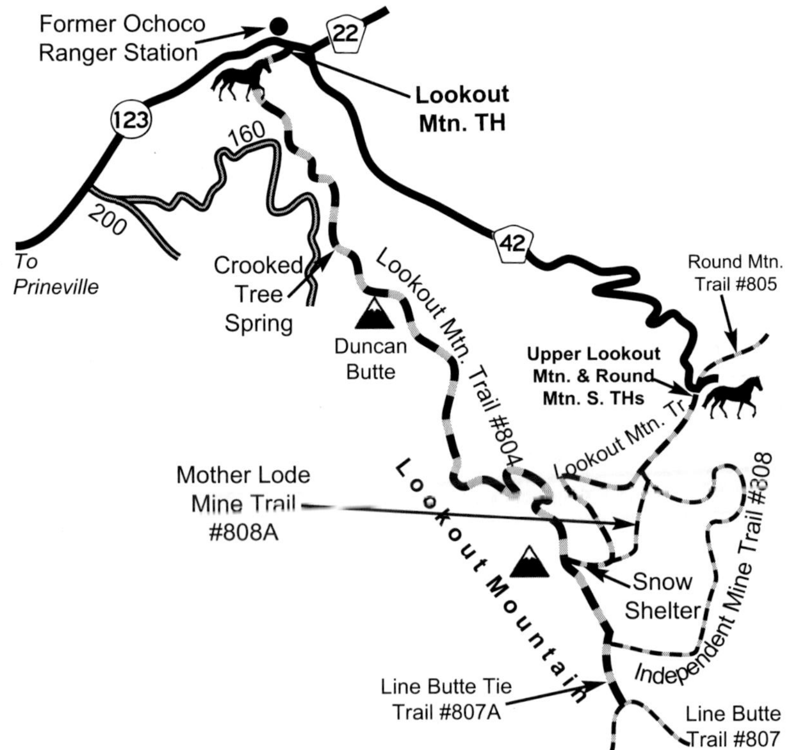

Connie and Lydia ride Moose and Shadow along the open summit of Lookout Mountain.

Finding the Lookout Mountain Trailhead: Take Hwy. 26 east from Prineville for 15 miles. Between the 34- and 35-mile markers, turn right on Hwy. 123 toward Walton Lake. Drive 8.3 miles. Just past the Ochoco Ranger Station, park on the right shoulder of the road, next to the trailhead sign.

The Ride: The trail climbs steeply for the first mile, then settles into a more moderate but steady ascent to the broad, flat summit of Lookout Mountain. Most of the ride is through beautiful ponderosa forest. Crooked Tree Spring is 2.5 miles from the trailhead, just to the right of the trail. About 3 miles after the spring, the trail makes a series of switchbacks through meadows loaded with wildflowers in season. Near the end of the switchback section you'll pass an interesting rock slide of columnar basalt, and 0.5 mile later the trail comes up a ridge and makes a switchback at the edge of a very steep drop-off. Fortunately, this breathtaking moment is over almost before it has begun. Very shortly you'll arrive at the tabletop summit and can enjoy the sweeping views. For a fun 13-mile variation on this ride, you can drop a trailer at the Lookout Mountain Upper Trailhead (see the Independent Mine pages), drive another trailer the 6.5 miles back to the Lookout Mountain Trailhead, then ride the Lookout Mountain Trail up and the Mother Lode Trail down to retrieve the dropped trailer.

Round Mountain North

Trailhead: Start at the Round Mountain North Trailhead

Length: 9 miles round trip

Elevation: 5,400 to 6,800 feet

Difficulty: Challenging -- rocky and steep in some places; trail is popular with mountain biker riders

Footing: Hoof protection recommended

Season: Summer through fall

Permits: None

Facilities: Parking for 5-6 trailers. Stock water is available on the trail.

Highlights: The trail leads through open forest, grassy meadows, and a flower-filled mountain meadow. The summit of Round Mountain is the highest point around, and you can see for miles in every direction.

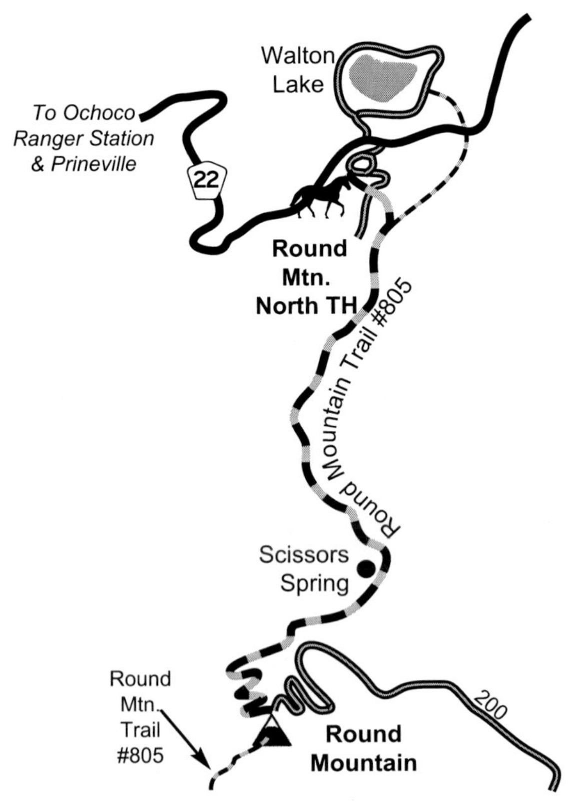

Connie rides Moose through a flower-filled meadow near the summit of Round Mountain.

Finding the Round Mountain North Trailhead: Take Hwy. 26 east from Prineville for 15 miles, and between the 34- and 35-mile markers turn right on Hwy. 123 toward Walton Lake. Continue 8.5 miles. Shortly after passing the site of the old Ochoco Ranger Station, turn left on Road 22. Go 6.7 miles. Just past the road to Walton Lake Campground, turn right at the sign to the Round Mountain Trailhead. Drive 0.2 mile farther to the trailhead. Park beside the trailhead loop.

The Ride: The first part of the trail goes through the forest and over a low, rocky ridge. After 2.5 miles you will reach a large meadow and Scissors Spring, where you can water your horses in the livestock troughs. Shortly after the spring you'll begin the switchbacks that traverse the forest and mountain meadows to reach the top of Round Mountain. The views from the mountaintop are vast, with Big Summit Prairie to the southeast, Lookout Mountain to the west, and rows of hills marching off in all directions. On a clear day you can see the Three Sisters and Mt. Jefferson.

Round Mountain South

Trailhead: Start at the Round Mountain South Trailhead
Length: 10 miles round trip
Elevation: 5,400 to 6,800 feet
Difficulty: Challenging -- rocky trail, a few steep stretches, and this trail is popular with mountain bike riders.
Footing: Hoof protection recommended
Season: Summer through fall
Permits: None
Facilities: Parking for 5-6 trailers. Stock water is available on the trail through early summer only.

Highlights: This trail to the summit of Round Mountain is slightly longer but not as steep as the Round Mountain North Trail. It has

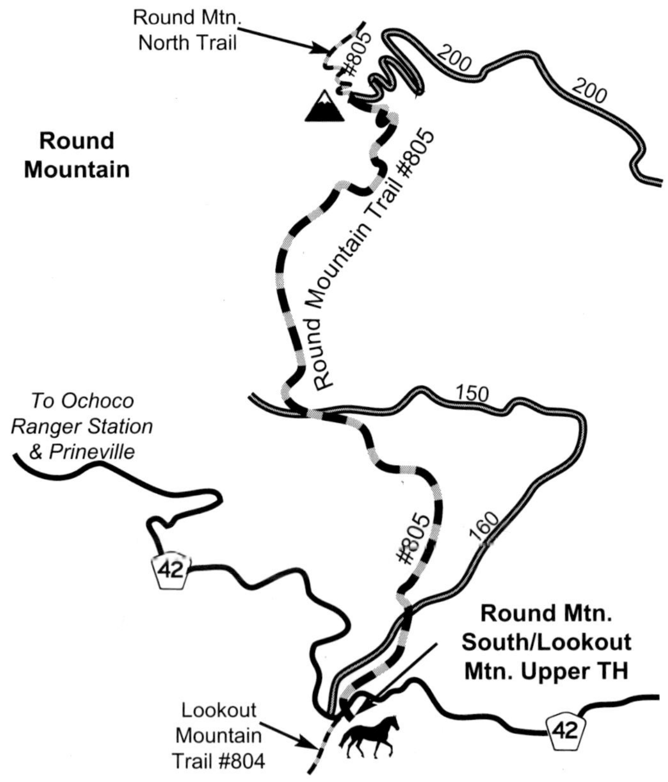

fewer mountain meadows to enjoy, but offers more shade. The views from the summit are impressive.

Finding the Round Mountain South Trailhead: Take Hwy. 26 east from Prineville for 15 miles and turn right on Hwy. 123 toward Walton Lake. In 8.5 miles, just after passing the site of the old Ochoco Ranger Station, veer right on Road 42. Drive 6.2 miles farther, then turn right into the Round Mountain South/Lookout Mountain Upper Trailhead.

The Ride: The trail departs from the north side of the parking area. In 0.3 mile it crosses Road 42, travels over a low ridge for the next 1.7 miles, then steadily climbs to the summit of Round Mountain in the last 3 miles. Most of the ride goes through ponderosa or hemlock/fir forest, so the route is fairly shady. However, the last 0.5 mile to the top runs through steep open meadows of corn lilies and other wildflowers. At various points on the ride you'll enjoy views of Big Summit Prairie on one side and Lookout Mountain on the other. On a clear day, you can see almost forever from the summit.

Mona and Roi take a breather at the summit of Round Mountain.

Twin Pillars Trail

Trailhead: Start at either the Twin Pillars South or Twin Pillars North Trailhead

Length: From the south trailhead, it is 7.5 miles round trip to where you can first see the Twin Pillars, or 12.5 miles round trip to the base of the pillars, or 17 miles round trip for the entire trail

Elevation: 3,800 to 5,400 feet

Difficulty: Moderate

Footing: Hoof protection recommended

Season: Late spring through fall

Permits: None

Facilities: Parking for 3-4 rigs at each trailhead. Stock water is available on the trail.

Highlights: From the south trailhead, the trail enters the Mill Creek Wilderness, and for the first 3.5 miles it follows the East Fork of Mill

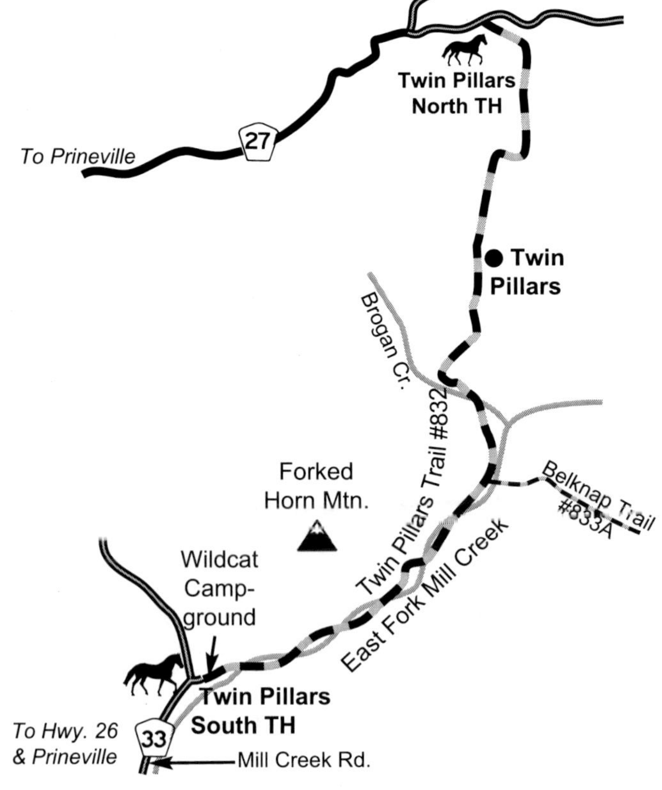

Cindy and Grace, with the Twin Pillars in the background

Creek. The creekside riparian vegetation contrasts sharply with the more arid ponderosa forest on the adjacent slopes. Then the trail leaves the creek and heads uphill into the area burned by the Hash Rock Fire in 2000. The Twin Pillars rise impressively from the top of a ridge. These plugs are all that remain of an eroded volcano that was active some 44 million years ago. Be sure to call the Forest Service before you ride to make sure the trail has been logged out, since fallen trees in the burned area can make the trail impassible.

Finding the Twin Pillars Trailheads: Twin Pillars South Trailhead: Take Hwy. 26 east from Prineville for 8 miles. Just past the 28-mile marker, turn left on Mill Creek Road (Road 33). Drive 9.5 miles to Wildcat Campground. The trailhead parking is on the right just before you enter the campground. Twin Pillars North Trailhead: From Prineville, go north on Main St., which turns into McKay Creek Rd. (Road 27). Follow it 14 miles to the trailhead.

The Ride: From the Twin Pillars South Trailhead, you'll head northeast and follow the East Fork of Mill Creek for about 3.5 miles, crossing the creek frequently. The trail then climbs steeply for 2.7 miles through badly-burned ponderosa forest to the Twin Pillars. From there it continues 2.3 miles to end at Bingham Spring on Forest Road 27.

Wildcat Trail

Trailhead: Start at the Wildcat South Trailhead
Length: 17 miles round trip
Elevation: 5,400 to 5,700 feet
Difficulty: Challenging -- the trail traverses some steep hillsides
Footing: Hoof protection recommended
Season: Summer through fall
Permits: None
Facilities: Parking for 2-3 trailers. Toilets and stock water at the trailhead at White Rock Campground. Stock water is only available on the trail at the far northern end.

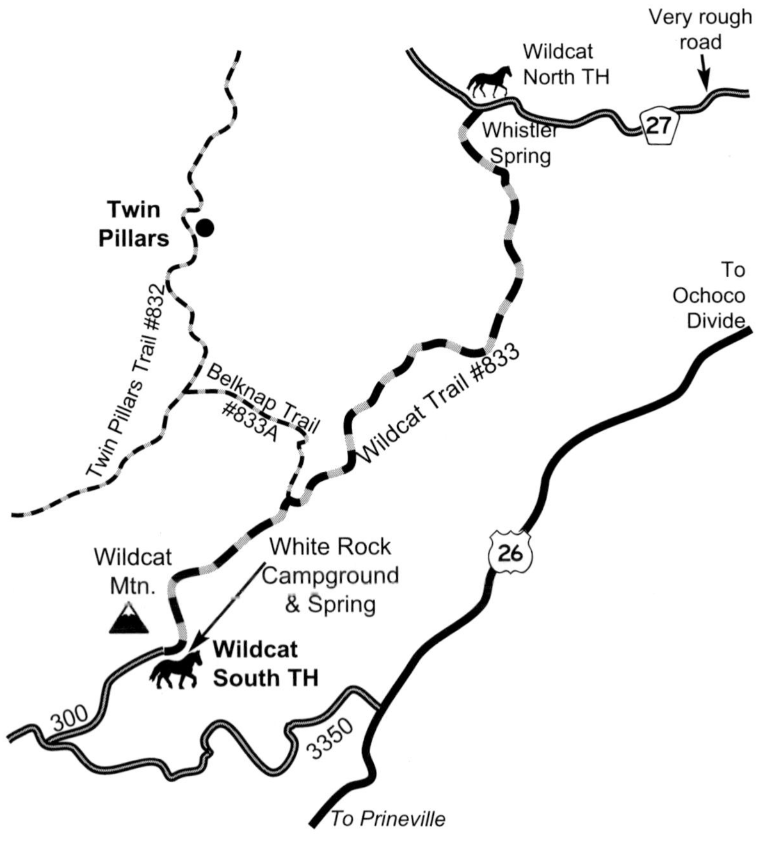

Highlights: This trail in the Mill Creek Wilderness travels along the east side of a ridge, traversing several very steep hillsides in the second half of the ride. Along the way you'll have views of Round Mountain and Lookout Mountain to the east and the Twin Pillars, Mt. Jefferson, and the Three Sisters to the west.

Finding the Wildcat South Trailhead: Take Hwy. 26 northeast from Prineville for 22 miles. Turn left on Road 3350 and continue 5.4 miles, up a steep and winding gravel road. Turn right on Road 300 and drive 1.5 miles to the trailhead at White Rock Campground. Park near the spring at the rear of the campground.

The Ride: Most of the trail runs through beautiful ponderosa and fir forest, but some of it was badly burned in the Hash Rock Fire in 2000. While the fire killed a lot of trees, it also opened up some views you wouldn't otherwise have. After 2.4 miles, the Belknap Trail that connects with the Twin Pillars Trail goes off to the left. The northern half of the trail has several very steep traverses. The trail ends at the Wildcat North Trailhead on Road 27 near Whistler Spring. Road 27 is very rough, and may not be suitable for trailers.

Linda and Beamer travel along the Wildcat Trail.

Cindy rides Grace along the Twin Pillars Trail.

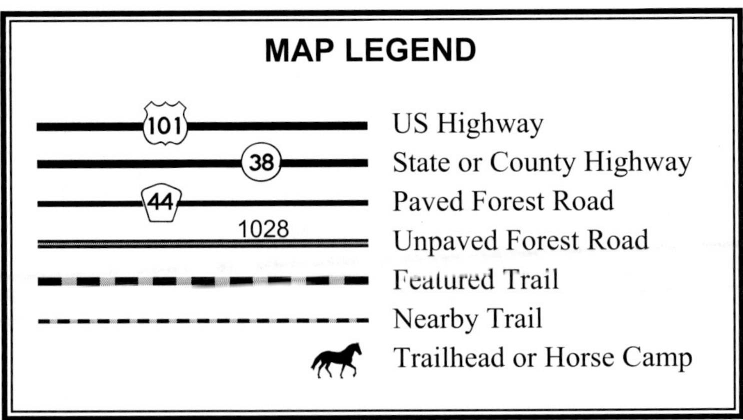

Whispering Pine Horse Camp

Trout Creek Butte Area

Deschutes National Forest

Whispering Pine Horse Camp is located a few miles southwest of Sisters, at the base of Trout Creek Butte. It's aptly named, as the afternoon breezes gently rustle the huge ponderosa pines that shade the campground. Whispering Pine provides nice accommodations for overnighters, and is a good starting point for day riders as well.

In late summer 2017, the Milli Fire burned through this area. Luckily, Whispering Pine Horse Camp was not harmed. However, when this book went to press, we had little information about how much damage the fire inflicted on the trails. For the next several years, it's likely you'll see plenty of dead trees. But you'll have the opportunity to observe firsthand how the forest regenerates after a fire. Before you ride, be sure to contact the Forest Service to make sure the trails have been cleared of fallen logs.

Pat and Ellen ride Secret and Tucker on a forest road near Whispering Pine Horse Camp.

Getting to Whispering Pine

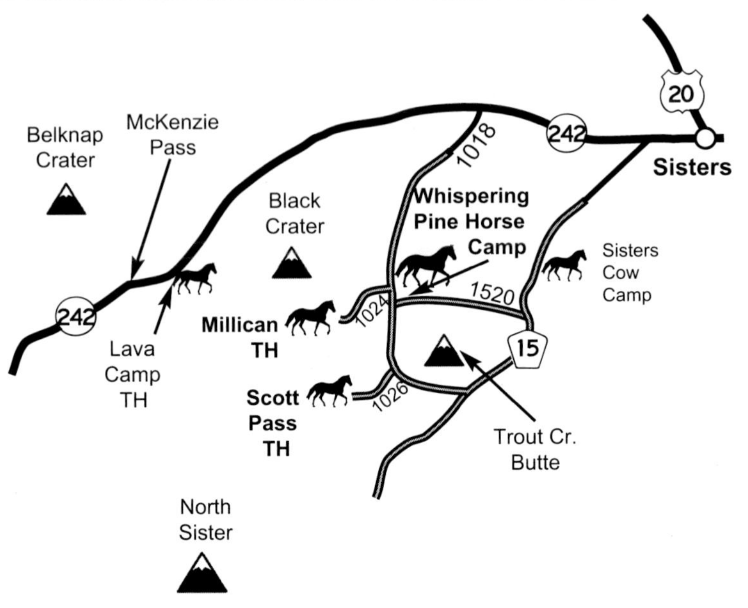

Jane waits impatiently for dinner in her corral at Whispering Pine.

Whispering Pine Horse Camp

Directions: From Sisters, take Hwy. 242 (McKenzie Hwy.) west for 6 miles, turn left on Road 1018, drive 4 miles and turn left on Road 1520. The campground is on the left in 0.1 mile. The route is well signed.

Elevation: 4,400 feet

Campsites: 9 sites, each with a 4-horse log corral. All sites have room for 2 vehicles. One site has pull-through parking and the rest are back-in. All sites have fire pits and picnic tables. Five sites are reservable; the other four are first-come, first-served.

Facilities: Vault toilet, manure bin, garbage cans. No drinking water, but stock water is available from Trout Creek, which runs along the west side of the horse camp. Whispering Pine doesn't have an official day-use parking area, but day riders can drive through the campground to turn around and then park on the side of Road 1520.

Permits: Camping fee

Season: Summer through fall

Contact: Sisters Ranger District: 541-549-7700
Hoodoo Recreation (Concessionaire): 541-338-7869, www.hoodoo.com
Reservations: www.recreation.gov or 877-444-6777

Whispering Pine Area Trails

Trail	Difficulty	Elevation	Round Trip
Scott Pass/Matthieu Lks.Lp.	Moderate	4,400-6,100	16 miles
Sisters Cow Camp	Moderate	3,400-4,500	11 miles
Trout Creek Butte	Easy	4,400-5,550	10 miles
Trout Creek Loop	Moderate	4,400-5,300	9 miles

Scott Pass/Matthieu Lakes Loop

Trailhead: Start at Whispering Pine Horse Camp
Length: 16 miles round trip
Elevation: 4,400 to 6,100 feet
Difficulty: Moderate
Footing: Hoof protection recommended
Season: Summer through fall
Permits: Camping fee for the horse camp. No fee to park beside Road 1520.
Facilities: Toilet and manure bin at the horse camp, stock water in nearby Trout Creek. Stock water is available on the trail.

Highlights: This ride goes through dense forest, along a huge lava flow, over Scott Pass, and past the picturesque Matthieu Lakes. Scott Pass offers expansive views of lava flows and cinder cones. Prior to the 2017 Milli Fire, many lodgepoles in the area had been killed by pine beetles, creating an abundance of fuel for the lightning-caused fire. While the Milli Fire burned through this area, as of our press date we do not know how much damage the fire did to these trails.

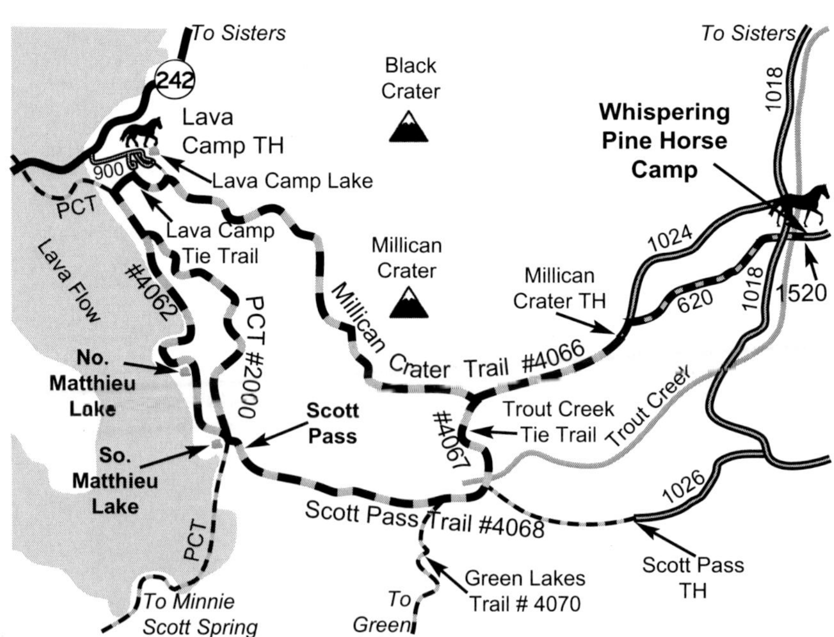

The Ride: From Whispering Pine Horse Camp, ride west on Road 1520, cross Road 1018, and pick up the single-track trail that leads up the hill. At the top of the hill, go straight ahead on Road 620. Follow it 1.4 miles, then veer left on red-cinder Road 1024 and ride a short distance to reach the Millican Crater Trailhead. Continue on the Millican Crater Trail #4066 for 1.1 mile and turn left on the Trout Creek Tie Trail #4067 toward Scott Pass. In 1.0 mile, turn right on the Scott Pass Trail #4068, toward Green Lakes and the PCT. After 0.4 mile, the Green Lakes Trail #4070 goes off to the left. Stay right and continue 1.8 miles to Scott Pass, with its impressive views. After a short distance, the trail intersects with the Pacific Crest Trail #2000. Turn right on the PCT and continue to South Matthieu Lake, which offers a good view of North Sister. From here you can either stay on the PCT or detour left on the North Matthieu Lake Trail #4062. Since the detour adds no distance and runs along an interesting lava flow, we recommend taking it. The trail rejoins the PCT in 2 miles. In another 0.5 mile, turn right on the Lava Camp Tie Trail and follow it 0.6 mile, passing the Lava Camp Trailhead, to reach the Millican Crater Trail #4066. Turn left and follow it 4.6 miles to the Millican Crater Trailhead. From here, retrace the first leg of your route to return to Whispering Pine. Note: In the vicinity of the Matthieu Lakes, dogs must be on leash July 15- September 15.

Lydia and Shadow take a breather on Scott Pass. An immense lava flow dotted with patches of snow is behind them.

Sisters Cow Camp

Trailhead: Start at Whispering Pine Horse Camp

Length: 11 miles round trip

Elevation: 3,400 to 4,500 feet

Difficulty: Moderate -- easy riding, but wayfinding skills, a Sisters Ranger District map, and a GPS will come in handy

Footing: Hoof protection recommended

Season: Summer through fall

Permits: Camping fee for the horse camp. No fee to park beside Road 1520.

Facilities: Toilet and manure bin at the horse camp, stock water in nearby Trout Creek. Stock water is also available in summer at Sisters Cow Camp.

Highlights: This fun road ride has good views of the mountains because it overlooks the area burned by the Black Crater Fire in 2006 and the Milli Fire in 2017. Most of the route is on gravel or dirt roads. (Please note that while we show road numbers in the text and on the map, some of the roads don't have road number signs on them.)

The Ride: From Whispering Pine Horse Camp, ride east on red cinder Road 1520 for 1 mile, then turn right on Road 570. In 0.2 mile,

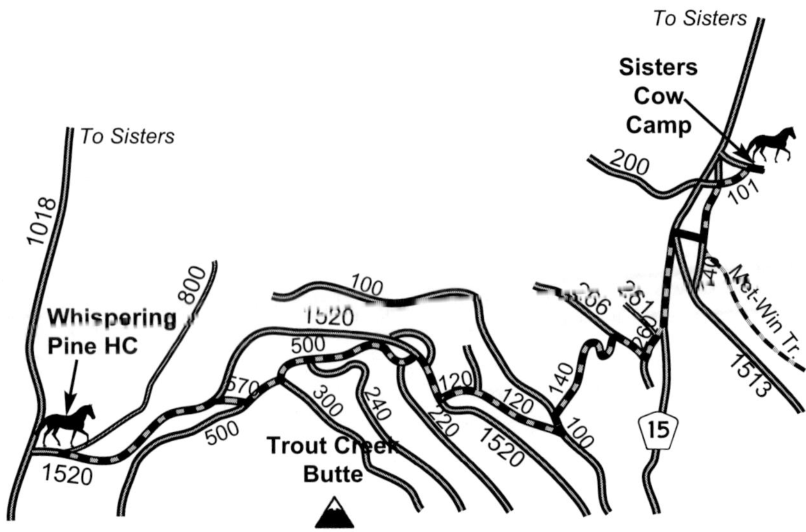

turn left on Road 500. In another 0.2 mile, Road 300 goes off to the right. Veer left to stay on Road 500. Soon you'll have views of Black Crater, North Sister, Mt. Washington, Three Fingered Jack, Mt. Jefferson, Black Butte, and even the tip of Mt. Hood. In 0.9 mile, Road 220 goes to the right. Again stay left on Road 500, and in 300 feet turn right on Road 1520. You'll pass an unsigned road on your left. At the second unsigned road, 0.3 mile after you turned onto Road 1520, turn left. You're now on Road 120. Follow it downhill for 0.2 mile, and at the next junction veer right, which will keep you on Road 120. In another 0.7 mile, turn left on Road 100, which is signed. In 0.2 mile, veer right on Road 140. Continue downhill for 0.7 mile, then turn right on Road 266. It will lead you to Road 260 in 0.3 mile. Turn left on Road 260, and in 0.2 mile you'll reach gray gravel Road 15. Turn left and ride beside Road 15 for 0.5 mile. At the junction of Roads 15 and 1513 (another gray gravel road), turn right and ride cross-country through the trees for 0.1 mile, then turn left when you come to a dirt road. (Be sure to mark this spot so you can find it again for your return trip.) You are now on the Metolius-Windigo Trail. Follow the yellow diamonds on the trees for 0.5 mile along Roads 140 and 101 to reach Sisters Cow Camp.

Suzi rides Tex, accompanied by Camo the dog, on the way to Sisters Cow Camp.

Trout Creek Butte

Trailhead:	Start at Whispering Pine Horse Camp
Length:	10 miles round trip
Elevation:	4,400 to 5,550 feet
Difficulty:	Easy
Footing:	Hoof protection suggested
Season:	Summer through fall
Permits:	Camping fee for the horse camp. No fee to park beside Road 1520.
Facilities:	Toilet and manure bin at the horse camp, stock water in nearby Trout Creek. No stock water on the trail.

Highlights: The Milli Fire of 2017 burned over Trout Creek Butte, and since the entire area was closed to the public until after this book went to press, we don't know how badly the trail was damaged. Note

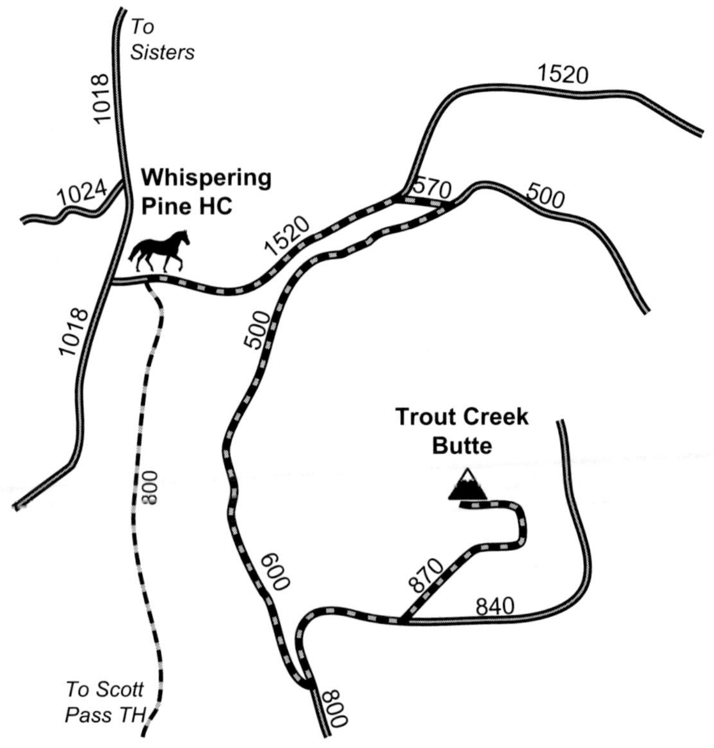

Lydia and Magic pause in front of the view of North Sister, en route to the top of Trout Creek Butte.

that a couple of user-created trails climb steeply to the summit of Trout Creek Butte, but this road ride is easier, safer, and much more scenic. About 2 miles into the ride, the trail goes through an old fire scar, providing great views (depending on which direction you look) of North Sister, Black Crater, Three Fingered Jack, and Mt. Jefferson. As you travel around the butte, you'll see Middle and South Sister, Broken Top, Tam McArthur Rim, and Whychus Creek Falls come into view. The summit was tree covered, but the Milli Fire may have changed that. In any case, the mountain views along the way are impressive.

The Ride: Ride east on Road 1520, the road that runs past the horse camp. After 1 mile, turn right on Road 570. In 0.2 mile, turn right on Road 500, which soon becomes Road 600. After 2.3 miles, turn left on red-cinder Road 800 and follow it for 0.5 mile, then turn left again on Road 870 and continue 1 mile to the summit.

Trout Creek Loop

Trailhead: Start at Whispering Pine Horse Camp
Length: 9 miles round trip
Elevation: 4,400 to 5,300 feet
Difficulty: Moderate
Footing: Hoof protection recommended
Season: Summer through fall
Permits: Camping fee for the horse camp. No fee to park beside Road 1520.
Facilities: Toilet and manure bin at the horse camp, stock water in nearby Trout Creek. Stock water is available on the trail.

Highlights: This loop takes you up into the Three Sisters Wilderness, through mostly-lodgepole forest. The first and last legs of the loop are on closed forest roads that take you to/from the Scott Pass and Millican Crater Trailheads. (Or, if you'd rather, you can ride the wide gravel Roads 1024, 1018, and 1026 to the trailheads.) From the trailheads, you can pick up the wilderness trails that make up the middle segment of this loop. Along the way you'll have tree-filtered views of

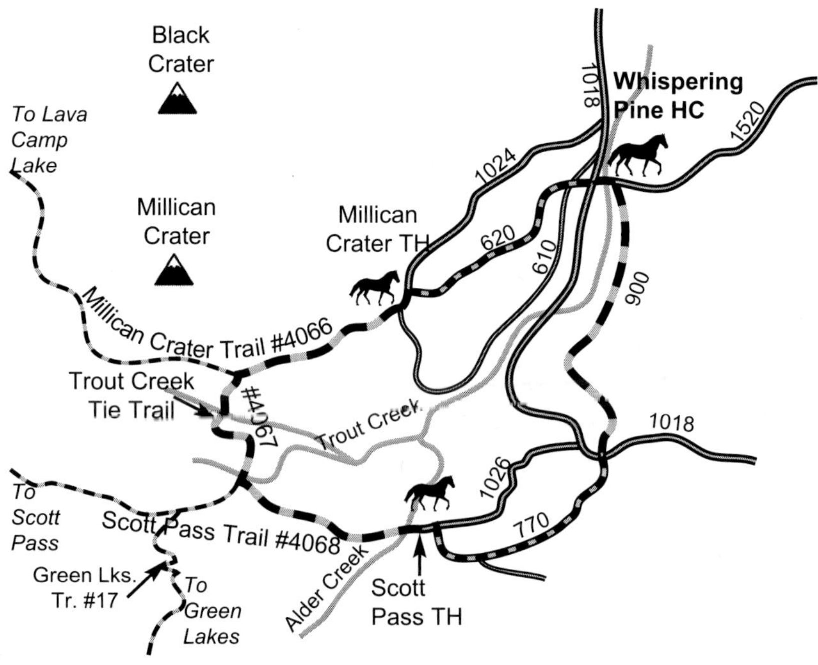

North Sister, Millican Crater, and Black Crater. The 2017 Milli Fire burned through this area, but at press time we did not know how hot the fire burned in this area or how much these trails were damaged.

The Ride: Ride out the entrance to the horse camp and turn left on Road 1520. In 200 feet, turn right on closed Road 900, which quickly becomes a single-track trail. Follow it for 1.8 miles, cross gravel Road 1018, and continue on Road 770 for 1.6 miles, ignoring any roads that go off to the left. When Road 770 intersects gravel Road 1026, turn left on Road 1026 and you'll reach the Scott Pass Trailhead in 0.2 mile. Fill out a wilderness permit and pick up the Scott Pass Trail #4068. Not long after leaving the trailhead, you'll cross Alder Creek, and 1.4 miles from the trailhead you'll reach a junction. The Scott Pass Trail goes to the left, and the Trout Creek Tie Trail goes to the right. Turn right (the sign points toward Lava Camp Lake), and immediately cross Trout Creek. About 0.4 mile later you'll cross another arm of Trout Creek, and 0.5 mile after that you'll reach the Millican Crater Trail #4066. Turn right toward Millican Trailhead, and in 1.1 mile you'll arrive at the trailhead. Ride down red cinder Road 1024 for 0.2 mile, then turn right on Road 620. Follow it 1.6 miles, cross Road 1018, and continue straight ahead for 0.1 mile to the horse camp.

Teresa and Pops enjoy the view of North Sister on the Scott Pass Trail segment of the Trout Creek Loop.

Debbie and Split cross Alder Creek, on the Trout Creek Loop.

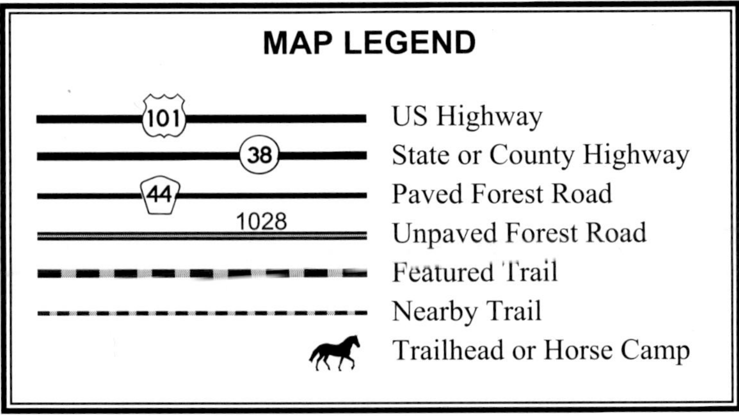

Whitefish Horse Camp

Diamond Peak Wilderness Area

Deschutes National Forest

Whitefish Horse Camp is the gateway to the Diamond Peak Wilderness, at the south end of the Deschutes National Forest. This area features several volcanic peaks and dozens of small lakes. At 8,744 feet, Diamond Peak is the tallest mountain in the area. It was named for John Diamond, a member of the party that explored the area in 1852 in search of a wagon route into Central Oregon.

Many rides are possible from Whitefish Horse Camp or from the nearby Fawn Lake and Windy Oldenberg Trailheads. This area is heaven for distance riders because many longer loop trails are available, and plenty of shorter-mileage riding is available as well. Mosquitoes can be fierce here in early summer, so the best time to come is late July through September.

Whitefish Horse Camp is on the shore of Crescent Lake.

Getting to Whitefish Horse Camp

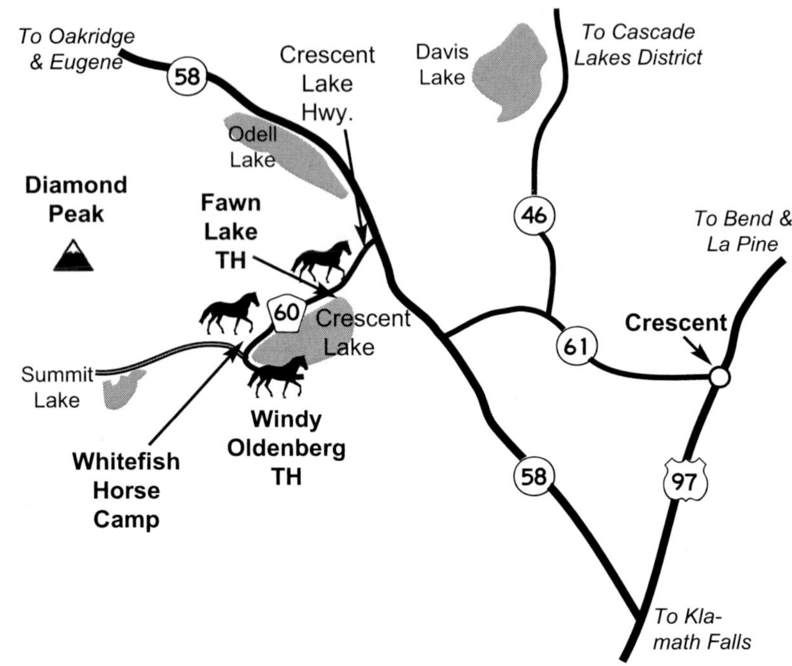

Whitefish Area Trails

Trail	Difficulty	Elevation	Round Trip
Diamond View Lake	Moderate	4,900-5,800	10.5 miles
Diamond View/Snell Loop	Moderate	4,900-6,250	17.5 miles
Fawn Lake	Moderate	4,900-5,600	15.5 miles
Fawn Lk./Whitefish Cr. Lp.	Moderate	4,900-6,300	16.5 miles
Meek Lake	Moderate	4,900-5,600	10 miles
Meek/Summit Lakes Loop	Moderate	4,900-5,950	16.5 miles
Oldenberg Lake	Easy	4,900-5,500	12.5 miles
Pretty/Fawn Lakes Loop	Moderate	4,900-5,900	16 miles
Pretty Lake	Moderate	4,900-5,800	13.5 miles
Snell Lake	Moderate	4,900-5,600	10 miles
Stag Lake	Moderate	4,900-5,800	10 miles
Summit Lake	Moderate	4,900-5,550	11.5 miles
Windy Lakes	Moderate	4,900-6,200	11.5 miles
Windy/Meek Lakes Loop	Moderate	4,900-6,200	15 miles
Windy/Oldenberg Lks. Lp.	Moderate	4,900-6,200	16.5 miles

Whitefish Horse Camp

Directions: From Bend, drive south on Hwy. 97 for 45 miles to the town of Crescent. Turn right on Hwy. 61 (the Crescent Cutoff) and drive west for 12 miles. At the junction with Hwy. 58, turn right and go north 3.4 miles. From Eugene, take Hwy. 58 to Oakridge and continue another 35 miles. All, turn southwest on Crescent Lake Hwy. Drive 2 miles, cross the railroad tracks, turn right on Road 60 (the first paved road on the right), and continue 4.3 miles to the horse camp.

Elevation: 4,900 feet

Campsites: 17 sites. Fourteen sites have 2-horse corrals and 3 sites have 4-horse corrals. All sites are level and graveled, with room for 2 vehicles.

Facilities: Toilets, potable water spigots, garbage cans, manure pit. Picnic tables and fire pits at each site. No day-use parking at Whitefish, but plenty of parking nearby at the Fawn Lake and Windy Oldenberg Trailheads.

Permits: Camping fee. Reservations required. No fee for day-use parking at the Windy Oldenberg or Fawn Lake Trailheads.

Season: June through September

Contact: Crescent Ranger District: 541-433-3200
Hoodoo Recreation (Concessionaire): 541-338-7869, www.hoodoo.com
Reservations: www.recreation.gov or 877-444-6777

FAWN LAKE TRAILHEAD

Directions: Follow the directions for Whitefish Horse Camp above. Before reaching the camp (about 0.9 mile after crossing the railroad tracks), turn left into the trailhead.

More Info: Parking for 8+ trailers, toilet, no permit needed, season is summer through fall. Contact: Crescent Ranger District, 541-433-3200.

WINDY OLDENBERG TRAILHEAD

Directions: Follow the directions to Whitefish Horse Camp above. Continue 1 mile past the horse camp and turn left into the trailhead road, which makes a loop back to Road 60.

More Info: Parking for 8+ trailers, toilet, no permit needed, season is summer through fall. Contact: Crescent Ranger District, 541-433-3200.

Diamond View Lake/Snell Lake Loop

Trailhead: Start at Whitefish Horse Camp or Windy Oldenberg Trailhead

Length: From Whitefish Horse Camp, round trip distances are: 17.5 miles for the entire loop, 10.5 miles to Diamond View Lake, or 10 miles to Snell Lake. From Windy Oldenberg Trailhead, round trip distances are: 19 miles for the entire loop, 12.5 miles to Diamond View Lake, or 10 miles to Snell Lake round trip.

Elevation: 4,900 to 6,250 feet for the entire loop. Diamond View Lake is at 5,800 feet and Snell Lake is at 5,600 feet.

Difficulty: Moderate

Footing: Hoof protection recommended

Season: Summer through fall

Permits: Camping fee at Whitefish; no fee for day-use parking at Windy Oldenberg Trailhead

Facilities: Toilets and potable water at the horse camp. Toilet and plenty of trailer parking at the trailhead. Stock water is available on the trail.

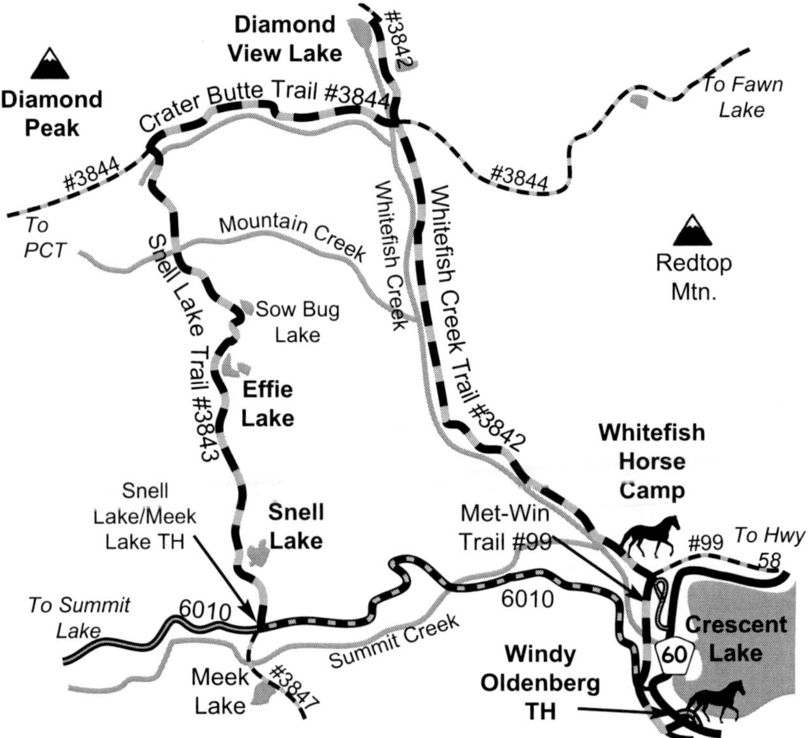

Highlights: As you might expect from the name, Diamond View Lake provides a wonderful view of Diamond Peak. Snell and Effie Lakes are also worthy destinations. The trail travels primarily through lodgepole forest, with stands of hemlock and fir at the higher elevations.

The Ride: From the Windy Oldenberg Trailhead, ride to the Metolius-Windigo Trail #99 and turn right. In 1.5 mile you'll reach the horse camp. From Whitefish Horse Camp, the Whitefish Creek Trail #3842 departs from the north end of the camp. The trail climbs fairly steadily as it follows Whitefish Creek through lodgepole forest for 5.0 miles to Diamond View Lake. The view of Diamond Peak across the lake is impressive. Backtrack 0.7 mile to the junction with the Crater Butte Trail #3844, turn west and travel 2.0 miles to the junction with the Snell Lake Trail #3843. Turn left and continue 2.6 miles to Effie Lake, and then 1.8 miles more to Snell Lake. About 0.6 mile after that you'll reach Road 6010. Turn left and ride 3.8 miles to the junction with the Metolius-Windigo Trail. Turn left again on the Met-Win and continue 0.7 mile to the horse camp, or turn right on the Met-Win and ride 0.8 mile to the Windy Oldenberg Trailhead.

If you want to ride to Snell Lake only, take the Met-Win Trail south (left) out of the horse camp for 0.7 mile. Turn right on Road 6010, go 3.8 miles, turn right on the Snell Lake Trail #3843 and go 0.5 mile north to the lake.

Diamond Peak across Diamond View Lake.

Fawn Lake/Whitefish Creek Loop

Trailhead: Start at Whitefish Horse Camp or Fawn Lake Trailhead

Length: From Whitefish Horse Camp, round trip distances are: 16.5 miles for the entire loop, 15.5 miles to Fawn Lake, or 18 miles to Stag Lake. From Fawn Lake Trailhead, round trip distances are: 16.5 miles for the entire loop, 8 miles to Fawn Lake, or 10 miles to Stag Lake.

Elevation: 4,900 to 6,300 feet for the entire loop. Fawn Lake is at 5,600 feet, Stag Lake is at 5,800 feet.

Difficulty: Moderate

Footing: Hoof protection recommended

Season: Summer through fall

Permits: Camping fee at Whitefish; no fee for day-use parking at Fawn Lake Trailhead

Facilities: Toilets and potable water at the horse camp. Toilet and plenty of trailer parking at the trailhead. Stock water is available on the trail.

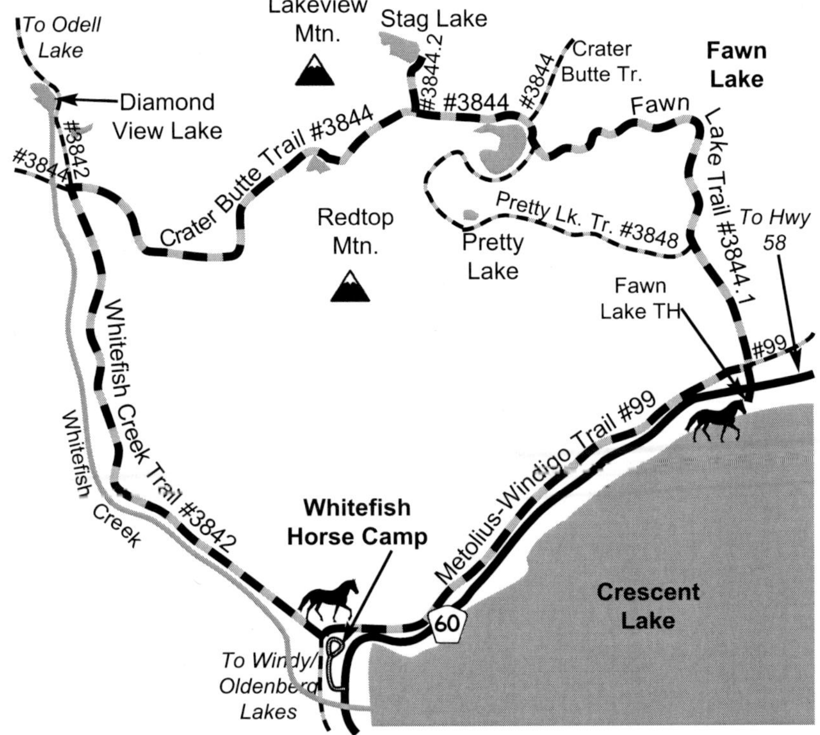

Lakeview Mountain from the south side of Fawn Lake.

Highlights: The Metolius-Windigo Trail runs along the shore of Crescent Lake, through stands of enormous old-growth trees. Fawn Lake is very pretty, and the views of Lakeview Mountain and Redtop Mountain are nice. Stag Lake is also a pretty destination.

The Ride: From Whitefish Horse Camp, pick up the Metolius-Windigo Trail #99 at the north end of the campground. Turn right on it and ride 4 miles to the junction with the Fawn Lake Trail. From the Fawn Lake Trailhead, pick up the Fawn Lake Trail, and in 0.1 mile you'll reach the junction with the Met-Win. All, head north on the Fawn Lake Trail #3844.1, and in 0.8 mile the Pretty Lake Trail #3848 goes off to the left. Stay right, and in another 2.5 miles you'll arrive at Fawn Lake. The loop trail to Pretty Lake comes in on your left. Stay to the right, and in 0.1 mile the Crater Butte Trail #3844 goes off to the right. Veer left and continue around Fawn Lake, and in about a mile you can take the 0.5-mile detour to the right to Stag Lake on the Stag Lake Trail #3844.2. Return to the Crater Butte Trail and continue riding west for 3.3 miles, then turn south on the Whitefish Creek Trail #3842 to return to the horse camp in approximately 4.4 miles. To return to the Fawn Lake Trailhead from the horse camp, turn left on the Met-Win Trail and ride 4 miles to the trailhead.

Meek Lake/Summit Lake Loop

Trailhead: Start at Whitefish Horse Camp or Windy Oldenberg Trailhead

Length: From either Whitefish Horse Camp or Windy Oldenberg Trailhead, round trip distances are: 16.5 miles for the entire loop, 10 miles to Meek Lake, or 11.5 miles to Summit Lake

Elevation: 4,900 to 5,950 feet for the entire loop. Meek Lake is at 5,600 feet, and Summit Lake is at 5,550 feet.

Difficulty: Moderate

Footing: Hoof protection recommended

Season: Summer through fall

Permits: Camping fee at Whitefish; no fee for day-use parking at Windy Oldenberg Trailhead

Facilities: Toilets and potable water at the horse camp. Toilet and plenty of trailer parking at the trailhead. Stock water is available on the trail.

Highlights: The portion of the trail that loops from Meek Lake to Summit Lake is shaded by old-growth hemlocks and firs, and festooned with lakes and lily ponds strung like beads on a necklace.

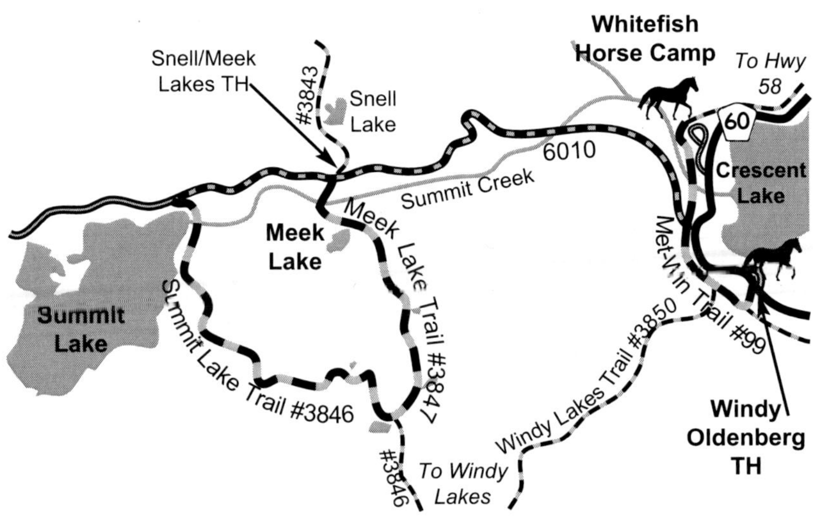

Beautiful Summit Lake is uncrowded compared to the more easily-accessible Crescent Lake. Don't be tempted to drive to the Snell/Meek Lakes Trailhead, as Road 6010 is too rutted for horse trailers, and the trailhead has nowhere to turn around. The road has good footing for horses, though, so you can easily ride to the trailhead.

The Ride: From Whitefish Horse Camp, pick up the Metolius-Windigo Trail #99 along the west side of the campground and turn left. Ride about 1 mile to Road 6010 and turn right. From Windy Oldenberg Trailhead, ride to the Met-Win Trail and turn right. Ride 0.7 mile to Road 6010 and turn left. All, ride west on Road 6010 for 3.8 miles to the Meek Lake Trailhead. Turn left onto the Meek Lake Trail #3847, which passes its namesake lake after 0.5 mile, winds through stands of old-growth mountain hemlock and fir and past dozens of lakes and ponds, including many with lily pads. Two miles after Meek Lake, the trail intersects with the Summit Lake Trail #3846. Turn right, and in 3.5 miles you'll reach Summit Lake. Turn right on Road 6010 and ride 4.8 miles, then veer left on the Met-Win to return to Whitefish, or right to return to the trailhead.

A lily pond on the trail between Meek and Summit Lakes.

Pretty Lake/Fawn Lake Loop

Trailhead: Start at Whitefish Horse Camp or Fawn Lake Trailhead

Length: From Whitefish Horse Camp, round trip distances are: 16 miles for the entire loop, or 15.5 miles to Fawn Lake, or 13.5 miles to Pretty Lake. From Fawn Lake Trailhead, round trip distances are: 8 miles for the entire loop or 7.5 miles to Fawn Lake, or 5.5 miles to Pretty Lake.

Elevation: 4,900 to 5,900 feet

Difficulty: Moderate

Footing: Hoof protection recommended

Season: Summer through fall

Permits: Camping fee at Whitefish; no fee for day-use parking at Fawn Lake Trailhead

Facilities: Toilets and potable water at the horse camp. Toilet and plenty of trailer parking at the trailhead. Stock water is available on the trail.

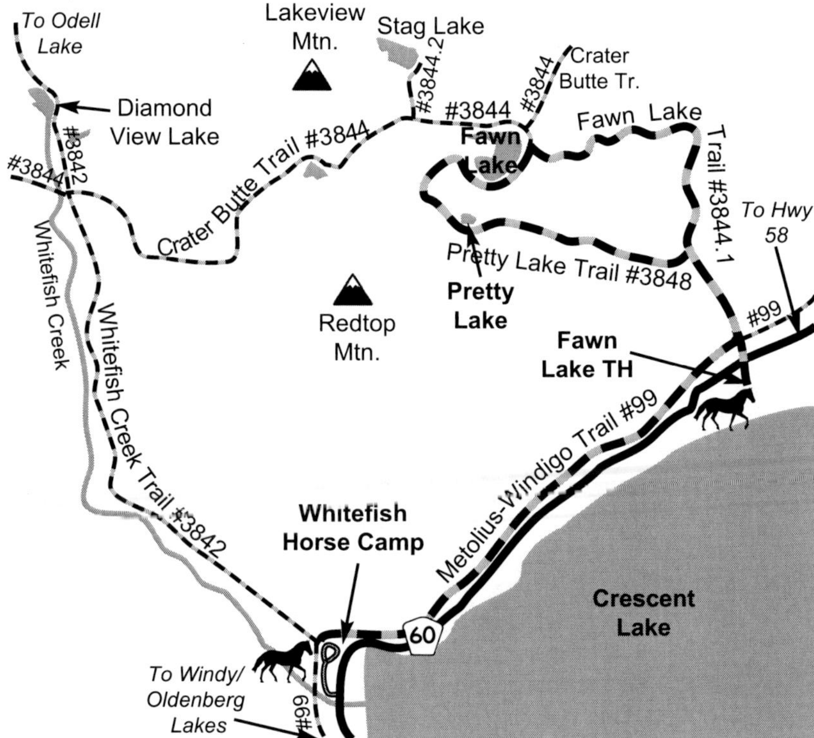

Connie rides Diamond and Lydia rides Shadow past Fawn Lake.

Highlights: This is a fun loop that takes you through varied terrain to two delightful lakes. If you start at Whitefish Horse Camp, you'll also enjoy the pleasant ride among the huge old-growth trees along the shore of Crescent Lake. The trail segment that goes from the Fawn Lake Trail to Pretty Lake is a good climb, gaining 900 feet of elevation in 1.8 miles.

The Ride: From Whitefish Horse Camp, pick up the trail at the north end of the campground and turn right on the Metolius-Windigo Trail #99. Follow it for 4 miles to the junction with the Fawn Lake Trail. From the Fawn Lake Trailhead, pick up the Fawn Lake Trail and in 0.1 mile you'll reach the Met-Win Trail. All, head north on the Fawn Lake Trail #3844.1, and in 0.8 mile turn left on the Pretty Lake Trail #3848. It climbs steadily for 1.8 miles to the shore of Pretty Lake, then continues 1.2 miles to Fawn Lake. Ride along the shore of Fawn Lake for about 0.5 mile, then veer right at the junction and take the Fawn Lake Trail 3.3 miles back to the Met-Win Trail. Go straight ahead to reach the Fawn Lake Trailhead, or turn right on the Met-Win to return to the horse camp.

Windy Lakes/Meek Lake Loop

Trailhead: Start at Whitefish Horse Camp or Windy Oldenberg Trailhead

Length: From Whitefish Horse Camp, round trip distances are: 15 miles for the entire loop, 10 miles to Meek Lake, or 11.5 miles to Windy Lakes. From Windy Oldenberg Trailhead, round trip distances are: 12.5 miles for the entire loop, 10 miles to Meek Lake, or 9 miles to the Windy Lakes.

Elevation: 4,900 to 6,200 feet for the entire loop. Meek Lake is at 5,600 feet and the Windy Lakes are at 6,200 feet

Difficulty: Moderate

Footing: Hoof protection recommended

Season: Summer through fall

Permits: Camping fee at Whitefish; no fee for day-use parking at Windy Oldenberg Trailhead

Facilities: Toilets and potable water at the horse camp. Toilet and plenty of trailer parking at the trailhead. Stock water is available on the trail.

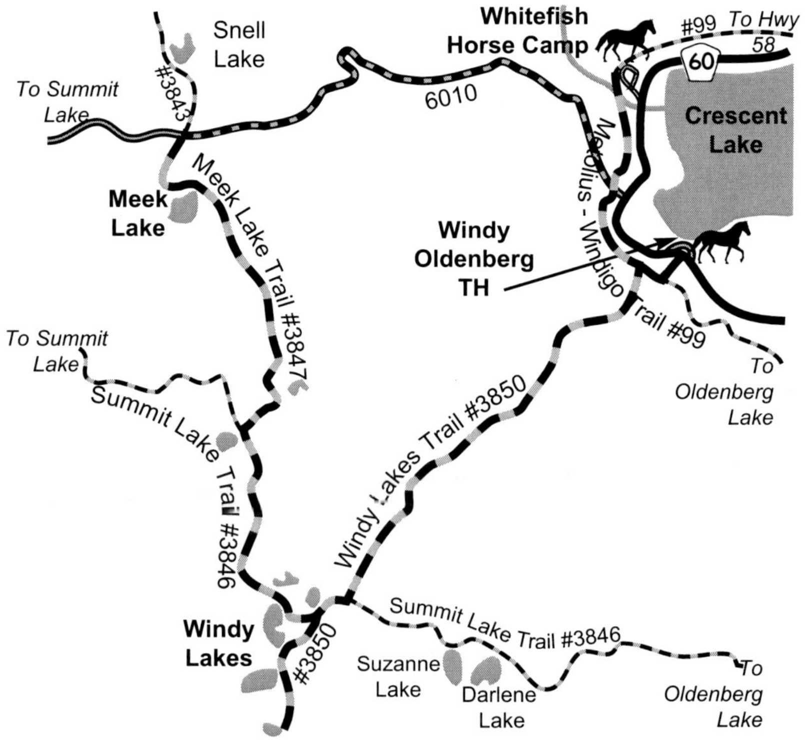

Diamond, Mo, Dixie, and their riders get ready to stop for lunch at the Windy Lakes.

Highlights: The Windy Lakes are beautiful, and the terrain between Meek Lake and the Windy Lakes features large mountain hemlock and fir trees and a smattering of picturesque lakes.

The Ride: From Whitefish Horse Camp, pick up the Metolius-Windigo Trail #99 along the west side of the campground and turn left. Ride about 1.3 miles and turn right on the Windy Lakes Trail #3850. From Windy Oldenberg Trailhead, ride to the Met-Win Trail and turn right. In 0.1 mile, turn left on the Windy Lakes Trail #3850. All, follow the Windy Lakes Trail for 3.3 miles to the junction with the Summit Lake Trail. You can go straight for 1.1 miles to explore all the Windy Lakes. Or you can turn right on the Summit Lake Trail #3846, continue 2 miles, then veer right on the Meek Lake Trail #3847 and ride 2.0 miles to Meek Lake. Continue 0.5 mile farther to reach Road 6010. Turn right and follow Road 6010 for 3.8 miles. Turn left on the Met-Win Trail to return to Whitefish Horse Camp, or turn right to return to the Windy Oldenberg Trailhead.

Windy Lakes/Oldenberg Lake Loop

Trailhead: Start at Whitefish Horse Camp or Windy Oldenberg Trailhead

Length: From Whitefish Horse Camp, round trip distances are: 16.5 miles for the loop, 11.5 miles to the Windy Lakes, or 12.5 miles to Oldenberg Lake. From the Windy Oldenberg Trailhead, round trip distances are: 14 miles for the loop, 9 miles to the Windy Lakes, or 10 miles to Oldenberg Lake

Elevation: 4,900 to 6,200 feet for the entire loop. Windy Lakes are at 6,200 feet and Oldenberg Lake is at 5,500 feet.

Difficulty: Moderate

Footing: Hoof protection recommended

Season: Summer through fall

Permits: Camping fee at Whitefish; no fee for day-use parking at Windy Oldenberg Trailhead

Facilities: Toilets and potable water at the horse camp. Toilet and plenty of trailer parking at the trailhead. Stock water is available on the trail.

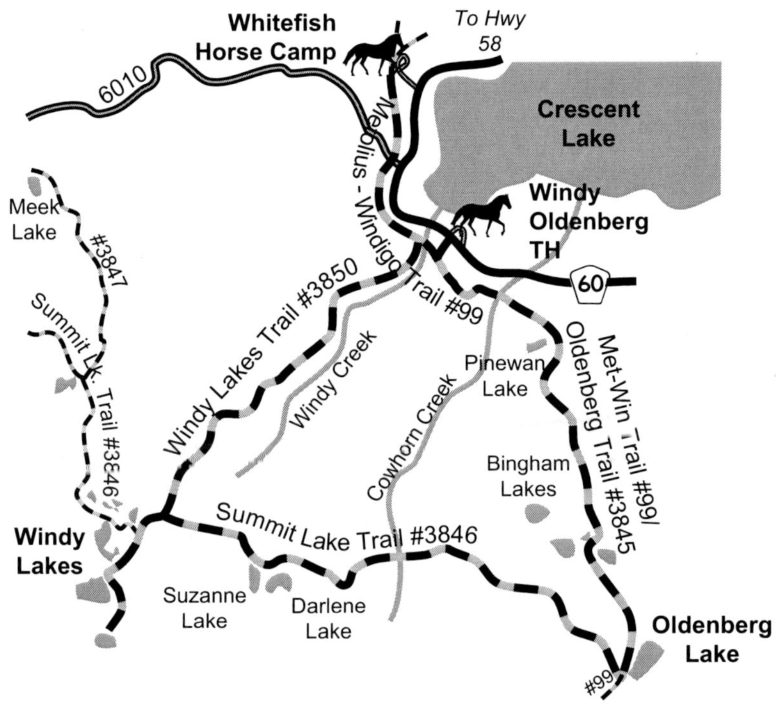

Highlights: The Windy Lakes and Oldenberg Lake are lovely and serene, and the trail between them runs through pretty fir and mountain hemlock forest. If you are doing the entire loop, the trail up to Windy Lakes is best done on the uphill leg of your ride, as it is steeper than the trail to Oldenberg Lake.

The Ride: From Whitefish Horse Camp, pick up the Metolius-Windigo Trail #99 along the west side of the campground and turn left. Ride about 1.3 miles and turn right on the Windy Lakes Trail #3850. From Windy Oldenberg Trailhead, ride to the Met-Win Trail and turn right. In 0.1 mile, turn left on the Windy Lakes Trail #3850. All, follow the Windy Lakes Trail for 3.3 miles to the junction with the Summit Lake Trail. You can go straight for 1.1 miles to explore all the Windy Lakes, or turn left on the Summit Lake Trail #3846, which takes you past Suzanne and Darlene Lakes to Oldenberg Lake in 4.6 miles. Turn left on the Metolius-Windigo (Oldenberg #3845) Trail and follow it 4.9 miles, then veer right to return to the Windy Oldenberg Trailhead. To return to Whitefish, stay on the Met-Win Trail for another 1.4 miles.

Whitney on Dixie, Diana on Mo, and Connie on Diamond, taking a break at beautiful Suzanne Lake.

Magic, Dixie, and Kodie enjoy a drink at Whitefish Creek, on the way to Diamond View Lake.

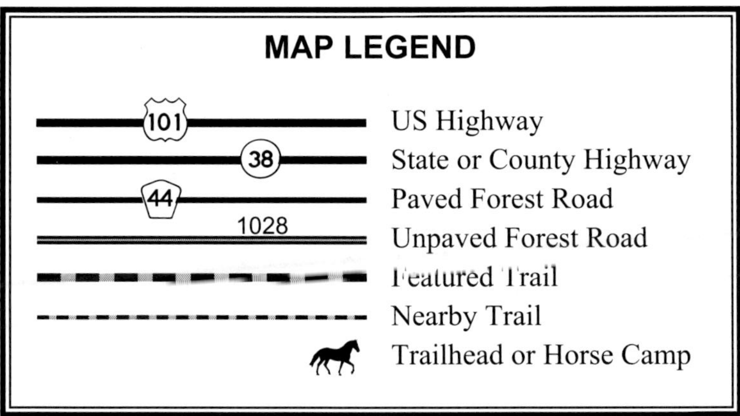

Index

T

U

W

Riding through Dry Canyon,
in the Cline Buttes Recreation Area.

In loving memory of Jane, an extraordinary trail horse who never spooked at anything, and who had an opinion about everything. She is missed.